PREFACE

The German post-war period as such, as a separate historical epoch, knows no continuous line of development other than that of the Free Corps and their successor organizations. The history of these Corps has not yet been written, but without an exact knowledge of it, the years between 1918 and 1924 are deprived of historical meaning. These were years of decision — years in which no decision was made but in which any decision was possible.

— Ernst von Salomon

On November 11, 1918, the Allied and Associated Powers announced in triumph that the object of a great crusade in Europe had been attained: German militarism was dead, her war machine crushed and broken. And yet, within a generation, a new and deadlier phoenix had arisen from the ashes of that defeat. It is the purpose of this study to trace the course of a movement which helped to make that resurrection possible.

The history of the Free Corps Movement is a necessary part of the larger problem of the rise of National Socialism in Germany. Various approaches have been made to that problem. Political and constitutional historians have sought the solution in the weaknesses of the Weimar Constitution, in its party structure and in its political leadership. Others urge the importance of economic factors and find the answer to the rise of Hitler in the inflation of the early twenties, or in the long German tradition of state socialism. Intellectual historians have pointed to the peculiar nature of the German mind and the continuity of a stream which has had many sources: Luther, Fichte, Hegel, von Treitschke, Nietzsche, Spengler, and Moeller van den Bruck. More recently, social psychologists — amateur and professional — have discovered that National Socialism is explicable only in psychopathological terms. Thus the Germans have become, variously: sado-masochists, paranoids, the victims of a big brother fixation, or the inevitable consequence of forced toilet training.

I have no serious quarrel with any of these major interpretations, provided that they are all brought into focus. For I am persuaded that here, as elsewhere in history, no one-line interpretation can give an adequate explanation of so complex a social phenomenon. Confronted by such a barrage of evidence from so many different sides, I am perfectly willing to fall back to the safety of a badly worn but well-tested cliché: it was a little of all of these things. Nor is there anything particularly startling about the conclusions reached in this study: in general, the years immediately following 1918 saw the germination of proto-Nazi thinking; and, more specifically, the Free Corps Movement made important, direct contributions to the growth of National Socialism.

My primary concern, however, has been to write a narrative history of the twentieth-century Freebooters. Since von Salomon urged the necessity of such a history, a number of German books have appeared; but they were written under the aegis of National Socialism and are consequently both heavily biased and flagrantly unreliable. They do not meet the long-felt need for a serious study of the movement.

The Nazi writers have just been accused of bias. Is this not simply the ancient case of the smudged pot belaboring the blackened kettle? It seems only decent to admit that I too have my biases and that I discovered early in my research that my sympathies were not with these "First Soldiers of the Third Reich." Indeed, I despise everything they stood for. The reason for this personal antipathy is understandable. Anyone reared in the traditions of Western civilization cannot but recoil from a philosophy of savage nihilism which is the very negation of all he cherishes. The leading spokesman of the Free Corps Movement has given a warning to prospective historians which strikes deeply here: "Anyone who judges Free Corps fighters by the standards of the civilization it was their task to help to destroy is utilizing the standards of the enemy." This warning must be taken seriously. The historian owes this much to the Freebooters: he must interpret

PREFACE

them in terms of their own *Weltanschauung*. But the historian
who subscribes to "the standards of the enemy" can not accept the
Freebooters solely on their own terms. He must evaluate them by
placing them within a larger frame of reference — that of Western civilization. In so doing he will employ precisely those criteria
which the Volunteers despised. To this extent such an historian
will be biased. To this extent this book is biased and marked by
the writer's personal predilections and sympathies; it nevertheless
attempts to maintain intellectual integrity. I have tried to be fair
to the fighters of the Free Corps. Indeed one of the reasons for
quoting the memoirs of the *Freikorpskämpfer* at such length in
this study was the desire to convey their spirit as accurately as
possible by letting them speak for themselves. And here spirit is
of the essence for it is my contention that the real importance of
the German Free Corps Movement lies in the ideas and attitudes
it brought to pre-Hitler Germany. Two other excuses may be
offered for drawing so heavily on the memoirs: they have not
previously been translated into English; and I have done it in
simple self-defense. Had I relied on paraphrase, it seems probable
that I would not have been believed.

The present book is the extensive revision of a thesis submitted
to the faculty of Harvard University in partial fulfillment of the
requirements for the degree of Doctor of Philosophy in Modern
European History. I am happy to acknowledge my indebtedness
to a number of sources. The staff of Widener Library kindly permitted me to use the then uncatalogued books of the Library of
Congress Mission to Germany. I wish to thank the President and
Trustees of Williams College for grants from the Class of 1900
Fund which helped to defray costs of research and publication. My debt to individuals is very great. Kenneth L. Holmes of
Macalester College first introduced me to Clio and instructed me
in techniques that might be used in wooing that illusive lady.
Sidney B. Fay of Harvard suggested the Free Corps as a thesis
subject and gave me sound advice and encouragement. I am
particularly grateful to H. Stuart Hughes who directed the dissertation and went over it with great care. In its revised form, the
manuscript was read by Orie W. Long, Richard A. Newhall,
Charles R. Keller, and Jack B. Ludwig of Williams College. Mr.

Ludwig and Mark H. Curtis, also of Williams, are largely responsible for smoothing out many of the rough spots in the narrative. John L. Clive, tutor in history in Harvard College, checked some of the more difficult translations. By their industry, perspicacity, and patience, the editors of the Harvard University Press have saved me time and spared me embarrassment. I have discussed aspects of the movement with Viscount Alexander of Tunis and former Chancellor Heinrich Brüning.

More is owed to my wife, Anne Barnett Waite, than is usually admitted in a preface. She listened to it all. She also supplied the index and ruthless criticism. Above all, she lent her unflagging sense of humor to the entire procedure. Geoffrey and Peter also helped. Their enthusiasm for things nonhistoric consistently drove me from my home to the peace of Widener and Stetson Libraries.

I am grateful to all these people. In no way, however, should any of them be held liable for the results of their assistance. The ideas and interpretations, the errors in fact and in judgment, are solely my own.

R. G. L. W.

Williamstown, Massachusetts
February 18, 1952

NOTE TO THE PAPERBACK EDITION

For this edition, minor factual errors have been corrected.

R.G.L.W.

Williamstown
October 16, 1968

CONTENTS

VANGUARD OF NAZISM

THE SONG OF THE LOST TROOPS

Remember that hour heavy with gloom,
Germany sinking to Communist doom,
Germany abandoned, betrayed, despised,
Street and Square with blood baptized:
Don't you remember?

Then out the trenches of the great World War,
From factory, schoolhouse, farm, and store,
Gathering to fight, united strong,
The Free Corps! Death to the Red Throng!
Don't you remember?

Baltic earth vibrates with song
Of German boot — we marched along,
Defended homeland, defeated foe,
United in blood, together we go!
Don't you remember?

Held Silesia's frontier to our last breath;
We'll never forsake you — true to the death —
Saint Annaberg, that sacred day,
Come insurgents, come who may!
Don't you remember?

Rhine! Ruhr! Palatinate! — and jail for our pay,
But awake! Dawns soon a glorious day!
Golzheimer Heath. Schlageter is dead!
The glowing flame, day breaks red:
Don't you remember?

Third Reich, thou wert our seed,
Thine our loyalty, thine our deed.
Thou art the Reich! Thou the Nation!
Germany's faith and adoration.
We remember!

I

THE REVOLUTIONARY SETTING AND
THE ARRIVAL OF NOSKE

> Amid the tremendous intellectual collapse of the German citizenry
> — it can hardly be called anything else than that — only one group
> kept its head. That was the German Officers' Corps . . . It became
> the decisive element of power.
>
> — Major E. O. Volkmann

I. THE EBERT-GROENER CONVERSATIONS

As revolutions go, the German Revolution was a rather disappointing affair. It lacked almost all of the parts which Professor Crane Brinton finds essential to his "Anatomy of Revolution." Most revolutions, Mr. Brinton observes, move to the extreme left as the early moderates give way to the radicals. In Germany, almost from the very beginning, the Revolution moved to the Right and stayed there.

Revolutions usually occur when the machinery of government has clearly shown itself to be inefficient. But historians would be hard pressed to find significant examples of such inefficiency in the government of Imperial Germany. The most reliable indication of a revolutionary situation would seem to be that the intellectuals have turned their backs on the established order. In Germany there was no such "desertion of the intellectuals." Quite on the contrary, the respected leaders of German thought agreed with one of the more circumspect of their colleagues when he insisted that Germany possessed the best system of government ever devised by modern man.[1]

[1] Hans Delbrück, *Regierung und Volkswille, Eine akademische Vorlesung* (Berlin, 1914), 186.

It would also be difficult to find examples in Germany of the overt class antagonisms which have helped to precipitate other revolutions in the past. Nor had widespread popular discontent preceded this upheaval of November 1918. There was war weariness — and that in abundance — but there was no concerted effort set upon overthrowing the existing regime.

When the Revolution came, it came as the logical consequence of military defeat. The war lords had been beaten; the army had been defeated; the navy had mutinied. The old system had collapsed. A great void had been created and into that void the German Socialists moved with hesitation and with distaste; for they had neither planned nor, indeed, wanted the Revolution.

Friedrich Ebert, the Socialist who looked like a prosperous bourgeois businessman, had been made Chancellor of the revolutionary government. And four days before the Republic was proclaimed, Ebert had pleaded with General Groener to save the monarchy by making one of the Imperial princes regent.[2] This was for good reason: the honest saddler from Heidelberg believed that the monarchy was the only alternative to social revolution, and he abhorred the very idea of revolution. "I want no part of it," he had said on the eve of the event, "I hate it as I hate sin." [3]

Apparently what Ebert really wanted was a constitutional monarchy. Since that was denied him by the abdication of the Kaiser and by what he felt was the foolish proclamation of the Republic by Scheidemann, he wanted a chance to think quietly. That too was denied him in the seething chaos of Berlin during the first weeks of November. Above all, he needed and needed desperately an armed force which could bring that *Ruhe und Ordnung* which was so dear to his heart. But there was no such force. There were plenty of armed men in Berlin but they were divided into half a dozen groups who were engaged in fighting each other for ascendancy. For now was the time, while the field army was still far from Berlin, for each political faction to build its own version of the Army of the Republic. Karl Liebknecht had

[2] Max von Baden, *Erinnerungen und Dokumente* (Stuttgart and Berlin, 1927), 592.

[3] Conversation with Prince Max, November 7, 1918, in *ibid.*, 600.

organized the "National Association of Deserters" (*Reichsbund der Deserteure*) to further the cause of Communism. Over at the *Polizeipräsidium*, Emil Eichhorn was building his "Security Force" (*Sicherheitswehr*) which he hoped would serve as the shock troops of the Independent Socialists. The notorious Peoples' Naval Division (*Volksmarine Division*) had taken over the Imperial Palace and Stables and was using them as headquarters for its looting forays.[4] Otto Wels, the Commandant of Berlin, was about to try to save the situation by organizing yet another army, the Republican Soldiers' Army (*Republikanische Soldatenwehr*). But this proved to be no solution; the men bickered and fought with other groups and preferred playing politics in the soldiers' councils to preserving law and order.[5]

The adjutant to the Commandant of Berlin has left a graphic account of the city during the first weeks of November:

Disorder, insecurity, plundering, wild commandeering and house-prowling had become the order of the day . . . The troops went their own way, the barracks were like so many bedlams. Sentry posts did not exist — only Soldiers' Councils in every corner and in every alley. Each group acted on its own hook . . . The only masters of Berlin were Disunity, Licentiousness and Chaos . . . Worst of all were the barracks. Crammed full to the bursting point when it was time for food or pay, but empty when the Commandant wanted a dozen soldiers to perform legitimate service . . . And day and night, senseless shooting — partly from exuberation, partly from fear. Berlin lived, danced, drank and celebrated.[6]

In the confusion of revolutionary Germany one thing was reasonably clear. Whoever controlled the field army might be able to control the course of the revolution. But at this point the field army was in the process of dividing itself into two parts and Ebert, in looking for an army to protect his government, had his

[4] See below, pp. 10–12.

[5] This is the testimony of one of the *Soldatenwehr's* commanders, Lieutenant Fischer, cited by Gustav Noske, "Die Abwehr des Bolschewismus," in *Zehn Jahre deutsche Geschichte, 1918–1928* (Berlin, 1928), 33. Emil Eichhorn admits that "friction was the daily order" between his men and the *Soldatenwehr*. See his memoirs, "*Ueber die Januar-Ereignisse: Meine Tatigkeit im Berliner Polizeipräsidium* (Berlin, 1919), 29.

[6] Fischer quoted by Noske in *Zehn Jahre*, 30–31. See also the memoirs of Philip Scheidemann, *Der Zusammenbruck* (Berlin, 1921), 214–217, 228–232, and his *Memoiren eines Sozialdemokraten* (Dresden, 1928), II, 327–332.

choice of the pieces. Either he could choose the Supreme Command and the group which it still controlled, or he could organize the rapidly mushrooming but terribly disorganized Soldiers' and Sailors' Councils. Lack of time and the gravity of a military problem to which the young Republic had fallen heir made him choose the former. By the terms of the Armistice, the German armies on the Western Front were to be withdrawn within thirty days. The OHL (*Oberste Heeresleitung* or Supreme Command) was the only authority in Germany capable of executing this incredibly complex military maneuver.[7]

The so-called "Ebert-Groener Deal" has been so distorted by historians of the Republic that it would be well to go into the actual scene of the conversation in some detail. On the evening of November 9, 1918, the harried Chancellor, his coat removed and his shirt stained with sweat, was pacing the offices of the Reichs-chancellery. The problem of the return of the field armies and a dozen others demanded immediate solution. He had put in a grueling day — a day that had seen him first fighting to preserve the monarchy and now trying desperately to save the Republic from extremism. Even his title of Chancellor rested on the legal fiction that Prince Max in conferring it was acting as Regent. He was exhausted and he was alarmed — not so much for himself but for the Germany his simple soul loved. The restless, milling crowds beneath his window did nothing to reassure him. In the gathering twilight, the signs that screamed "Down with the Traitors of the Revolution," "Down with Ebert-Scheidemann" were still plainly visible. He winced as the strident strains of the

[7] Rosenberg says that Ebert's decision to use the Supreme Command was the first great mistake of the Republic and suggests that the withdrawal could have been effected without relying on the Imperial generals. Arthur Rosenberg, *Geschichte der deutschen Republik* (Karlsbad, 1935), 44. But two competent military authorities contend that Ebert made the only decision possible under the circumstances: Herbert Rosinski, *The German Army* (New York, 1940), 167–168, and J. Benoist-Méchin, *History of the German Army,* translated by Eileen R. Taylor (Zurich, 1939), I, 58–61. Lutz calls the evacuation ". . . the last great act of the army of Frederick, Scharnhorst and Moltke." Ralph H. Lutz, "The German Revolution, 1918–1919" in *Stanford University Publications* (Stanford University Press, 1922), Vol. I, No. 1, 76.

Internationale crowded up from the Wilhelmstrasse below. Suddenly the telephone rang. It was the secret line which connected the Chancellery with Army headquarters at Spa. Ebert's hand trembled as he lifted the receiver. Then he breathed more easily. It was all right after all! It was only his old friend General Groener. After exchanging nervous amenities, Ebert requested that the OHL supervise the withdrawal of the field armies. That was agreed to. The conversation continued:

EBERT: What do you expect from us?
GROENER: The Field Marshal expects that the government will support the Officers' Corps, maintain discipline, and preserve the punishment regulations of the Army. He expects that satisfactory provisions will be made for the complete maintenance of the Army.
EBERT: What else?
GROENER: The Officers' Corps expects that the government will fight against Bolshevism, and places itself at the disposal of the government for such a purpose.
EBERT: [after a slight pause] Convey the thanks of the government to the Field Marshal.[8]

All that Ebert had done in his conversations with Groener, it needs to be emphasized, was to promise to combat Bolshevism in return for the support of the Supreme Command. He did not, as recent writers have implied, deliberately deliver up the entire Revolution into the hands of the reactionary Army. Hans Fried's sensationalistic book is fairly typical of the interpretation which seeks to make Ebert the "sabotager-in-chief of the revolution."

[8] The conversation is recorded in Erich Otto Volkmann, *Revolution über Deutschland* (Oldenburg, 1930), 68. Volkmann apparently reconstructed the conversation from Groener's testimony at the Munich Dolchstoss Trial of November, 1925. Professor Rosenberg doubts the reliability of Groener's testimony. He points to the fact that Groener was obviously mistaken when he also testified that Ebert had slept through the entire period from December 24 to December 27, 1918. (Rosenberg, *op. cit.*, 244–245.) I do not, however, believe that Groener's inaccuracy in one statement necessarily invalidates his entire testimony. Moreover, the OHL certainly proceeded on the assumption that such an understanding had been reached and so did the Majority Socialists. *Vorwärts* was satisfied with the arrangement when it wrote on December 24, 1918: "At this moment there is no danger of a counter-revolution . . . the danger which threatens the success of the Revolution in this hour is anarchy."

Fried quotes a director of the Reichsarchiv to substantiate his charge: " 'General Groener pointed out [in the Dolchstoss Trial] that as far back as November 9 and 10 [1918] he had concluded an alliance with Ebert for the suppression, as he expressed it, of the Revolution . . .' " [9] This is a deliberate distortion of both Groener's testimony and Volkmann's interpretation of that testimony. Volkmann's statement needs to be given in its entirety because his qualifying phrase is important: ". . . an alliance with Ebert for the suppression of the Revolution, *that is, of the purely internationalist-proletarian tendencies inherent in socialism as it was concentrated in the radical socialist wing.*" [10]

Fritz Ebert was not prompted by any sinister motives when he appealed to Groener for help. It was the pressure of events which forced him to turn to the Supreme Command just as it had been the pressure of events which had forced him into office. Ebert's real mistake was not made on the night of November 9. At that time, he made the only decision possible. His mistake — and it proved to be a fatal one — was in continuing to rely on the Army even after it had proved faithless and in failing to try to build an army sympathetic to the Republic until it was much too late. So much can be said for Ebert. But the fact remains that in one telephone call he had made the OHL the protector of his government. This gave the Army the opportunity it wanted to reintroduce the "Doctrine of Responsibility" (to use Rosenberg's apt

[9] Hans Ernst Fried, *The Guilt of the German Army* (New York, 1942), 90. For a similar interpretation see R. T. Clark, *The Fall of the German Republic* (London, 1935). Mr. Clark writes (p. 47), "It was only afterwards that the details of the bargain became known and the real role of Ebert as the sabotager-in-chief of the revolution was understood."

[10] E. O. Volkmann, "Der internationale sozialistische Gedanke in seiner Einwirkung auf die deutsche Wehrmacht im Weltkrieg," in *Wissen und Wehr,* 1927, VIII Jahrgang, 168–269 (italics are mine). Groener's actual testimony at the Dolchstoss trial supports Volkmann's interpretation and refutes Fried. When asked directly if the alliance was aimed at overthrowing the Republic or whether it was directed solely against Communism, Groener replied: "This alliance was directed against the danger of Bolshevism and against the soviet system . . . Our purpose on November 10, was the erection of an orderly governmental power, the support of that power by troops, and the holding of a national assembly as soon as possible. I advised the Field Marshal not to take up arms against the Revolution . . . I proposed to him that the O.H.L. might ally itself with the Majority Socialist Party." *Der Dolchstoss-Prozess in München* (Munich, 1926 [?]), 223–225.

phrase[11]) which had been so successfully employed by Ludendorff during the war. This doctrine was a variety of political extortion. Whenever the Supreme Command decided that it did not like a government measure, it would announce that it could not feel "responsible" for the results of its execution. Since the government in power could not stand without the Army's support, it invariably respected the feelings of the OHL. The first new application of the old doctrine occurred on December 6, 1918. On that day, Ebert was forced to ask for assistance to cope with unrest caused by the ludicrous attempt by Count Wolff Metternich to stage a putsch, and the melee which followed one of Karl Liebknecht's demonstrations.[12] In answer to Ebert's call for help, General Lequis in command of sections of the Division of Horse Guards was dispatched to Berlin. When the Independent Socialists objected, Kurt von Schleicher was sent to inform the government that the OHL would withdraw its support unless Lequis was allowed to enter the city. Ebert had no trouble making up his mind; Lequis entered Berlin on December 12.

Meanwhile the first sections of the field armies began to arrive from the Western Front. The Socialist government made elaborate preparations for their homecoming. As the first of the troops filed under the Brandenburger Tor, Ebert welcomed them with the amazing assertion: "As you return unconquered from the field of battle, I salute you." [13]

The Chancellor's intentions were probably good. He was simply trying to win the support of the Army for the new Republic. But in one brief sentence he had helped to absolve the Army and

[11] Arthur Rosenberg, *Die Entstehung der deutschen Republik* (Berlin, 1928), 117 ff. See also John W. Wheeler-Bennett, *Wooden Titan: Hindenburg in Twenty Years of German History, 1914–1934* (New York, 1936), 82–84.

[12] The details are given in Friedrich Wilhelm von Oertzen, *Die deutschen Freikorps, 1918–1923*, 5th ed. (Munich, 1939), 239–242; Volkmann, *Revolution*, 122 ff., and Rosenberg, *Geschichte*, 48–49.

[13] The text of the speech is given in *Freiheit*, December 11, 1918. The best description of the returning troops is to be found in the memoirs of the Berlin Correspondent of the *Temps*, Paul Gentizon, *La Révolution Allemande* (Paris, 1919), 124–131. On the evening of December 9, Ebert had entertained a group of staff officers in the Steglitzer Rathaus. At that time he expressed the hope that the Army would aid him in the solution of his tasks. *Vorwärts*, December 10, 1918.

to condemn his own government for the defeat. His speech was taken up eagerly by those who were already spreading the "stab-in-the-back" theory throughout the Reich. Nor had he accomplished his objective of wooing the Army to his cause. The reaction of Major Pabst, who was to play a leading role in the putsch of 1920, is only typical of the average front soldier's attitude:

> The "reception committee" under Ebert's leadership and his speech had no effect on us. We were only aware of one fact: that the fight against "the masses of mankind" would be hard and bloody . . . it would now be necessary to fight all physical and psychological resistance, to become hard — even against ourselves — to become free of all sentimentality. A great task lay before us.[14]

The Left-wing socialists were spurred into feverish activity by the arrival of the field army and the presence of Lequis in the city. They wanted desperately to create an armed force which would free the Republic from its dependence on the old army. On December 12, the Council of Peoples' Commissars passed a law which organized a Volunteer Civil Guard (*Freiwillige Volkswehr*). The Guard was to be recruited from volunteers sympathetic to the Republic; it would choose its own officers and would be completely independent of the Supreme Command's jurisdiction.[15] The Supreme Command was, of course, furious at this affront. There was more to come. In the meeting of the Congress of Soldiers' Councils held in Berlin on December 17, 1918, three new decrees were passed: Hindenburg and the entire OHL were to be dismissed; the previous decision to dissolve the Cadet Schools was ratified; and the so-called "Hamburg Program" was adopted. This program incorporated the law of December 12 and further insulted the Army by decreeing that all badges of rank were to be abolished.[16] General Groener conveyed the news to

[14] Major W. Pabst, "Spartakus," in *Deutscher Aufstand: die Revolution des Nachkriegs,* edited by Curt Hotzel (Stuttgart, 1934), 30–31.

[15] The law of December 12, 1918, is given in General Ludwig R. Maercker, *Vom Kaiserheer zur Reichswehr, Geschichte des freiwilligen Landesjägerkorps,* 3rd ed. (Leipzig, 1922), Appendix I.

[16] The Congress actually convened on December 16, but a group of sailors, daubed with war paint, and led by Dorrenbach, broke up the meeting. The next day Lampl, a delegate from Hamburg, presented Dorrenbach's demands in the form of a seven-point program. It was ratified by a "thunderous majority." *Allgemeiner Kongress der Arbeiter und Soldatenräte Deutschlands,* Stenographische Berichte, Section 130, 61–65.

von Hindenburg and asked the old gentleman what the Army should do. The Field Marshal was beside himself with anger. He replied:

> What do these people dare to ask? ·That I should tear off my insignia that I have worn since my youth? That I should surrender my sword that has served my King and my Fatherland through three wars? . . . Tell Herr Ebert that I do not recognize the decisions of the Congress . . . [and that] I will fight it to the last ditch . . .[17]

Thus informed, the Chancellor decided that it would be wise to negotiate between the two military authorities who were jockeying for power. He invited representatives of the General Staff to come to a joint meeting of the Peoples' Commissars and the Soldiers' Councils. General Groener and Major von Schleicher, the OHL delegates, arrived in Berlin resplendent in their Imperial uniforms. On their way from the railway station, they were insulted by a group of sailors. The offenders were immediately arrested. Socialist writers have pointed out the significance of the incident:

> On the way from the station to the Chancellery, Groener and Schleicher achieved their first victory over the Revolution . . . Three weeks after November 9, a person could be arrested in Berlin for casting aspersions on an Imperial officer's uniform . . . That is what had happened to the German Revolution! [18]

In the stormy session of December 20, the "Doctrine of Responsibility" once more proved effective. Ebert was flatly told that unless the insane demands of the radicals were rejected, the Supreme Command could not be responsible for the existence of the government. The result was a foregone conclusion: The Army remained in the hands of the Imperial officers. The decision had two highly significant results. First, it consolidated, for the life of the Republic, the power of the Army. Second, it infuriated the radical wing of the Socialist party. By calling the joint meeting, Ebert had rather naïvely hoped that he could reconcile the Army and the leftists. He had driven a wedge between them.

[17] Quoted in Volkmann, *Revolution*, 143–144.
[18] Kurt Caro and Walter Oehme, *Schleichers Aufstieg, Ein Beitrag zur Geschichte der Gegenrevolution* (Berlin, 1933), 8.

II. THE IMPERIAL ARMY FAILS TO CRUSH THE RADICALS

The Independent Socialists were incensed by Ebert's "betrayal" and they began to stir up the highly inflammable Soldiers' and Sailors' Councils. Their work produced immediate results. The most violent and irresponsible section of the Councils was composed of a group of sailors led by Dorrenbach, one of the leaders of the Kiel mutiny. The looting and pillaging which he did nothing to discourage soon attracted the dregs of the Berlin underworld. Adventurers and oafs of all sorts found that by calling themselves revolutionaries they had free run of the city. The first commander of the Division characterized the group succinctly when he observed, "My men are an organized band of robbers." [19] Dorrenbach's merry men had taken over the Imperial Palace and Stables (the *Schloss und Marstall*) as their base of operations and began to blackmail the government. Early in December they promised to leave the Schloss if the government would pay them 125,000 marks. Ebert paid the money. In the meantime, however, the men found that the Imperial wine cellars were well stocked and that the palace afforded excellent accommodations for their women. So, supported by the Police President of Berlin, Emil Eichhorn, they decided to stay on. The money was soon spent, however, and since Christmas was coming they decided that they needed more. Dorrenbach suggested that it would be worth an additional 80,000 marks to the government to have the Schloss vacated. Ebert had had enough; he flatly refused to pay any more money. Dorrenbach thereupon surrounded the Chancellery, took several Majority Socialists as hostages and cut all the telephone wires he could find. Fortunately for Ebert, he was unable to locate the secret line. Once again the Chancellor called for assistance. And once again the Supreme Command proved an ever present — if expensive — help in time of trouble. The Army responded with alacrity because it saw in the task of clearing out the sailors a

[19] Count Wolff Metternich, quoted by Volkmann, *Revolution*, 133. This seems to be the unanimous opinion of all responsible writers. See for example, Gerhard Schultze-Pfaelzer, *Von spa nach Weimar: die Geschichte der deutschen Zeitwende* (Leipzig, 1929), 165–169 and Rosenberg, *Geschichte*, 52–56.

splendid opportunity to settle once and for all the question of whether the Imperial officers or the revolutionary sailors and soldiers would hold the key to power in Republican Germany.

The battle before the Schloss began at 7:40 on the morning of Christmas Eve when General Lequis opened an artillery barrage on the Schloss.[20] The first phase of the battle went to the soldiers of the Imperial Army. The sailors had no artillery, their amunition was rapidly running out, and the reinforcements expected from Kiel did not arrive, thanks to Gustav Noske. At this time, as governor of Kiel, he had made the sailors there promise that they would not send help to "the mutineers who had revolted against the government." [21] At 9:30 the sailors raised a white flag and obtained a twenty-minute truce.

A startling change took place during the course of those twenty minutes. As soon as the shooting had begun, Emil Barth and other USPD and Spartacist leaders[22] had jumped into open cars and driven through the streets of Berlin shouting: "Monarchist counter-revolution! . . . Imperial officers are seizing the Schloss! . . . The Republic is in danger! . . . Come to the Schloss and save the Republic!" [23] By 9:45 a large crowd had gathered and within a few minutes the confused soldiers were confronted by a hostile mob. Surprisingly enough, the soldiers held their fire and some of them went over to the opposition. Dorrenbach's sailors were quick to take advantage of the general melee. They pulled down

[20] The "campaign" is described in too much detail in every nationalist account. See, for instance, Edgar von Schmidt-Pauli, *Geschichte der Freikorps* (Stuttgart, 1936), 177–181.

[21] Gustav Noske, *Von Kiel bis Kapp: zur Geschichte der deutschen Revolution* (Berlin, 1920), 54.

[22] In the early stages of the Revolution, it is extraordinarily difficult to differentiate between the Left wing of the USPD and the Spartacist League. *Freiheit*, the organ of the Independent Socialists, and the Spartacists' *Rote Fahne* often followed identical policies and USPD leaders such as Emil Barth fluctuated between the two groups. For some light on the tangled relationships between the USPD and the *Spartakusbund* (after January 1, 1919, the German Communist Party), see Ruth Fischer, *Stalin and German Communism: A Study in the Origins of the State Party* (Cambridge, Mass., 1948), 14, 71–72, 74, 140–146 and *passim*.

[23] Ludwig Freiwald, *Der Weg der braunen Kämpfer: Ein Frontbuch von 1918–1933* (Munich, 1934), 37.

their white flag, grabbed women and children as shields,[24] and opened fire on the soldiers. Completely surrounded by a crowd of jeering women and children, the once glorious Division of Horse Guards threw down its rifles, took to its collective heels, and ran away. Sailors and civilians joined in the general rout. On the night before Christmas, Major Harbou, chief of staff to General Lequis, sent the following telegram to the Supreme Command:

> The troops under the command of Lequis are no longer capable of action . . . I do not see how it is possible to support or defend the government with the means at our disposal. The government could only be saved by the intervention of an entire army . . . I consider it best that the local troops be demobilized . . . Lequis, in my opinion, is impossible. I suggest his dismissal.[25]

Thus the first and the only attempt of the Supreme Command to crush the Revolution directly failed and failed miserably.[26] This is not to say that the OHL had abdicated. On the contrary, it was to continue to play a decisive role in the management of the ephemeral German Republic. But for the moment it was seriously embarrassed. Its prestige had already been badly shaken by the recent war; and now the unthinkable had happened. It had actually been insulted and defeated by the civilian rabble. The Supreme Command must control the Republic — that much was obvious; but for the present it could not afford to take the risk of doing so directly.

Why not follow the suggestion of that clever young major who was getting along so well with the old Field Marshal? Major von Schleicher had suggested that the government be encouraged to organize volunteer corps recruited from the old army and commanded by former Imperial officers. The idea had much to recommend it. The Supreme Command would maintain just enough interest in the venture to live comfortably while it reorganized

[24] General Freiherr von Lüttwitz, "Einmarsch der Garde-Kavallerie-Schutzen Division in Berlin," in *Deutsche Soldaten*, edited by Hans Roden (Leipzig, 1935), 52.

[25] Quoted in Volkmann, *Revolution*, 163.

[26] A competent military authority calls Christmas Eve, 1918, the absolute nadir of the OHL and describes the Imperial German Army as "a disorganized mob" (*zusammengelaufenen Haufen*). E. O. Volkmann, "Das geistige Gesicht des deutschen Offizierkorps in der Zeitwende," in *Deutsche Rundschau*, CCXLIII (April 1935), 2. See also Rosinski, *op. cit.*, 169.

its own corporation. If the enterprise failed, the OHL would not be compromised because it was the Ebert government which was really responsible for hiring and paying the volunteers. If the enterprise succeeded — that is, if these Free Corps were able to stabilize the Revolution at a respectable level — that was fine; unless, of course, they began to usurp the Army's prerogative of controlling the state.[27] If that were to happen, the Supreme Command's interest was still strong enough to see to it that the Free Corps were put in their proper place. Supported by Groener, von Schleicher was able to convince the *Oberste Heeresleitung*. It agreed to the formation of volunteer corps.[28]

III. THE ARRIVAL OF NOSKE

The first stage of the Revolution, which had seen the ascendancy of the Spartacists, passed quietly into the second, which was to see the rise of the Free Corps. The second stage began in a manner similar to the first. Once again Ebert picked up the telephone and called Groener. The two men had learned a great deal in the preceding days. The Chancellor of the Republic had learned that his policy of mediation between the Imperial officers and the Soldiers' and Sailors' Councils was futile. Groener had learned that the Imperial Army could not handle the situation. They both realized that a new military basis and a new leader would have to be found. So in the telephone conversation of December 26, 1918, Groener demanded a new strong man to replace the Independent Socialists who had resigned from Ebert's cabinet after the Schloss affair. Ebert suggested his old friend Gustav Noske.[29] General Groener was quick to second the nomi-

---

[27] For a typical expression of a German general's attitude toward the state, see below, p. 184.

[28] Heinz Brauweiller, *Generäle in der deutschen Republik: Groener, Schleicher, Seeckt* (Berlin, 1932), 36, and Konrad Heiden, *Der Fuehrer,* translated by Ralph Manheim (Boston, 1944), 243.

[29] It was at Ebert's suggestion that Prince Max appointed Noske the military governor of Kiel. (Noske, *Von Kiel bis Kapp,* 8). Noske's longstanding friendship for Ebert is attested both in Noske's memoirs and in his contribution to a memorial volume dedicated to Ebert and published shortly after the President's death. Gustav Noske, "Seine letzten Tage," in *Friedrich Ebert Kämpfe und Ziele, Mit einem Anhang: Erinnerungen von seinen Freunden* (Dresden, n. d.), 376.

14 VANGUARD OF NAZISM

nation. The Army had heard good things about Noske. For years he had enjoyed the reputation of spokesman for that group of Socialists who advocated a strong armament policy.[30] His reputation during the Revolution spoke for itself: he had brought order out of chaos at Kiel, and he had prevented the Kiel Naval Council from sending reinforcements to Dorrenbach during the Christmas Eve fiasco. Besides, Noske showed the proper deference to and great enthusiasm for the Imperial Army — an enthusiasm which perhaps only an old N.C.O. who had sat at officers' mess with von Moltke could feel for the German Army. Noske's subsequent career served to increase the Army's high opinion of him. General von Maercker, founder of one of the first Free Corps writes: "In the first contact with the new Supreme Commander we [the German generals] got the impression that we were dealing with a man of human understanding and tremendous activity. Noske showed an excellent comprehension of military questions . . . and of the spirit of troops and officers." [31] And after Noske's Free Corps had crushed the Spartacists, the Field Marshal himself wrote a personal letter to Noske in which he said: "The Army has confidence in the Government, limited confidence in the ministry, and unlimited confidence only in the Minister of National Defense." [32]

Thus the "Woodcutter from Brandenburg" who was shortly to become the "Bloodhound of the Revolution" was called to Berlin on December 27, 1918. As soon as he arrived in the capital he gave an indication of the type of policy he would pursue. At his first cabinet meeting he was asked if he were prepared to assume all the responsibilities of the Minister of National Defense. He replied: "Of course! Somebody will have to be the bloodhound

[30] In a Reichstag debate of 1907, Representative Oldenberg had charged that the Social Democrats wanted to disarm Germany. Noske's rebuttal was a spirited defense of national armament. *Verhandlungen des deutschen Reichstags* (Stenographische Berichte), April 25, 1907, 1908.

[31] *Vom Kaiserheer zur Reichswehr*, 65.

[32] Noske, *Von Kiel bis Kapp*, 168–169. After his retirement in 1920, Noske continued to receive testimonials of confidence from the generals. See his last book, published posthumously, *Erlebtes aus Aufstieg und Niedergang einer Demokratie* (Offenbach-Main, 1947), 173 ff.

— I won't shirk the responsibility." [33] The cabinet gave Noske carte blanche to deal with the situation as he saw fit. If his instructions were not precise, so much the better; he would have all the more freedom of action. The new Supreme Commander wrote with satisfaction: "My authority as Supreme Commander (*Oberfehlshaber*) was complete. I have never read the actual wording of my commission, and the appointment as Supreme Commander was never placed in my hand." [34] As Noske left the Chancellery he was greeted by an enthusiastic crowd who hoisted him on their shoulders and began to parade him through the streets. The massive, walrus-mustached Minister yelled good naturedly, "Let me down! I will bring order back to Berlin." [35]

He lost no time in going about his work. In the months which followed, his direct, decisive action stood out in sharp contrast to the worried, uncertain vacillations of his colleagues in the cabinet. Two main problems confronted the new Minister of National Defense. First, it was necessary to reorganize what little police authority existed in Berlin. Secondly, he had to find an army.

The first was quickly solved. Eichhorn, the Chief of Police who had aided and abetted Dorrenbach[36] and had flirted with the Spartacists,[37] was replaced by Eugen Ernst, a man Noske felt he could trust. With the approval of the Supreme Command, General von Lüttwitz, former commander of the Imperial Third Corps, became commander of the troops around Berlin in place of the disgraced Lequis. In the months which lay ahead, this strange combination — the son of a Brandenburg weaver and former N.C.O. and the scion of Prussian nobility and former Imperial general — reorganized the military strength of Germany.

[33] Noske's sobriquet has been variously translated: "The Butcher," "The Executioner," "The Bloody," and "The Bloody Executioner." What he actually said was, "*Meinetwegen! Einer muss der Bluthund werden, ich scheue die Verantwortung nicht!*" (*Von Kiel bis Kapp,* 69.)

[34] *Ibid.,* 68.

[35] *Ibid.,* 69.

[36] Eichhorn admits the charge in his memoirs, *Ueber die Januar-Ereignisse,* 47–48, 50. See also von Oertzen, *op. cit.,* 254 and Lutz, *loc. cit.,* 74.

[37] For a Communist's tribute to Eichhorn, see Clara Zetkin, *Les Batailles Révolutionnaires de L'Allemagne en 1919,* Publication No. 47 of Editions de L'Internationale Communiste (Petrograd, 1920), 4.

With key positions of control in safe hands, Noske began to look for his army. On the morning of January 4, 1919, Noske and Ebert accepted an invitation to go to Camp Zossen on the outskirts of Berlin to review a group of volunteer soldiers whom General von Maercker had just organized into a Free Corps. It was the first time in the long history of the Prussian Army that German troops had passed in review for the benefit of two civilians. The demonstration exceeded the wildest hopes of the two ministers. An army seemed to have suddenly sprung from the frozen ground of the old drill field. Noske thrilled to the sight of rank after rank of well-equipped, beautifully drilled soldiers marching past in perfect cadence. As the civilians left the field, Noske clapped Ebert on the back and said, "You can relax now. Everything will be all right!" [38]

Noske had found his army! At least he had found in the first of the postwar Free Corps the model on which he would pattern his army. But before discussing the recruitment and organization of the Volunteers, it seems advisable at this point in the narrative to pause and examine some of the formative factors which conditioned and molded those self-confessed freebooters who were to form the vanguard of Hitler's Germany.

[38] General Maercker, *op. cit.*, 64.

II

ORIGINS OF THE FREE CORPS

In order to understand the new . . . associations of the post-war
period, one must first understand the psychological transformation
which had begun by the influence of the Youth Movement of pre-war
Germany.

— Ernst Posse

I. THE INHERITANCE OF THE PREWAR YOUTH MOVEMENTS

It is the enormously difficult task of the social psychologist, and
not the historian, to disentangle and analyze those psychological
and social forces which influence the behavior of men. For obvious reasons, no such attempt will be made in this place. And yet
the whole problem of the "psycho-sociological factor" is of such
primary importance to an understanding of the German Free
Corps Movement that it cannot be completely ignored even in a
narrative history of the movement.

The generation to which the *Freikorpskämpfer* belonged — the
generation born in the 1890's — participated in two experiences
which were to have a tremendous effect on his subsequent career
as a Volunteer. The first of these was the prewar Youth Movement; the second, World War I.

During the twenty-odd years which preceded the war, German
youth by the thousands were captivated by a movement which
swept their native land. The social factors which produced the
phenomena of the *Wandervogel* and its allies have titillated the
imaginations of sociologists for years.[1] They seem to have in-

[1] See Theodora Huber, *Die soziologische Seite der Jugendbewegung* (Inaugural dissertation, University of Munich, Munich, 1929), 30–82; Howard
Becker, *German Youth: Bond or Free* (London, 1946), 35–53 and the attached bibliographies.

cluded, among other things, the following: the influence of late nineteenth-century industrialization; the manifold effects produced by urbanization; transformation of the traditional German family structure; psychological aspects of adolescence and the peculiar nature of the German educational system.

In a very real sense, there was no single German Youth Movement — there were dozens of separate groups which display a bewildering complexity and a range of programs which included everything from open homosexuality[2] and sexual excess to extreme self-abnegation; from vegetarianism to epicurianism; from atheism to religious fanaticism; and from pacifism to folkish nationalism. There are a few dominant threads, however, which may serve to lead us through the labyrinth; on these virtually all writers are in accord. And the point which needs to be emphasized here is that all these main aspects are, without exception, characteristic of the Free Corps and subsequently of National Socialism.

The Youth Movement was above all else the revolt of discontented bourgeois youth against a liberal bourgeois society and all its works.

> Specifically, they thought that parental religion was largely sham, politics boastful and trivial, economics unscrupulous and deceitful, education stereotyped and lifeless, art trashy and sentimental, literature spurious and commercialized, drama tawdry and mechanical . . . family life repressive and insincere, and the relations of the sexes, in marriage and without, shot through with hypocrisy.[3]

A characteristic voice raised in this revolt against the bourgeois world is that of Gustav Wyneken, who coined the term *Jugendkultur* to differentiate his ideal completely from the liberalbourgeois culture he despised. The only way to attain this Youth Culture, he said, was to wage a relentless fight against the school,

[2] Hans Blüher, *Wandervogel: Geschichte einer Jugendbewegung,* sixth edition, two parts in one volume (Prien, 1922). Few social psychologists would agree with Blüher's Freudian interpretation of social structure, and his methodology may well be questioned; but his evidence on the preponderance of homosexuality in the *Wandervogel* is beyond dispute.

[3] Becker, *op. cit.,* 51. Of dozens of other witnesses, see especially Huber, *op. cit.,* 7, 10–12, 125 and *passim;* Blüher, *Wandervogel,* 53 ff and Günther Ehrenthal, *Die deutsche Jugendbünde: ein Handbuch ihrer Organisation und ihrer Bestrebungen* (Berlin, 1929), 6–10, 14–15.

the home, and the church, "to tear the youth away from all the old ties and replace them with the free colony of the *Jugendgeistes*." [4]

A familiar picture of the movement is one which shows a group of sun-tanned young Nordics, wearing leather shorts, tramping through the woods and singing the Song of the Freebooters (*Landsknechtslied*). The Leader gives a signal and they stop at dusk to build a great fire. They sit in silence listening for "the messages from the Forest" and feeling the mystic forces of the *urdeutsch*, folkish soul. Their eager, tense, young faces light up as, in the light of the campfire, someone reads from his favorite writer: Nietzsche, or perhaps Stefan George who, as early as 1907, had pleaded: "Volk and high counsel yearn for The Man! — The Deed! . . . Perhaps someone who sat for years among your murderers and slept in your prisons, will stand up and *do the deed*." [5] One of the group who has obviously heard the forest message jumps up. He makes an exhortation which shows perfectly two aspects of the movement characteristic toọ of both the Free Corps and of National Socialism: the eagerness to submit to a Leader and the lust for action — action simply for the sake of action itself. He cries out:

Leaders, Leadership, that is our need; and obedience and great wordless activity. . . . Discussion can be left to the leaders round the council fire. . . . The new religion must be inarticulate . . . convictions must be sealed in the dark. . . .

I want the fight, and man naked and unashamed with his sword in his hand; and behind, the stars sweeping westward, and before, the wind in the grass. It is enough, Brothers. Action! The word is spoken.[6]

It is extremely difficult for the uninitiated to understand the mysteries of the *Führer* principle. Charismatic qualities are not amenable to rational exposition; they must be *felt* by the Leader.

[4] Quoted in Huber, *op. cit.*, 12.

[5] Quoted by Peter Viereck, "Stefan George's Cosmic Circle," in *Decision* (October, 1941), 49. (Italics are in the original.) For intellectual influences see Wilhelm Hedemann, "Die geistigen Strömungen in der heutigen deutschen Studentenschaft," in *Akademisches Deutschland*, edited by Michael Doeberl (Berlin, 1930–1931), Vol. III, and Wilhelm Fabrizius, "Der Aufstand der Bündischen Jugend," in *Deutscher Aufstand*, edited by Curt Hotzel (Stuttgart, 1934).

[6] Quoted in Becker, *op. cit.*, 59.

Wyneken, the leader of one of the wings of Free German Youth, was once asked how he became a Leader. His answer is worthy of Der Führer himself: "I do not know *whose* Führer I am; but I do know *that* I am Führer even if no one chose me to be his leader. How do I know this? Laotse would say, 'From Tao.'" (*"Vom Tao," würde Laotse sagen.*)[7]

The desire for action without any conscious purpose, without any goal whatsoever, is so marked in the German Youth Movement before the war that an able American sociologist concludes, "'Goallessness' in the relative sense of inability or unwillingness to specify the objective, was so marked a trait in the Roamers [*Wandervogel*] and the branches sprouting from them that it would be hard to find a 'purer' type of irrational social action in any society."[8] This "goalless" activity, motivated more by feeling than by thought, was encouraged by the leaders. One of them writes:

Where lively people gather together, there is no need for any *program*. Our happiest hours are those in which nothing was planned beforehand . . . There is nothing more valuable and fruitful than the communion of a small circle of confidants [moved by] the spirit which "bloweth where e'er it listeth." The spirit which unites and enthralls us . . . You must say yes only to that which finds an echo in your hearts of strength and true human worth.[9]

Finally, the movement emphasized the mystic fellowship of the *Volk* as opposed to the rights of the individual. An incessant refrain throughout the literature of the movement is the one so familiar to the readers of Baldur von Schirach and Josef Goebbels: The individual is nothing, the *Volk* is everything.[10] This emphasis

[7] Quoted in Hans Blüher, *Führer und Volk in der Jugendbewegung* (Jena, 1924), 10. Italics are in the original.

[8] Becker, *op. cit.*, 95–96. See also Blüher, *Wandervogel,* 61.

[9] Wilhelm Stählin, *Fieber und Heil in der Jugendbewegung* (Hamburg, 1924), 59–60, 68. Stählin is addressing the postwar youth he helped to organize but his advice applies just as well to the earlier period.

[10] See Richard Braun, *Individualismus und Gemeinschaft in der deutschen Jugendbewegung* (Inaugural dissertation, University of Erlangen, 1929), 53–56 and *passim,* and Ernst H. Posse, *Die politischen Kampfbünde Deutschlands,* in *Fachschriften zur politik und staatsbürgerlichen Erziehung,* Ernst von Hippel, general editor (Berlin, 1931), 14.

on folkish corporatism inevitably led to an attack on the democratic processes which were struggling for expression in prewar Germany. A recent writer has taken pains to point out, however, that this attack was not aimed at the state:

People have said that the battle [of the youth] . . . was a battle against the state. Very wrong indeed! It was solely . . . the battle against . . . a state system which through its parties and through the accident of possessing a majority will (*Zufallsmehrheitswillen*) opposed the concept held by the movement: the concept of corporative spirit and the Führer principle.[11]

In all fairness, it must be said that there was another side to the prewar Youth Movement. It is characterized by high idealism, hopeful — if naïve — optimism and gentle good will. It is the side expressed by Friedrich Wilhelm Foerster:

The Youth Movement is the snowdrop on the hard German winter snow. It announces the German spring. It is a real consolation for every German who was ready to doubt whether the German soul would ever escape from the enchantment in which its pursuit of Power seemed to have inextricably involved it . . . The *Jugendbewegung* is a moral rejuvenescence of the German people, the return of the German soul to its best traditions.[12]

It is this side which appeals to Mr. Gooch. He therefore quotes Foerster — and nobody else — and considers the eminent German humanitarian the "best interpreter" of the movement. Dr. Foerster may well have been the best interpreter, if one gives a qualitative moral meaning to the adjective, but he was certainly not the most representative spokesman. In point of historical fact, the future belonged to those who pursued Power and not to those who formed snowdrops on the hard German snow. But the point which really concerns us here, is the fact that it was not the gentle aspects of the movement which appealed to and conditioned the *Freikorpskämpfer* in the impressionable days of his youth.

[11] Gerhard Bergmann, "Akademische Bewegungen," in *Akademisches Deutschland*, II, 81.
[12] Friedrich Wilhelm Foerster, *Jugendseele, Jugendbewegung, Jugendziel* (Munich and Leipzig, 1923). The quotation appears in G. P. Gooch, *Germany* (London, 1925), 312–313.

II. THE INHERITANCE OF THE WAR

> War, the Father of all things, is also our father. He hammered us,
> chiselled us, hardened us into that which we now are. And forever,
> as long as the wheel of life still turns in us, War will be the axis on
> which it revolves. He trained us for war, and warriors we will remain
> as long as we draw the breath of life.
>
> — Ernst Jünger

On August 3, 1914, a young law student who was to die within
the month at Chalons-sur-Marne wrote the following letter to
his family:

Hurray! At last I have my orders. I report tomorrow morning at 11
o'clock . . . We are bound to win! Nothing else is possible in the
face of such a determined will to victory. My dear ones, be proud that
you live in such a time and in such a nation and that you too have the
privilege of sending those you love into so glorious a battle.[13]

Thus that famous Austrian corporal who was "overwhelmed by
impassionate enthusiasm" and who fell on his knees and thanked
God for the coming of the War,[14] was no exception. German
youth by the thousands welcomed the War and eagerly waited
the great opportunity of their lives — the chance to defend the
Fatherland from the attack of the common foe. To a man, they
were sincerely convinced of the righteousness of the cause.[15] As
the jubilant, singing throng left for the front, only one thought
disturbed them: the war, everyone predicted, would be over in
a month or so and they might be too late.

As the war dragged on year after year, the youthful enthusiasm
vanished. The war diary of Ernst Jünger is a case history of the
terrible psychological transformation which took place. As a
sensitive, idealistic volunteer he was nauseated by the sight of
blood; and, on a lovely April day, he wrote that his sympathy was
with the poet:

[13] The letter is reprinted in *Kriegsbriefe gefallener Studenten,* edited by
Professor Doktor Witkop (Munich, 1928), 7–8.

[14] Adolf Hitler, *Mein Kampf* (Reynal and Hitchcock edition, New York,
1940), 210.

[15] This is true of even the pacifist poet, Ernst Toller, who writes in his
memoirs: ". . . I was proud. I was a soldier at last, a privileged defender
of the Fatherland." *Eine Jugend in Deutschland* (Amsterdam, 1936), 53.

> Surely this day that God has given
> Was meant for better uses than to kill.

In the course of two war years, that boy of nineteen was changed into a hard, ruthless killer; the veteran of twenty wounds, the proud wearer of the *Pour le Mérite;* the commander of a Storm Battalion. He now wrote:

The turmoil of our feelings was called forth by rage, alcohol and the thirst for blood. As we advanced heavily but irresistibly toward the enemy lines, I was boiling over with a fury which gripped me — it gripped us all — in an inexplicable way. The overpowering desire to kill gave me wings. Rage squeezed bitter tears from my eyes . . . Only the spell of primaeval instinct remained.[16]

While the spirit of Ernst Jünger merits our attention because it was to become the spirit *par excellence* of the postwar Volunteers, a more specific contribution was made to the Free Corps by the War: the concept of the Storm Troops. The breakdown of the Schlieffen Plan at the Marne forced Falkenhayn to dig in defensively. The war of attrition had begun and the mobile warfare, the tradition of a century — the tradition of Clausewitz, the elder Moltke and Schlieffen — was abandoned as a strategic concept. Army commanders, however, began to experiment on the tactical level with compact, well-armed, highly mobile units in a desperate attempt to break through the trenches and end the war of attrition. As early as the autumn of 1914, these "Shock Troops" (*Stosstrupps*) had been used in the Argonne. It was here that the hand grenade was used successfully for the first time. But on the whole, the experiment failed.[17] It remained for a certain Captain Rohr, now famous in the annals of German military history, to perfect the concept of the Storm Troops. Briefly, what Rohr did was to organize superlatively conditioned, well-trained elite troops whose

---

[16] *In Stahlgewittern: Ein Kriegstagebuch,* 16th edition, 125th thousand (Berlin, 1926), 152 and 257, 265. The sentiments here expressed are manifest through out the war letters. In addition to the collection already cited see also *Der deutsche Soldat: Briefe aus dem Weltkrieg,* edited by Rudolf Hoffmann (Munich, 1937).

[17] Major Ernst Schmidt, *Argonnen: Schlachten des Weltkrieges* (Berlin, 1927), 136.

task it was, literally, to "storm" the enemy lines and force a breakthrough for the regular infantry.[18]

Special equipment was designed for the Storm Troops. A light carbine replaced the more accurate, but more unwieldy, model "98" rifle; small flamethrowers and portable machine guns were issued; and Rohr is given credit for inaugurating the use of the steel helmet.[19] But the hand grenade remained the favorite weapon of the new troops.

After a period of intensive training under live fire behind the lines, these hard-hitting, self-sufficient units were ready for the front. Rohr's concept was used so effectively at the Somme that in October 1916 the Supreme Command ordered every army to build combat units patterned after the Rohr Storm Battalion. "In the course of one short year," writes Dr. Gruss, "the Storm Battalion had succeeded in forcing the entire army to recognize their new battle art." [20]

Concessions of all sorts were made to the Storm Troops and they were encouraged to look upon themselves as an elite troop. Special uniforms and insignia were designed for them — they were even authorized to wear the coveted silver death's head, previously worn only by the aristocratic Cavalry.[21] They were given the best food, the best equipment and were authorized to wear pistols, previously issued only to officers. They were given

[18] The whole question of World War I Storm Troops is the subject of a German doctorate dissertation, Hellmuth Gruss, *Aufbau und Verwendung der deutschen Sturmbataillone im Weltkrieg* (University of Berlin, 1939). The résumé given here is based largely on this study. See also Curt Jany, "Sturmtruppen," in *Geschichte des deutschen Heeres im Weltkrieg*, edited by Hermann Cron (Berlin, 1937); Ernst Jünger, "Stosstrupps," in *Das Antlitz des Weltkrieges. Fronterlebnisse deutscher Soldaten* (Berlin, 1930) and the same writer's *In Stahlgewittern: Ein Kriegstagebuch* (Berlin, 1936); Ferdinand von Ledebur, *Die Geschichte des deutschen Unteroffiziers* (Berlin, 1939), 481 ff; W. Hoeppener-Flatow, *Stosstrupp Markmann greift an! Der Kampf eines Frontsoldaten* (Berlin, 1939), 51–59; and Hans Zoberlein, *Der Glaube an Deutschland* (Munich, 1938), 151 ff.

[19] Colonel Bauer, *Der Grosse Krieg*, cited in Gruss, *Deutschen Sturmbataillone*, 21.

[20] *Op. cit.*, 80.

[21] When the Storm Troops entered the Free Corps, they took their insignia with them. The death's head was by all odds their most popular emblem. See pictures of the insignia in *Das Buch vom deutschen Freikorpskämpfer*, edited by Ernst von Salomon (Berlin, 1938).

fourteen-day furloughs at the discretion of their Storm Troop leaders. They had their own military entity, and were classified by Storm Battalions and not by regimental number. They were billeted far behind the lines, where they lived comfortably, and were transported in trucks up to the lines for dramatic break-throughs and then returned to the safety of the rear. In short, in dozens of those little things so important to a soldier, the elite Storm Trooper lorded it over the common foot soldier. The inevitable result was that friction arose between the two. Witness the bitter testimony of a lowly doughboy:

The men from the Storm Battalions arrived in fast trucks early in the morning from their quiet quarters behind the front . . . they would take a few prisoners and then go back to their quarters. But the trench fighters had to stay and sweat out the heavy return fire throughout the whole day until by midnight, only a handful of men was left. They [the Storm Troops] were always mentioned by name and praised as the best troops in the war bulletins, while the trench fighters never even dreamed of being mentioned at all.[22]

Franz Schauwecker gives a clear picture of the World War Storm Trooper, a type which he considers to be "the perfected form" of the German soldier. His description is worth quoting at some length:

Even in externals, the "Western Fighter" had become very different from the soldiers of the beginning of the war. In his most refined and perfected form (*durchgebildetsten, vollendesten Form*), in the battle soldier of the *Sturmbataillon,* he did not march with shouldered rifle but with unslung carbine. His knees and elbows are protected with leather patches. He no longer wears a cartridge belt, but sticks his cartridges in his pockets. Crossed over his shoulders are two sacks for his handgrenades . . . Thus he moves from shell hole to shell hole through searing fire, shot and attack, creeping, crawling like a robber, hugging the ground like an animal, never daunted, never surprised . . . always shifty, cunning, always full of confidence in himself and his ability to handle any situation . . . to capitalize on every advantage. A new type of man. A man who has achieved the highest intensification

[22] Werner Beumelburg in the introduction to *Eine ganze Welt gegen uns,* edited by Wilhelm Reetz (Berlin, 1934), 7. Beumelburg is also the author of the immensely popular, savage diatribe against the Weimar Republic, *Deutschland in Ketten* (Berlin, 1931), a book which had reached over 75,-000 copies before it was reissued by the Nazis in 1940.

of all human qualities and blended them so harmoniously and yet so violently that one can only describe him with one word: "Fighter." [23]

German military writers often regret that modern mechanized warfare has tended to ruin the noble concept of the true warrior. They note that infantry fighting, for instance, deteriorated during World War I into uninteresting mass slaughter. But Ernst Jünger, the proto-Nazi philosopher and glorifier of the Storm Troop mentality (he was himself a commander of a Storm Battalion), emphatically denies the charge. He shows that among the Storm Troops, at least, the true spirit of the German warrior remained very much alive. He writes:

Combat during the World War also had its great moments. Everyone knows that who has ever seen these princes of the trenches (*Fürsten des Grabens*) in their own realm, with their hard, set faces and bloodshot eyes; brave to the point of madness, tough, quick to leap forward or back. Trench warfare is the bloodiest, wildest, most brutal of all warfare and it produced its own type of men — men who grew into their Hour — unknown, crazy fighters. Of all the stimulating moments of war, none is so great as the meeting of two Shock Troop Leaders (*Stosstruppführer*) in the narrow confines of a trench. There is no retreat and no mercy then. Blood wrings forth from their shrill war cries which are wrenched from the heart like a nightmare.[24]

The peculiarly close relationship between officers and men which we shall find to be an essential characteristic of the Free Corps, was fostered by these combat units. Discipline in the Storm Troops was strict, but it was not the traditional "discipline to the death" (*Kadaverdiszipline*) cherished by the officers of the old army. It was rather an almost friendly type of loyalty: "a rougher, but more hearty tone existed between Storm officers and Storm troopers," Dr. Gruss tells us.[25] One simple fact is eloquent of this "new discipline." The Storm Troopers often used

[23] *Im Todesrachen, Die deutsche Seele im Weltkriege,* first edition (Halle, 1919), 282–283.

[24] *In Stahlgewittern,* 240. The introduction to the English translation by Basil Creighton, *Storm of Steel* (New York, 1929) is worth recording here: "He (Jünger) displays the truly adventurous spirit. He is no more brutal or insensitive than any other explorer, arctic or equatorial. He snipes at English Tommies or French *poilus* . . . in a spirit of sportsmanship which contains no sting for us because we know the inevitable outcome." (Page references above are to the German edition.)

[25] Gruss, *op. cit.,* 24–25.

the familiar "du" in addressing their officers — a degree of familiarity unheard of in the old Army. The relationship is well expressed by the biographer of one of the Storm Troop Leaders:

> Markmann knew precisely how he stood with his men. To them he was not their commanding officer; he was their Leader! And they were his Comrades! They trusted him blindly and would have followed him into hell itself if it were necessary.[26]

The direct carry-over of this new discipline to the postwar Volunteers is best illustrated from the semiofficial history of German noncommissioned officers:

> During these years [1917–1918] there developed between troops, officers and non-commissioned officers a comradely relationship which was cemented by their blood — a relationship such as was never known before in time of peace. This famous relationship, founded on mutual respect, was one of the foundation stones on which was built the Free Corps . . . who were to fight for the rebirth of the German *Volksseele*. This foundation of the old Front Fighter was above all of a spiritual nature.[27]

By its very nature, the Storm Troop system made two things apparent: First, there was a tremendous increase in the number of young commanders. The ratio of officers, or noncommissioned officers, to enlisted men sometimes reached as high as one to four.[28] Secondly, only a very special type of officer could be used. He must be unmarried, under twenty-five years of age, in excellent physical condition (former athletes were given preference), he must be mentally alert, and above all he must possess in abundance that quality which German military writers call "ruthlessness." The result was that at the time of the Armistice Germany was flooded with hundreds of capable, arrogant young commanders who found an excellent outlet for their talents in the Free Corps movement.[29]

To summarize, it may be said that the postwar Volunteers learned a great deal from the Storm Troop system. From it they

[26] Hoeppener-Flatow, *Stosstrupp Markmann*, 95.
[27] *Geschichte des deutschen Unteroffiziers*, edited by Ferdinand Freiherr von Ledebur (Berlin, 1939), 481.
[28] *Akten des Heeresarchives*, Potsdam, quoted by Gruss, *op. cit.*, 43.
[29] For the role of the junior officer in the postwar period, see below, pp. 45 ff.

received their organizational form, that of small self-sufficient combat units; they received much of their leadership and with it the "new discipline" which was an extension of the Führer principle; and above all, they were imbued with what Storm Troop glorifiers call the spirit of the "new men of Europe." Since much of the literature of the postwar period is a paean of praise to this "new man," it would be well to look at him closely. Ernst Jünger, who knew him best, paints his picture in words that are at once a description and a prophecy for the future:

This is the New Man, the storm soldier, the elite of *Mitteleuropa*. A completely new race, cunning, strong, and packed with purpose. What first made its appearance openly here in the War will be the axis of the future around which life will whirl faster and ever faster . . . The glimmering sunset of a declining period is, at the same time, the morning light of another day in which men are called to new and harder battles. Far behind them await the mighty cities, the hosts of machines, the nations whose inner foundations will be torn asunder by the attacks of this New Man—of the audacious, the battle-proven, the man merciless both to himself and to others. This war is not the end. It is only the call to power. It is the forge in which the world will be beaten into new shapes and new associations. New forms must be molded with blood, and power must be seized with a hard fist.[30]

Franz Schauwecker endorses Jünger's characterization with enthusiasm, calls the Storm Troops the "Troops of Destiny," and adds: "The dissolution of these battalions after the war did not hinder the inner development of such troops. Here was born and made virile that pure culture (*Reinkultur*) which we call the culture of the front-line soldiers." [31]

If Jünger and Schauwecker seem to have been quoted at too great length in this chapter it is not only because the leading authority on the Storm Troops considers them to be the most reliable spokesmen for the system and quotes liberally from their works; nor is it solely because of the tremendous popularity of their books in postwar Germany. They have been quoted because

---

[30] *Der Kampf als inneres Erlebnis,* 5th edition, 40th thousand (Berlin, 1933), 76–77.

[31] In his introduction to Hoeppener-Flatow's biography of Markmann, previously cited, 20–21.

the spirit they describe was to become the prevailing spirit of those latter-day "Storm" or "Shock" formations: those of the Free Corps[32] and their successors, Hitler's *Sturmabteilungen*.

This writer certainly does not wish to suggest that the attitude of these "Heroic new men" is typical of all German soldiers in World War I. The reader can find a convenient antidote to Jünger and Schauwecker in Erich Maria Remarque's *All Quiet on the Western Front*. And there are dozens of other testimonials to a totally different type of soldier. One need only read the sensitive, tragic war letters written by German students to realize that thousands of young Germans loathed an abominated war but fought and died in the belief that they were helping to build a more humane world.[33] It may well be that these, and not the men we have found it necessary to discuss, constituted the most representative type of German soldier; but it was not this type which characterized the Free Corps. It is also true that after the Armistice, the vast majority of the German veterans returned to quiet civilian lives. It can also be argued that many men of moderate, liberal convictions enlisted in the Volunteers. But we are here concerned with the men who set the spirit and tone of the Free Corps movement; and these men are best described by one of Hermann Goering's favorite remarks: "fighters who could not become de-brutalized." A famous Free Corps fighter depicts them well:

The war could not release them from its grip . . . The most active part of the Front marched simply because it had learned to march. It marched through the cities enveloped in a cloud of sullen rage — a cloud of vaulting, purposeless fury — knowing that now it had to fight, to fight at any cost . . . This then was the one problem of the Free

[32] The Free Corps preserved both the *esprit* and the actual terminology of their predecessors, that of either "Storm" or "Shock" to describe their formations. Thus we have the *Stosstrupps* of the Stephani Free Corps, Ehrhardt's *Stosstrupp* section, and we will find Schlageter leading a *Stosstrupp* of the Special Police in Upper Silesia. The adjective "Storm" is, if anything, more widely used: *Sturmbataillon* Schmidt, *Sturmabteilung* Rossbach, *Sturmabteilung* Heinz, *Sturmfahne* of the Oberland Free Corps, etc. *Sturmbataillon* Ruhr followed their leader directly into the Hindenburg Free Corps.

[33] See, for example, the letters collected by Witkop, in *Kriegsbriefe gefallener Studenten,* previously cited.

Corps fighter: to give his utmost so that the real meaning of the War could be made manifest to the very limit of his power.[34]

III. THE STAB IN THE BACK

The theory that the German Army was really never defeated but was forced to surrender solely because it had been traitorously stabbed in the back by the civilian revolutionaries is of course a legend. Time and again it has been pointed out that the Supreme Command first threw in the towel four months before the Revolution; that during the war years it had exercised absolute military, political, and economic control over the civilian government; and finally that it was Ludendorff who forced an unwilling civilian government to sue for peace.[35] These incontrovertible facts should be sufficient in themselves to give the *Dolchstoss* a decent burial and it would seem not only indelicate but totally inadvisable to exhume it here. Yet it is not enough for the historian to record "how it actually took place" — difficult as that is. It is sometimes far more important to record what men *believed* actually took place. The important historical fact here is not that the stab-in-the-back theory is false; but rather that *it was believed to be true*. It is important because, as Professor Brinton reminds us, "Though beliefs may change in time, they are at any given moment among the hardest of facts; harder than logic — harder even than statistics." [36]

By the psychological process of rationalization born of humiliation and wounded pride, the German soldier believed, or came to believe, completely and thoroughly, that the Army had never been defeated after all. Apart from the very real fact that he *wanted* desperately to believe it, two other factors helped him. During the course of the War he had come to distrust and despise everything connected with the home front and what he loosely called the "Rear" (*Etappe*). Any one of the War memoirs shows the feeling:

[34] Ernst von Salomon, *Die Geächteten* (Berlin, 1930), 106–107; and "Die Gestalt des deutschen Freikorpskämpfers," in *Das Buch vom deutschen Freikorpskämpfer,* 11.

[35] For a recent study of the *Dolchstoss* legend see Harry R. Rubin, *Armistice, 1918* (New Haven, 1944), 54–55, 392–394.

[36] *The United States and Britain* (Harvard University Press, 1945), 25.

. . . yes, and then we have the Rear!! The Rear lies far, far behind the front and there is plenty of everything there: plenty of comfort, food, conveniences, peace — all the enjoyments of life combined in that one little enticing word: The Rear! . . . we called them "Chair-born goldbricks" (*etappenhengste*) and the word was never spoken without an undertone of contempt . . . Front and Rear — between them lies a chasm between Action and Words.[37]

This statement must not be dismissed as merely the usual "gripe" of a soldier. The chasm between front and rear is recognized by one of Germany's leading military authorities, a member of the Potsdam Research Institute for War and Military History, as the primary cause of friction in the Army. Major Volkmann writes:

If we feel obligated to state . . . that there was a rift within the Army, the line of demarcation was not between officers and men. For the masses of the officers were up in the trenches and underwent all the privations and dangers of the men. The rift was rather between the Front and the Rear . . . It was here that misunderstanding and hostility developed . . .[38]

Given this background, it was perhaps inevitable that when the defeat came, the front-line soldier would blame it on the people behind the lines. And he was encouraged to do so not only by the effective and widespread propaganda disseminated by the Army, but also by the bungling attempts of the civilian government to win his support by flattery. One of the government's incredible pamphlets tells the soldier:

A new Germany greets you! . . . Perhaps you do not return as victors who have completely crushed the enemy to the ground . . . But neither do you return as the vanquished, for the war was stopped at the wishes of the leadership of the Reich (*Reichsleitung*) . . . so you can hold your heads high.[39]

[37] Schauwecker, *Im Todesrachen*, 116–120.
[38] "Das Soldatentum des Weltkrieges," in *Die deutsche Soldatenkunde*, Bernhard Schwertfeger and Erich Otto Volkmann, editors (Leipzig, 1937), I, 166–167.
[39] *Deutschland als freie Volksrepublik: Den aus dem Felde heimkehrenden Volksgenossen*, an anonymous pamphlet issued by the executive committee of the Social Democratic Party (n.p., November 1918). Representative pamphlets issued by the army include the following suggestive titles: *Armee und Revolution: Entwicklung und Zusammenhänge*, by "a German general staff officer" (Berlin, 1919), and *Deutschlands Zusammenbruch: Seine Ursachen und Folgen, Eine Flugschrift zur Aufklärung und Rechtfertigung*, by Haupt-

It is not difficult to predict what the attitude of the front-line soldier will be when he returns home. He is convinced that the Army which had fought through four years of cruel war has been stabbed in the back by the cowards and pacifists of the home front.

The War memoirs are crowded with pictures of homecoming scenes. One example must suffice here. Hans Zöberlein is returning to revolutionary Munich. At the station he is accosted by a group of Socialists who insult him and tear off his military insignia. He continues:

> If I had taken the streetcar, I could have been home in 15 minutes. But I didn't feel like hurrying. No joy of arrival hastened my heavy steps. I went on a long detour as once before . . . when as a boy I had to go to the dentist. What would I do at home anyway? What could I do in this cold, strange place which had once been my homeland? How could I talk to people who had become strangers to me?

Confused, lonely, and terribly bitter, Zöberlein can find solace only in thinking back over his life as a soldier. Snatches of his soldiers' oath come back to him: "I swear by Almighty God . . . never to be faithless . . . in storm and battle . . . in war as in peace — in war *as in peace.*" The last phrase makes him feel better. He repeats it to himself and concludes his memoirs: "The war is over. But the battle for Germany goes on. Volunteers, to the front!" [40]

---

mann Vorweck (Oldenburg, 1919). It was not until years later that the Reichstag investigating committee published its laborious report on the causes of the collapse. *Untersuchungsausschuss über die Weltkriegsverantwortlichkeit. 4. Unterauschuss, Die Ursachen des deutschen Zusammenbruches in Jahre 1918. Unter Mitwirkung von Dr. Eugen Fischer, Dr. Walther Bloch, herausgegeben von Dr. Albert Philipp, M.d.R.* (12 vols., Berlin, 1925–1929). The question of the stab-in-the-back is discussed in volume VI, 1–29. The historian must congratulate the committee for its careful investigation. The report is a monument to German industry and objectivity. It is nevertheless a pathetically ineffective answer to the cheaply inaccurate but highly successful propaganda of the opposition.

[40] *Der Glaube an Deutschland: Ein Kriegserleben von Verdun bis zum Umsturz,* 25th edition, 275th thousand (Munich, 1938), 879–890.

III

ORGANIZATION AND CHARACTER
OF THE FREE CORPS

> Anyone who judges Free Corps fighters by the standards of the
> civilization it was their task to help to destroy is utilizing the standards
> of the enemy.
>
> — Ernst von Salomon

I. NOSKE COLLECTS HIS ARMY

After reviewing Maercker's Volunteer Rifles at Camp Zossen,
Gustav Noske began at once to collect an army based on the
volunteer system. Since the Spartacists were the masters of Berlin,
the new Supreme Commander of all German forces moved his
headquarters to the dormitories of a girls' boarding school on the
outskirts of the city.

As might be expected, National Socialist writers virtually dismiss Noske as a factor in the development of the Free Corps
system. They suggest that the Volunteers suddenly sprang forth
full grown from out of the German *Boden* in answer to one of the
many *urdeutsch* calls for strong men. Socialist writers, who
habitually refer to all Volunteer formations as "Noske Guards,"
or "The Bloodhound's Bastards" (to give two of their less pungent
epithets), give Noske far too much credit for initiating and organizing the system. What Noske did was simply to give official
authorization to a movement which was already sweeping the
country. He did not organize an army, he collected one.

The Volunteers took their names from their point of origin or
from well-known military leaders: The Ehrhardt Brigade; The
Haase Free Corps; Maercker's Volunteer Rifles; The Hindenburg
Free Corps; The Thuringian Free Corps, and so forth. It would be

both impossible and unrewarding to try to discuss all the volunteer bands that were springing up throughout Germany in the early months of 1919.[1] A few examples must suffice. Since we are concerned, at this point, with the immediate origins and the organizational form of the Free Corps, Maercker's Volunteer Rifles (*Freiwilligen Landesjägerkorps*) are worth studying in some detail. They were the first of the Volunteers to establish a well-articulated organization, and later groups used them as their model. But it is a mistake to assume, as it has been assumed, that Maercker and his men were typical of all Free Corps. General Maercker was an almost uniquely attractive figure in the history of the movement, and his corps was characterized by strict discipline, moderation, and a military bearing that was beyond reproach. The best compliment that can be paid to the little, florid-faced General is that other Volunteers consider his men woefully lacking in "the true Freebooter spirit." [2]

[1] See the note in the Appendix.

[2] Hans Fried calls General Maercker ". . . one of the most embittered enemies of the Republic (yet who, under the Republic, could now make his own law)," and again, ". . . one of the most aggressive antagonists of the Republic." *The Guilt of the German Army* (New York, 1942), 176, 395. This is a flagrant misrepresentation of both Maercker's purpose and his actions. He probably did not like the Republic, but more than any of his colleagues he supported it because he felt that the only other alternative was anarchy. His refusal to endorse the Kapp putsch is not the action of "an embittered enemy" or "an aggressive antagonist." Indeed the biographer of Kapp lays heavy blame on Maercker for the failure of his hero's project. (Ludwig Schemann, *Wolfgang Kapp und die Märzunternehmung vom Jahre 1920: Ein Wort der Sühne,* Munich and Berlin, 1937, 148–150). See below, p. 156. In writing the founding orders for his Rifles, Maercker indeed made "his own law"; but it was because no other law had been written. The government not only endorsed it but incorporated its main features into the law of March 6, 1919, which established the Provisional Reichswehr. Maercker systematically weeded out all freebooter elements from his corps. He organized vocational skills, sports, and music programs to raise the morale of his troops and established political discussion groups in which Republican and Socialist spokesmen participated. See his memoirs, *Vom Kaiserheer zur Reichswehr, Geschichte des freiwilligen Landesjägerkorps,* 3rd ed. (Leipzig, 1922), 57–59, 178 ff. For typically adverse opinions of Maercker given by leading Volunteers, see Rudolf Mann, *Mit Ehrhardt durch Deutschland, Erinnerungen eines Mitkämpfers von der 2. Marinebrigade* (Berlin, 1921), 38–39, and Hermann Ehrhardt, *Kapitän Ehrhardt, Abenteuer und Schicksale,* edited by Friedrich Freksa (Berlin, 1924), 103, 125.

On December 12, 1918, General Maercker, the former commander of the old 214th Infantry Division submitted a memorandum setting forth his ideas for the creation of a Free Corps to his superior officer, General von Morgan. It was immediately approved, and on December 14 — just two days after the Council of People's Commissars had published their law creating the Volunteer Civil Guards[3] — he wrote the "First Constructive Order of the Volunteer Rifle Corps."[4] The founding order provided for strict discipline; established "Trusted Men" (*Vertrauenleute*) to serve as intermediaries between officers and men and sit as judges on courts-martial; and it made extensive changes in the old Army's military courtesy and punishment regulations. This program was approved by the Supreme Command without change. The single fact that an individual commander could take it upon himself to change the sacrosanct German Army Regulations is eloquent testimony of the depths to which the *Oberste Heeresleitung* had sunk in December 1918.

Maercker at first used older officers as commanders of troops,[5] because he felt that younger men lacked the requisite poise and experience to deal with problems of civil war. He soon changed his mind, however, and began to use younger men as much as possible. He writes: "I learned that my earlier theory was completely wrong. I have observed many very young officers in difficult situations in which they conducted themselves admirably . . . Youth has the advantage of carelessness, of enterprising spirit, and above all, of patriotic fervor on its side — qualities that are not to be despised."[6] It is this use of young officers, usually lieutenants and captains, which is a distinguishing feature of the

[3] See above, p. 8.

[4] *Grundlegender Befehl Nr. 1 der Freiwilligen Landesjägerkorps* is reprinted in Maercker, *op. cit.*, 45–47.

[5] The Second Constructive Order called for the following table of organization: brigades were to be commanded by major generals or colonels; sections (*Abteilungen*) by lieutenant colonels and majors; and companies by captains. (*Ibid.*, Appendix 2.) Parenthetically, the date of *Grundlegender Befehl Nr. 2* is incorrect. The date given is December 14, 1920, but *Grundlegender Befehl Nr. 3* (which deals with conditions of enlistment) is dated December 22, 1918, and Maercker was relieved of his command in the autumn of 1919.

[6] *Ibid.*, 50.

movement. The qualities which Maercker calls *Unbekümmertheit, Unternehmungsgeist,* and *Vaterländischen Schwungen,* we shall presently see, served, in other formations at any rate, as an excuse for the savage excesses of "the Freebooter spirit."

Since his Free Corps was to be used to crush isolated pockets of resistance throughout the Reich, Maercker combined several military functions and created small, self-sufficient units precisely as the Storm Troops of the war had done. Each company had its own machine gun and trench mortar section. As the occasion demanded, light and heavy artillery, flame-throwers, armored cars and even aircraft were added.

Having set forth the organization and technique of deployment, Maercker was ready to recruit volunteers. Recruiting headquarters were established in a Franciscan convent near Salzkotten, Westphalia. Maercker had no difficulty in enlisting recruits. By the end of December, he could review his first section of four thousand men. The main problem facing the General was in outfitting his men. He tells in his memoirs how he hurried from one depot to another only to find that the Spartacists had already looted them, or that the officials in charge would not authorize supplies because the Rifles did not meet the specifications of the law of December 12. He writes: "I appealed to General von Lüttwitz and he told me that he could not supply me . . . I went personally to the War Ministry and asked the General Director of the War Department for some overcoats. He threw his hands in the air and said, 'I haven't any!' " [7] Thus at the end of 1918, neither the commander of troops around Berlin, nor the Minister of War, both of whom enjoyed the confidence of the Supreme Command, could equip four thousand men!

In the closing weeks of 1918, Maercker's example was being followed with enthusiasm throughout the Reich. On December 26, Colonel Reinhard met with a few officers of his old 4th Guard Regiment in the State Library on Unter den Linden and began to organize the Free Corps which bore his name. "My purpose," he tells us in his memoirs, "was the creation of a troop that could annihilate the Republican gangs, and in so doing, re-establish order in Berlin . . . and serve as an impetus to the redevelop-

[7] Maercker, *op. cit.,* 62.

ment of Germany's military strength."[8] The organization of the Reinhard Brigade is strikingly similar to that of Maercker's Rifles. He too uses the *Vertrauenleute*, and provides exactly the same regulations in regard to punishment and military courtesy. In fact the similarity is much too close to be coincidental. Yet, the man who was to become S.S. Oberführer of Berlin under Hitler gives no credit to Maercker. He speaks of the "innovations" which he inaugurated and intimates that he alone was responsible for revolutionizing the entire Free Corps movement.[9]

Revolutionary Berlin gave birth to a phenomenon absolutely unique in the annals of Prussian military history. Here, in the early days of December 1918 was born a troop of men of battalion strength who were commanded by a noncommissioned officer. When the Second Guard Regiment returned from the Western front they were insulted by the solicitations of the Soldiers' Councils. A group of the regiment's soldiers appealed to their sergeant-major to organize them into a Free Corps. Sergeant-Major Suppe called an organizational meeting at the Zirkus Busch, and founded the Suppe Free Corps. His brigade of some 1,500 men was divided into companies, each of which was commanded by a sergeant. After the Schloss and Marstall fiasco, Suppe joined the Reinhard Brigade, but kept command of his own battalion.[10]

[8] Colonel Wilhelm Reinhard, *1918–1919: Die Wehen der Republik* (Berlin, 1933), 59. Reinhard's reference to *"republikanischen Banden"* and later to "the Government's soviet troops" (p. 77) is typical of the effort of irresponsible nationalistic writers to discredit the Republic. He is insinuating, not at all subtly, that the Government supported the Spartacist terrorists. The exact opposite is the truth. It was the Free Corps who were the "Republican gangs" hired by the Government to defeat the Spartacists.

[9] Reinhard, *op. cit.*, 60–61.

[10] It should be noted, however, that non-commissioned officers did not normally command Free Corps. When Heinz Oskar Hauenstein was asked to praise the work of N.C.O.'s in the postwar period, he stressed their general importance but was forced to admit, "I can recall only two cases: [where N.C.O.'s served as commanders of Free Corps]: Non-Commissioned Officer Battalion Suppe of the Reinhard Regiment and deck officer companies of the Third Marine Brigade." *Geschichte des deutschen Unteroffiziers*, 449. Suppe was later promoted to Deputy Officer (*Offizierstellvertreter*) by Reinhard for his work in holding the Chancellery in the street fighting of January, 1919. See his own account, "Zwischen Soldatenwehr und Freikorps in roten Berlin," in *Das Buch vom deutschen Freikorpskämpfer*, edited by Ernst von Salomon (Berlin, 1938). Hereafter cited as *Freikorpskämpfer*.

About this time in Kiel, Admiral Loewenfeld founded his
Third Naval Brigade as a companion to Ehrhardt's more famous
Second Brigade. Like Ehrhardt's Free Corps, the Third Brigade
also consisted predominantly of officers, naval cadets, and
seasoned petty officers. According to one of its members, each
of the company commanders had been a former U-boat commander and all of them wore the coveted *Pour le mérite*, Germany's highest military award. Its "Storm Battalion" was led by
Arnauld de la Pierre, the famous submarine hero who had sunk
550,000 tons with his own ship.[11] Loewenfeld writes proudly of his
Corps:

[It became] . . . on the whole the strongest Free Corps in Germany,
not only in numbers — about 8,000 men — but also in its articulation
of infantry, pioneers, artillery (of four calibers), trench mortars, flame-
throwers, armored vehicles, tanks, aircraft, and trucks. We could
handle every demand of war.[12]

Meanwhile, from Düsseldorf to Königsberg; from Hamburg to
Munich, similar groups were forming everywhere. And Noske,
from his office in the girls' dormitory, encouraged them all and
launched a drive for more troops. Separate recruiting offices were
established throughout the Reich and provocative advertisements
appeared on billboards and in newspapers:[13]

VOLUNTEERS!

From the West — March to the East!
FLAME-THROWER PERSONNEL
Enlist in the Flame-thrower section of
THE LUETTWITZ CORPS
Immediate pay plus 5 marks daily bonus.
Free food and equipment.

[11] Friedrich Glombowski, *Organisation Heinz (O. H.): das Schicksal der
Kameraden Schlageters* (Berlin, 1934), 16–17.
[12] "Das Freikorps Loewenfeld," in *Deutsche Soldaten, vom Frontheer und
Freikorps über die Reichswehr zur neuen Wehrmacht,* edited by Hans Roden
(Leipzig, 1935), 156. Hereafter cited as *Deutsche Soldaten.*
[13] The *Berliner Tageblatt, Vorwärts,* and the *Vossische Zeitung* printed
these, or similar advertisements. In January 1919, a special newspaper was
established for the Volunteer army. Its first issue contains, in addition to
recruitment advertisements, an editorial by Noske which sets forth the purposes of the Free Corps. *Volkswehr,* January 25, 1919. Representative posters
are reprinted in *Deutsche Soldaten* and in *Freikorpskämpfer.*

COMRADES

The Spartacist danger has not yet been removed.
The Poles press ever farther onto German soil.
Can you look on these things with calm?
NO!
Think what your dead comrades would think!
Soldiers, Arise! Prevent Germany from becoming
the laughing stock of the earth. Enroll NOW in
THE HUELSEN FREE CORPS
Recruiting offices: Bauer Cafe, Unter den Linden,
Potsdam Beer Gardens . . . [etc.]

VOLUNTEERS, FALL OUT!
Patriotic Germans, join the fierce and foolhardy
LUTZOW FREE CORPS.

Measured in terms of sheer quantity, the recruiting campaign
was immensely successful. By the summer of 1919, thousands of
Germans had entered one or another of the volunteer formations. It is extraordinarily difficult to give even a very loose approximation of the size of the movement. Contemporary sources
are in flat disagreement. The Independent Socialist, Hugo Haase,
in a speech to the National Assembly, pointed with alarm at an
illegal army of over a million men.[14] Noske estimates the number
at 400,000.[15] Ernst von Salomon has difficulty making up his mind.
In one place he says "between 50,000 and 70,000"; in another,
"150,000." [16] In part, the difficulty arises from the fact that a
"Volunteer" may be defined in a variety of different ways. All the
postwar military and semimilitary formations were recruited on
a volunteer basis. These formations included not only the Free
Corps (Freikorps) as such, but Emergency Volunteers (Zeitfrei-
willigen), Civil Guards (Einwohnerwehr), and Security Police
(Sicherheitzpolizei), as well as a host of armed student formations

[14] Speech of July 16, 1919, Verhandlungen der verfassunggebenden deutschen Nationalversammlung (Stenographische Berichte), 67 Sitzung, 1962.
[15] Von Kiel bis Kapp, 167. This is the number usually given. See also
Rosinski, The German Army, 171.
[16] The first figure is given in his article, "Der verlorene Haufe," in Krieg
und Krieger, edited by Ernst Jünger (Berlin, 1930), 120. The second is in
Nahe Geschichte: Ein Ueberblick (Berlin, 1936), 96.

such as the *Münster Akademische Wehr*. What further compli-
cates matters is that these latter types sometimes served as local
civilian guards and sometimes conducted regular military campaigns along with the Free Corps. Even if we accept the rule-of-
thumb criterion suggested by von Salomon and confine ourselves
to the "real" Free Corps, that is, only to "those troops capable of
coping with any military problem," there is still no agreement.
Schmidt-Pauli in the foreword to his history of the movement
complains about the difficulty of discussing "over two hundred
well organized Free Corps";[17] while von Salomon insists that the
number of such formations never exceeded eighty-five.[18]

Let us estimate, then, that the number of men directly involved
in the movement was somewhere between 200,000 and 400,000.
The numbers — imprecise as they admittedly are — are nevertheless important. These men practiced a doctrine which differed in
no essential way from that political and social cannibalism which
was to call itself National Socialism. It is worth remembering
that by the summer of 1919 the Free Corps may well have been
the most important single power in Germany.[19]

In 1919, the contrast between the strength of the Free Corps
and the weakness of Adolf Hitler's movement is glaring. While
the Volunteers were sweeping the country with their gospel of
race and power, what was Hitler doing? One afternoon during
that same summer an obscure political agitator raised his strangely
compelling voice to demand that the struggling, newly formed,
little German Workers' party purchase three rubber stamps in
order to improve its office equipment.

II. REASONS FOR ENTERING THE FREE CORPS

In addition to general appeals to patriotism, the recruitment
campaign emphasized the very real material advantages offered
by the Free Corps. Conditions varied in each Corps, but a hypo-
thetical average Volunteer could expect to receive a daily base

---

[17] Edgar von Schmidt-Pauli, *Geschichte der Freikorps, 1918–1924* (Stuttgart, 1936), 9.
[18] *Nahe Geschichte*, 96.
[19] At any rate, this is the considered judgment of a leading historian of the
Republic, Arthur Rosenberg, *Geschichte der deutschen Republik* (Karlsbad,
1935), 75–76.

pay of from 30 to 50 marks; he was guaranteed 200 grams of meat and 75 grams of butter a day; service in the Free Corps counted toward workers' and farmers' pensions; his family received the regular family allotment; at the end of his period of enlistment, the Volunteer drew the pay allotted to all demobilized soldiers; he was, of course, completely clothed at government expense.[20] Officers received extra bonuses which varied with the area in which they served. The Volunteers were satisfied with the arrangements. One of them writes: "Noske added 5 marks [to the regular pay], and the Bavarian government another 5. Then too, we got plenty of beer and cigarettes and a quarter of a liter of wine a day. We had a good time." [21]

Why, then, did they join the Free Corps? Because as patriots they wanted to save the Fatherland from internal anarchy and the threat of invasion? Because of assurances of material well-being? These, indubitably, were factors. But they only supply a part — and not a very important part — of the answer. There was a better reason for entering the movement. It was that the Free Corps gave high promise of solving the basic psychological and social problems which confronted this generation which was indeed "the Generation of the Uprooted and Disinherited." [22] It is not possible to understand the appeal of the Volunteers without first understanding the tremendous psychological repercussions which the defeat of 1918 had on the German mind. It left a generation of men bewildered, embittered, and filled with a terrible hatred against the world which had betrayed them. Let us look more closely at the motivations of the two groups which together formed the great majority of all Volunteers: the front soldiers and the student youth of Germany.

The type of veteran discussed in the previous chapter returned from the War with roots which could not find nourishment in the soil of a *bürgerlich* society. He saw in the new Republic a feeble government of pacifists which had betrayed the Army. Such a society could neither appreciate nor understand him; conse-

[20] In addition to recruitment advertisements, see Benoist-Méchin, *op. cit.*, I, 150–151.

[21] Mann, *Mit Ehrhardt durch Deutschland*, 78.

[22] The phrase is Konrad Heiden's. Used to characterize the postwar youth of Germany, it is as apt as his "armed intellectuals" is unfortunate.

quently, after the first weariness of the front had passed, he joined
the Free Corps. Here he found comradeship, understanding, economic security, and a continuation of the military life he had
learned to love. Friedrich Wilhelm Heinz, a War volunteer at sixteen, member of the Ehrhardt Brigade, and subsequently supreme
S.A. Leader for Western Germany, is representative of the men
who could never demobilize psychologically:

> People told us that the War was over. That made us laugh. We our-
> selves are the War. Its flame burns strongly in us. It envelops our whole
> being and fascinates us with the enticing urge to destroy. We obeyed
> . . . and marched onto the battlefields of the postwar world just as
> we had gone into battle on the Western Front: singing, reckless and
> filled with the joy of adventure as we marched to the attack; silent,
> deadly, remorseless in battle.[23]

The Free Corps leader who was to become Minister President
of Saxony under Hitler tells us that this "pure Freebooter type"
was the most common of all Volunteers, and the type most sought
after by the *Freikorpsführer*:

> The pure *Landsknechte* didn't much care why or for whom they
> fought. The main thing for them was that they *were* fighting . . . War
> had become their career. They had no desire to look for another . . .
> War made them happy — what more can you ask? I liked this group
> . . . such freebooters were useful to our purposes in every respect.[24]

Next to the war veterans, students formed the largest group in
the Free Corps. For the most part, they were young idealists who
had been brought up to believe in the moral righteousness of
Germany's cause. They were stunned by the magnitude and the
suddenness of the collapse. They demanded immediate and drastic action to save the Fatherland. This was no time for moderation, for the half-measures proposed by those bungling politicians
in Weimar. An astute observer of his generation has caught the
attitude perfectly in one phrase: "Radicalism is trumps." [25] Some

[23] Friedrich Wilhelm Heinz, *Sprengstoff* (Berlin, 1930), 7. The author
explains the title in his introduction (p. 14): ". . . we ourselves are the
Sprengstoff (Explosives)."
[24] Manfred von Killinger, *Das waren Kerle!* (Munich, 1944), 54–55.
[25] E. Günther Gründel, *Die Sendung der Jungen Generation: Versuch
einer umfassenden revolutionären Sinndeutung der Krise* (Munich, 1932),
226.

of them entered politics with results that are succinctly described by Dr. Edgar J. Jung in an often-quoted article entitled, "The Tragedy of the War Generation":

> One after the other of them, in danger of starvation . . . resignedly bowed under the yoke of a period whose catch word was peace and money-grabbing. . . . But others would not give in to so hard a fate. Clumsily ignorant but intransigent . . . they entered domestic politics with the courage of despair. . . . They drew up programs without knowledge, enthused over actions without forces, and concocted projects without reality.[26]

And many of them enlisted in the Volunteers. During the War, they had identified themselves with the front soldier; and now they felt the impact of the defeat as keenly as did their heroes. The accident of age and what they felt was a traitorous armistice had cheated them of their right to fight for the Fatherland and to participate in the glories and the romance of battle. The Free Corps gave them another chance. And above all, like the National Socialism which was in a real sense its heir, the Free Corps movement answered the pressing psychological need of the confused and the insecure. It gave them a chance to forget their own inefficacy by identifying themselves with a movement which promised them everything which they lacked as individuals: the opportunity for dramatic action and power. They welcomed this chance to barter personal freedom for a new security and a new pride in participating in power.[27]

A great deal of the literature of postwar Germany is unreadable, irresponsible bombast. But the writings of Ernst von Salomon are an honest reflection of the chaotic and embittered mind of his generation. As a boy of sixteen, he watched the defeated Army return to Berlin. His reaction is worth quoting at some length, for it was the reaction of thousands of his fellow students:

> Their eyes were hidden in the shadow thrown by the peaks of their caps, sunk in dark hollows, grey and sharp. These eyes looked neither to

[26] Edgar J. Jung, "Die Tragik der Kriegsgeneration," in *Süddeutsche Monatshefte*, Heft 8, 27. Jahrgang (May 1930), 526. Mr. Fried wrongly attributes the quotation to Gründel. (Fried, *Guilt of the German Army*, 201.)

[27] For a social psychologist's discussion of the relationship between psychological insecurity and political dictatorship, see Erich Fromm, *Escape from Freedom* (New York, 1941).

the right nor to the left. They remained fixed before them, as if under
the spell of a terrifying goal . . . God! What a look they had, those
men! Those thin faces, impassive under their helmets, those bony limbs,
those ragged clothes covered with dirt! They advanced step by step
and around them grew the void of a great emptiness . . .

But here was their home, here warmth and fellowship awaited
them — then why did they not cry out with joy? Why didn't they laugh
and shout? . . . Why didn't they even look at us? . . . Oh, God!
This was terrible! Somebody had lied to us. These were not our heroes,
our defenders of the Homeland! These men did not belong to us at all.
Everything we had hoped, thought and said had become terribly wrong
. . . What a mistake! What a ghastly mistake! . . . These men had
come from a totally different world! . . . Yes, that was it! Suddenly
I understood.

These men were not workers, farmers, students . . . These men
were soldiers . . . united in the bonds of blood and sacrifice. Their
home was the Front — it was for them Homeland! Fatherland! *Volk!*
Nation! That is why, yes, that is why they could never belong to us.
That is the reason for this stolid, moving, spectral return . . . War
moved them; war dominated them; they could never abandon it;
never come home. They would always carry the Front in their blood:
the approaching death, the glorious suspense, the suffering, the smoke,
the cold steel . . .

And suddenly they were supposed to become peaceful citizens in a
bürgerlich world! Oh, no! That was a transplanting, a counterfeit
which was bound to fail . . . The war is ended but the warriors still
march! . . .

Posters hung in the street corners, volunteers were sought. Formations were to be organized to defend our Eastern frontiers. On the day
after the entrance of the troops into the city, I volunteered. I was accepted, I was equipped. I too was a soldier.[28]

[28] *Die Geächteten* (Berlin, 1930), 26–35. Ernst von Salomon was born in
1902. He was active in the Free Corps and its successor organizations from
1918 to 1921. Imprisoned for his part in the assassination of Walter Rathenau,
he served sentences intermittently from 1921 to 1928. He survived World
War II and has recently published a new autobiographical sketch which
reaffirms his bombastic nationalism and his hatred for democracy. See his
Fragebogen (Hamburg, 1951). Although his earlier books are quoted ex-
tensively by the National Socialists, Salomon never joined the party. For an
attitude similar to that of Salomon quoted above, see Heinz Schauwecker's
article, "Erinnerungen eines Freikorps-Studenten," in *Deutscher Aufstand:
Die Revolution des Nachkriegs,* edited by Curt Hotzel (Stuttgart, 1934);
Gerhard Bergmann, "Akademische Bewegungen," in *Akademisches Deutschland,* edited by Michael Doeberl, 4 vols. (Berlin, 1930–1931), II; Theodore
Abel's interesting study, *Why Hitler Came to Power: An Answer Based on
the Original Life Stories of Six Hundred of His Followers* (New York, 1938).

III. THE CAPTAINS AND LIEUTENANTS

Not nearly enough attention has been paid to the role which the junior officers played in the history of postwar Germany. Not the colonels and the generals, but the lieutenants and the captains — Röhm, Schlageter, Ehrhardt, Rossbach, Schultz and the rest — formed the backbone of the Free Corps movement. And — to change the metaphor — it was they who were the link between the Volunteers and National Socialism. The problem of the junior officer is essentially a social-psychological problem and it was a direct inheritance of the War.

During the course of World War I, the German Officers' Corps underwent a tremendous transformation. It had never been a large corps, and the demands of modern warfare in general, and of the Storm Troop system in particular, forced it to expand. At the beginning of hostilities it consisted of some 22,112 active and 29,230 reserve officers. By the time of the Armistice the total number of Germans who enjoyed all the social prerogatives attendant on being an officer in the Imperial German Army was well over 270,000. In other words, the active Officers' Corps of the prewar years formed only about a twelfth part of the total officers at the end of the war.[29]

But far more important than the numerical increase was the social transformation which had taken place. The Corps had changed so markedly in respect to both age and social background that a leading military authority considers the transformation to be a main cause of Germany's defeat.[30] Professor Rosenberg no doubt exaggerates when he suggests that the old Officers' Corps ceased to exist after the battle of the Marne,[31] but the final statistics do show an appalling toll of casualties. Of the 22,112 active

Thirteen per cent of the Columbia sociologist's sampling had been active members of the Free Corps. See also Gründel, *Die Sendung der Jungen Generation*, 26–27 and *passim*.

[29] Karl Demeter, *Das deutsche Heer und seine Offiziere* (Berlin, 1930 [?]), 220.

[30] Major E. O. Volkmann, "Sozial Heeresmissstände als mitursache des deutschen Zusammenbruches von 1918," in the Reichstag committee's report: *Die Ursachen des deutschen Zusammenbruches*, XI, Zweiter Halbband.

[31] *Die Entstehung der deutschen Republik*, 89 and 109.

officers entering the war, 11,357 — over half of them — were killed.[32]

The Supreme Command used two means of filling in the gaps in the military tables of organization. The overwhelming majority of officer replacements came from one-year volunteers (*Einjäh-rig-Freiwilliger.*) These young men of seventeen or eighteen served a brief period at the front, were hastily trained in officers' candidate schools and commissioned second lieutenants. The social and military position of these young officers was not an altogether happy one. The enlisted men despised them and referred to them jeeringly as "90 day wonders," [33] and the regulars of the Officers' Corps looked down on them as "civilian officers." With virtually no hope of securing regular commissions, their one ambition was to ape the mannerisms and attitudes of the "real officers" so that they might be mistaken for them. Their "naive reverence" for the regular officers, a staff officer of the old school tells us, made them "more Catholic than the Pope." [34]

Although more than 200,000 *Einjährigen* were commissioned during the course of the war,[35] still more officers were needed. The Supreme Command finally decided to promote men from the ranks. This was, of course, against all tradition, and it was only with the greatest of regret and much soul-searching that the rigid old principles of selection were finally modified. It is important for us to notice that the field appointments occured only among the battle veterans of the front lines — men who would one day become Free Corps commanders. Everywhere else the old techniques of promotion were adhered to with loving tenacity.[36]

[32] Demeter, *op. cit.*, 220.

[33] For the attitudes of enlisted men toward the *Einjährigen*, see *Die Geschichte des deutschen Unteroffiziers,* edited by Ferdinand, Freiherr von Ledebur (Berlin, 1939), 493–494; and Generalleutnant Bernhard Ramcke, *Vom Schiffsjungen zum Fallschirmjägergeneral* (Berlin, 1943), 83.

[34] *Das Alte Heer,* by "a Staff Officer" (Charlottenburg, 1920), 43, quoted in Morgan, *Assize of Arms,* 142.

[35] Rosinski, *op. cit.*, 160.

[36] Christian Walter Gässler, *Offizier und Offizierkorp der alten Armee in Deutschland als Voraussetzung einer Untersuchung über die Transformation der militärischen Hierarchie* (Inaugural Dissertation, University of Heidelberg, 1930), 71.

Forced by necessity to admit into their ranks those whom they deemed to be "socially impossible," [37] the members of the world's most exclusive military club hit upon an interesting method of promotion. The exigencies of war might require that young social upstarts be made officers; but there were ways of seeing to it that the social tone of the Officers' Corps would not be harmed permanently by the influx of enlisted men. Commissions to the rank of a regular officer were avoided as much as possible. Instead, the enlisted man was appointed to the temporary rank of "Sergeant-Major-Lieutenant" (*Feldwebel-Leutnant*) or of "Deputy Officer" (*Offizierstellvertreter*).[38] As such he could be an acting officer for the duration of the war, but it was made very clear to him that he was neither the military nor the social equal of the "real officers." He was definitely considered to be a "second-class officer" and, throughout most of the war, he might at any time be "degraded" when an officer was available to take his place.[39]

Nevertheless, the junior officer — regardless of whether he was an *Einjährigen*, a "Deputy Officer," or a genuine officer — looked and felt and acted like an officer. He had tasted the power of command. He had worn the uniform of an officer in the Imperial German Army. It is not in the least surprising that "when peace broke out" [40] he did not want to surrender his newly won power, his uniform, and the prestige and social status he enjoyed among

[37] Von Salomon, *Nahe Geschichte*, 97.

[38] Fried exaggerates when he implies that no enlisted men were commissioned. (*Guilt of the German Army*, 108.) But the number of men commissioned from the ranks was certainly very low. The more or less official history of the German noncommissioned officers sets the total number at 150. (Ledebur, *op. cit.*, 494.) See also Volkmann's "Sozial Heeresmissstände" in *loc. cit.*, XI, 36. For a conflicting impression see General Ernst von Wrisberg, who maintains that the number of enlisted men commissioned was "really considerable." *Der Grosse Krieg 1914–1918*, edited by Max Schwarte, 10 vols. (Leipzig, 1921), Vol. VIII, 34. Wrisberg repeats this impression in his *Heer und Heimat 1914–1918* (Leipzig, 1921), 200. General Morgan misreads Wrisberg and uses him as a source to prove that very few officers came from the ranks. (*Assize of Arms*, 140–141.)

[39] See Wrisberg's article in *Der Grosse Krieg*, XVIII, 33–34, the same writer's *Heer und Heimat*, 200, Gässler, *op. cit.*, 72, and Morgan, *op. cit.*, 142–143.

[40] The expression is usually attributed to Captain Röhm, but it occurs repeatedly in other memoirs.

civilians. In a word, he felt that he could not face the "soul-destroying" [41] life of a civilian. One of Captain Röhm's comrades was speaking for hundreds of his fellow junior officers when he coined what Röhm considered a "classical expression": "I hereby declare that I no longer belong to these people [the civilian rabble]. I can only remember that I once belonged to the German Army." [42]

The melancholy prospect of becoming civilians did seem to be the fate of the junior officers. For the regular army authorized by Versailles allowed for only 4,000 officers. Since the organizers of the new army were formerly Imperial generals, and since they wanted above everything else to carry on their cherished traditions, the select Four Thousand were chosen from the officers of the old school and not from the war-made officers who formed over 50 per cent of all the German officers who had fought in World War I. [43]

This, then, was the dilemma of the junior officer of 1918: he wanted to remain a military commander, but the regular Army did not want him. Given his problem, and the attitude expressed by Röhm's friend, the number of junior officers entering the Free Corps Movement is about what one would expect. A detailed case study of more than 9,000 Bavarian officers shows that 22.6 per cent of all the second lieutenants who had served in the war and 27.6 per cent of the first lieutenants continued their military careers in the Free Corps. The percentage of higher officers so engaged is definitely lower. [44] "From staff officers on up," says von Salomon, "the senior officers showed surprisingly little inclination to enter Free Corps service. Furthermore, majors were received by the troops themselves as an unwelcome burden." [45]

The Free Corps Movement was an almost perfect answer to the psychological and social needs of the junior officer. Indeed,

[41] Glombowski, op. cit., 14.

[42] Ernst Röhm, Die Geschichte eines Hochverräters, 7th ed. (Munich, 1934), 10.

[43] Demeter, Das Deutsche Heer und seine Offiziere, 220.

[44] J. Nothaas, Beiträge zur Statistik Bayerns, cited by Fried, op. cit., 124–125. The percentage of "Deputy Officers," not given in Nothaas's study, would presumbly be higher than that of the regular officers.

[45] Ernst von Salomon, "Der verlorene Haufe," in Krieg und Krieger, 120.

life in the Volunteers was even better than it had been in the Imperial Army. In those days he had commanded a platoon or at best a company; now he was the master of mixed formations of battalion or even regimental strength.[46] In the Imperial Army men were assigned to him and he had to train them according to rigid Army regulations; now he could recruit his own men and train them as he saw fit. He no longer was rigorously supervised by military superiors; under the Free Corps system he was responsible to no one. In brief, the life of the *Freikorpsführer* was eminently satisfactory. Indeed it was so satisfactory that the young leader did everything in his power to perpetuate the system. Hence, in the days when the Free Corps were theoretically dissolved, the captains and the lieutenants turned to the various military and semimilitary organizations sponsored by National Socialism as the nearest approximation of the Free Corps system.

IV. TWENTIETH-CENTURY FREEBOOTERS

By urging individual commanders to recruit and organize their own troops, Noske had attained his immediate objective, that of getting men under arms in a hurry. But he had also created a situation which was, as he rather ruefully admits, "not unlike the days of Wallenstein." [47]

As historical analogies go, this one is pretty apt. As everyone knows, the distinguishing characteristic of seventeenth-century *Landsknechte* warfare was the absence of any central military agency to coördinate and control the unruly freebooters, whose only allegiance was to their immediate commanders. By granting unlimited authority to each *Freikorpsführer* and by failing to force the separate Corps into any effective over-all military organization, Noske encouraged precisely the same type of military atomization.[48]

[46] Von Salomon, *Nahe Geschichte*, 97–98; "Junius Alter" (Franz Sontag), *Nationalisten, Deutschlands nationales Führertum der Nachkriegszeit* (Leipzig, 1932), 76–77. The best National Socialist history of the movement notes that a main cause of the friction between the Free Corps leaders and the old-line generals developed over this marked discrepancy between rank and size of command. Von Oertzen, *Die deutschen Freikorps*, 23.

[47] Noske, *Von Kiel bis Kapp,* 116.

[48] It is true that an effort was made to absorb the Free Corps into the "Provisional Reichswehr" as planned by the law of March 6, 1919. But the

Each separate Free Corps was and remained not only the unit but the heart and soul of the system. It was the focus of each Volunteer's loyalty and it was the constant preoccupation of the leader to preserve his Corps' independence at all costs. As one of literally dozens of examples, let us take the case of Heydebreck's Wehrwolves. Republican officials had asked Lieutenant Heydebreck to organize a Free Corps to help defend the Republic. The one-armed war hero was happy to oblige. But when the officials transferred his men to another commander, Heydebreck was beside himself with rage, he screamed: "Somebody stole my troops!" The exclamation introduces a passionate and untranslatable indictment of the government's entire military system — a system which simply could not understand the peculiarly close bonds which connected the Free Corps fighters with their leader.[49] Heydebreck swore revenge and proceeded at once to organize an illegal formation with the avowed purpose of overthrowing the government. It would be difficult to carry military anarchy much further.

The Führer principle which we saw developing in the prewar youth movement and among the Storm Troops of the War reached new heights in the Free Corps movement. The principle is manifested on two levels. First, the individual commander — he is often referred to as "Der Führer" — is idolized as the concrete embodiment of all those qualities which the Volunteer wanted to possess in himself. This tribute to Ehrhardt is typical: "Captain Ehrhardt is the flesh and blood of the soldier and the *Führernatur* of York, Blücher, Nelson and Ney; iron in self assertion, . . . rough and dominating in action, . . . the word danger is unknown to his heart. His unflagging energy has no bounds." [50]

military provisions of the Treaty of Versailles put an abrupt end to this faltering attempt to bring some order out of the chaos. On the Provisional Reichswehr, see below, pp. 78 ff.

[49] Peter von Heydebreck, *Wir Wehrwölfe: Erinnerungen eines Freikorpsführers* (Leipzig, 1931), 76. For an almost identical reaction, see the biography of Berthold, the commander of the *Eiserne Schar*, Ludwig F. Gengler, *Kampfflieger Rudolf Berthold, Sieger im 44 Luftschlagen, Erschlagen im Brüderkampfe für Deutschlands Freiheit* (Berlin, 1934), 152 f.

[50] Friedrich Wilhelm Heinz, *Die Nation greift an: Geschichte und Kritik des soldatischen Nationalismus* (Berlin, 1932), 88. For another example of the same type of thing, see Carsten Curator, *Putsche, Staat und Wir!* (Karlsruhe, 1931), 164–166.

But the Führer is also an abstraction. In the twentieth-century version of Barbarossa's beard growing around the table in the Kyffhauser, he is seen as the great Leader who will come to lead the Free Corps to victory over all their enemies. Thus in the black days of despair which followed the defeat of the Volunteers in the Baltic, we have the leader of the *Eiserne Schar* writing to his sister: "Someday a Man will come to lead us — a Man who unites German spirit and German power! Believe me . . . things will be just a little better for us then!" [51] And Ernst von Salomon writes: "We looked around us and asked who the Man would be who would be able to speak for us . . . Where was this man filled with the stuff of history; one who had more than just passing greatness — more than the silent Seeckt, the prudent Ebert, the hesitant Scheidemann?" [52]

Social psychologists would probably be interested in the fact that the Volunteers delighted in picking up and applying to themselves the worst epithets enraged citizens had hurled at them. They gloried in calling themselves outlaws, traitors, nihilists, and murderers. "But," says Ernst von Salomon, "the term most often applied to the Volunteers by the soldiers themselves, was the same one the frightened citizens used: Freebooters (*Landsknechte*)." [53] The true Landsknechte type which the National Socialists were later to extol as the possessor of "the moral strength of the race," [54] is personified in Gerhard Rossbach, the notorious Free Corps leader who became the first adjutant of Hitler's S.A. Rossbach looked back on the period of the Volunteers with nostalgia:

It was the beautiful old Freebooter class of war and post-war times . . . organizing masses and losing them just as quickly, tossed this

[51] The letter is given in Gengler, *Kampfflieger Rudolf Berthold*, 178.

[52] Von Salomon, *Die Geächteten*, 267.

[53] Von Salomon, "Der verlorene Haufe," in *Krieg und Krieger*, 118. Notice how they titled their memoirs: *Die Geächteten* (von Salomon); *Landsknechte wurden wir* (Erich Balla); *Geschichte eines Hochverräters* (Ernst Röhm); and so forth.

[54] Gerhard Günther, *Deutsches Kriegertum im Wandel der Geschichte* (Hamburg, 1934), 81. He goes on to say that the Nazi Storm Trooper "feels his kinship with the Freebooters in his *unbürgerlichen*, carefree spirit and his sheer love of battle" (p. 216). Ernst Jünger had already used the term "Freebooter" interchangeably with "the new elite" to describe the Storm Troops of World War I (*Der Kampf als inneres Erlebnis*, 56).

way and that way just for the sake of our daily bread; gathering men about us and playing soldiers with them; brawling and drinking, roaring and smashing windows — destroying and shattering what needs to be destroyed. Ruthless and inexorably hard. The abscess on the sick body of the nation must be cut open and squeezed until the clear red blood flows. And it must be left to flow for a good long time 'till the body is purified.[55]

And Heinz Oskar Hauenstein, the twenty-year-old noncommissioned officer who founded and led both the Heinz Storm Battalion and the Organization Heinz describes his comrades: "Fighting was the whole content and meaning of their lives. Nothing else made any sense . . . It was battle alone that they loved . . . the battle that was hard, brutal, pitiless." [56] But while he revered and respected the seventeenth-century Landsknecht warrior, the twentieth century Freebooter sometimes felt that he had gone beyond his precursor and had reached a higher plane of cultural development. One of Captain Ehrhardt's commanders writes:

I have often tried to comprehend the soul of the Free Corps soldier . . . I think that one can say that "The Eternal German" was the most usual type. He was drunk with all the spirit of "The Eternal German." Naturally in varying degrees. Some had taken only a little "shot" — but enough to make them voluble and carefree; many had taken a big "shot" — enough to make them psychopathic (*Psychopathische*) . . . thus they became an ennobled troop of Freebooters (*veredelte Landsknechtstruppe*) and far surpassed their predecessors by reason of the intensification of culture which had taken place during the preceding centuries.[57]

V. THE BOURGEOIS REVOLT AGAINST A BOURGEOIS WORLD

National Socialist writers like to think that the Free Corps movement — like the Nazi movement — was a tremendous patriotic upsurge in which all true Germans rose as one man to save the Fatherland. All social and class distinctions, they say, were dissolved in the crucible of white hot patriotic fervor.

[55] Quoted in Heiden, *Der Fuehrer*, 145.
[56] Hauenstein, in the introduction to Glombowski's memoirs, *Organisation Heinz (O.H.): Das Schicksal der Kameraden Schlageters*, 5. Hauenstein later became the editor of the National Socialist newspaper *Niederdeutscher Beobachter*.
[57] Rudolf Mann, *Mit Ehrhardt durch Deutschland: Erinnerungen eines Mitkämpfers von der 2. Marinebrigade* (Berlin, 1921), 214–215.

It is true that social extremes are represented in the Volunteers. Destitute laborers did rub cartridge belts with the nobility. In the more or less official Who's Who of the National Socialist party, for example, there appears the name of Carl Eduard, Duke of Saxe-Coburg-Gotha. The Duke was as proud of his Free Corps activity as he was of his other distinctions. Along with his work as member of the staff of the Supreme S.A. Leadership, his membership in the Kaiser Wilhelm Society and his presidency of the German Red Cross, he lists his other accomplishments: In 1919 he served on the staff of the Franconian Volunteer Rifle Regiment. During the same year he was a leader of the Bavarian *Einwohnerwehr*. In 1920 he was Thuringian district leader for the Ehrhardt Brigade and subsequently of Ehrhardt's murder organization, the Organisation Consul.[58] Other examples might be cited, but they too would be exceptions to the rule. The overwhelming majority of the Volunteers — like the majority of the National Socialists — came from lower middle-class and peasant backgrounds. This is true not only of the common *Freikorpskämpfer* but of the leaders and heroes of the movement: Schlageter, Ehrhardt, Schultz, Berthold, and the rest.[59]

The laboring classes did not tend to join the volunteer army of the Republic. In the first place, many of them suspected the purposes of the Free Corps. Secondly, men with a job and a family did not feel disposed to risk their economic position in the unstable postwar period by joining the Volunteers. Thus Emil Eichhorn found to his regret that the laboring class would not even join his socialist Security Force. The *Sicherheitswehr*, he admits, was dominated not by "stable elements" but by buccaneering soldiers of fortune. He writes: "There were plenty of good men around, married Berliners and organized workers, but only a few of them joined." [60] Finally, Free Corps commanders made it a

[58] *Das deutsche Führerlexikon, 1934–1935* (Munich, 1934), 399–400.
[59] While no statistical study of this matter has yet been made, the conclusion is apparent from the autobiographies and the short biographical sketches given in the *Führerlexikon;* Baldur von Schirach, *Die Pioniere des Dritten Reiches* (Essen, 1933[?]); Wilhelm, Freiherr von Muffling, *Wegbereiter und Vorkämpfer für das neue Deutschland* (Munich, 1933); and in *Die Braunhemden im Reichstag, Die Nationalsozialistische Reichstagsfraktion, 1932* (Munich, 1933). See also Theodore Abel's study *Why Hitler Came to Power,* previously cited.
[60] Eichhorn, *Ueber die Januar-Ereignisse,* 22–24.

point to exclude "the proletariat inferiors of the great cities." [61]

After a time, the Socialist government began to suspect that there might be danger inherent in the fact that Rightist nationalists of the middle class were gaining control of the government's army. *Vorwärts,* the government organ, on September 11, 1919, entreated the working class to join the Civil Guard:

> Party Comrades! Enter the *Einwohnerwehr* at once! Weapons in the hands of a reactionary citizenry are dangerous; in the hands of our party comrades they are the guarantee of the existence of the Republic. If you workers encounter any difficulties in trying to join, tell us immediately.

But the laboring class continued to stay away from the Free Corps and the government did not press the point.[62] It is, of course, true that the Socialist parties later organized their own volunteer formations in a belated effort to repair the damage done by the Freebooters. But this was years after the Free Corps as such had been officially dissolved. The Majority Socialists' *Reichsbanner Schwarz-Rot-Gold,* moribund from the start, was not founded until 1922; and the *Rote Frontkämpferbund* of the Communists did not appear until two years later.

Thus the Free Corps movement remained essentially a bourgeois movement. And its members dedicated themselves to the task of destroying the very society which had given them birth. The basic social causes which produced this species of social cannibalism await the analysis of the sociologists.[63] All this

---

[61] Gengler, *Kampfflieger Berthold,* 139. See also Ernst H. Posse, *Die politischen Kampfbünde Deutschlands,* 2nd enlarged edition, in *Fachschriften zur politik und staatsbürgerlichen Erziehung,* Ernst von Hippel, general editor (Berlin, 1931), 60 ff, and Richard Bernstein, *Der Kapp-Putsch und seine Lehren,* Revolutions-Bibliothek Nr. 10 (Berlin, 1920), 6.

[62] Posse, *op. cit.,* 60, 72, and Noske, *Erlebtes aus Aufstieg und Niedergang einer Demokratie,* 99, 266.

[63] Erich Fromm, the psychiatrist, gives an analysis that is deceptively simple. It is that the German middle class turned on itself in response to its own masochism and its own will to destruction (*Escape from Freedom,* 163, 172, 211–215). This solution to a complex social problem is based on what would seem to be a highly debatable premise. Dr. Fromm proceeds on the assumption that completely valid conclusions can be reached by arguing solely from analogy. He presupposes that the ills of social classes can be accurately diagnosed by applying to them the terminology of the psychiatrist. Other psychiatrists have used Fromm's methodology to arrive at different but no

writer has the courage to do is to record the historical fact that bourgeois men *did* revolt against liberal bourgeois society and to suggest two factors which may have prompted them to do so. In the first place, their experience in the prewar youth movement had taught the *Freikorpskämpfer* in the days of their youth to look with disgust and loathing at the whole bourgeois-liberal world — a world which they found shallow, tawdry and insincere.[64] The second factor is more important. To many of the Volunteers, World War I was more than a military campaign. It was a crusade in which German *kultur* had been pitted against the corrosive ideals of the liberal western world. One thing and one thing alone was responsible for its failure: the crusaders had been stabbed in the back by the government of the "November traitors." Not only that, but that government had turned around and had adopted the very principles against which the Volunteers had fought. In this they were quite right: the Weimar government was indeed a liberal-bourgeois government. And since it was, the Freebooters intended to smash it. Here is the testimony of a German student:

These people still believe that they could build on the same lies and false sentiments with which — in spite of unheard of sacrifices on the part of the soldiers — they had lost the war against the Western world. Now this lie was fulfilled through the acceptance of Western democracy. Now this blasphemy (*Gottlosigkeit*) was made official. The western bourgeois had triumphed . . . We [the students of 1918] replied: We must become nihilists in order to crush this rottenness underfoot.[65]

---

less interesting diagnoses. Dr. Brickner pronounces the Germans paranoid (Richard M. Brickner, *Is Germany Incurable?* [New York, 1943]), and Dr. Erikson writes, "Psychologists overdraw Hitler's father attributes . . . He is the Führer: *a glorified older brother* who replaces the father . . . (Erik Homburger Erikson, writing in *Psychiatry*, November 1942, Vol. V, 480. Italics are Dr. Erikson's). Harold Lasswell, on the other hand, finds that Hitler plays the maternal role in German society. ("The Psychology of Hitlerism," in *The Political Quarterly*, Vol. IV (1933), 380.)

[64] See above, p. 18.

[65] Curt Hotzel, "Student, 1918" in *Deutscher Aufstand*, 5. Readers of Moeller van den Bruck will recall a similar passage: "We can only speak with scorn of those intellectuals who lured the German *Volk* to its doom and who now stand with their stupid faces aghast before the result to which their own ideology led them! . . . These blockheads have still not learned anything. They still . . . mouth the eternal validity of their principles: world democracy . . . International Arbitration . . . Peace on Earth. They will neither

The accepted authority on the Freebooter mentality suggests another reason why he and his comrades revolted against their class. He argues that since the very *raison d'être* of the Free Corps was total destruction, the movement obviously could not draw its rationale from the *Weltanschauung* of the bourgeois-liberal world. Of necessity, therefore, that world must be destroyed. In a revealing essay von Salomon writes:

When we probe into the make-up of the [Free Corps fighter] we can find all the elements which ever played a role in German history except one: the *bürgerlich*. And that is only natural because the peculiar experience of these men . . . had forged them into one single force of consuming destructiveness. Their purpose could only be accomplished by the emphatic renunciation of what they felt most strongly to be the falsification of the true German substance. The spirit of the past centuries [i.e., of bourgeois-liberalism] had not been able to meet the uniquely severe test — that of the hardness of war. That is why the warrior, of necessity, despised the whole system which this spirit had created. The task required of him was not only to build up a new spirit . . . More than that. The task required . . . that all ballast, all sentimentalism, all other values must be ruthlessly cast aside so that his whole strength could be set free . . . Ecstasy and death, tumult and adventure, heroism and excess, cold deliberation and burning idealism, robbery and plundering, arson and murder — a mixture of every passion and demoniacal fury formed . . . the fighters who dominated the postwar period.[66]

The memoirs left by the fighters of the Free Corps movement are a veritable Hymn of Hate directed against the Weimar Republic which was the symbol and hence the target of their revolt against bourgeois society. Three short excerpts are enough to convey the feeling. The leader of the Wehrwolves writes:

But my idea was not to husband and preserve my troops until the new state had established itself. On the contrary, it was war against

---

see, nor hear, nor confess that through their guilt men all around us are suffering under foreign domination . . ." *Das Dritte Reich,* 3rd ed. (Hamburg, 1931), 11–12.

[66] Ernst von Salomon, "Der verlorene Haufe," in *Krieg und Krieger,* 122–123. Von Salomon has been quoted at length in this study because all writers, both Socialists and Nationalists, unanimously agree that he is the most reliable spokesman of the Free Corps movement. When the Volunteers themselves wanted to publish a memorial volume, *Das Buch vom deutschen Freikorpskämpfer,* Ernst von Salomon was chosen to edit it.

this state of Weimar and Versailles. War daily and by every means. For as I loved Germany, so I hated the Republic of November 9th.[67]

On January 21, 1919, the commander of the *Eiserne Schar* made the following entry in his diary:

> I will set down here in my journal . . . that I will not forget these days of criminals, lies and barbarity. The days of the Revolution will forever be a blight on the history of Germany . . . As the rabble hates me . . . I remain strong. The day will yet come when I will knock the truth into these people and tear the mask from the faces of the whole miserable, pathetic lot . . .[68]

Finally, a former member of the Ehrhardt Brigade who later marched on the Feldherrnhalle during the ill-fated Beer Hall Putsch writes:

> The state, born of this Revolution — whatever constitution it gives itself, and whoever is at the head of it — this state will forever be our enemy. The strength of its first years was treason, cowardice, lies, corruption, weakness and selfishness . . . *Out of the experience of the Revolution came the conviction that our task for the next decade would be: For the Reich! For the Volk! Fight the Government! Death to the Democratic Republic!* [69]

Such were the men who formed the German Free Corps movement and such their attitudes and their beliefs. History records few ironies more bitter than this one: the Republic hired these men to save it from destruction.

[67] Heydebreck, *Wir Wehrwölfe*, 70.
[68] Quoted in Gengler, *Kampfflieger Berthold*, 123–125.
[69] Heinz, *Sprengstoff*, 26 and 29. Italics are in the original.

IV

THE FREE CORPS CRUSH
LEFTIST REVOLTS

I will bring you freedom with a young republican army.

— Gustav Noske (January 1919)

I. THE CONQUEST OF BERLIN, JANUARY 1919

Throughout the decade that preceded Adolf Hitler, German nationalists liked to point with alarm at every little flurry of Leftist activity and claim that the Fatherland was about to be engulfed by the "Red Peril." Actually there was probably only one brief period in the entire history of the Republic when Communism had a good chance of coming to power in Germany. That time was during the first weeks following the Schloss and Marstall fiasco of Christmas Eve, 1918.

The orderly withdrawal of the troops from the Western Front, executed with such consummate skill by the Supreme Command, stands out in sharp contrast to the chaos of the demobilization process. No adequate machinery for demobilization had been constructed and the mighty Imperial Army simply fell apart. Battle-tough veterans wandered aimlessly and noisily through the streets of German cities and thousands of them forgot their hunger and found warmth and new excitement in Communist meetings and demonstrations.[1]

In Berlin, the ranks of the motley army of the Spartacists had swollen to alarming proportions by the first week of January 1919. There was no visible means of stopping a Communist

[1] See J. Benoist-Méchin, *History of the German Army*, I, 100–102.

putsch: the OHL had touched the absolute nadir of its power and prestige; and although Noske had placed his want ads in newspapers throughout the Reich, he had not yet collected his army. In January, an American army officer wrote in his diary, "The city is mad . . . I begin to believe that the Government has only a phantom army. It never appears." [2] Furthermore, the Spartacists controlled transportation, public utilities, the Berlin munitions factories, and during the first days of January, they had seized and fortified the offices of the chief Berlin newspapers at a time when the national elections were imminent. Above all, a majority of the population was probably on their side.[3]

Berlin waited tensely for a catalytic event. It was not long in coming. When Noske dismissed Eichhorn from the Polizeipräsidium, the Independent Socialists joined the Communists[4] in staging the largest public demonstration ever seen in Berlin. Everything seemed ready for a Communist seizure of power. The situation in Berlin in January of 1919 was not unlike the November days of 1917 in Petrograd, except that in Berlin nothing happened. A year later, *Die Rote Fahne* recorded this impression of one of the most decisive forty-eight hours in German revolutionary history:

What was seen that Monday in Berlin was probably the greatest proletariat manifestation in history . . . From the statue of Roland to the statue of Victory, the proletariat was massed shoulder to shoulder. The mob extended right into the Tiergarten. They had brought their weapons and were waving red flags . . . it was an army of 200,000 men . . . Then an unheard of thing happened. The crowds had been standing in the cold and fog since nine in the morning. And their leaders were seated — no one knew where — deliberating. The fog grew thicker and the throngs were still waiting. Noon came; the cold and hunger increased. The crowds were feverishly impatient. They demanded an act — even a word — anything to quiet the suspense. But no one knew what; for the leaders were deliberating . . . The fog became more dense and night began to fall. The people went sadly home.

[2] Knowlton Ames, Jr., *Berlin after the Armistice* (Privately printed, n.p. 1919), 36. See also the vivid description of the Berlin correspondent of the *Temps,* Paul Gentizon, *La Révolution Allemande* (Paris, 1919), 189–195.
[3] Rosenberg, *Geschichte der deutschen Republik,* 55, 68–69.
[4] The incendiary proclamation calling forth the demonstration was signed by both parties and appeared simultaneously in both their newspapers on Sunday, January 5, 1919. See *Freiheit* and *Die Rote Fahne* of that date.

They had hoped to accomplish great things; they had done nothing because their leaders were deliberating. They had sat first at the Marstall and then at the Polizeipräsidium . . . outside in the Alexanderplatz, the proletariat waited with rifle in hand, heavy and light machine guns ready . . . and behind closed doors the leaders deliberated. They sat all evening; they sat all night. They were still sitting the next day at dawn. The crowd came back once more and gathered along the Siegesallee and the leaders were still in session: they deliberated, deliberated, deliberated . . . (*sie bereiten, bereiten, bereiten* . . .)[5]

While the leaders of the Left bickered, and did nothing,[6] the government leaders acted. Even though Noske had not yet gathered the full strength of the Free Corps, they decided to attack the Spartacists with what Volunteers were available in Berlin. The Spartacists were entrenched in two parts of the city which were of immense strategic importance: the Spandau district, where the great munitions factories were located, and the Belle-Alliance-Platz, the home of the leading Berlin newspapers. After a hurried conference with Lüttwitz, the new commandant of the troops around Berlin, an immediate offensive against these two areas was set in motion.

While Noske was organizing the Free Corps from his Headquarters in Dahlen, Colonel Reinhard's Brigade had remained in Moabit. It was the only force available to the government. On the morning of January 10, Reinhard received a hurried penciled order to attack the Spandau area. The order was signed "Ebert-Scheidemann."[7] After a sharp fight, the district fell to Reinhard.

Meanwhile, Major von Stephani's Potsdam Free Corps, which had been placed under the general command of Lüttwitz,[8] at-

[5] Quoted by Noske, *Von Kiel bis Kapp*, 69–70.

[6] Eichhorn writes bitterly, "The single positive result of the sessions was the creation of a number of sub-committees which, to my knowledge, never met." *Ueber die Januar-Ereignisse*, 72.

[7] Schmidt-Pauli, *Geschichte der Freikorps*, 185.

[8] Parallel to the development of Maercker's Rifles, General von Lüttwitz had collected a group of separate Free Corps around him which are loosely called the Lüttwitz Free Corps. In addition to the Division of Horse Guards, under his direct command, they included Major von Stephani's Potsdam Free Corps, General von Roeder's *Landeschützen*, the Kuntzel Free Corps, the Reinhard Brigade, and other smaller groups. "All these formations," writes Lüttwitz, "I brought together under the name of the 'Lüttwitz Free Corps' . . . its strength was about 10,000 men, but it soon increased with

tacked the Belle-Alliance-Platz. On December 12, 1918, von Stephani had taken command of what remained of his former regiment, the First Regiment of Foot Guards, and had added to it from former members of the old Imperial Potsdam Regiment. In January, his Free Corps numbered about 1,200 men. Its three companies were composed chiefly of young officers, doctors, cadets and students.[9] While awaiting orders to attack, Stephani disguised himself as a Spartacist and entered the *Vorwärts* offices to reconnoiter. Finally on the afternoon of January 9, he too was handed a scrap of paper signed "Ebert-Scheidemann"; it authorized an all-out offensive. Spearheaded by the "Potsdam Shock Troops" and supported by flame-throwers, machine guns, trench mortars and artillery, the Potsdam Free Corps subdued the Belle-Alliance-Platz by 8:15 on the morning of January 11.[10] The defenders had had enough; they came out of the newspaper buildings waving white flags and asking for terms of surrender. Von Oertzen says without comment, "The furious soldiers of the Potsdam Regiment rounded up the Spartacists and shot them without any court-martial." [11]

On January 11, Noske entered the city marching at the head of his "Iron Brigade" of 1,600 men from Kiel,[12] and Maercker's Volunteer Rifles. These troops, reinforced by Roeder's Scouts, converged on the south and west of Berlin. By January 13, the centers of resistance had been crushed and Noske could occupy

the addition of other volunteers." General Walther, Freiherr von Lüttwitz, *Im Kampf gegen die November-Revolution* (Berlin, 1933), 25.

[9] Major von Stephani, "Freikorps Potsdam," in *Deutsche Soldaten,* 44; and Colonel Reinhard, *1918–1919: Die Wehen der Republik* (Berlin, 1933), 77. For Reinhard's subsequent career, see the Appendix.

[10] No effort will be made in this study to discuss the military campaigns of the postwar period in any detail. The interested reader will find more than enough coverage in any of the pertinent memoirs and in the general secondary accounts of the Free Corps movement. For the so-called "Battle of the Belle-Alliance-Platz" see Stephani's own account, "Der Sturm auf das Vorwärtsgebäude," in *Deutsche Soldaten,* 39–44; Reinhard, *op. cit.,* 77 ff; and von Oertzen, *Deutsche Freikorps,* 262–269.

[11] Von Oertzen, *Die deutschen Freikorps,* 269. Stephani had thus carried out Colonel Reinhard's orders: "I ordered him not to negotiate and to win unconditional surrender with mercy or without mercy." Reinhard, *op. cit.,* 75.

[12] This group had been organized while Noske was governor of Kiel. It was a motley, ill-organized, ill-equipped outfit. Noske greatly exaggerates when he calls it the "Kerntruppe" of the Free Corps. *Von Kiel bis Kapp,* 74.

the city. By a secret order of that date,[13] the various Free Corps
were assigned to different parts of the capital. By midnight of
January 14, the occupation had been carried out according to
plan. The national elections took place without incident on
January 19, 1919.

In the meantime, on the evening of January 15, the Freebooters
committed the first of what was to be a long series of political
murders.[14] That afternoon officers of the Volunteer Division of
Horse Guards arrested Rosa Luxemburg and Karl Liebknecht,
brought them to the Division's headquarters in the Eden Hotel,
and delivered them to Captain Pabst, the Free Corps' adjutant.
The same evening a group of officers escorted first one and then
the other of the Spartacist leaders out the back door of the hotel.

Liebknecht was the first to appear. The sentry, one Runge, acting on orders of his officers,[15] raised his rifle butt and clubbed the
prisoner. Liebknecht was dragged into a waiting automobile and
driven to a lonely spot along the Charlottenburg Highway. There
he was asked if he could walk. He staggered forward a few
steps and was shot "while attempting to escape."

A few minutes after Liebknecht had left the hotel, more
officers appeared escorting Rosa Luxemburg. Again Runge
swung his rifle, and struck down the intellectual leader of
German Communism. Her inert body was pushed into the back
seat of a second automobile. As the car drove way, a certain
Lieutenant Vogel emptied his revolver into her battered head.
Some days later her body was found floating in the Landwehr
canal. Runge was dismissed from his Free Corps for "leaving his
post without being properly relieved" and for "improper use of
his weapons." He was sentenced to two years in prison. Oberleutnant Vogel was brought to trial some time later. The judge
pointed to his fine war record, agreed with the court physician

[13] For the text of the order, see Maercker, *Vom Kaiserheer zur Reichswehr*,
Appendix 4.
[14] See below, pp. 212 ff.
[15] Runge later wrote a confession which reads, in part: ". . . I had strict
orders from the officers to club those scoundrels (*Lumpen*) to death with my
rifle butt as soon as they came out." Quoted in E. J. Gumbel, *Vier Jahre
politischer Mord*, 5th ed. (Berlin, 1922), 12.

that he was "psychopathic," hence not responsible for his actions, and sentenced him to two years in prison.[16]

Rosenberg, a former Communist historian, has called the January fighting for Berlin, "The Battle of the Marne of the German Revolution," and two Socialists write: "Noske's Free Corps had conquered Berlin . . . he had not fulfilled his promise, 'I will bring you freedom with a young republican army.' He did not have a young republican army, but an old ultra-reactionary army . . . Neither had he brought peace, but the quiet of death. Not freedom, but the unfettered terror of the Freebooter." [17]

This last statement needs to be qualified on two counts. In the first place, bad as the occupation was in January, the "unfettered terror" did not come until the following March. Philip Scheidemann, no friend of the Volunteers, admits that when the Free Corps entered Berlin in January, "The troops were joyfully welcomed all along the way; the vast majority of the populace was up in arms over the Communist Reign of Terror." [18] In the second place, it is an oversimplification common to Leftist writers to characterize the proto-Nazi Freebooters as "ultra-reactionary."

[16] The account given above is based on the National Minister of Justice's report, *Denkschrift des Reichsjustizministers zu "Vier Jahre politischer Mord,"* edited by E. J. Gumbel (Berlin, 1924), 12 ff and Gumbel's own book, *Vier Jahre,* 10 ff. F. W. von Oertzen, at the time of the murder an officer of the intelligence section of the Horse Guards, gives a different version. He insists that the attack was unpremeditated and that the officers were trying to smuggle their prisoners to the safety of a Moabit prison to protect them from the patriotic fury of the soldiers. Quite apart from the contradictory testimony of Runge and the findings of the Minister of Justice, this version leaves some pertinent questions unanswered. Knowing the feeling of their men, why did the officers bring the prisoners to the Free Corps headquarters? In escorting them to the automobiles, why did they not draw their pistols and order the sentry to let them through? Finally, if the attack on Liebknecht was "an accident," why did they bring Luxemburg out a few minutes later and why did they do nothing to stop a repetition of the same accident? Von Oertzen's account is given in his *Kamerad, reich mir die Hände: Freikorps und Grenzschutz Baltikum und Heimat* (Berlin, 1933), 49–55.

[17] Rosenberg, *Geschichte der deutschen Republik,* 71; Kurt Caro and Walter Oehme, *Schleichers Aufstieg: Ein Beitrag zur Geschichte der Gegenrevolution* (Berlin, 1933), 48–49.

[18] Scheidemann, *Memoiren eines Sozialdemokraten,* 2 vols. (Dresden, 1928), II, 345. This was written after members of the Free Corps had attempted to kill the author.

We shall have to deal with this point later, but here it will be sufficient to notice the comment made by the leading German historian of the movement:

> What Walter Oehme says — when he talks about the "ultra-reactionary" army of Noske . . . and means the Free Corps — is just as false as what others have thought and said about the spirit of the Free Corps. These soldiers and officers were certainly no Republicans; . . . and they did not conceal their distrust of Noske. Neither could they set out to support a government whose leading personalities and ideas were so foreign to them . . . They did not bother their heads with complicated political matters. And above all, one thing these young Free Corps men were not was "ultra-reactionary." In them slumbered the as yet unrecognized strength of the national revolutionary force . . .[19]

The fires of revolt in Berlin had been stamped out, but the embers still glowed. In the middle of March, fanned by Communist revolts in middle Germany, they were to burst forth into one of the most intense conflagrations of the postwar period. But in January, Berlin was calm and Noske was confident. He withdrew his Volunteers to the outskirts of the city, and did not even think it necessary to dissolve Dorrenbach's unruly People's Naval Division, the group which had been greatly responsible for the disturbances of December and January.[20]

II. THE FREE CORPS DEFEND THE NATIONAL ASSEMBLY

With the Communist uprising in Berlin apparently crushed, the government could turn its attention to Weimar. Professor Rosenberg,[21] among others, attaches symbolic significance to the fact that Weimar, and not Berlin, was chosen as the meeting place for the National Constituent Assembly. It is suggested that the republican leaders chose Weimar because they wanted to

---

[19] Die deutschen Freikorps, 282.

[20] Colonel Reinhard maintains that he had disarmed the Volksmarine Division on his own initiative, but "Noske ordered me to come to a conference . . . sitting under a portrait of His Majesty the Emperor . . . he demanded the immediate re-armament of the Volksmarine Division. Since His Excellency von Lüttwitz also agreed, it was carried out." (1918–1919: Die Wehen der Republik, 83–85.)

[21] Rosenberg, Geschichte der deutschen Republik, 85–86.

divorce themselves from the cold militarism associated with Potsdam and hoped that the gentle, persuasive atmosphere that had stimulated Goethe and Schiller might usher in a new era of democratic liberalism. The sentiment is attractive, but actually political and military reasons were more decisive elements in the choice than was sentiment. Since Berlin was the center of German radicalism, the Independent Socialists and Communists were as anxious that the Assembly be held there as the Majority Socialists were determined that it meet elsewhere. As early as December 23, Ebert had advised moving the seat of government to either Weimar or Rudolfstadt, but Hasse and Barth had raised such strenuous objections that the idea was dropped.[22] In January, when the question was raised again, Noske and Scheidemann reminded their colleagues how Dorrenbach's sailors had broken up the meeting of December 16 and had captured the government on December 23. Noske also expressed concern that the soldiers might be won over to the radicals and refuse to protect the assembly. The Defense Minister clinched the argument by pressing military reasons for leaving the capital. Great, sprawling Berlin, he said, could not be defended without converting it into an armed camp — scarcely the setting for democratic deliberations. Weimar was small, relatively isolated, and easy to defend.[23]

On January 30, General Maercker was ordered to Weimar to police the city. At first only an advance force of two officers and 120 men was sent. The detachment was attacked, disarmed, and imprisoned by the Communists. Maercker observes, not without irony: "These events showed, public opinion to the contrary, that Weimar was by no means the quiet little city of the muses where the National Assembly could meet without any disturbance." [24] During the first three days of February 1919, the main body of the Rifles, totaling well over 7,000 men, arrived in Weimar and encircled the little city with a ring of steel. The Assembly could proceed with its business.

Maercker had hoped to utilize his stay at Weimar to consolidate

[22] Volkmann, *Revolution über Deutschland*, 152.
[23] Noske, *Von Kiel bis Kapp*, 85–86.
[24] Maercker, *Vom Kaiserheer zur Reichswehr*, 90.

his forces and weed out the undesirable Freebooter elements who had joined his Rifles. But new Spartacist disturbances soon called him elsewhere.

III. THE FREE CORPS CRUSH SPORADIC REVOLTS

It is neither possible nor necessary to discuss all the interventions of the Free Corps in the Leftist uprisings which spread through the Reich in the early months of 1919. The events followed a fairly well-defined pattern. In various German cities, the extreme Left took advantage of the lack of a republican army to establish extremist governments. Then Noske moved the Free Corps into the offending cities, the Spartacist governments were ruthlessly crushed, and the former governments reëstablished. The actions at Bremen, Mühlheim, and Halle had particular significance for future events.

During the first weeks of January 1919, the Spartacists had established a thinly veiled dictatorship in Bremen. To Noske, the issue was clear-cut: either the dominant power in Germany was to be Spartacism or it was to be "law and order." The vitally important seaport of Bremen would serve as a test case. By the end of January, the news leaked out that Noske planned to send a detachment of Maercker's Rifles, Gerstenberg's Free Corps, the Kiel Iron Brigade and sections of Roeder's Scouts to restore order in Bremen. Leaders of various Workers' and Soldiers' Councils throughout the Reich covered Noske's desk with telegrams of protest. They threatened immediate retaliatory action if any of the Free Corps were sent. General strikes were promised by the Councils of Cuxhaven, Hamburg, and the Ruhr. The threats only served to convince the Defense Minister that decisive action was imperative. He stuffed the unread telegrams into the pockets of his baggy tweed coat and observed: ". . . if order were not restored immediately in Bremen, the Government could consider itself lost, for no one would respect it. Any risk was better than that." [25] A Storm Troop led by Fritz Fuhrmann, later a notorious murderer of the Feme, first stormed the Weser and attacked the city. By February 5, Bremen was occupied, the council of Peoples Commissars thrown out of office and the bourgeois government

[25] Noske, *Von Kiel bis Kapp,* 82.

reëstablished.[26] Bremerhaven, Cuxhaven, and Wilhelmshaven were similarly subdued.

The North had scarcely been conquered when the threatened general strike broke out in the West. After a bloody struggle, Mülheim was occupied by Lichterschlag's Free Corps and the revolt was crushed by mid-February. With Westphalia restored to relative peace, the wave of insurrection moved on to middle Germany. Noske relied largely on Maercker's Volunteer Rifles to stem the tide. After a particularly bloody campaign in Halle, Maercker moved on to Magdeburg. Here, with the help of the Gorlitz Free Corps and men from the recently formed *Stahlhelm*, order was quickly restored.[27] On April 18, Maercker, reinforced by the Ehrhardt Brigade, subdued Brunswick. Dresden fell April 14. By May 10, with the assistance of the Von Oven Regiment, the Von Hülsen Free Corps and a tank section of the First Saxon Frontier Brigade, Maercker had conquered Leipzig. "By the middle of June," concludes Schmidt-Pauli, "Order had been sufficiently established so that martial law could be lifted from the cities . . . the Free Corps had again proven their worth brilliantly." [28]

The front soldier suffering the humiliations of the defeat of 1918 found balm for his injured pride in this triumphant procession through the cities of Germany. One of the "Conquerors of Brunswick" writes: "The entry into Brunswick was the first ray of sunshine after the long night of rain . . . Those of us who had smelled powder in the past years . . . were happy that this first campaign in the Homeland had ended so brilliantly. . . . Now we could hope for the future." [29]

The confused and insecure student found new confidence and exhilarating strength by identifying himself with the victorious

[26] Schmidt-Pauli, *Geschichte der Freikorps*, 191 ff, and A. W. Rose, "Sturm auf die Weserbrücken," in *Freikorpskämpfer*, 63 ff.

[27] Later nationalist accounts, however, exaggerate the contributions made by the *Stahlhelm* in the military campaigns of the period. See, for example, Fritz Carl Roegels, *Der Marsch auf Berlin: Ein Buch vom Wehrwillen deutscher Jugend* (Berlin, 1932), 51–53 and *passim*. For the Rifles' campaigns in Middle Germany see, in addition to von Oertzen and Schmidt-Pauli, Maercker's own account in *Vom Kaiserheer zur Reichswehr*, 128–158; and Hans Roden, "Einmarsch in Mitteldeutschland," in *Deutsche Soldaten*.

[28] *Geschichte der Freikorps*, 195.

[29] Mann, *Mit Ehrhardt durch Deutschland*, 43–45.

march of the Freebooter army. The Free Corps spelled power and
he gloried in participating in it — even at the price of surrender-
ing his youthful idealism: "The precisely constructed military
machine [of the Free Corps] rolled on blindly and without any
concern whatsoever for ideological purposes. And like a machine
it rolled over and crushed everything which tried to oppose it
with revolutionary ideas of its own . . ." [30]

Apart from the boost it provided for the Volunteer's morale, a
modification of the Free Corps system was the most important
result of the spring campaigns. Since the Volunteers were
needed urgently to put down scattered pockets of insurrection at
short notice, General Maercker was caught without sufficient
strength to garrison the conquered cities. He therefore left only
enough men to organize smaller groups recruited from the
civilians of each city. Successively at Halle, Magdeburg, Brunswick, and Leipzig, these Civil Guards (*Einwohnerwehren*) were
organized. Parallel to their organization, Maercker set up a series
of volunteer formations theoretically independent of the Civil
Guards but actually drawing strength from them. Thus the
Magdeburg Regiment developed from the Magdeburg *Einwohnerwehr*. Similar formations were organized elsewhere: at
Halle, the Halle Free Corps; and at Brunswick, the Brunswick
Rifle Regiment (*Jägerregiment Braunschweig*).[31] Here too,
Maercker's work served as the model for later developments.
During the period of the 100,000 man army, as we shall see in a
later chapter, these local Civil Guards, when organized by Dr.
Escherich into the *Orgesch* (*Organisation Escherich*), formed
a reserve militia for the German Army.

IV. THE WEEK OF BLOODSHED IN BERLIN

The results of the revolts of January and February forced the
Communists to change their tactics. In Bremen, Mülheim, and
Halle, three serious insurrections had been attempted. All three
had ended in overwhelming victories for the Volunteers. In defeat, the Spartacists had learned three valuable lessons. First,

[30] Von Salomon, *Nahe Geschichte*, 64.

[31] The system is described by Maercker, *Vom Kaiserheer zur Reichswehr*,
142–149.

power was rapidly slipping from their grasp. If there was any chance left of carrying out a complete revolution, Communism would have to act quickly. Second, German Communism had dissipated its strength in isolated areas. The cost had been ruinous. All its waning power must be concentrated in one huge demonstration in the capital. Third, it was abundantly clear that the Spartacists were no match for the Free Corps when they met in pitched battle. They must avoid giving battle and rely on a disciplined general strike.[32]

Some of these conclusions were embodied in the notice calling out the great general strike which appeared in *Die Rote Fahne* the morning of March 3, 1919:

WORKERS! PROLETARIANS!

Once again the hour has struck! Once more the dead arise! . . . The "Socialist" government of Ebert-Scheidemann-Noske has become the mass executioner of the German proletariat. They are only waiting for the chance to bring "peace and order." Wherever the proletariat rules, Noske sends in his bloodhounds:

Berlin, Bremen, Wilhelmshaven, Cuxhaven . . . Gotha, Erfurt, Halle, Düsseldorf — these are the bloody stations of the cross of Noske's crusade against the German proletariat.

Thousands of your brothers are being mishandled, thrown into prison, murdered . . . struck down, butchered like mad dogs! Remember your Spandau Comrades . . . remember Rosa Luxemburg and Karl Lieb-knecht. Remember them all and consider this: The murderers go their way with the benediction of Ebert-Scheidemann-Noske while your comrades rot in prison . . . The Revolution can only go forward by tramping on the graves of the Majority Social Democrats. . . .

On to the General Strike!
On to the new struggle for the Revolution!
On to the new battle against the Oppressors!

WORKERS! PARTY COMRADES!

Let all work cease! Remain quietly in the factories. Don't let them take the factories away from you. Gather in the factories! Explain things to those who want to hesitate and hang back. Don't let your-

[32] The clearest statement of the reasons for the shift in Communist strategy is given in a Spartacist pamphlet by "Cains," *Generalstreik und Noske-Blud-Bad in Berlin* (Berlin, 1919), 2–4 and 7–9. See also Clara Zetkin, *Les Batail-les Révolutionnaires de L'Allemagne en 1919*, Publication No. 47 of Editions de L'Internationale Communiste (Petrograd, 1920), 8–9.

selves be drawn into pointless shooting. Noske is only waiting for you to do that as an excuse for spilling more blood. Stay together in the factories so that you will be ready for action at a moment's notice.

> *Höchste Disziplin!*
> *Höchste Besonnenheit!*
> *Eiserne Ruhe!*
> *Aber auch eiserner Wille!*

Workers! Proletarians! The fate of the world is in your hands! . . . On to Battle! On to the General Strike! . . .[33]

The government answered the strike by making Noske virtual dictator of Berlin. Noske, as usual, acted with decision and proclaimed martial law. His order of March 3 prohibited all public meetings, suspended Leftist newspapers, and gave notice that anyone found looting or pillaging would face a court-martial.[34] On the same night and during the next day, street fighting broke out in the city and Noske called in the Free Corps to restore order.[35]

If the strike leadership really wanted to avoid open warfare with the Volunteers, why did street fighting break out? Nationalist writers object to the interpretation given above. They insist that the Communists never intended to achieve their aims by any means other than armed insurrection and had made detailed plans for the active fighting they anticipated.[36] It is true that the incendiary wording of the strike proclamation hardly seems conducive to promoting "the strictest discretion." But the discrepancy

[33] The entire front page of the special morning edition of *Die Rote Fahne* is given over to the proclamation. *Freiheit,* organ of the Independent Socialists, later apologized to its readers for failing to publish the proclamation. *Freiheit,* March 8, 1919.

[34] The text of Noske's order appears in the morning edition of *Vorwärts,* March 4, 1919. Throughout the period, *Vorwärts* published the official orders.

[35] Caro and Oehme maintain that the disorders of March 4 were instigated by *agents provocateurs* hired by the Supreme Command (*Schleichers Aufstieg,* 67). Independent Socialists later charged that Noske himself had deliberately provoked the disorders (Benoist-Méchin, *op. cit.,* I, 194) and the Communists claimed that it was Colonel Reinhard who had hired the *agents provocateurs.* (Ambroise Got, *L'Allemagne après le Débâcle: Impressions d'un Attaché à la Mission Militaire Française à Berlin,* Strasbourg, 1919, 170). It seems highly unlikely that the revolters needed added encouragement from any source.

[36] Von Oertzen, *Die deutschen Freikorps,* 288 and Volkmann, *Revolution über Deutschland,* 211.

must be accounted for by the psychological difficulty any radical revolutionary party has in urging moderation and discipline. For months the German Communist leaders had used the most violent rhetoric in exhorting their followers to fight the government. They could not now phrase their new program in moderate terms and expect support. The street fighting was led by the ragged, desperate remnants of the *Volksmarine Division* and the *Republikanische Soldatenwehr,* who feared that their dissolution was imminent and decided to make one last effort to seize power. Nationalist writers to the contrary, the strike leadership did not encourage the fighting. The reverse is true. As soon as the fighting started, the Central Committee of the KPD distributed handbills which disavowed any connection whatever with these "Hyenas of the Revolution" and urged their followers not to support them.[37]

In the confused street fighting which followed, three main battles emerged. On March 5, the Reinhard Brigade stormed and held the Alexander Platz and the Berlin subway. On the same day the Marstall fell. On March 6, the heaviest fighting of the opening stages of the campaign took place in the battle for the Polizeipräsidium, which had been converted into a veritable fortress by the Spartacists. It was finally taken after a squadron of bombing planes,[38] trench mortars, howitzers, and heavy machine guns had softened up the defenses.

In the face of the Free Corps attack, the Spartacists retreated to the Lichtenberg suburbs. Once again the revolution of the proletariat had degenerated into unequal street fighting with the advantage all going to the better armed, better organized, and better led Volunteers. On March 8, 1919, the strike committee

[37] Noske, *Von Kiel bis Kapp,* 110; Friedrich Wilhelm Heinz, *Der Nation greift an,* 32; and von Salomon, "Der Berliner Märzaufstand, 1919" in *Freikorpskämpfer,* 44. The interpretation given above agrees with Benoist-Méchin, *op. cit.,* I, 191–195. A contemporary Communist pamphlet calls the *Volksmarine Division* and the *Soldatenwehr* "the most loyal helpers of the government . . . for the government wanted an armed conflict . . . The Communists were at no time and never the allies of these troops." ("Cains," *Generalstreik und Noske-Blud-Bad,* 7.)

[38] Benoist-Méchin, *op. cit.,* I, 198. Von Oertzen insists that the aircraft were not bombers and that they were used only to drop supplies and munitions to the attacking Free Corps. *Die deutschen Freikorps,* 291.

withdrew the general strike and made peace overtures to the government.[39]

But the breathing space was short-lived. On March 9 and 10, Berlin was swamped with wild stories of Spartacist terrorism. Among other things, newspapers published reports that the entire Lichtenberg police garrison had been massacred. Actually no such wholesale slaughter had taken place. When the fog of rumor had lifted, it was established that five policemen had been killed, and it was never determined whether they had lost their lives during the fighting or whether, as first alleged, they had been shot down in cold blood by the Communists.[40]

In a confused period of charges and countercharges, Noske issued his famous order of March 9, 1919: "The brutality and

[39] *Vossische Zeitung*, March 8, 1919 (morning edition). The Volunteers had been so successful that the same newspaper, in its evening edition, commented, "Today it has become perfectly certain that the Spartacist revolt in Berlin is over."

[40] The number is that given by Herr Ziethen, Bürgermeister of Lichtenberg, in his official report published in *Vorwärts*, March 13, 1919 (morning edition). Earlier reports of the so-called "Lichtenberg Atrocity" were conflicting, but they all grossly exaggerated the extent of the "massacre." On March 10, *Vorwärts* informed its readers that "Sixty police officials and several dozen of the government soldiers have been shot down like animals." The *Berliner Tageblatt* of the same day set the number at 57 and castigated the Leftist press for demanding the dissolution of the Free Corps. The *Vossische Zeitung* screamed, ". . . over 150 officers, soldiers and officials of the Lichtenberg Polizeipräsidium were shot . . . in an unheard-of mass murder" (March 10, morning edition). The Berlin correspondent of the London *Times* cabled in a delayed dispatch of March 12: "Men of the Volunteer Army [*sic*] inform me that prisoners were being shot in batches of eighteen." Even after the facts were known, National Socialists insisted on falsifying the extent of the "massacre" by using noncommittal terms: Von Oertzen says, ". . . *eine Reihe* of Police officials were murdered in a bestial manner" (*Die deutschen Freikorps*, 516); Reinhard says, "*Zahlreicher*" (*Die Wehen der Republik*, 104), and Schmidt-Pauli says, "*Eine grosse Anzahl*" (*Geschichte der Freikorps*, 190). The Lichtenberg Atrocity was used by later National Socialist writers as an example of the type of thing that took place under the Republic. (See, for example, the officially authorized book, *Das Buch der NSDAP: Werden, Kampf, und Ziel der N.S.D.A.P.* edited by Walter M. Espe, Berlin, 1933.) Both in a speech in the National Assembly on March 13 (*Verhandlungen der verfassunggebenden deutschen Nationalversammlung*, Stenographische Berichte, 27 Sitzung, 741–742) and in his memoirs (p. 108) Noske admitted that the number of victims had been grossly exaggerated. On March 13, 1919, both *Vorwärts* and the *Vossische Zeitung* established the total number killed at five policemen and printed shamefaced apologies for misinforming their readers.

bestial behavior of the Spartacists fighting against us obliges me to issue the following order: From now on, any person who bears arms against government troops will be shot on the spot." [41] This order served as a hunting license for the Freebooters. The number of their victims was further increased by an order of the day issued by the Division of Horse Guards. This order of March 10 announced that anyone found with arms in his possession would be shot without trial. [42] Thus a citizen of Berlin could be shot not only for bearing arms against the Free Corps; he could be shot simply for owning firearms. The result of these two orders was that hundreds of Berliners were killed in retaliation for an atrocity which had never taken place.

The exact role which Gustav Noske played in this matter is open to dispute. Two authorities, Professor Lutz and M. Benoist-Méchin, imply that Noske diabolically invented the "Lichtenberg Atrocity" in order to prepare public opinion for an all-out offensive against the Spartacists; and that after fabricating the incident out of whole cloth, he deliberately encouraged the reprisals which followed. [43]

[41] *Vorwärts,* March 10, 1919 (morning edition). The order was first issued on the afternoon of March 9. (See note 43 on page 74.) Mr. Gooch incorrectly dates it March 8. (G. P. Gooch, *Germany,* 187.)

[42] It is typical of the general confusion of the time that this order, whose existence the Government had apparently denied, was not made public until eight days after it was issued. On March 18, *Freiheit* published it under the headline: "Denied murder order finally disclosed."

[43] Mr. Lutz says flatly, "To inflame the people against the Communists, Noske falsely accused them of a general massacre of prisoners at the Lichtenberg Police Station, and therefore ordered them to be exterminated." R. H. Lutz, "The German Revolution, 1918–1919," in *Stanford University Publications,* I, No. 1, 128. M. Benoist-Méchin writes in his dramatic way, ". . . the atmosphere is relaxing . . . If hostilities are suspended all the sacrifices of the preceding days will have been in vain . . . A new event must come to shake up public opinion . . . Noske has no intention of stopping half way . . . A false piece of news . . . will serve him as a pretext to take up the offensive again." *History of the German Army,* I, 200. The French historian gives this sequence to the events of the period from March 9 to March 11, 1919: (1) After spreading the false atrocity story through Berlin, (2) Noske published his decree, and (3) launched his offensive against the Spartacists. It is an interesting theory, but the chronology of the events in question works against it. The crucial point in the chain of events is the time at which the Lichtenberg atrocity story was disseminated. Benoist-Méchin says newspapers spread the story through Berlin on March 9. But none of the leading Berlin newspapers carried any such story in their editions

The present writer cannot subscribe to this interpretation. Available evidence seems to indicate that Noske did not invent the false rumor; it resulted from general hysteria and faulty newspaper reporting. If Noske profited from the rumor, it was only indirectly. There was nothing underhanded about the Defense Minister's activity in March 1919. In Berlin he did exactly what he had already done in Bremen, Mühlheim, Leipzig, and Halle and as he would do in Munich: without consulting or trying to influence public opinion, he bluntly ordered the Volunteers to go in and crush the Spartacists.

of March 9. This is true not only of liberal newspapers which normally endorsed the Free Corps against their Leftist critics such as the *Vossische Zeitung* and the *Berliner Tageblatt,* it is also true of *Vorwärts,* the government organ — the place where one would expect Noske to plant such a story. The first mention of the Lichtenberg story is in the morning editions of *March 10,* the day *after* Noske issued his "shoot-on-the-spot order." (Noske's order was released through the Wolf telegraph agency on the afternoon of March 9, but it did not reach the newspapers in time for publication; see *Vossische Zeitung* for March 10.) By his own statement, Benoist-Méchin sets the beginning of the final offensive against Lichtenberg "*on the morning of Sunday, March 9*" (*op. cit.,* I, 201; italics are mine). The events in question, therefore, must have taken place in this order: (1) the offensive (morning, March 9); (2) the Noske order (afternoon, March 9); (3) the publication of the atrocity story (morning, March 10). The conclusion would seem to be that Noske did not deliberately manufacture the atrocity story. Even if we grant — which we do not — that Noske felt it necessary to create an incident, he certainly would have waited until the story had had its desired effect before he began his offensive. It would have been more logical, for example, to have published the story on the 9th, issued his decree and begun his attack on the 10th. But even if he had taken this course, it would have been entirely out of character. It would have been the first time in the history of the period that the "Bloodhound" felt it necessary to consult public opinion before attacking the Spartacists. Benoist-Méchin feels that Noske's guilt is "Clearly established" by the single fact that *Vorwärts* endorsed Noske's decree as the only answer to the alleged Lichtenberg murders (Benoist-Méchin, I, 201, note 1). The argument is worthless. *Vorwärts* not only supported this specific action of the Defense Minister; it consistently supported virtually everything he did. It should be emphasized that the interpretation given by Benoist-Méchin to the whole affair is precisely the same as that given by such flagrantly biased accounts as the Communist pamphlet by "Cains," *Generalstreik und Noske-Blud-Bad,* 12–13, the speech given by U.S.P.D. delegate Hugo Haase to the National Assembly, *Verhandlungen der verfassunggebenden deutschen Nationalversammlung* (Stenographische Berichte), 30 Sitzung, March 27, 1919, Vol. 327, 842–851, and the U.S.P.D. pamphlet, *Die Wahrheit über die Berliner Strassenkämpfe* (*Freiheit* verlag, Berlin, 1919).

Beginning on Sunday morning, March 9, the Volunteers converged on Lichtenberg.[44] After a full-scale military offensive, in which tanks, flame-throwers, artillery, and trench mortars were used, the Free Corps subdued Lichtenberg with savage brutality.[45] While the suburbs were being cleared, the most sanguinary event of this "Week of Bloodshed" was taking place in another part of the city.

At long last, Noske had decided that the Volksmarine Division should be dissolved. On the night of March 10, 1919, the sailors were instructed to go to the office of the Volksmarine Division at 32 Französischestrasse between the hours of nine and one o'clock on March 11 to receive their pay and demobilization certificates. Hundreds of them went and fell into a well-laid Free Corps trap. The "Paymaster" was Lieutenant Marloh, one of Colonel Reinhard's most ruthless officers.[46] But the ruse worked too successfully. As the sailors crowded into the building, Marloh found that his detachment was not strong enough to handle them all. He telephoned twice to Reinhard for reinforcements. In the first conversation, he was told that the Reinhard Brigade had no men to spare. The future SS Oberführer of Berlin records the second conversation: "Again he asked for help . . . 'Bullets are the best help,' was my answer — he could go ahead and shoot." [47] Marloh carried out this suggestion with great élan. He chose twenty-nine sailors at random and had them machine-gunned. At his trial he testified that he had intended to kill three hundred of the sailors but an unnamed officer had stopped him. After his acquit-

[44] While Reinhard's Brigade cut off retreat to the North and East, the Von Hülsen Free Corps and Roeder's Scouts entered from the West and Ehrhardt's Brigade from the South.

[45] See the account of a participant, Alfred Arnold, "Freiwilligen-Detachment Tüllmann im Roten Lichtenberg," in *Freikorpskämpfer*, 52 ff.

[46] This account is based on the report given by the French military attaché in Berlin, Ambroise Got, *La Contre-Révolution Allemande* (Strasbourg, 1920 [?]), 136–139; *Blut und Ehre*, edited by Maximilian Scheer, herausgegeben vom ueberparteilischen deutschen Hilfsausschuss (Paris, 1937), 17, and the account of eyewitnesses quoted in Haase's speech to the National Assembly on March 27, 1919. *Verhandlungen* (Stenographische Berichte), 30 Sitzung, 844–845. The Nazi account is quite different. Von Oertzen insists that the sailors had come to reorganize their scattered forces for a new attack on the Free Corps, *Die deutschen Freikorps*, 297. Reinhard (*op. cit.*, 104) aggrees with von Oertzen.

[47] Reinhard, *op. cit.*, 105.

tal, Reinhard appointed him to a "judgeship" in the judiciary section of the Reinhard Free Corps. In later years, Marloh became
an ardent Nazi and joined a wholesale cigarette firm. He wrote
sales production letters in which he reminded prospective cus-
tomers that he had been a War hero and had killed twenty-nine
sailors during the November Revolution. He ended his letters:
mit deutschen gruss und Hitler heil! [48]

By March 13, the last Spartacist in Lichtenberg had either
surrendered or been liquidated, and Berlin's second great prole-
tarian uprising had been crushed by the Free Corps. The "Week
of Bloodshed" had ended with the death of between 1,200 and
1,500 citizens.[49]

The enthusiasm with which the Berliners had greeted Noske
and his Volunteers in January cooled perceptibly during these
March days of terror. The answer which von Oertzen gives to
charges of wanton savagery on the part of the Free Corps is both
interesting and illustrative of National Socialist reasoning. First
he dismisses all such charges as the "lies and slanderous abuse
of the Leftist press." He then offers a number of reasons *why*
the Freebooters were forced to act with what he calls "decision."

(First:)   One must always be cognizant of the fact that the
                officers and men of the various Free Corps formations
                had long years of war service behind them and con-
                sequently their entire attitude had become extremely
                unbürgerlich.

(Second:)   In addition to that, their nerves were frayed by the
                intervention of the citizenry in the civil war and by
                the inner chaos which is always more wearing on the
                nerves than war against an external enemy . . .

(Third:)   Not only this, but the daily slanderous abuse of their
                angered countrymen necessarily brought on a condi-

[48] Minutes of the trial and a sample letter are given in Scheer's *Blut und
Ehre,* 17–19. Von Oertzen hurries to the defense of a *Freikorpskämpfer*
and explains the massacre by saying that Marloh was an unusually brave
man who had been wounded in heroic action at the Front. (*Die deutschen
Freikorps,* 297.) Noske calls the action, "terrible and indefensible." (*Von
Kiel bis Kapp,* 110.)

[49] Noske fixes the total at 1,200. Schmidt-Pauli concludes, "Approxi-
mately 1,500 human lives were sacrificed to the Bolshevist [*sic*] insanity."
(*Geschichte der Freikorps,* 191.)

tion of unstrung nerves (*Nervenüberreizung*) . . .
which often lead to unexpected explosions.

(Conclusion:)   Because of these conditions, which were unfortunately unavoidable, naturally the best efforts of the
[Free Corps] leadership to establish "honorable and
disciplined behavior" by drawing up directives to
that effect, were not sufficient . . . the men frequently kicked over the traces.[50]

The March days of 1919 served to stimulate the already active
persecution complex of the Volunteers. Filled with a "black
hatred" against the *feige Bürgergeschmeiss* and the "systematic
slander of the Leftist press," the men took vengeance against
society in general during the rest of their activity in the Reich.
Actually, the German press was surprisingly patient with Freebooter excesses. It is only *Freiheit* and, of course, *Die Rote Fahne*
which engage in the type of criticism the National Socialists
describe. The policy of *Vorwärts,* the Majority Socialist paper,
which the Free Corps historians consider one of the worst perse-
cutors and insist on classifying as "Bolshevist," is illuminating.
The day after the "Week of Bloodshed," *Vorwärts* published the
following résumé of the period:

Now that the battle is over, a great criticism had begun over what
has happened . . . The laboring classes are particularly passionate in
their judgment . . . It would naturally be nonsense to deny that the
government troops have not perpetrated actions which would fill any
thinking man with loathing and indignation . . . but in a struggle to
the death in which the Spartacists gave no quarter, it is only natural
that the Volunteers should fulfil their duty with resolute firmness
(*entschlossener Derbheit*). They have performed a very difficult task,
and if isolated acts of brutality have occurred, our judgment can only

[50] Von Oertzen *Die deutschen Freikorps,* 307–308. He cites as an example of the moderating directives issued by Free Corps leaders that of
Maercker during the siege of Halle. This almost unique order is certainly
not typical of the average Freebooter commander. In another place, Von
Oertzen writes: ". . . destructive elements, in the *bürgerlich* meaning
of the term, frequently made the best and most energetic soldiers . . .
precisely this type of man frequently attained leadership. Thus it was
obvious that often enough the commanders simply closed their eyes when
their best troops (in a military sense) did something which did not meet
with the approval of bourgeois-democratic standards of morality." *Kamerad,
reich mir die Hände,* 101–103. The title of the book is taken from the first
line of Ehrhardt's marching song.

be that their actions were only human . . . Certainly no one would
be happier than the Government if such men [as the Free Corps]
could be found in greater numbers . . .[51]

Noske was also pleased with the work of his volunteer army.
He realized, however, that the Free Corps required better organization. What was needed was an amalgamation of all separate
corps into one united and centrally controlled army. He introduced this proposal to the National Assembly. After protracted
and stormy debates in which the Defense Minister and other
Majority Socialists defended the Freebooters against their Leftist
critics, the Law for the Creation of the Provisional Reichswehr[52]
was passed on March 6, 1919. The law envisaged the creation of
a national army "built on a democratic basis through the articulation of already existing Volunteer formations . . . and the recruitment of similar formations." [53] It was designed as a stop-gap
measure pending the terms of the peace conference and the creation of a permanent Reichswehr.[54] It did not end the Free Corps
system, nor did it end the military anarchy which that system —
rather, lack of system — had produced. Many of the "real Free
Corps" simply refused to enter the provisional army. Supported
by industry and conservative landed interests,[55] they maintained
their separate existence. The government made no serious effort
to dissolve these irregular formations. In fact, as we shall see in a
later chapter, it either gave them its tacit approval or, as in the
case of the Ehrhardt Brigade, paid them and paid them hand-
somely.[56] Other formations, notably Rossbach's Storm Troops,
entered, left, and reëntered the Reichswehr at the whim of their
Freikorpsführer. And so cherished was the tradition of independ-

[51] *Vorwärts,* March 15, 1919 (morning edition); see also the *Vossische
Zeitung's* handling of the Marloh massacre (March 12, 1919).
[52] "Gesetz über die Bildung einer vorläufigen Reichswehr," *Reichsgesetzblatt,* Jahrgang 1919, Nr. 6755, 295 ff.
[53] *Loc. cit.,* 295.
[54] "Wehrgesetz vom 23 March 1921," *Reichsgesetzblatt,* Jahrgang, 1921,
Nr. 8050, 329 ff.
[55] See below, pp. 137, 189–190.
[56] See below, pp. 150, 170. The deleterious effect of the government's
army policy on the national economy is discussed in Paul Beuter, *Wesen
und Organisation des Reichsheeres und seine Bedeutung für die deutsche
Wirtschaft,* inaugural dissertation, University of Giessen (Giessen, 1926).

ence and the follow-the-leader principle that even those better organized formations which entered the temporary army almost without change often insisted on being called by their old Free Corps names rather than by their new Reichswehr designations. General Hülsen's Free Corps, for instance, entered as the Third Brigade and Colonel von Epp's formation as the Twenty-first Brigade, but von Hülsen never speaks of his troops as anything but "my Free Corps" [57] and von Epp's men remained the "Von Epp Free Corps." In short, as a monographic study has pointed out,[58] the law of March 6, 1919, only tended to confuse further the military situation in Germany and it did not, we repeat, end the Free Corps movement.[59]

V. THE CONQUEST OF MUNICH, MAY 1919

Munich was to play such an important part in the subsequent history of the Free Corps movement that it would be well to sketch in the main outlines of its revolutionary history. That history is a sorry tale of the rapid succession of regimes which were, in turn, inefficient, confused, corrupt, and terroristic. It is a history which served as excellent grist for the mills of Nazi propaganda. For the National Socialists did not allow the German people to forget that they had saved the Fatherland from the horrors of democracy — from the time, for example, "When Israel was King of Bavaria." [60]

[57] Lieutenant General Bernhard von Hülsen, "Freikorps in Osten," in *Deutsche Soldaten.*

[58] Beuter, *op. cit.,* 8–11.

[59] For a different impression, see Benoist-Méchin, *op. cit.,* I, 172–174. The French writer, who is anxious to show the continuity of the Imperialist tradition of the German Army, leaves the impression that the Free Corps were completely absorbed into the Provisional Reichswehr. He writes: "Just as we have seen the former Imperial units give forth, in the month of December 1918, little independent formations . . . we now see the *Freikorps* in their turn integrate into the Reichswehr and melt into the framework of the new army" (I, 173). Perhaps the best evidence is that given by Defense Minister Noske. He supports the interpretation given above (Gustav Noske, *Erlebtes,* 267).

[60] The expression was first used in Jean Jerome Tharaud's account of Bela Kuhn's government in Hungary entitled *Quand Israel est roi.* It was eagerly adopted by the National Socialists and applied to Bavaria. Thus Colonel von Epp's biographer calls his chapter on Bavaria, "Wenn Israel König ist." Walter Frank, *Franz Ritter von Epp: Der Weg eines deutschen*

After the collapse of the Imperial armies on the Western Front, Kurt Eisner, the Jewish leader of the Bavarian USPD raised the old cry of *los von Berlin!* and on November 8, 1918, proclaimed a Socialist Republic in conservative, Catholic Bavaria. Eisner was one of the best-hated and the best-loved figures in the history of the German Revolution. His nationalist enemies damn him for his traitorous pacifism in accepting Germany's war guilt and call him "that hated Jewish ideologist . . . that caricature of a statesman." [61] His Leftist friends idolize him and insist that he was "the single creative statesman who had come forth since November 1918." [62]

Fair evaluation of Eisner lies somewhere between these two extremes. On the one hand, he was personally one of the most attractive figures in Bavarian history. He was at once an accomplished scholar of broad interests, an idealist of generous thoughts, a great and sincere humanitarian and the prophet of a new world order based on the reconciliation of all nations. But he totally lacked the political capacity to realize his ambitions for the world. A French journalist was once invited to visit the new Minister President. He found the gentle little patriarch in his shiny black suit and greasy skull cap sitting in the midst of amiable confusion in what had once been the luxurious, ordered halls of the Wittelsbachs:

Diplomatic acts, parchments, revolutionary proclamations, even telegrams, cover tables and armchairs in a confusion suggestive of the

Soldaten (Hamburg, 1934), and von Oertzen captions pictures of Bavaria's revolutionary leaders "Wenn Juda König ist" (*Die deutschen Freikorps,* 305).

[61] Schmidt-Pauli, *Geschichte der Freikorps,* 199. One of Eisner's first acts as Minister President of Bavaria was to join Maximilian Harden and F. W. Foerster in publishing carefully edited and selected German documents relative to the outbreak of World War I with the purpose of showing Germany's war guilt. Some of Eisner's speeches did nothing to win the affection of German patriots. On more than one occasion, he regretted that Germany had no Clemenceau to govern her. See Ernst Müller-Meiningen, *Aus Bayerns schwersten Tagen: Erinnerungen und Betrachtungen aus der Revolutionzeit,* 2nd ed. (Berlin and Leipzig, 1924), 68, 75 ff., and Volkmann, *Revolution über Deutschland,* 90–91.

[62] Rosenberg, *Geschichte der deutschen Republik,* 78. See also the enthusiastic appraisal of a young admirer, Ernst Toller, *Eine Jugend in Deutschland* (Amsterdam, 1936), 137 ff.

backroom of a shop, and he hardly tries to conceal the most compromising documents from the indiscretion of the journalists who besiege
him. On the contrary, in his desire to break entirely with the past,
Eisner himself offers to their curiosity the acts concerning his own
politics. Would you like the telegram that was sent today to the government of Berlin? Here it is . . . Would you like the order of the day
for the coming council of ministers? Here it is . . . Sometimes some
hurried visitor, tired of waiting, bursts all at once into the first office,
where several young men and women secretaries . . . work, smoking
cigarettes and eating sandwiches in a chaos of tables and chairs piled
high with newspapers and proclamations . . . For no method and no
organization seems to prevail in the functioning of this odd ministry.[63]

Eisner's popularity dwindled rapidly during the three short
months of his ministry. A week before the January elections he
had boasted that ninety-five per cent of the Bavarian people stood
behind him; in the elections he received less than two per cent of
the total vote and his party returned three members to the Diet.[64]
In a desperate effort to stay in office, Eisner tried first to win the
support of the Majority Socialists and then of the Communists.
He was rebuffed by both. Finally on the morning of February 21,
1919, the lonely, defeated idealist made his way to the government
buildings to convey his resignation to Auer, the leader of the
Majority Socialists. En route, he was shot down in the street by
Count Arco auf Valley, a member of the proto-Nazi Thule
Society.[65] That same morning in the Diet, Auer was assassinated

[63] Paul Gentizon, *La Révolution Allemande* (Paris, 1919), 61–63, quoted
in Benoist-Méchin, *op. cit.*, I, 256. See also the memoirs of the French
military attaché, Ambroise Got, *La Terreur en Bavière* (Paris, 1922), 34–40.

[64] Müller-Meiningen, *op. cit.*, 109. It is indubitably true that Eisner had
more actual support than these figures indicate, but Professor Rosenberg exaggerates the extent of that support. Rosenberg contends that forty-five per
cent of the Diet still supported Eisner, but he bases his conclusion on the
highly doubtful assumption that Eisner had the backing of both the Majority
Socialists and the Communists. (Rosenberg, *Geschichte der deutschen Republik*, 78.)

[65] The *Thule Gesellschaft* was one of the dozens of extremist racist groups
common in the early twenties. It formed its own Free Corps, the *Thule
Kampfbund,* and as early as 1918 it used the swastika as its symbol and
"Heil!" as its greeting. The founder and leader of the society comments:
"Count Arco auf Valley had Jewish blood . . . from his mother's side . . .
and since he was partly Jewish, he was excluded from both the *Thule
Gesellschaft* and the *Kampfbund*. He wanted to show that even a half-
Jew could carry out an act of heroism." Rudolf von Sebottendorff, *Bevor
Hitler Kam: Urkundliches aus der Frühzeit der nationalsozialistischen Be-*

by a young Communist butcher's apprentice. It was an amazing scene. The assassin simply walked calmly into the Diet, shot the leading government official, and calmly walked out again. Guards were summoned, but they did not detain him.[66]

While thousands of Münchners mourned the death of their beloved Eisner,[67] two rival groups disputed his political inheritance: the Majority Socialists, now led by Adolf Hoffman, and an odd assortment of intellectual radicals led by Ernst Toller. On March 7, Hoffman put together a shaky coalition cabinet and assumed office.

On March 20, 1919, Communism had been given a new impetus throughout central Europe when Bela Kuhn installed his dictatorship of the proletariat in Hungary. A wave of Communist enthusiasm swept up the Danube. By April it had reached Bavaria. On the night of April 6, in the Queen's bedroom in the Wittelsbach Palace, Ernst Toller and his friends proclaimed that Bavaria was now a Republic of Soviets (*Räterepublik*). Hoffman's coalition government fled to Bamberg, and a group of "Coffee House Anarchists" began one of the most fantastic experiments in government in European history.

Ernst Toller, the neurotic young poet and essayist, became President of the Executive Council. While Munich starved, he began his government by issuing a decree suggesting that the people should turn to free art; it was there, he said, that one would find solace and the regeneration of the human soul. Silvio Gesell, the

---

wegung (Munich, 1934), 82. The book is in general an attempt to prove that the *Thule Gesellschaft* was the real nucleus of National Socialism. As a result, the book was placed in the closed archives of the N.S.D.A.P. and stamped with a large red V before its call number. Other books that vary from the party line or whose authors were purged, such as Ernst Röhm and Peter Heydebreck, also have the V mark. Does it stand for *Volkswiderlich*?

[66] An eyewitness account of the murder is given by a deputy who was present at the scene, Müller-Meiningen, *Aus Bäyerns schwersten Tagen*, 122–127.

[67] Large portraits of Eisner were garlanded with flowers and set up in the streets of Munich. Members of the *Thule Gesellschaft* soaked burlap sacks in the sweat of bitches in heat and dropped them near the pictures. The scent attracted the dogs of Munich, who tore at the pictures and defiled them. The revolting story is repeated here for one reason. It is because the Freebooters found the incident highly amusing and publicly bragged about it.

leader of a free-money clique, found ample opportunity to experiment with his monetary theories as Minister of Finance. Gustav Landauer, the anarchist philosopher, was the new Commissar for Public Instruction. He proclaimed that everyone would be educated according to his own ideas, that the University was open to all Bavarians over eighteen years of age, and that "history, that enemy of civilization, is suppressed." [68] Dr. Franz Lipp, the new Commissar for Foreign Affairs, was thoroughly enjoying a full-blown psychosis. His foreign policy consisted in writing a series of letters. To Lenin, he wrote:

The proletariat of Upper Bavaria is happily united. Socialists plus Communists plus Independents fused together like a hammer. However, the hairy gorilla hands of Gustav Noske are dripping with blood. We want peace forever. Immanuel Kant, *Vom ewigen Frieden,* 1795, Theses 2–5.[69]

He complained to the Pope that the cowardly Hoffman had stolen the key to his toilet,[70] and to the Minister of Transport he wrote:

My dear Colleague: I have just declared war on Württemberg and Switzerland because these dogs did not send me 60 locomotives immediately. I am certain of victory. Moreover, I have just sent a supplication to the Pope — a very good friend of mine — begging him to bless our arms.[71]

The Commissar for Public Housing requisitioned all the houses in Bavaria and decreed that henceforth no home could contain more than three rooms and that the living room must always be placed above the kitchen and bedroom.[72]

The happy, irresponsible government of the Coffee House Anarchists was continually sabotaged by the Communists,[73]

---

[68] Quoted in Volkmann, *Revolution über Deutschland,* 222.

[69] Quoted in Got, *La Terreur en Bavière,* 128.

[70] Toller, *Eine Jugend in Deutschland,* 151.

[71] Quoted in Noske, *Von Kiel bis Kapp,* 136. Lipp's previous letter to the Pope had ended with his favorite quotation, "Peace forever!"

[72] Volkmann, *op. cit.,* 222.

[73] See Ernst Toller's memoirs, *Eine Jugend in Deutschland,* 144 ff. Communist writers despise this caricature of the true Republic of Soviets. For their indictments, see Clara Zetkin, *Les Batailles Révolutionnaires de L'Allemagne en 1919* (Petrograd, 1920), 14. Paul Levi, writing under the name of Paul Werner calls its leaders "anarchistic Don Quixotes" and "opportunists" (Paul Werner, *Die Bayrische Räterepublik,* Petrograd, 1920, 15);

and, of course, by the Nationalists. It did very well to last for six days.

On the lovely[74] Palm Sunday of April 1919, the Communists seized power in Bavaria. Leadership was vested in the Russians, Leviné, Axelrod, and Levien,[75] and their arrival in Munich brought a reign of terror which was mitigated only by inefficiency and confusion. Violent decree followed decree, soldiers of the "Red Army" ran drunkenly through the streets plundering and looting; schools, banks, newspaper offices, and the National Theater were closed; a series of unauthorized "General Strikes" was proclaimed; prisoners were released from the jails and police dossiers burned — this last for very good reason. The new Police President, one Köberl, was intimately concerned with police records. In 1903 he had served a sentence for moral turpitude, and during the years 1903–1907 he had been arrested on an average of once every year for burglary, forgery, assault, and a variety of lesser crimes. The mad sex orgies which took place in the new Communist headquarters, the Palace of the Wittelsbachs, shocked even sophisticated Munich.[76]

During the "Red Terror" the Communist Army, led by Rudolf Eglhofer, enrolled thousands of men in its ranks largely because it was probably the best paid army in history. Privates received 25 marks a day; officers, 100 marks a day, plus a bonus which rose

and Rosenberg says that they were "patently pathological." (*Geschichte*, 81.) Ruth Fischer, who quotes Werner, is more sympathetic. (*Stalin and German Communism*, 102.)

[74] It is an interesting coincidence that while the important days of the Revolution in Berlin were almost uniformly cold and miserable, those in Munich were usually pleasant: November 7–8 and April 13–14, balmy; May 1–3, clear and warm. For comments on the weather, see Müller-Meiningen, *Aus Bäyerns schwersten Tagen*.

[75] Towia Axelrod was born in Moscow. Banished to ·Siberia under the Czar, he became Chief of Press under Lenin. In July 1918 he was sent to Berlin to foment revolution and subsequently took over the same assignment in Munich. Eugen Leviné and Max Levien had similar careers. For biographical sketches of Communist leaders see Ambroise Got, *La Terreur en Bavière*, 163–167, 167–172, 172–177, 177–182.

[76] Of the literally dozens of accounts of the "Red Terror," see especially the memoirs of the Hoffman democrat, Josef Karl, *Die Schreckensherrschaft in München und Spartakus im bayr. Oberland* (Munich, 1919[?]), 27–37, 265 and *passim*. See also the dispatches of the London *Times* correspondent for May 1 to May 5, 1919, and Got, *La Terreur en Bavière*, 192, 214–235.

as high as 15,000 marks. The pay was collected in advance every ten days. The families of all Red soldiers were given free living quarters; and the men were supplied with free liquor and free prostitutes. The army cost the Bavarian people some 500,000 marks a day at first, but when that proved inadequate, Eglhofer started the printing presses rolling and special currency to supply the army's needs appeared in abundance.[77]

With the news from Munich more and more distressing, Hoffman and his War Minister, Schneppenhorst, tried frantically to build an army which would enable them to regain power in Bavaria. Their efforts were not successful and, sometime in April,[78] Hoffman asked Noske for help. Noske suggested that the Von Epp Free Corps[79] now stationed at Ohrdruf in Thuringia, be used to

---

[77] On the question of the Red Army in Munich, see the account of the French military attaché, Ambroise Got, *La Terreur en Bavière*, 190 ff.; Major E. O. Volkmann, *Revolution über Deutschland*, 227; and the *Berliner Tageblatt* for April 26, 1919.

[78] It is not clear when Hoffman asked for help. The chronology and organization of Noske's memoirs are extremely bad. He writes, "During the time of the Councils' domination of Munich, I talked twice with President Hoffman in Berlin." (*Von Kiel bis Kapp*, 137.) *Räteherrschaft* might, of course, refer to either Toller's or Leviné's councils.

[79] Colonel Franz Ritter von Epp became one of the great heroes of National Socialism. In January 1919, Noske had urged him to form a Free Corps. When both the Eisner and Hoffman governments refused to allow him to recruit men in Bavaria, Noske intervened and a compromise was agreed to: Epp was permitted to recruit men in Bavaria, but he was to train them across the Thuringian border. The Epp Brigade was one of the strongest Free Corps in Germany. In 1919, Epp and his men entered the official Republican army but continued to call themselves the Von Epp Free Corps. During this period, Colonel von Epp actively supported the efforts of Hitler and Röhm to overthrow the Republic. He joined the NSDAP at an early date and was one of their first deputies to the Reichstag. Under Hitler, he became the Reichsstatthalter of Bavaria. Prominent Nazis belonging to his Free Corps included: Karl Fritsch, later Minister-President of Saxony; Hühnlein, the Supreme Leader of the National Socialist *Kraftfahrerkorps;* Rudolf Hess; and Friedrich Wilhelm Brückner, Hitler's personal adjutant. Nazi propaganda later maintained that Hitler himself had belonged, but I am unable to find substantiation for this claim which is made in the party-endorsed version edited by Walter M. Espe, *Das Buch der NSDAP: Werden, Kampf, und Ziel* (Berlin, 1933), 11. In addition to the biographies of von Epp, written by Walter Frank, *op. cit.*, and Josef H. Krumbach, editor, *Franz Ritter von Epp: Ein Leben für Deutschland* (Munich, 1939), see also *Das deutsche Führerlexikon, 1934–1935* (Munich, 1934), and Edgar von Schmidt-Pauli, *Die Männer um Hitler* (Berlin, 1932).

rout the Communists. Members of his own cabinet-in-exile also pleaded with him to call in the Epp Free Corps, but to all entreaties Hoffman replied, "I don't need any foreign help. We Bavarians can do it ourselves." [80] So Hoffman and Schneppenhorst's little army advanced on Munich. The result of their offensive was the military fiasco at Dachau on April 18, 1919. Schneppenhorst's "anti-militaristic Republicans" either fled at the first sight of bloodshed or went over to the Communists. Von Oertzen comments with fine scorn, "Anti-militarist soldiers are and remain a contradiction *per se*." [81]

Hoffmann had now no other choice but to call for the Volunteers, though well he knew that in the past Free Corps help invariably led to Free Corps domination. Noske was not unhappy either at Hoffman's military defeat or at the prospects of subduing Munich. Aid was granted to Hoffman, but only under Noske's conditions: Command of the expedition was vested in the Minister of National Defense; and the tactical commander, General von Oven, was ordered not to accept any instructions from the Bavarian government until Munich was under control. The conditions were extremely unsatisfactory, but the harried Majority Socialist Premier had no other alternative. He accepted them.

A tactical plan for the conquest of Munich was available in a surprisingly short time. It was accepted and ready to be put into operation between April 20 and April 23, 1919. The fact that such a plan, complete with the disposition of all forces, was already in existence at this early date lends some credence to the story that the Red unrest in Munich was stirred up deliberately by *agents provocateurs* employed by Army leaders in order to give them an excuse for occupying the city.[82]

[80] And when a deputy asked him how many troops he had to oppose the Red Army's 30,000 men he replied that he supposed he had about 8,000. (Müller-Meiningen, *Erinnerungen*, 185.)

[81] Von Oertzen *Die deutschen Freikorps*, 331.

[82] Hans Fried, *The Guilt of the German Army*, 185, gives the earlier date. Von Oertzen says the plan was ready by April 23 (*Die deutschen Freikorps*, 333). As early as April 20, Noske had given verbal orders to Major von Unruh, chief of staff to von Oven, to begin gathering Volunteers for the liberation of Munich. See von Unruh's own account, "Einmarsch in München," in *Deutsche Soldaten*, 85. We do not know precisely when Hoff-

The military plans called for an encirclement of Munich by concentric maneuver. By April 27, the Volunteers had taken up their positions and formed an iron ring around the city.[83] During the next two days the circle began to contract and Dachau fell to the Görlitz Free Corps on April 30. The plan of operations called for moving into Munich proper on the morning of May 2, but an earlier attack was precipitated by a Communist act of terror.

As the Free Corps approached Munich, the orders and proclamations issued by Rudolf Eglhofer, Commander of the Red Army, became increasingly hysterical. The "Prussians" were coming and his men were doing exactly what wise rodents do when sea vessels are about to capsize. On April 29 he issued the following appeal to his deserting soldiers:

WORKERS! SOLDIERS OF THE RED ARMY!

The enemy stands before the doors of Munich! The officers, students, sons of the bourgeoise and White guardist soldiers of capitalism are already in Schleissheim. There is not an hour to be wasted! Out from the factories! Immediate General Strike! Defend the Revolution! Defend yourselves! Out to the battle! . . . Stand firm! . . . Everything is at stake! [84]

But his soldiers continued to desert and the news from the front was more and more alarming. On the morning of April 30, Eglhofer was told that there was absolutely no hope of defending the

man agreed to Noske's terms, but it must have been sometime after April 18 (the defeat at Dachau). Noske's laconic comment, "Agreement on the methods of executive action (*Reichsexekution*) was not reached without some discussion . . ." (Noske, *Von Kiel bis Kapp*, 138) may, of course, indicate a delay of a few hours or a few days. The theory that the Army used *agents provocateurs* is advanced in Fried, *op. cit.*, 184; Ambroise Got, *L'Allemagne après la Débâcle. Impressions d'un Attaché à la Mission Militaire Française* . . . (Strasbourg, 1919[?]), 135; Konrad Heiden, *Der Fuehrer*, 88; and by Kurt Caro and Walter Oehme, *Schleichers Aufstieg: Ein Beitrag zur Geschichte der Gegenrevolution* (Berlin, 1933), 68. It seems highly doubtful if the thesis will ever be proved or disproved. It is very unlikely, however, that the OHL would employ a psychotic, Dr. Franz Lipp, as their chief agent as Oehme and Caro maintain (*ibid.*, p. 68).

[83] A detailed list of the disposition of each of the Corps is given in Schmidt-Pauli, *Geschichte der Freikorps*, 202–204. The activity of each group is discussed in elaborate detail in *Das Buch vom deutschen Freikorpskämpfer*, Ernst von Salomon, editor (Berlin, 1938). Most of the accounts are based on the diaries of men who participated.

[84] Quoted in Karl, *Die Schreckensherrschaft*, 71.

city. That afternoon the terrified Commander ordered the shooting
of the hostages he had seized and held captive in the Luitpoldgymnasium. Ernst Toller rushed to the place and managed to save
some of the prisoners, but twenty of them, including some of the
most prominent citizens of Munich, were killed and their bodies
so horribly mutilated that it was not possible to identify them
all.[85] The citizens of Munich, long since fed up with Communist
misrule, were shaken and alarmed by the Luitpoldgymnasium
atrocity. They had already formed small self-defense groups;
these now attacked the Reds and helped to accelerate the speed
of the Free Corps conquest.[86]

Students slipped through the Red lines and reported the atrocity to Ehrhardt and Epp. Both their Free Corps began to attack
immediately on the evening of April 30. By the second of May,
Munich was in the hands of the Volunteers.

The following days saw a reign of terror which made the "Red
Terror" of the preceding weeks pale in comparison.[87] The London

[85] The *Times* (London), May 7, 1919, reported that the native soldiers
of the Red Army refused to carry out Eglhofer's order. The actual shooting
was therefore done by Russians who had been sent by the Third International. This version is corroborated by the *Berliner Tageblatt*, May 5,
1919. For a detailed report of the event, see Sebottendorff, *Bevor Hitler
kam*, 135–162. The author, as founder of the Thule Gesellschaft, was
particularly interested, since several of the hostages had belonged to his
society. Von Oertzen maintains that the shooting was done by the commandant of the Gymnasium, one Seidel. (Von Oertzen, *Kamerad, reich mir
die Hände*, 86–87.

[86] Mr. Fried, in his eagerness to indict all things connected with the Free
Corps, calls these self-defense formations a "fifth column." (*Guilt of the
German Army*, 185). In so doing, he weakens his case against the Volun-
teers by distortion and misrepresentation. The attacks from within the
city were led by Lieutenant Lautenbacher's *Freischar*. After the conquest
of Munich, Lautenbacher's group joined the Von Epp Free Corps. Later,
as a separate *Sturmbataillon*, it actively supported Adolf Hitler in the Beer
Hall Putsch. Many of the early members of the Nazi Party, including
Heinrich Himmler, had been members of Lautenbacher's Volunteers. See
Lieutenant Friedrich Lautenbacher, "Widerstand im Roten München," in
Freikorpskämpfer, and von Oertzen, *Die deutschen Freikorps*, 342.

[87] Nationalist writers have grossly exaggerated the extent of the Red
Terror in Munich. It is true that the Communist regime was guilty of
extortion, licentiousness, and general misrule, but its actual tyranny was
mitigated by the inefficiency of its government. The terrible massacre of
the hostages is the only such act reported during the period. It was done
by men who were half-crazed with fear; men who believed that they would
all be killed as soon as the approaching "Prussians" arrived. While the

Times correspondent, who had previously reported that the people of Munich had received "the government troops with great joy," [88] now cabled from Berne:

A journalist just returned from Munich confirms the view that the "White Terror" of the Prussian military rule is far worse than the Red Terror of Communism. All suspected of extreme views are shot without trial. Numerous notables suspected of even moderate Socialist views disappear without a trace. The press is completely muzzled . . .[89]

On May 4, Major Schulz of the Lützow Free Corps set the tone of the occupation in a speech to his fellow officers. He said:

Gentlemen! Anyone who doesn't now understand that there is a lot of hard work to be done here or whose conscience bothers him had better get out. It is a lot better to kill a few innocent people than to let one guilty person escape . . . You know how to handle it . . . shoot them and report that they attacked you or tried to escape.[90]

That afternoon Major Schulz gave a dramatic example of what he had meant in his speech. He sent Lieutenant Georg Pölzing to the town of Perlach near Munich to arrest a group of citizens. Pölzing chose a dozen people, apparently at random, brought

---

socialist writers who normally defend the Communists unanimously condemn this act of terror, the nationalists unite in unanimous defense of the literally hundreds of systematic murders committed by the Volunteers. Ernst Toller indubitably exaggerates when he says that the Communists' "Revolutionary Tribunal" did not rob or mishandle a single person, but there is no record of it ever handing down a death penalty (Toller, *Eine Jugend in Deutschland,* 164). See also the anonymous pamphlet, published by *Freiheit,* entitled, *Die Münchener Tragödie; Entstehung, Verlauf und Zusammenbruch der Räte-Republik München* (Berlin, 1919).

[88] *Times* (London), May 3, 1919.

[89] *Loc. cit.,* May 16, 1919. The French military attaché, who was present at the time, says that when the Volunteers first arrived, "The people breathed a sigh of relief — they naïvely imagined that it meant an end to the terror of dictatorship . . . It would require a volume to narrate all the atrocities committed by the Whites . . . organized barbarism was given free reign . . . a savage debauchery, an indescribable orgy . . ." (Ambroise Got, *La Terreur en Bavière,* 269–286). Even Josef Karl, who writes the most bitter and most detailed account of Communist terrorism, notes sadly that "misfortune seldom comes unaccompanied" and in a new preface to his memoirs dated May 1919 expresses the hope that he will see no more human sacrifices such as he witnessed during the first days of May. (*Die Schreckensherrschaft in München,* 149 and iii–iv.)

[90] Quoted in the Report of the State Commission for Public Order, August 28, 1919. Cited in E. J. Gumbel, *"Verräter Verfallen der Feme," Opfer, Mörder, Richter, 1919–1920* (Berlin, 1929), 89. The title of the book is a direct quotation from the bylaws of the Organization Consul.

them back to Munich, and had them shot without trial in the Hofbräuhaus. The lieutenant was brought to trial seven years later (January 1926). It was established that none of the victims had been a Communist. It is not at all surprising that Pölzing was acquitted of all charges when one considers the fact that the "expert witnesses" called to testify were his former commanding officers.[91]

On the evening of May 6, 1919, a group of Catholic workers of the Saint Joseph Society held a meeting to discuss educational and cultural matters. In the middle of a quiet discussion of the role of the theater, the door was suddenly yanked open, and Free-booters entered and arrested the group. Captain Alt-Sutterheim picked out twenty of them and had them shot as "Communist terrorists."[92] Herr von Oertzen gives the losses suffered by the Free Corps during the "Battle of Liberation" as 68 killed and 170 wounded. "The losses of the Reds," he says, "were significantly higher. Including those shot by courts-martial, the total can be estimated at from 1,000 to 1,200."[93] The estimate is conservative. The sheer number of bodies posed a difficult problem for city health officials. Undertaking establishments simply could not handle the volume of business and the decaying corpses which littered the streets became a health menace. The Freebooter's solution to the problem was the one which would be used by their Nazi successors: shallow trenches were dug and the unnamed, stinking corpses were shoved in.[94]

Apart from the hundreds of Münchners who were shot infor-mally by the Freebooters, dozens of citizens were sentenced to death by hurriedly summoned "Courts-martial." The commander of the Baltic *Landeswehr* describes the procedure of one of these courts. He is speaking of one which met in the Baltic, but the example is equally applicable to either Munich or the Ruhr. In this case, a government official who was unfriendly to the Freebooters was brought before the *Freikorpsführer:*

[91] *Ibid.*, 90–96, and Maximilian Scheer, editor, *Blut und Ehre* (Paris, 1937), 37–38.

[92] *Times* (London), May 15, 1919; and E. J. Gumbel, *Vier Jahre politischer Mord,* 5th ed. (Berlin, 1922), 41–42.

[93] Von Oertzen *Die deutschen Freikorps,* 346.

[94] Toller, *Eine Jugend in Deutschland,* 232.

I said, "I hereby summon a court-martial. Members are myself, the chief of staff and ordnance officer. I order that the death penalty by hanging be applied immediately. Agreed?" After agreement by the two other gentlemen, the Minister was hanging . . . over the market-place in less than two minutes.[95]

What von Schmidt-Pauli calls the "stern justice of the people's courts"[96] was not the only characteristic of the occupation. The period was not without its lighter side. Prisoners herded into improvised prisons were confronted with jocular signs which read, "This is were we make Leberwurst out of Spartacists. Reds executed free of charge."[97] The future Minister President of Saxony under the Nazis wrote an account of his experiences as a Free Corps leader under the revealing title, *Ernstes und Heiteres aus dem Putschleben*. In the book he recalls an incident which he classifies as one of the more frivolous episodes in his life as a "putschist." After the troops had conquered Munich, the author recalls:

Two of my men approached a woman we found on the street. She tried to bite them. A blow on the mouth brought her to reason. In the yard, she was laid over the tongue of a wagon and hit so often with sticks that not a white spot remained on her back.[98]

Lieutenant Rudolf Mann, at that time regimental adjutant of one of the two Ehrhardt regiments, found aspects of the mopping-up operations equally amusing. He writes:

[95] Major Fletcher, "Die Eroberung Tuckums," in *Freikorpskämpfer*, 146. After the occupation, the regular Bavarian courts sentenced 407 persons to fortress confinement, 1,737 to prison and 65 to hard labor. Franz Neumann, *Behemoth: The Structure and Practice of National Socialism* (New York, 1942), 21. See below, p. 162.

[96] *Geschichte der Freikorps*, 208.

[97] Toller, *op. cit.*, 213.

[98] Manfred von Killinger, *Ernstes und Heiteres aus dem Putschleben*, 6th ed. (Munich, 1934, Zentral verlag der NSDAP), 15. The first edition appeared in 1927. The book contains a dedication which commends itself to the attention of a psychiatrist: "To the memory of my little tiger . . . a creature who loves me and whom I love above everyone else and who looked at me questioningly with his great brown eyes whenever I had to leave him. I took his head in my hands and kissed him between the nostrils and I wept. I am not ashamed of my tears. My tiger was better than any human being because he never gossiped." Other examples of his heavy-footed humor may be found in his *Das waren Kerle!* (Munich, 1944), a book published to raise the morale of World War II soldiers by reminding them of the spirit of the Freebooters. For brief facts about Killinger's career, see Appendix at the end of this study.

92 VANGUARD OF NAZISM

The supreme commander tacked proclamations to the walls: "Warning! All arms are to be surrendered immediately. Whoever is caught with arms in his possession will be shot on the spot!" What could the poor citizen of average intelligence do? Surrender — but how? If he took his rifle under his arm to take it to the place were arms were collected, he would be shot on the steps of his house by a passing patrol. If he came to the door of his house and opened it, we all took shots at him because he was armed. If he got as far as the street, we would put him up against the wall. If he stuck his rifle under his coat it was still worse . . . I suggested that they tie their rifles on a long string and drag them behind them. I would have laughed myself sick if I had seen them go down the street doing it.[99]

Rudolf Mann was apparently interested only in the first part of General von Oven's order of May 5, 1919. The rest of the order is worth reading because it shows, Leftist writers to the contrary, that the Supreme Commander of the forces of liberation did try to stop indiscriminate shooting. Mann's interpretation of the order, however, is eloquent testimony to the fact that such orders did not effectively dampen the "Freebooter spirit." Oven's order reads:

1. Whoever is caught with arms in his possession will be shot on the spot.
2. Whoever is taken prisoner can only be sentenced by legal channels, i.e., by duly constituted courts of martial-law (*Standrechtliche Gerichte*).
3. The martial-law courts will hold their sessions in the regular court buildings.
4. Every other sort of proceedings against prisoners is not recognized (*unzulässig*). This applies especially to the sentences by military field courts-martial (*Feldgericht*). Whoever forms that sort of court-martial will be arrested immediately. Sentences rendered by such courts are not binding . . .[100]

In Munich the reaction to the Volunteers' occupation was so violent that the commander of the Bavarian Army found it necessary to remind the citizens of their debt to the forces of liberation

[99] Rudolf Mann, *Mit Ehrhardt durch Deutschland, Erinnerungen eines Mitkämpfers von der 2. Marinebrigade* (Berlin, 1921), 71–72.
[100] Quoted in Gumbel, *Vier Jahre*, 111–112. It hardly needs to be pointed out, however, that the victims of the proscribed "courts-martial" — which continued to function — were scarcely in a position to appeal the legality of their sentences. See Josef Karl's memoirs, *Die Schreckensherrschaft in München*, 150.

and warn Münchners to stop complaining about Freebooter atrocities:

TO THE CITIZENS OF MUNICH:

The North German troops in liberating our home from Spartacistic-Communism and from the Russian leaders . . . have earned the gratitude of every citizen regardless of his party affiliation. But in spite of this, an evil hatred has developed against the Prussian troops. It is your duty to apprehend those persons who criticize [the "Prussians"] . . . and bring them to justice.

(signed)
Möhl.
Bavarian Commander.[101]

By May 6, 1919, General von Oven was able to inform Noske that the city was under control and that the Hoffman regime could return. The shaky government of the Social Democrats lasted until March 1920, when military leaders used the opportunity afforded by the Kapp Putsch to install Gustav von Kahr as the virtual dictator of Bavaria. The story of the Kahr government and the Beer Hall Putsch will be continued in a later chapter. The intimate relationship between those events and the Freebooter conquest of May 1919 is emphasized by F. W. von Oertzen:

Munich became the matrix of National Socialism and if we search in the history of the National Socialist movement for its earliest contact with the Free Corps of the postwar period, we must conclude that this contact, with all its direct and indirect consequences, was the liberation of Munich, carried out by Free Corps from all over Germany — even though at that time Adolf Hitler was still a completely unknown corporal about whom the officers and men of the Free Corps knew nothing.[102]

Before following the career of the Volunteers during the rest of their activity within the Reich, we shall turn to one of the most turbulent chapters of their colorful history: "The Baltic Adventure."

[101] Reprinted in the *Berliner Tageblatt,* May 5, 1919. It is highly significant that throughout the period of the "Liberation of Munich" *Vorwärts* had no major criticism to make of the Volunteers' conduct.

[102] Von Oertzen *Die deutschen Freikorps,* 346–347. Edgar von Schmidt-Pauli is more rhapsodic: "Here was sounded the *first anacrusis which preceded the mighty Germanic symphony* which could only be conducted by the National Socialist leadership in the Third Reich." *Geschichte der Freikorps,* 215. (Italics are in the original.)

V

THE BALTIC ADVENTURE

Today, with pounding hearts, we can ask ourselves what would have become of Germany if the Bolshevist hordes — those animal-men who knew nothing save their own lustful passions — had broken into Germany and united with the Spartacists. And where, indeed, would Europe be today?

— Edgar von Schmidt-Pauli

On the Western Front during the month of August 1918, the German Army experienced the blackest day of its history. But in the East things were very different. The Treaty of Brest-Litovsk had been signed and Germany's centuries-long dream of *Drang nach Osten* seemed about to be fulfilled.

That August, monocled eyes flashed with approval as they scanned the map of Eastern Europe. They saw that Posen, incorporated into the Reich since 1772, was being safely and sternly administered by its military commander, General von Bock und Polach. The Kingdom of Poland, conquered in 1915, was also a part of the Greater Reich; it was being governed from Warsaw by General von Beseler. And still farther to the east, they saw a vast, continuous belt of land stretching from the Baltic to the Black Sea. The Eastern campaign had indeed been triumphant. But seldom has a triumph been so short-lived. It ended with the collapse of the Western Front. The war map was rolled up and put away for future reference.

I. THE LOSS OF POSEN

In Eastern Europe the period immediately following the Armistice of 1918 was made turbulent by the fact that no final settlement of Germany's Eastern border could be made until the diplomats had met to determine the peace. But the Poles could not wait for Versailles. Sensing the rebirth of their ancient independence and heartened by Mr. Wilson's thirteenth point, they began to carve out a new country.

During the course of the War, the Poles in Posen had organized a fairly effective underground movement. Now, with the collapse of Germany, it was not difficult for Polish nationalists to organize and consolidate their positions. This was done in two ways: First the Poles won the support of the German Workers' and Soldiers' Councils by promising them representation. Then, after getting their support, they by-passed or dominated the Councils. Secondly, they created a strong Polish volunteer army and furnished it with the weapons they had seized from the Germans. In a matter of weeks, the Poles were the masters of Posen.[1]

Meanwhile, with conflicting reports reaching the Chancellor's office about conditions in Posen, Ebert sent Helmuth von Gerlach, an undersecretary of state, to investigate. After a thorough and remarkably fair-minded investigation, von Gerlach recommended a policy of arbitration and conciliation. Above all, his report insisted that no military action should be taken to reconquer Posen. It should be noted that this last point was not just von Gerlach's own idea. It had been urged on him by members of the staff of the Commanding General of Posen, who were convinced that any German attack at that time would only result in victory for the Poles.[2] But here again, as in the case of the Armistice and the signing of the Versailles treaty, the onus for "cowardly surrender" was placed squarely on the shoulders of the civilians. The Cabinet approved von Gerlach's report, but the Supreme Command had no intention of submitting to the civilian government. Field Marshal von Hindenburg was particularly fu-

---

[1] Karl Rzepecki, *Powstanie grudniowe w Wielkopolsche*, 27, 12, 1918 (*The December Revolt in Greater Poland*, December 27, 1918, Posen, 1919), cited in A. Loessner, *Der Abfall Posens: 1918–1919* (Volume VI of *Ostland Schriften*, Danzig, 1933), 5–6, 12–14 and 20–22. See also Erich Otto Volkmann, *Revolution über Deutschland* (Oldenburg, 1930), 92–93.

[2] In addition to Gerlach's memoirs, *Der Zusammenbruch der deutschen Polenpolitik*, Flugschriften des Bundes Neues Vaterland Nr. 14 (Berlin, 1919), 13–15, see also Zygmunt Wieliczkas, *Wielkopolska a Prusy w dobie powstania 1918–1919* (*Greater Poland and Prussia during the Revolt of 1918–1919*, Posen, 1932), cited in Loessner, *Der Abfall Posens*, 36.

rious. He refused to entertain the thought that the province of Posen, for two hundred years a part of the "sacred soil of the Fatherland" and the place where he was born, should be handed over to the despicable Poles.

On November 24, 1918, unknown to the Ebert government and in open defiance of the Gerlach report, Hindenburg sent secret orders to all divisional commanders in the East to prepare for an attack on Posen.[3] But the Field Marshal was forced to postpone his plans. It will be recalled that December 1918 was the low-water mark in the prestige and power of the Supreme Command. Among other things, General Lequis had suffered an embarrassing and decisive defeat before the doors of the Marstall, and Hindenburg decided that another such defeat — a defeat such as General von Bock had predicted — would be ruinous. The old gentleman called off the attack, trembled in impotent rage, and waited for an opening. He did not have long to wait. The arrival of Noske and his Free Corps system greatly improved the military situation in Germany. In the course of a few weeks the Volunteers had subdued Berlin and Weimar, and Maercker's Rifles were about to start on their victorious march through Middle Germany. The Supreme Command took a new lease on life. "What it could not bring about with the old Imperial Army," says Benoist-Méchin, "it hopes to accomplish with the *Freikorps . . .*"[4]

A strategic plan for the reconquest of Posen was drawn up quickly, and an invading army of Free Corps under the command of General von Bulow moved across the border and conquered Culmsee. But in the meantime, Paderewski in Paris was having no difficulty convincing the Allies of the dangers of a revival of German power.[5] On February 16, Marshal Foch called the Armistice Commission together at Trier and issued an ultimatum to

[3] J. Benoist-Méchin, *History of the German Army since the Armistice,* translated by Eileen R. Taylor (Zürich, 1939), I, 219.

[4] *Ibid.,* I, 227.

[5] Even before Paderewski's storm of protest to the Allies, the Archbishop of Gnesen and Posen, as early as January 15, 1919, had been writing letters to Foch complaining about the sacrilege, atrocities, and terror perpetrated by the Free Corps which were already assembling in Posen. The letters are reprinted in Wieliczkas, *Wielkopolska a Prusy,* quoted in Loessner, *op. cit.,* 27–28. See also von Gerlach, *Zusammenbruch,* 16–17.

the Ebert government which demanded the immediate withdrawal of all German troops in Posen under the threat of an Allied
occupation of Westphalia. Ebert ordered the Volunteers to withdraw. It is difficult to see how the President could have done
otherwise, but the Volunteers chose to ignore the reality of Entente power and convinced themselves that a glorious victory had
once more been torn from them by the cowardly pacifists of the
November Revolution.[6]

Thus thwarted in Posen, the Supreme Command turned its attention to the Baltic. Here their agent, General Graf Rudiger von
der Goltz, was already busy organizing Free Corps to serve as his
instrument for wresting the Baltic provinces from the advancing
Red Army of Soviet Russia — and, if need be, from the little native states which had recently established precarious governments
there.

II. THE CALL OF THE BALTIC

For seven hundred years the fog-bound, forbidding land along
the shores of the Baltic Sea has had a compelling attraction for
Teutonic adventurers. Generations of German Romanticists have
fallen under the spell of the *Baltikum*, and have chanted the
praises of this weird land of the Teutonic Knights in story, song,
and sentimental novel.[7]

Modern Germany, as Peter Viereck has pointed out,[8] has suffered acutely from the lingering hangover produced by the heady

[6] As one example of this attitude, see the article written by the commander
of the Hülsen Free Corps, Bernhard von Hülsen, "Freikorps im Osten," in
Deutsche Soldaten, vom Frontheer und Freikorps, edited by Hans Roden
(Leipzig, 1935).

[7] Recent examples of the type of poetry dedicated to the Baltic may be
found in virtually every issue of the official organ of the Baltenverband,
Baltische Blätter (Berlin, 1917 ff). *Die baltische Tragödie, eine Romantrilogie*
by Siegfried von Vegessack (Bremen, 1934) is no worse than dozens of other
novels on the Baltic. Youthful Nazis were nourished on the same fare; see
Hans zur Megede's "Die baltische Tragödie" in the June 1934 issue of *Der
Schulungsbrief,* official publication of the Reichsschulungsamt. For the sentimental panegyric of a typical Pan-Germanist, see the essay by Hans Siegfried
Weber, "Das deutsche Baltentum" in *Das grössere Deutschland: Wochenschaft für deutsche Welt und Kolonialpolitik,* Nr. 50 (December 9, 1916),
1584 ff.

[8] See his provocative study, *Metapolitics: From the Romantics to Hitler*
(New York, 1941).

wine of nineteenth-century Romanticism. But it was not romance
which called Germans to the Baltic in 1919. It was opportunity.
The *Oberste Heeresleitung* and influential members of the Foreign Office had long been interested in the Baltic as a sphere for
German expansion.[9] Their interest was increased during and after
World War I. Just before signing the treaty of Brest-Litvosk,
Kühlman asked von Hindenburg why he wanted to annex the
provinces. The hero of Tannenberg replied, "I need them for the
maneuvering of my left wing in the next war." [10] And as soon as
the Western Front showed signs of crumbling, both Hindenburg
and Ludendorff seriously considered the possibility of continuing
the war from bases in Courland.[11]

Now, with the Armistice signed and a disastrous peace settlement in the offing, the OHL once again looked to the Baltic; for
here in the East they saw the chance to redeem the defeat in the
West. With this in mind, they moved their headquarters from
Cassel to Colberg and drew up plans for seizing the border states.
The clearest statement of those plans is given in a revealing passage in the memoirs of the man who was to be responsible for
their execution. Count Rudiger von der Goltz, the Supreme Commander of all the Free Corps in the Baltic area, writes:

I wanted to salvage from the unfortunate war whatever was still
salvageable. In the East, Germany was the victor . . . In alliance with
the "White" Russians and under the banner of fighting the Bolshevists
(*unter der Flagge der Bolsheviken-Bekämpfung*) why could not our
Eastern politics, which had been blocked by the events of 1918, be
achieved in a somewhat altered and more adaptable form . . . ?
Above all, why could not an economic and political sphere be created
next to Russia? Russia's own intelligentsia was ruined and her land
hungered for German technicians, merchants and leaders. Her devas-
tated and depopulated border provinces required German settlers to
cultivate their fertile soil. Especially, I had in mind discharged soldiers

[9] A good statement of German annexationist plans for the Baltic is given
by Stanley Page, *The Formation of the Baltic States (Lithuania, Latvia,
Estonia) 1917–1920* (unpublished Ph.D. thesis, Harvard University, 1946),
159–166.

[10] Quoted in John W. Wheeler-Bennett, *Wooden Titan: Hindenburg in
Twenty Years of German History, 1914–1934* (New York, 1936), 126.

[11] Arthur Rosenberg, *Die Entstehung der deutschen Republik* (Berlin,
1928), 126 f.

. . . Russia was no longer in a position to object to these plans as she had been before the war.

With such a goal before my eyes, was I to be stopped by a blade of straw (*Strohalme*)? [12]

The author of these lines had been an enthusiastic Pan-Germanist for years; he was to become an ardent supporter of Adolf Hitler.[13] It is one of the lesser ironies of postwar history that he had come to the Baltic at the invitation of the Latvian Republic and with the endorsement of the British government — that is, at the request of those "blades of straw" which von der Goltz was determined would not stand in his way. Let us see how this came about.

The situation in the Baltic at the time of the arrival of the Free Corps was confused by the presence of at least three groups which were competing for the control of the provinces which the late Czar had bequeathed to a troubled Eastern Europe. The Baltic Barons were determined to organize the provinces under their leadership. They were in competition with the recently formed native governments, which were equally determined to shake off the control which the Barons had held over them for centuries. The nationalist governments were actively supported by the Entente, and more especially by a squadron of British warships under Admiral Sinclair, which had come to the Baltic ostensibly to clear it of mine fields.[14] The third element was the advancing Red Army, which threatened to engulf the borders states and reclaim them for Russia.

As early as November 1918, the Allies had anticipated the threat of Soviet Russia to the area and had hit upon what seemed

[12] General Graf Rudiger von der Goltz, *Meine Sendung in Finnland und im Baltikum* (Leipzig, 1920), 127.

[13] In addition to his memoirs, see the entry in *Das deutsche Führerlexikon: 1934–1935* (Munich, 1934), 150–151. In this more or less official "Who's Who" of the NSDAP, von der Goltz lists his "special interest" as "the restoration of Germany's military power on National Socialist foundations." He welcomed Hitler to power in an article in *Deutschlands Erneurung*, entitled "Die deutsche Revolution," June 1933 (XVII Jahrgang). See also "Junius Alter" (Franz Sontag), *Nationalisten, Deutschlands nationales Führertum der Nachkriegszeit*, new enlarged edition (Leipzig, 1932), 169–170.

[14] The *Times* (London), December 31, 1918.

at the time to be a happy — and a very inexpensive — way to deal with the problem. They decided to use German troops to combat the Soviet threat. Article XII of the Armistice terms reads:

All German troops at present in territories which before the war formed part of Russia must . . . return to within the frontiers of Germany (as they existed on August 1, 1914) as soon as the Allies shall think the moment suitable having regard to the internal situation of these territories.[15]

The significance of this use of their former enemy to fight a former ally was not lost on the United States Senate Commission which was sent to write a report on the situation in the Baltic. The Hale Report concludes:

The Germans were, therefore, present in the Baltic Provinces with the full consent of the Allies and, indeed, by their implied command. The framers of the Armistice recognized that the red tide could not be held by any bulwark which any of the native states could maintain . . .[16]

But the Allies were not to get off that easily. The Germans, smarting under the humiliation of the Armistice, were in no mood to fight their late enemy's battles. They mutinied, laid down their arms, and began to leave the Baltic.[17]

In the meantime, M. Ulmanis, who had once taught agronomy at the University of Nebraska[18] and who was now the president of the new country of Latvia, was trying desperately to organize a native army to fight the Bolsheviks. But his pitifully inadequate forces could not even maintain order among the Latvians, much less stem the tide of the advancing Red Army. His army had staged a number of minor revolts during the first days of Decem-

[15] The full text of the revised Armistice terms may be found conveniently in Harry R. Rudin, *Armistice, 1918* (New Haven, 1944), Appendix G.

[16] *Senate Documents, 66th Congress, 1st Session,* Vol. XV, "Report of the Mission to Finland, Estonia, Latvia, and Lithuania," by Robert Hale (Washington, D.C., 1919), 8. Hereafter cited as *Senate Documents.*

[17] The London *Times* was surprised and infuriated by what it considered the duplicity of the Germans. It maintained that the Germans deliberately encouraged the advance of the Red Armies (October 27, 1919). See also the pamphlet of the Royal Institute of International Affairs, *The Baltic States: A Survey of the Political and Economic Structure and the Foreign Relations of Estonia, Latvia, and Lithuania* (London, 1938), 24.

[18] *New York Times,* October 11, 1919.

ber 1918. On each of these occasions Ulmanis had gone to the office of the German plenipotentiary in the Baltic, Herr August Winnig,[19] and asked for help. Each time Winnig stalled him off. The Latvian Army's revolt of Christmas Day was particularly threatening. Once more the harried Latvian President hurried to Winnig's office and "with beads of perspiration on his forehead" [20] pleaded for assistance.

Winnig realized that the stakes were big and he played his cards carefully. The future Nazi pseudophilosopher wanted complete control of the Baltic[21] and he saw in the Free Corps movement the instrument for attaining that goal. But first of all it was necessary to convince the worried Latvian President that Germany and Germany alone could help him. Consequently, when Ulmanis came to him on Christmas Day, Winnig told him to go and take his troubles to the British. The finesse worked. The British, as Herr Winnig well knew, were unable to give Ulmanis much help. They assured him of their sympathy, said something

[19] Prince Max had sent Winnig, a Majority Social Democrat, to the Baltic in October 1918 to establish good relations with the newly formed governments in the Baltic. After the November Revolution, the Ebert government authorized him to stay on as "the general plenipotentiary of the Reich. "In 1920 Winnig was dismissed from the SPD for suppporting the Kapp government. He later became a loyal champion of the Nazis and wrote a series of books and articles filled with mystical nonsense about blood, soil, and destiny. See, for example, his *Befreiung* (Munich, 1926) and *Die Hand Gottes* (Berlin, 1940). Still later, during World War II, he turned against Hitler and flirted with the Canaris-Beck-von Hassell opposition group. See Ambassador Ulrich von Hassel, *The Von Hassel Diaries 1938–1944: The Story of the Forces against Hitler inside Germany as Recorded by Ambassador Ulrich von Hassell, a Leader of the Movement* (New York, 1947), 82, 295 and *passim*.

[20] The Ulmanis-Winnig conversations are recorded in Winnig's memoirs, *Am Ausgang der deutschen Ostpolitik: Persönliche Erlebnisse und Erinnerungen* (Berlin, 1921), 75 ff.

[21] As early as 1915, Winnig had shocked his Socialist colleagues by demanding that Germany expand into the Baltic area. (In addition to his *Am Ausgang der deutschen Ostpolitik*, 37–38 and 50–54, see F. W. Heinz, "Der deutsche Vorstoss in das Baltikum," in *Deutscher Aufstand*, 48.) His hopes for the Baltic as compensation for the defeat in World War I parallel the aspirations of von der Goltz. One of his warm admirers quotes Winnig as saying: "Prestige on the seas is lost, the way to the West blocked off. But here in the East the way must be kept open — it is the way to the World . . . (quoted by Harald von Rautenfeld, "Der 16. April, 1919" in *Baltische Blätter*, 12 Jahrgang, Nr. 5, April 15, 1929, 119–120).

about helping him from the sea, but refused to participate in land warfare on his behalf. When Ulmanis came back empty-handed, Winnig played his ace. He writes:

> When Ulmanis finally came to the conclusion that the English had no idea of defending the land . . . our mutual understanding was immeasurably improved . . . We talked about the consequences of the fall of Riga. Riga was not all of Latvia. We could retreat to Mitau and, if the recruitment [of Free Corps] was successful in the Reich, we could reconquer Riga and the rest of Latvia from bases in Courland. *Ulmanis grabbed at this proposition with both hands.*[22]

M. Ulmanis thought it was a splendid idea, but first he wanted to find out what the British thought of it. In a conference on board the *Princess Margaret,* His Majesty's representatives gave their approval.

Since the success or failure of the Volunteers' Baltic adventure depended, in large measure, on the approval of Great Britain, it is worth examining the reasons for this endorsement. They were dictated by two main factors: fear of Bolshevism and war weariness. British reaction to the Russian Revolution was an unhappy mixture of instinctive fear of the unknown and whistling in the dark. Members of the House of Commons asked uncertainly, "What is a Bolshevist anyway?" and spoke with dread of "that government of Jews and all sorts of other people." [23] But the Prime Minister, the Secretary of State for War, and the Foreign Secretary were reassuring. Mr. Lloyd George gazed into a clouded crystal ball and made the following prediction to the British people: "Bolshevism itself is rapidly on the wane. It is breaking down before the relentless pressure of economic facts. This process must inevitably continue. You cannot carry on a great country upon such rude and wild principles . . ." [24] "Mr. Churchill expressed the conviction . . . that in his view Bolshevism in Russia represented a mere fraction of the population and would be exposed

---

[22] Winnig, *Am Ausgang der deutschen Ostpolitik,* 82–83. (Italics are mine.)

[23] *The Parliamentary Debates, Official Report, House of Commons,* Vol. 118, 5th session, 2066. (Hereafter cited as *H. C. Debates,* with appropriate volume and column.)

[24] 114 *H. C. Debates,* 2944.

and swept away by a General Election . . ." [25] Mr. Balfour was also hopeful, but a little more realistic. Bolshevism, he agreed, was rotten to the core, but it might take a little push from the outside to topple it over. "I do not despair," he said on one occasion, "of our being able to do something material to restore the economic and political unity and nationality of that great country." [26]

This statement of Mr. Balfour's of June 20, 1918, may be considered an epitome of the policy Britain was to pursue in the Baltic. Bolshevism was the real enemy and "something material" would have to be done about it; but not too much, for Britain was already feeling the serious economic consequences of the war and her people were tired. Furthermore, Labour was constantly reminding the Government that its belief in self-determination applied to Russia as well as to other areas, and was asking embarrassing questions about the cost in lives and money of the British intervention on behalf of the anti-Bolshevist forces.[27] The Prime Minister was also concerned with the cost. In an early speech, which the Labour Party was not to let him forget, Lloyd George had said, "I share the horror of all Bolshevik teachings but I would rather leave Russia Bolshevik until she sees her way out of it than to see Britain bankrupt." [28] The problem, then, was to stop the Bolshevist menace, but to do it as cheaply and painlessly as possible. In December of 1918 it seemed to the British that the German Volunteers provided a perfect solution. Thus in the conference on the *Princess Margaret*, British representatives agreed with M. Ulmanis that Herr Winnig's suggestion was an excellent one — that he should go ahead and invite the Free Corps to come and fight the Red Army.[29]

Thus encouraged, Ulmanis hurried back to the Germans and drew up the treaty of December 29, 1918. By its terms the Pro-

[25] David Lloyd George, *Memoirs of the Peace Conference* (New Haven, 1939), I, 214–215.
[26] 118 *H. C. Debates*, 1970.
[27] 118 *H. C. Debates*, 1969, 1970, and 1980.
[28] 114 *H. C. Debates*, 720.
[29] J. Benoist-Méchin, *Histoire de L'Armée Allemande, 1919–1936* (Paris, 1938), II, 17.

visional Latvian Government agreed to use the German Free Corps and to allow German officers to command them. It was further stipulated that any increase in the number of native Latvian troops would necessitate a corresponding increase of German troops. In return for their services, all German soldiers who had fought for at least four weeks in the Baltic would be granted full Latvian citizenship.[30]

It needs to be emphasized, however, that the agreement of December 29 did not promise land to the Volunteers. M. Benoist-Méchin, and virtually all the memoirists, are simply wrong when they say that the agreement promised each of the Volunteers about 90 acres of land for settlement.[31] August Winnig himself tells of his numerous and frustrating efforts to pin Ulmanis down and force him to sign a definite land-grant provision. All these efforts failed; the final treaty of December 29 contained no such provision:

> The treaty still contained no promise of land settlement (*kein Siedlungsversprechen*). The Latvian Government had committed itself not to granting land, but only to promising full rights of citizenship (*vollen Bürgerrechts*). To be sure, the treaty was often interpreted in Germany as a colonization treaty (*Siedlungsvertrag*), but in so interpreting it, people went too far.[32]

It is important to remember that although no land had ever been promised by Ulmanis, the Volunteers coming to the Baltic were confident that they would be given free land upon arrival. The elaborate recruitment campaign within the Reich encour-

[30] The short, four-point treaty is reprinted in its entirety in Winnig, *Am Ausgang der deutschen Ostpolitik*, 83.

[31] Benoist-Méchin, *op. cit.*, II, 17. The French historian relies heavily on von Salomon, and may have taken his information from him. Von Salomon writes: ". . . the Latvian government of Ulmanis . . . promised the German Volunteers 80 *morgen* of land for colonization" (*Die Geächteten*, 68). See also Claus Grimm, *Jahre deutscher Entscheidung im Baltikum, 1918–1919* (Essen, 1939), 254; and Ludwig Gengler, *Kampfflieger Rudolf Berthold: Sieger im 44 Luftschlägen, Erschlagen im Brüderkampfe für Deutschlands Freiheit* (Berlin, 1934), 158.

[32] August Winnig, *Heimkehr*, 3rd ed. (Hamburg, 1935), 91. In his earlier book, the wily Winnig shows that he did nothing whatever to correct the misinterpretation. He says that as soon as the treaty was signed, he transmitted it, without comment, to the recruitment offices within the Reich ". . . so that it might help them in winning recruits." (*Ostpolitik*, 83)

aged them to think so. One of the chief selling-points of the campaign was that the Volunteers were assured of great estates in the "beautiful Baltic" [33] — this in contrast to the unemployment and misery at home. It was this type of extravagant promise which prompted Noske to comment laconically, "What was not promised in posters, the recruitment officers promised verbally." [34]

Recruitment directors found that the "Red Peril" was another effective means of enrolling recruits for Baltic service. The Rightist press warned that German *Kultur* was about to be trampled under foot by the approaching Asiatic hordes and billboards were covered with gruesome predictions of imminent disaster. A typical recruitment poster shows a picture of ravaging wolves crossing the Eastern border of Germany with blood (or is it only saliva?) dripping from their extended tongues. The copy reads: "Germans! Defend the Fatherland from the Russian Bolshevists!" [35]

It is no doubt true that many sincere young men went to the Baltic to fight the Communists, but the numbers were not as great as the National Socialist historians suggest. It is significant that the books written before 1933 generally do not emphasize the Red Peril as a motivating factor. Indeed they consider it — quite rightly — as an excuse rather than a cause. Von der Goltz himself, it will be recalled, considered the crusade against Bolshevism a pretext to disguise his real motives;[36] and Ernst von Salomon says, "What made our war in Courland possible was the fear of the West for Bolshevism . . . We never took the slogan 'Fight Bolshevism' seriously." [37] The biographer of the notorious Gerhard Rossbach, writing, it should be observed, before the advent

[33] See, for example, the advertisement which appeared in the special soldiers' newspaper, the *Reichswehr,* on June 18, 1919. It begins, "Wonderful Settlement Opportunity! Anyone who wants to own his own estate in the beautiful Baltic, report to one of the following recruitment offices . . ." An advertisement in the *Vorwärts* for March 10, 1919, promised bonuses, family allotments, and good food, in addition to "excellent colonization opportunities."

[34] Gustav Noske, *Von Keil bis Kapp, Zur Geschichte der deutschen Revolution* (Berlin, 1920), 177.

[35] Reprinted in *Das Buch vom deutschen Freikorpskämpfer,* edited by Ernst von Salomon (Berlin, 1938), 144.

[36] See above, p. 98.

[37] Von Salomon, *Die Geächteten,* 108, 114.

of Hitler, has caught the attitude of the *Freikorpsführer* succinctly:

His attitude was neither anti-Bolshevist nor pro-Bolshevist; it was simply German. An anti-Bolshevist cloak had been thrown over the shoulders of the enterprise to shield it from the probing eyes of the Entente . . . basically they [Rossbach and his comrades] fought for nothing else than for German land, for German conquest and for German colonization on the Baltic Sea.[38]

The commander of the Iron Division adds another reason which the Volunteers always considered a logical corollary to the conquest of the Baltic: they planned to use the Baltic as a base of operations from which they could attack and overthrow the Berlin government and end the ignominy of Versailles.[39] In the light of these admissions, the later National Socialist line that the gallant, altruistic Germans had gone to the Baltic solely to fight the Red Peril and to protect the independence of the struggling little border states can be dismissed as the most transparent Nazi propaganda.[40]

Many different types of Volunteers answered the call of the Baltic in the first months of 1919. There were — and this must not be forgotten — idealistic young patriots like Albert Leo Schlageter[41] who went to defend the soil of the Fatherland from the menace of Bolshevism and to redeem the Western defeat. A member of the Iron Brigade describes this group:

Despairing over the collapse of Germany and the dissolution of her army and disgusted with conditions in the homeland, they refused to give up the battle for Germany. In mind and in deed they were deter-

[38] Arnolt Bronnen, *Rossbach* (Berlin, 1930), 70.

[39] This purpose is implicit in all the memoirs, but see especially Major Joseph Bischoff, *Die letzte Front, Geschichte der Eisernen Division im Baltikum, 1919* (Berlin, 1935), 9, 171, 243 and 247. The point will be taken up later. See below, pp. 136–137.

[40] For this treatment see the officially authorized National Socialist account: *Soldaten der Freiheit: Ein Parolebuch des Nationalsozialismus, 1918–1925,* edited by Hermann Kretschmann (Berlin, 1935), 84 and *passim.* Major Fletcher, the commander of the aristocratic Baltic Landeswehr, had a different opinion of the local inhabitants. His main purpose, he says, was to organize all "noble elements" in order to destroy "this rabble." Alfred Fletcher, "Die baltische Landeswehr," in *Baltische Blätter,* 12. Jahrgang, Nummer 5 (March 1, 1929), 70.

[41] See below, pp. 233 ff.

mined to make this last attempt to resist the horror of German defeat and to hope for a better future. Or — even if they could no longer believe in that — they still felt that it was their German duty to risk life and limb in this last effort.[42]

Old men went to the Baltic to claim the land promised them by the recruitment offices and thus to fulfill lifelong dreams of owning their own soil.[43] Men from well-established German families went, like Major Fletcher, because they could not stomach the "miserable socialist rabble" of the new government of the Reich. They found kindred spirits among the Baltic Barons. Major Fletcher speaks for this group: "In the common life and common battle shared with the Balts, my sick German heart, which had lost faith in the German people during the Revolution, was made well once more. In retrospect, I can say that I only found loyalty and honor among the Balts!"[44]

But the type most common among the *Baltikumers* was the restless Freebooter who had learned war and did not want to learn anything else. He went to the Baltic in the spring of 1919 for the same reason that he would later go to Mexico, Ireland, China, Bolivia, and India: he went to seek adventure, excitement, and war; he went to escape the monotony and boredom of civilian life. Whatever their motivations, the Volunteers were all convinced that it was to be a glorious adventure. They went with their hopes high and the battle cry of their medieval predecessors on their lips: *Gen Ostland wollen wir reiten!*

For the first time since the days of the German Orders, German warriors gathered from virtually every gau and province of the Reich where the German tongue rings forth . . . Volunteers came from the endangered Eastern provinces, from the Rhine . . . Bavaria, Württemberg and Baden; from Bohemia and the Tyrol; from Alsace and Switzerland.[45]

[42] Fritz Büchner, writing in the preface to Major Bischoff's memoirs, *Die letzte Front*, 14.
[43] For pathetic examples of this type of homesteader-volunteer, see August Winnig, *Heimkehr*, 105.
[44] Fletcher, "Die baltische Landeswehr," in *Baltische Blätter*, 12. Jahrgang, Nummer 5 (March 1, 1929), 70.
[45] Claus Grimm, *Jahre deutscher Entscheidung im Baltikum 1918–1919* (Essen, 1939), 460.

National Socialist historians assure their readers that all undesirable elements were ruthlessly weeded out and that only good elements remained. It is instructive to examine the Freebooter conception of what constituted the "good elements." Von Oertzen's definition is interesting:

> The good elements of the Free Corps of this time . . . were the exact opposite of "*bürgerliche Menschen.*" Their training and their form of life were emphatically front-soldierly; i.e., raw and *antibürgerlich* . . . The men of these Free Corps were better soldiers to the extent to which they were rougher, tougher and more *antibürgerlich* . . .[46]

A good example of this "pure-souled type of fighter" [47] is found in a novel written by one of the battalion commanders of the Iron Division. The story records an incident in which a soldier of the Red Army is taken prisoner, shot, and robbed by his Free Corps guard. The author soliloquizes:

> Bernhard [the guard] showed himself to be what in normal times would be called a bandit-murderer . . . But actually these primitive men are to be envied. They have no nerves and no moral scruples . . . They are just like nature — instinctively good and instinctively cruel. All the strength of life lies waiting within them and the direction in which it manifests itself depends entirely on the opportunities and circumstances in which they are placed.[48]

Ernst von Salomon elaborates on the concept of the "primitive man":

> We were cut off from the world of *bürgerlich* norms. . . . The bonds were broken and we were free. The blood surging through our veins was full of a wild demand for revenge and adventure and danger . . . We were a band of fighters drunk with all the passions of the world; full of lust, exultant in action. What we wanted, we did not know. And what we knew, we did not want! War and adventure, excitement and destruction. An indefinable, surging force welled up from every part of our being and flayed us onward.[49]

[46] Von Oertzen, *Die deutschen Freikorps*, 21–22.

[47] Edgar von Schmidt-Pauli uses the term to describe the majority of the men who fought in the Baltic (*Geschichte der Freikorps*, 62).

[48] Erich Balla, *Landsknechte wurden wir: Abenteuer aus dem Baltikum* (Berlin, 1932), 123–124. Von Oertzen calls it an "excellent book" and recommends it because he says it gives an accurate picture of the Free Corps spirit (*op. cit.*, 35).

[49] Von Salomon, *Die Geächteten*, 72–73.

III. THE SPRING OFFENSIVE OF 1919

General Graf Rudiger von der Goltz, the supreme commander of all Free Corps in the Baltic, arrived in Libau on February 1, 1919, after a miserable trip in an unheated, fourth-class railway coach.[50] The disgruntled General set to work at once on his task of transforming the border provinces into German states. He first saw to it that the Ulmanis army was so weakened that the Latvians were completely dependent on German arms to fight off the advancing Red Army.[51] That accomplished, he began to organize the Free Corps into an effective fighting force. The two largest groups of Volunteers comprising von der Goltz's army were the Baltic *Landeswehr* and the Iron Division.

The *Landeswehr* had originally been organized by the Ulmanis government and in theory it remained under its jurisdiction. But the aristocratic Baltic Barons like crusty old Baron Engelhardt and Count Lothar zu Dohna-Willkühnen despised the native government, and soon gained ascendancy over its army. Toward the end of January 1919, Count Lothar called on Major Fletcher[52] at his home in Königsberg and asked him to assume command of the *Landeswehr*. Fletcher accepted on one condition: that he would have absolute command of the native troops. Supported by von der Goltz and the Baltic Barons, Fletcher systematically dismissed the native elements and placed German officers in all key positions. By mid-February of 1919, Latvians composed less than one fifth of their own army.[53] In reorganizing the *Landeswehr*,

[50] Von der Goltz, *Meine Sendung*, 123.

[51] See the testimony of an anonymous British naval officer, "With the Baltic Squadron, 1918–1920," in *Fortnightly Review* (May 1921), 707, and the report of the British representative, "Dispatch from Sir Walter Gowan," the London *Times*, April 12, 1920. Von der Goltz himself admits the charge. He says that it was necessary to disarm the Ulmanis army because it was "Bolshevik." (*Meine Sendung*, 154.)

[52] After the failure of the Baltic venture, Major Fletcher organized a series of secret military societies in East Prussia. A great friend of Wolfgang Kapp, he was the chief supporter of the Kapp government in East Prussia. He delivered Kapp's funeral oration. The speech ends: "Fare thee well, my dear friend Wolfgang Kapp — I shall carry on." (Ludwig Schemann, *Wolfgang Kapp und die Märzunternehmung vom Jahre 1920: Ein Wort der Sühne*, Munich and Berlin, 1937, 135–137, 232.)

[53] Eugen Freiherr von Engelhardt, *Der Ritt nach Riga: Aus den Kämpfen der baltischen Landeswehr gegen die Rote Armee, 1918–1920* (Berlin, 1938),

Fletcher relied heavily on the advice of General Staff Captain Pabst, the man who was to figure so largely in the Kapp Putsch. It was at Pabst's suggestion that Fletcher adopted the system already employed by General Maercker — the use of small, mixed formations of troops each of which was militarily self-sufficient.[54]

One of the first men von der Goltz met in the Baltic was the half-legendary commander of the Iron Division, Major Joseph Bischoff. When the Supreme Commander noticed the ease with which Bischoff lit his cigarette in a high wind, Bischoff replied, "Oh, you learn that, Count. This is my twelfth year of war-making — eight years in Africa, then the World War. I'm an old Free-booter." [55] On January 11, 1919, Bischoff had been called to the office of the Supreme Command of the East (*Oberkommando-Ost*) in Königsberg and ordered to the Baltic to help organize Free Corps there. By the time von der Goltz arrived, the work of organizing the Iron Division was well under way. By the time of the spring offensive, thanks to the recruitment campaign within the Reich, his Division numbered well over 14,000 men. Unlike the *Landeswehr* and most Volunteer formations, the Iron Division was not composed of individually self-sufficient groups; it followed the organizational scheme of the old field armies. Bischoff lists its component parts: a divisional staff, three infantry regiments, trench mortar and machine gun companies, one field artillery regiment, a regiment of cavalry; aircraft, intelligence, flame-thrower and balloon section; a field hospital and an armored vehicle company.[56] On paper, the Iron Division looks like an extraordinarily well-coördinated and disciplined force. Actually Bischoff, like von der Goltz and other Imperial officers who tried to coördinate the Free Corps, had a great deal of trouble coping with that "Freebooter spirit" which the National Socialists extol.

11–18, 98; Alfred Fletcher, "Das Wesen der baltischen Kämpfe vom Frühjahr 1919: Erinnerungen an die baltische Landeswehr" in *Baltische Lande*, Vol. IV (1939); the same writer's article in *Baltische Blätter*, March 1, 1929; Grimm, *Jahre deutscher Entscheidung im Baltikum*, 421; and Georg Hartmann, "Aus den Erinnerungen eines Freiwilligen der baltischen Landeswehr," in *Deutsche Revue*, Januar bis März, 1921 (46 Jahrgang).

[54] Fletcher in *Baltische Blätter*, March 1, 1929, 70.

[55] Quoted in von der Goltz, *Meine Sendung*, 133.

[56] Bischoff, *Die letzte Front*, 77–78.

Bischoff ruefully admits that the Hamburg Free Corps, one of his infantry regiments, was one of his better formations. This outfit flew the ancient Hansa flag, sang old pirate songs, swaggered through the towns and villages of the Baltic coast with smoking carbines and used streetlights and windows for target practice. One of its members describes their *esprit:*

> They let their hair and beards grow long and they saluted only the officers they knew and liked. And it was a great honor for any officer to be saluted by the men of Hamburg. For this crazy outfit recognized none of the usual military regulations. They had been formed by no particular authority and they recognized none save their own. The only thing that counted was the will of their own Führer . . .[57]

The attack against the Red Army was launched from Libau during the second week of February.[58] Goldingen and Windau fell in quick succession, and by the first of March, the Baltic coast was cleared from Libau north to Windau. Mitau fell to the Iron Division in the first week of March. The Brandis and Count Yorck Free Corps captured Bausk and groups under Major Fletcher took Stalgen. After consolidating his positions, von der Goltz prepared for his next goal objective, the capture of Riga. But before moving on to Riga, the Free Corps became involved in a political situation which was to have important consequences for the Baltic Adventure.

IV. THE PUTSCH OF APRIL 16, 1919

When Latvian nationalists seized the opportunity afforded by the Russian Revolution to form their own government, they were striking for their independence not only from the late Czar's

---

[57] Von Salomon, *Die Geächteten,* 70.

[58] The military campaigns in the Baltic are described in overwhelming detail and exaggerated out of all proportion to their historical significance by German writers. Under Hitler, the Army prepared a comprehensive study of all military campaigns of the postwar period: *Darstellungen aus den Nachkriegskämpfen deutscher Truppen und Freikorps: Im Auftrage des Oberkommandos des Heeres, bearbeitet und herausgegeben von der Kriegsgeschichtlichen Forschungsanstalt des Heeres,* 7 vols. (Berlin, 1938–1939). The second and third volumes discuss the Baltic campaigns. See also von Oertzen, *Die deutschen Freikorps,* 24–115; von Schmidt-Pauli, *Geschichte der Freikorps,* 35–172, and, for personal accounts, the memoirs of von Engelhardt, von der Goltz, Bischoff, and those given in *Das Buch vom deutschen Freikorpskämpfer,* 127–215.

control, but from the social and economic domination of the German-Balts. The Baltic Barons would have considered any native government an intolerable usurpation of their ancient right to dominate and control the border provinces, but they were particularly opposed to the Ulmanis government. They were totally unrepresented in the new government[59] and every proposal they made to change the situation was flatly and defiantly rejected by the social upstarts who were now, in theory at least, masters of the government of Latvia.

But the issues involved in Latvian politics in April 1919 were far more important than the local issue of the conflict between Balts and Latvians. The German Free Corps, as von der Goltz's memoirs constantly remind us, had come to the Baltic to conquer provinces and to avenge Versailles. They did not propose to let the native governments stop the fulfillment of an ancient dream and a modern opportunity. The Free Corps, then, were as determined as the Baltic Barons to get rid of the Ulmanis government.

As early as February 1919 a certain Landmarschall Baron von Stryck greeted von der Goltz by laying before him a plan for overthrowing all the native governments and creating a German-Balt state which would be friendly to Germany. At this time, von der Goltz rejected the proposal for a number of reasons: the plan was not carefully worked out,[60] it did not guarantee the German domination of the Baltic which von der Goltz's own political objectives envisaged, and above all it came at the wrong time. In February, the military problem was of pressing importance; some headway would have to be made against the Bolsheviks before attending to the unsatisfactory political situation.

[59] In fact it is doubtful if the Ulmanis government was representative of the broad masses of the Latvian population. This is, of course, the opinion of all German writers. See, for example, the biased but factually accurate study by Claus Grimm, *Jahre deutscher Entscheidung im Baltikum*, which gives the party affiliations of all members of the government (pp. 131–132). But it is also the verdict of the United States investigating committee. The Hales Report says: "The Government [of Ulmanis] had no real mandate from the people; it could not possibly have been upheld by a popular election; it entirely lacked the support of large elements of the community." (*Senate Documents*, XV, 17.) See also Page, *Formation of the Baltic States*, 206.

[60] See Friedrich Wilhelm von Oertzen, *Baltenland, Eine Geschichte der deutschen Sendung im Baltikum* (Munich, 1939), 310–311.

During the second week of April, domestic tension between the Balts and the Ulmanis government reached a breaking point when Ulmanis once again refused to consider a surprisingly moderate Balt request for better representation and more equitable treatment.[61] After the flat rejection of their petition, the Balts and their Reichsdeutsch friends were convinced that the Ulmanis government would have to go.

In connection with the Stryck affair, the Latvian government had arrested a German *Freikorpskämpfer,* one Lieutenant Stock, and charged him with conspiring to overthrow the legal government. On the morning of April 16, men of the von Pfeffer[62] Free Corps rushed to the help of their comrade-in-arms. They released him from prison and took captive the entire staff of the Latvian army — some 550 officers.[63] About noon of the same day, the youthful commander of the Landeswehr's *Stosstrupp,* Baron von Manteuffel, arrested the Ulmanis government. "Unfortunately," says Schmidt-Pauli, "Ulmanis escaped to the English. His pernicious influence was to be felt in the future." [64] General von der Goltz had gone for a long walk during the putsch and was, he says, taken completely by surprise by these events. He had the presence of mind, however, to declare that the "unstable conditions in Latvia" forced him to declare martial law. After the conditions had become more stable, he lifted the martial law and

[61] The fourteen-point petition is quoted in von Oertzen, *Baltenland,* 312–313. See also Harald von Rautenfeld, "Der 16. April 1919," in *Baltische Blätter,* Nummer 5, 12. Jahrgang (April 15, 1929), 123–125.

[62] Franz Pfeffer von Salomon was the brother of Ernst von Salomon. He appears to have dropped the latter part of his name out of deference to National Socialist Semitic sensitivities. The founder of the Westphalian Free Corps, he was active in the Baltic, Upper Silesia, the Kapp Putsch, and the Ruhr. He was a charter member of the O.C. murder organization. Under the Nazis he was variously, SA Oberführer for Westphalia, Supreme Leader of the SA (*Osaf*), and National Socialist deputy in the Reichstag.

[63] F. W. Heinz, "Der deutsche Vorstoss in das Baltikum," in *Deutscher Aufstand,* 57.

[64] Schmidt-Pauli, *Geschichte der Freikorps,* 87. Actually the British had a great deal of trouble with Ulmanis. Viscount Alexander told me that he and other members of the British Mission found Ulmanis arrogant, opinionated, and very difficult to work with. (Interview with His Excellency Viscount Alexander of Tunis, Governor General of Canada, in Government House, Ottawa, September 7, 1950.)

placed the government of Latvia in the unwilling hands of a meek little quisling, Pastor Andreas Needra.

Herr von Oertzen stresses the importance of the putsch because he feels that it is indicative of the growing political consciousness of the Free Corps. This is important for the future because the Volunteers, he says repeatedly, are to become the "political soldiers" of the Third Reich. His conclusion is also interesting in light of the fact that he previously insisted that neither von der Goltz nor any of the *Freikorpsführer* had anything whatever to do with the coup. He writes:

The putsch of April 16 . . . shows the development of political sensitivity and political thinking on the part of the German Free Corps. The most interesting proof of this is that here we see a military leader with far-reaching national-political concepts — whether they were feasible or not will not be investigated here — and we see the Free Corps themselves engaged in political activities . . .[65]

The political situation thus settled in favor of the Free Corps, and their rear protected from possible Latvian sabotage, Count Goltz made plans to conquer Riga.[66]

[65] *Die deutschen Freikorps,* 50.

[66] The exact role which von der Goltz played in the April putsch will probably never be known. But I believe, on the basis of indirect evidence, that he aided and abetted — if he did not personally plan and direct — the coup. With the single exception of the unreliable anti-Nazi account, Berthold Jacob, *Das neue deutsche Heer und seine Führer* (Editions du Carrefour, Paris, 1936), every German writer I have read says that von der Goltz had nothing to do with the affair. The general himself pleads innocent. He argues that the single fact that he did not support the proposed putsch of Baron von Stryck in February proves that he did not authorize the April coup and that military factors were so "unclear" that he had no time to become involved in domestic political matters. (*Meine Sendung,* 169, 179–181.) The military situation was indeed unclear in February but conditions had changed by April. The Reds had been defeated in the campaigns of March, the front stabilized, and an unusually heavy thaw had made it absolutely impossible to continue military operations. The Free Corps commanders utilized the time to reorganize their forces and *to wait for the political situation to change in their favor* (see Bischoff, *Die letzte Front,* 76–78, and Heinz's article in *Deutscher Aufstand,* 55). The General thus had both the time and the opportunity to settle the unsatisfactory political situation behind his lines. Herr von Oertzen says that "neither Count Goltz himself nor Captain von Pfeffer wanted a putsch and . . . even young Baron von Manteuffel up to the last moment, had not thought of a putsch . . . [their] actions were absolutely accidental and were neither premeditated nor planned." (*Deutsche Freikorps,* 48; see also the same author's *Baltenland,* 316.) The truth of the matter is

In the meantime, however, the British had become alarmed over the April putsch. They now suspected, quite rightly, that von

rather that both von Pfeffer and Manteuffel had made plans to seize the Latvian government and that von der Goltz, who knew of their plans, nevertheless ordered Manteuffel to go to Libau, the seat of the government, ostensibly for a rest. (See Rautenfeld's article in the *Baltische Blätter* of April 15, 1929, 125, and the second edition of von der Goltz's memoirs. *Als politischer General im Osten*, Leipzig, 1936, 110–111.) After Pfeffer had arrested the entire staff of the Latvian army, von der Goltz felt the moment opportune to take a long walk while Manteuffel captured the Ulmanis government. When the British asked if the government would be released, the General replied that it was impossible to do so because it was a Bolshevik government and a menace to the peace and stability of Latvia. (Sir Walter Gowan's report, the London *Times*, April 12, 1920.) His only regret was that the putsch had not been comprehensive enough and had allowed Ulmanis to escape to the British. (*Meine Sendung*, 181, and *Als politischer General*, 111.) Other portions of the General's memoirs throw an illuminating — if indirect — light on the affair. From the beginning of his mission he found that the Ulmanis government was "a thorn in my eye" and "simply impossible"; and in March he confided to his diary: "someday we'll kick these rascals (*Knechtseelen*) in the teeth." (*Als politischer General*, 106.) On other occasions he found it useful to let his subordinates bear the responsibility for executing difficult or unauthorized actions. For example, when he first assumed command, he was ordered by the OHL not to go beyond the Libau-Murajewo-Schaulen-Kowno line. Count Goltz allowed Fletcher to go beyond that line and conquer Tuckum and Mitau (von Oertzen, *Baltenland*, 309–310). And witness his comment on the proposed attack on Riga, which was forbidden by the Entente and frowned on by von Seeckt: "One could easily protect oneself from the Entente by placing the entire responsibility for the further advance on the shoulders of an insubordinate general." (*Meine Sendung*, 190.) It would seem that this is precisely the tactics he used in the April putsch. Notice his reply to the British representative in the Baltic, Admiral Sir Walter Gowan, when asked to explain the coup: "He denied all responsibility or knowledge . . . saying that his troops were out of hand and that the Baltic Germans were not under his orders." (*Times*, April 12, 1920.) He told members of the American mission a different story: "He admitted that the troops which participated in this coup d'état were under his command and that their acts constituted a breach of military discipline." (*Senate Documents*, XV, 17.) His comment on an unfriendly Lithuanian government is particularly interesting: "Perhaps with the aid of my Free Corps leaders I could have put in a cabinet more friendly to German and [White] Russian interest. *But at that time* [October 1919] such a seizure of power would have alienated all sympathy for the Bermondt project and would have caused the German Free Corps great difficulties." (*Meine Sendung*, 254; italics are mine.) To conclude: the whole affair fitted the "political general's" plans for the Baltic so perfectly that it is impossible to believe that he was not involved in the plot. The direct connection between the putsch and the march on Riga is emphasized by Rautenfeld, who writes: "The political purpose of the coup had been reached: concentration of political strength of the land

der Goltz wanted not only military but political control of the Baltic, and the idea did not appeal to them. His Majesty's Government acted on impulse and demanded the immediate recall of von der Goltz and his Volunteers in a series of notes (April and early May, 1919) to the German government. But Berlin's replies forced the British to reconsider their demand. The German notes reminded His Majesty's Government that the recall of the Free Corps would leave the defense of the Baltic in British hands. Was His Majesty's Government, they asked, prepared to send an expeditionary force to the Baltic? It was not. So it was finally agreed that the Germans could remain, but only with the understanding that the Volunteers were not to engage in any offensive campaigns.[67]

This agreement was totally unsatisfactory to von der Goltz for it meant that he would be forced to abandon his aspirations for the Baltic. And the scope of those aspirations had enlarged with each easy military and political victory won by his Free Corps:

I [now] calculated that the whole of southern Livonia could be reconquered and, if supported by a few divisions, St. Petersburg could be taken and thus a place in the East would be won which would considerably change the Versailles Treaty.[68]

As an absolute minimum he demanded the conquest of Riga; for this ancient Ordenstadt of the Teutonic Knights held not only symbolic importance. It also possessed the finest seaport on the Baltic. Determined that he would not be stopped by the cowardly traitors at home who had once more kowtowed to Entente demands, he hurried to Berlin. But he got no satisfaction. The Ebert government was in no position to defy the Entente; it refused to authorize a Free Corps offensive. The frustrated General then

---

was obtained, the way was open to the liberation of Riga and the common task of reconstructing the ravaged homeland." ("Der 16. April 1919," in *Baltische Blätter*, April 15, 1929, 128.)

[67] A convenient digest of the texts of the notes can be found in the *Deutscher Geschichtskalender*, edited by Friedrich Purlitz, the volume entitled, "Vom Waffenstillstand zum Frieden von Versailles" (Leipzig, 1920), 470–476 and *passim*. Britain's dilemma of either keeping the dangerous Freebooters in the Baltic or allowing the Reds to move in is discussed by the London *Times*, April 22, 1919.

[68] Von der Goltz, *Meine Sendung*, 190.

asked what the Government would do if the Baltic *Landeswehr* were to attack. The Government replied that it had no jurisdiction over the Latvian army. Heartened by this reply, von der Goltz sent the following telegram to his staff in the Baltic: "Tax on flour not approved. But if the *Landeswehr* puts a tax on flour, the Iron Division can join them." The General explains the message: "In conversations with my staff before my departure it was understood that . . . '*Mehlabgabe*' was code for attack on Riga." [69]

The *Landeswehr* quickly obliged by attacking the Reds and the Free Corps began a general offensive. Again, there is no direct evidence that von der Goltz or his staff actually ordered the *Landeswehr* to advance, but the opportune timing of the attack is too fortuitous to be dismissed as merely one more lucky event in a long series of coincidences.[70]

Von der Goltz's tactical plan for the storming of Riga had originally called for the use of the same "swinging door" maneuver which he had used in taking Mitau. At the last moment, however, the plan had to be changed when the all-important right wing was weakened by the withdrawal of the First Reserve Division.[71] His right wing now consisted of the Free Corps Count York, Brandes, Eulenberg, and Rieckoff and the theoretically dissolved von Pfeffer Free Corps.[72] It engaged in a holding action while Riga was

[69] Von der Goltz, *Als politischer General im Osten*, 118.

[70] It should be remembered that the *Landeswehr* was only theoretically the "Latvian Army"; it was by this time composed predominantly of Baltic-German and Reichsdeutsch troops. Furthermore, it was commanded by a German, Major Fletcher, and von der Goltz worked in closest coöperation with Fletcher. The General's high opinion of the Major is seen in the fact that he accepted without change Fletcher's tactical plan for storming Goldingen. (See *Meine Sendung*, 131.) The Free Corps commanders did not bother with the subtleties of the message. Major Bischoff says simply that the telegram ordered a general offensive (*Die letzte Front*, 90).

[71] This division was composed of various formations which had been recruited within the Reich. It was withdrawn to Germany over von der Goltz's protest in order to protect the Reich from possible Polish attack.

[72] After the April putsch, the British had demanded the dissolution of the Von Pfeffer Corps. Von der Goltz complied by transferring its members to the Schaulen Brigade and the Rieckoff Free Corps. This method of meeting Entente demands was typical of the period. (See Schmidt-Pauli, *op. cit.*, 95 ff.) In a protracted debate with Noske in the National Assembly, Haase, the USPD deputy from Berlin, charged that as late as July, von Pfeffer was

stormed by frontal attack. The Free Corps made their triumphal entry into Riga on May 22, 1919.

V. REACTION AGAINST THE FREE CORPS

The fall of Riga marks the high point of Free Corps success in the Baltic. German nationalists never forgot the glory of that day of May, 1919. "It was as if all the stars in the heavens shone once more in the interminable night of Germany's self-imposed weakness and atrophy and illuminated the brilliance and greatness which is eternal soldierdom," says Heinz.[73] To von Schmidt-Pauli, "It was the symbol of the victory of European civilization over Asiatic barbarism." [74] It was also the beginning of the end of the entire Baltic adventure.

What had happened was that the Free Corps had been much too successful and their success had alarmed everyone concerned: the local inhabitants, the Allies, and the home government. The situation was epitomized aptly by a remark made by the commander of the Iron Division to his chief of staff: *"Um Gottes Willen, wir haben uns totgesiegt!"* [75]

The people of the border provinces were the first to take action against the Free Corps. The suspicion with which they had first greeted the German Volunteers had been intensified by the April putsch. It now turned into cold fury when they learned what it meant to be "liberated" by the Freebooters. Five hundred Latvians had been shot without trial in Mitau, two hundred in Tukkum, one hundred and twenty-five at Dunamunde — all under the single excuse that they had been pro-Bolshevik.[76] What Herr von Oertzen is pleased to call "the glorious victory of Riga" meant that some three thousand inhabitants lost their lives as the un-

recruiting men for Baltic service from offices in Giesen. Noske admitted the charge. *Verhandlungen der verfassunggebenden deutschen Nationalversammlung* (Stenographische Berichte, 67 Sitzung, 1963.)

[73] Friedrich Wilhelm Heinz, *Die Nation greift an: Geschichte und Kritik des soldatischen Nationalismus* (Berlin, 1932), 67.

[74] Schmidt-Pauli, *Geschichte,* 94. See the special commemorative issue of the *Baltische Blätter* published on the tenth anniversary of the fall of Riga (May 22, 1929, Nummer 10, 12. Jahrgang).

[75] "For God's sake, we have conquered ourselves to death!" (Bischoff, *Die letzte Front,* 123.)

[76] Benoist-Méchin, *Histoire de L'Armée Allemande,* II, 28.

bridled terror of the Freebooters made the "Red Terror" of the Bolsheviks pale in comparison. Quite apart from the hundreds of informal shootings, the martial law imposed by Major Fletcher pronounced the death penalty for such crimes as failure to report to a drumhead court-martial, sympathy for Bolshevism, being found in the streets of Riga after 6:00 P.M., and using a private telephone.[77]

After the fall of Riga, the Latvians had another good reason for being unimpressed by the argument that the Free Corps was saving them from the terrors of Bolshevism. For in the last days of May the miserable little group of ill-equipped, ill-organized Russians who constituted the "Red Peril" withdrew completely from the entire Baltic area.

Tired of Freebooter domination and helped materially by the British, the local inhabitants organized a creditable army of their own.[78] And when von der Goltz ordered the *Landeswehr* to clear the Estonian ports in preparation for his march on St. Petersburg, an Estonian-Latvian army attacked and routed Fletcher's forces near the village of Wenden just beyond Riga. Furious at this affront, the General dispatched the Iron Division and other Reichsdeutsch Volunteers to crush the natives. But once again the attack was repulsed and the Free Corps defeated.

It is not surprising that the National Socialist accounts do not discuss the unfortunate Wenden campaign in any detail. But the explanations for the defeat offered by the memoirists are worth noting for they show the chronic jealousy and rivalry which existed between the Volunteer formations. Von der Goltz blames Bischoff's Iron Division for the defeat; Major Fletcher places the blame on von der Goltz and both agree that "virus of the German

[77] The French delegate of the Interallied Military Mission to Latvia reprints Fletcher's order of May 27, 1919, and contrasts the "White Terror" of the Freebooter occupation with the Bolshevik rule. (Lieutenant Général Du Parquet, *L'Aventure Allemande en Lettonie* (Paris, 1926), 72–74. See also Ambroise Got, *La Contre-Révolution Allemande* (Strasbourg, 1920[?]), 146.

[78] Immediately after the fall of Riga, Britain sent the Latvians 19,500 rifles, 500 machine guns, light artillery, and ammunition. (Benoist-Méchin, *op. cit.*, II, 36, and *House of Commons Debates*, Vol. 120, 1287.) By mid-June the Latvian army was two divisions strong. See Général A. Niessel, *L'Évacuation des Pays Baltiques par les Allemands* (Paris, 1935), 20.

revolution" had taken its toll of the Volunteers and made them apathetic in their support of the Baltic Barons.[79] Ernst von Salomon notes bitterly that some of the Freebooters actually enlisted in the Estonian-Latvian army and joined it in attacking their former comrades,[80] and even von Oertzen admits that "the general feeling was a good deal less than gratifying." [81]

The scene now shifts to the peace conference in Paris. After the April putsch of the *de facto* government of Ulmanis and the unauthorized Free Corps attack on Riga, the Allies began to suspect that all was not well in the border states. Although the American Secretary of State's confidence in the good faith of von der Goltz was unshaken,[82] the British Foreign Secretary insisted that a special committee be appointed to outline a new policy for the border states. In its report of May 23, the committee recommended that an Allied mission be sent to the Baltic to organize a native army which could free the Baltic governments from their reliance on the dangerous Free Corps.[83]

The Gough mission was composed solely of British personnel, and when it arrived in the Baltic in mid-June, it began at once to carry out the orders transmitted to it directly by the British War Office.[84] Those orders instructed General Gough to clear the

[79] See Major Fletcher's preface to Baron Engelhardt's memoirs, *Der Ritt nach Riga,* 13; and von der Goltz, *Meine Sendung,* 214. Bischoff answers the charges in his book, *Die letzte Front,* 128.

[80] Von Salomon, *Nahe Geschichte,* 52, and *Die Geächteten,* 87–88. The Baden Sturmbataillon was one of the formations which was attacked by troops who had deserted the Free Corps.

[81] Von Oertzen, *Die deutschen Freikorps,* 73.

[82] David Hunter Miller reported to his diary that "In his [Mr. Lansing's] opinion, there existed no danger of German misbehavior." *My Diary at the Conference of Paris, with Documents* (private printing, 1925), XVI, 253.

[83] The Committee's report is reprinted in Miller, *My Diary,* XVI, 363–364.

[84] The United States Senate committee in its official report states: "Although General Gough is acting in the name of the Allies, none but British officers are attached to his staff . . . if General Gough's mission is to have the name and exercise the authority of an Allied mission, it would seem that Allied officers should be attached to him." (The Hale Report, *Senate Documents,* XV, 30.) On July 15, 1919, the British Secretary of State for War was asked in the House of Commons to define the Gough Mission. Mr. Churchill replied, "This mission was sent out in consequence of the agreement [of the Allies] . . . General Gough and all the officers of his mission are under the War Office." (118 *H. C. Debates,* 183.) Gough's orders, marked "Secret" and

Baltic of German Free Corps. First of all, Andreas Needra, the German puppet, was removed from office and Ulmanis restored to power as the *de facto* President of Latvia. Next, the Baltic *Landeswehr* was slowly purged of its German elements and returned to the Latvian government. To facilitate the transfer, it was placed under the command of a British officer, Lieutenant Colonel Alexander — subsequently Governor General of Canada.

The transfer of the *Landeswehr* raised an interesting problem. It was done over the vehement protests of von der Goltz, but with the open approval of its former commander, Major Fletcher. Von der Goltz wanted the *Landeswehr* to enter the service of the White Russian adventurer, Count Awaloff-Bermondt and was enraged at their "desertion to the British." His subordinate, however, despised Bermondt as much as he admired Alexander. He countermanded von der Goltz's orders and actively facilitated the transfer. He writes: "The last favor that I could do for my beloved Balts was this: I did not lead the Baltic *Landeswehr* into the ranks of the so-called Bermondt Army . . . My successor, the English Lieutenant Colonel Alexander, was an English nobleman and front fighter of the West . . . a true gentleman." [85] Alexander felt the same way about Fletcher. He told me that he found Fletcher to be "the best type of German officer and a fine gentleman." [86]

After taking the *Landeswehr* out of the hands of von der Goltz,

---

dated June 4, 1919, originated in the office of General Wilson, Chief of the Imperial General Staff. They are reprinted in *Senate Documents*, XV, 37–38.

[85] Fletcher writing in the preface to Baron Engelhardt's memoirs, *Der Ritt nach Riga*, 13–14. Von der Goltz was furious at "the desertion to the British" but in the 1936 edition of his memoirs he was able to explain how it had happened: "Only since January 1, 1933, could Germans living outside the Reich hope again. At that time [June 1919] thanks to the spirit of Weimar and Versailles, they were without hope . . . Therefore the resolution of the Baltic *Landeswehr* to desert their brothers is understandable." (*Als politischer General im Osten*, 132.)

[86] Alexander was not aware, at the time, of a conflict between von der Goltz and his subordinate. When he was apprised of the conflict, he said, "I didn't know this before. It helps explain Fletcher's eagerness to coöperate with me. He was certainly very helpful." (Interview with His Excellency Viscount Alexander, Governor General of Canada, in Government House, Ottawa, September 7, 1950.)

it seemed that Gough was well on the way to the completion of his mission. On July 3, 1919, he succeeded in forcing the German Commander in Chief to sign an agreement which promised that all German Volunteers would withdraw from the Baltic.[87]

VI. REVOLT AND ENTRY INTO WHITE RUSSIAN SERVICE

General Gough and the Allies soon discovered that it was a good deal easier to make the Volunteers sign agreements than it was to make them abide by them. Week after week during the summer of 1919, angry notes demanding the recall of von der Goltz and his Freebooters shuttled from London to Paris, from Paris to Berlin, and from Berlin to Count von der Goltz. And week after week the Free Corps remained in the Baltic. Their commander either invented excuses or flatly refused to obey the orders issued both by his own government and by the Allies. He records a typical interview with General Gough:

> Once again Gough handed me an Entente "order" to clear out [of the Baltic] under his supervision. I told him that an order from the Entente meant absolutely nothing to me . . . Gough asked me once again,
> "Will you obey the order of the Entente or will you not?"
> "No!"
> I then asked him if he had anything more to say. If not, I would take my leave.[88]

The Free Corps commander was defiant but by mid-June he knew that he could not go on with the game indefinitely. His own part in the great adventure was over. But he was still determined that his cherished plans for the Baltic would be carried out. His only hope now lay in stalling for time and in transferring the titular command of the Free Corps to someone else. Thus it came about that the fantastic White Russian, Awaloff-Bermondt, led the Freebooters in the last sorry chapter of the Baltic adventure. Colonel Bermondt had served without distinction in the Im-

---

[87] H. W. V. Temperley, *A History of the Peace Conference of Paris* (London, 1924), VI, 300.

[88] *Meine Sendung*, 241; and see also 228–235, 237–240. Serviceable guides to the tangled negotiations are the London *Times* and Purlitz's *Deutscher Geschichtskalender.*

perial Russian Army during the war. After the Revolution, he advertised his sentiments — and flaunted his somewhat dubious pedigree — by adopting his maternal uncle's name. He thus became General Prince Pawel Michaelovich Awaloff-Bermondt. He liked to think of himself as a dashing adventurer, a great — if syphilitic — lover, and a brilliant military leader. He believed that he had been sent by destiny to reconquer the whole of Bolshevik Russia and thus make it a land fit for aristocrats like himself.[89] With some of these things in mind, he had come to the Baltic early in the year and had begun to organize a few former Russian prisoners of war into what he was pleased to call the "Russian Army of the West." After General Judenitsch had coldly rebuffed him, Bermondt turned to the Germans.

The Free Corps commanders had little respect for either Bermondt or his fantastic schemes. They agreed with the French military observer who said that he was "the colonel of operettas and the prince of comedies." [90] Nevertheless, they realized that he could be very useful to them. For by giving this Russian formal command over their troops, the German Free Corps leaders could always tell the Berlin government and the Entente that they had nothing whatever to do with "the Russian Army of the West." It is not surprising, therefore, that as soon as the reaction against the Free Corps set in, von der Goltz did everything in his power

[89] See his astonishing memoirs, General Fürst Awaloff-Bermondt, *Im Kampf gegen den Bolshevismus* (Glückstadt and Hamburg, 1925) and the character sketch given by the French delegate of the Inter-Allied Military Mission to Latvia, Lieutenant General Du Parquet, *L'Aventure Allemande en Lettonie*, 147–150.

[90] Captain René Vanlande, *Avec le Général Niessel en Prusse et en Lithuanie, la Dernière Défaite Allemande* (Paris, 1921), 27. Friedrich Wilhelm Heinz calls Bermondt's plan "a dream that was as romantic as it was grotesque." ("Der deutsche Vorstoss in das Baltikum," in *Deutscher Aufstand*, 65.) Fletcher, who had refused to carry out von der Goltz's orders to join Bermondt, writes: "I considered this man to be a political visionary and a military incompetent and did everything to prevent such an elite troop as the Baltic *Landeswehr* from falling into the hands of such a character." (Fletcher, writing in the preface to Baron Engelhardt's memoirs, *Der Ritt nach Riga*, 13.) Even von der Goltz, who supported Bermondt from the start and speaks glowingly of his "black, shining eyes and bristling mustache" and of how "his men worshipped him like a God," had so little respect for his military ability that he tried — in vain — to find a competent German staff officer to help him run his army. (*Meine Sendung*, 255.)

to champion the cause of the Russian poseur. He is quite clear
about this:

I was determined to hinder the withdrawal of the German troops
which had already been officially ordered by the German government
since the middle of May . . . Obviously I wanted as slow a withdrawal as possible for in the meantime Bermondt could complete the
recruitment of his corps . . . [and again:] So much did I believe that
the Bermondt Project was the last *Heil* of Germany, that I was determined to do everything possible to see it go through.[91]

And on July 31, he issued the following secret order to all the
Freikorpsführer in the Baltic:

Mitau, 31 July 1919

SECRET:

Some progress is to be noted in the Russian question. But the financial
aspects remain unsolved . . . Certain [Free Corps] Leaders are
spreading propaganda against entrance into Russian service . . . Anyone who agitates against entrance into Russian service is to be informed that such agitation is fomented by Spartacist-Germans, the
English and the Latvians. I order that this type of agitation be opposed
by every means at your command.

(Signed) Count von der Goltz.[92]

For a moment, however, it looked as if von der Goltz's plans
to carry on the venture by using Bermondt as his instrument
would be thwarted. For the Allies, disgusted by German stalling,
sent an ultimatum to the Ebert government demanding that it
either withdraw all Volunteer troops from the Baltic area or suf-
fer the consequences of economic sanctions. On August 5, 1919,
Ebert ordered the Free Corps to return to the Reich by the end
of August. Von der Goltz took this final order in his stride and set
off at once for Weimar. What would the government's attitude
be, he asked, if the Free Corps were to enter Russian service?
Ebert, Noske, and Müller (the foreign secretary), all replied that
the German government would have no jurisdiction over such a
privately organized army.[93]

Thus the stage was set in Weimar for the revolt that took place

[91] *Meine Sendung*, 189, 235 and 264.

[92] The order is reprinted in Ambroise Got, *La Contre-Révolution Allemande*,
148–149.

[93] Von Oertzen, *Baltenland*, 322–323, and von der Goltz, *Meine Sendung*,
242–243.

in Mitau on August 24, 1919. On that day the first detachment of Volunteers from the Iron Division was to leave the railway station at Mitau for their return to Germany. As the bitter, angry Free-booters milled about in the station, awaiting the arrival of the train which was to carry them away from the Baltic, Major Bischoff appeared on the platform and announced amid the cheers of the troops: "I hereby forbid the departure of the Iron Division!" [94]

The news of Bischoff's declaration set off a chain reaction of rebellion among the Volunteer formations. On August 25 a group of officers from assorted Free Corps met in Mitau and organized the German Legion. The Legion was commanded by Naval Captain Siewert, and after his death in battle, by his chief of staff, Captain Otto Wagener.[95] Within a few days men representing a dozen Free Corps had swollen its ranks to over 14,000 men. Its equipment included 64 airplanes, six cavalry units, 56 field pieces, armored sections, a field hospital, and 156 machine guns.[96] Thus by the thousands Freebooters from the Legion, the Iron Division, the Plehve Free Corps,[97] and a dozen smaller formations replaced their old insignia with the huge oblong cockade of the "Russian Army of the West." Bermondt estimates its total strength at 55,000 men. "Of this number," he writes, "40,000 were German volunteers." [98]

[94] Von Salomon gives an eyewitness account of the mutiny. (*Die Geächteten*, 110–111.)

[95] Wagener subsequently became leader of the economic bureau of the Brown House and then Reichskommissar for economics under Hitler.

[96] Hauptmann Otto Wilhelm Heinrich Wagener, *Von der Heimat geächtet* (Stuttgart, 1920), 48. Free Corps entering the Legion included the Baden Storm Battalion (which, it will be recalled, had once before mutinied and joined the enemy of the Free Corps, the Latvian Army), the Stever, Diebitsch, Von Brandis, and Von Weickham Free Corps, the Regiment von Jena, and others.

[97] The Plehve Free Corps (also called the 2nd Guard Reserve Regiment) had been formed within the Reich at the orders of the OHL. After the siege of Riga it was withdrawn to defend West Prussia from Polish attack. It returned to the Baltic in July and joined Bermondt's forces in September. See the memoirs of its commander, Captain Karl von Plehve, *Im Kampf gegen die Bolschewisten: die Kämpfe des 2. Garde-Reserve-Regiments zum Schutz der Grenze Ostpreussens, Januar–November, 1919* (Berlin, 1926).

[98] Awaloff-Bermondt, *Gegen den Bolshevismus*, 217. On November 4, 1919, in a written answer to the House of Commons, Mr. Churchill, then Secre-

In spite of the fact that he had planned and secretly encouraged such a rebellion since mid-June, von der Goltz was, he says, astonished that German soldiers should actually revolt against the orders of their government. Nevertheless, since he felt that he could not "leave the men in the lurch," he hurried back to the Baltic, accepted an invitation to review the rebellious troops on the anniversary of the battle of Sedan, and in general resumed his function as the guiding and directing force behind what was called, for the sake of convenience, the "Bermondt Project." [99]

An interesting facet of the Freebooter mentality is seen in their attitude toward the mutiny of August. So tenacious was the hold of traditional German discipline and respect for authority that even these men who gloried in the name of "outlaws" and "nihilists" found it necessary to explain at length why they had mutinied. Their rationalizations are interesting. Some of them deny that the term mutiny is applicable at all and either avoid using the word or else put it in quotation marks. Von der Goltz argues that, seen in the proper light, no mutiny really took place: "The German troops within the Reich may have felt that they should abide by their oath to the usurper Ebert but . . . we *Baltikumers* had never obeyed him so we broke no oath." [100] Schmidt-Pauli also objects to the use of the term: "When one understands the reasons for the action, he knows that to call Bischoff's decision

---

tary of State for War, estimated the number of Freebooters in the Bermondt army at about 20,000. (120 *H. C. Debates,* 1329).

[99] See his *Meine Sendung,* 245–247. Benoist-Méchin's treatment of the relationship between von der Goltz and Bermondt is misleading. He says that von der Goltz surrendered his command and returned to the Baltic on his own hook (*à titre privé*) to serve as Bermondt's technical adviser. (*Histoire de L'Armée Allemande,* II, 41.) It is true that on September 21 von der Goltz officially handed over the command of the German Volunteers in Russian service to Bermondt. But von der Goltz had not surrendered his command of other German volunteers. As late as September 26 he received a telegram from Noske in his capacity as commander of all German troops in the Baltic. He did not relinquish his command until October 12, 1919. (*Deutscher-Geschichtskalender,* 35. Jahrgang, II, 759, and *Als politischer General,* 280.) Furthermore he certainly considered himself far more than the term *"conseiller technique"* would seem to imply. In the last chapter of his memoirs — which he calls "Tragedy in the Baltic" — he assumes complete responsibility for the Bermondt Project and speaks of the "West Russian Army which I had organized." (*Meine Sendung,* 282.)

[100] Von der Goltz, *Als politischer General,* 140.

'mutiny' is completely false . . . If the Free Corps mutinied it was against the Revolution and against Versailles." [101] Bischoff himself, on the other hand, brags about his mutiny, compares it favorably with the equally patriotic revolt of Count York of Wartenburg in 1813,[102] and comments: "Dared we not also believe that a great part of them [the front soldiers within the Reich] who saw the fruits of their fighting denied them, would understand our call and follow us? No government in the world could have stopped that." [103]

In order to explain their action and to answer the indictments leveled at them by the German democratic press,[104] a number of *Freikorpsführer* drew up the following proclamation:

TO THE GERMAN FATHERLAND AND TO ALL CIVILIZED PEOPLE OF THE EARTH:

With heavy hearts we have decided to reject the order which our government has issued under pressure from the Entente and have decided to stick it out on the Bolshevist front.

We are soldiers trained in the duty of obedience. Nevertheless we believe that the commands of our own conscience are a higher authority than obedience to orders given under duress. And our conscience tells us to defend the Fatherland from the unspeakable terrors which the break-through of the Bolshevist hordes would bring to our people . . .

In our ears we hear the shrieks of raped women, and butchered children; before our eyes, the picture of bestially mutilated bodies!

We will not aim our guns at you. No! It is for you that we stay on here to fight . . . for you!

What evil-minded men tell the world about our motives does not matter. Do not believe them. They are in the pay of the Spartacists who have been bought out by the Bolshevists. They only want to slander us in the eyes of the world in order to put us aside so that they will have a free hand . . .

We tremble for our sisters and brothers. We fear for the culture of the entire world!

[101] Schmidt-Pauli, *Geschichte der Freikorps*, 127.

[102] Bischoff was not the only one to compare his work with that of the heroes of 1813. Nationalists in general and National Socialist and Volunteers in particular liked to think that the postwar period was directly analogous to the War of Liberation.

[103] Bischoff, *Die letzte Front*, 197.

[104] See, as one example, the editorial in the *Vossische Zeitung*, August 28, 1919.

If the Fatherland and the statesmen of the world . . . abandon us,
then good! Then we will be the only ones who emerged from the
Great War . . . with our sense of human duty and honor unsullied.
Perhaps there is still a God who will stand beside us! [105]

In view of the simple fact that the entire Red Army had long
since withdrawn from the Baltic area, those volunteers who entered Bermondt's army because they really "feared for the culture
of the entire world" were certainly in the minority. The forces
which held the Free Corps in the Baltic were stronger than the
myth of the Red Peril. The Volunteers had come with high hopes
of winning a great victory — a victory which would wipe out the
memory and the shame of the western defeat. They could not
bear the thought of returning, once again, to the Reich as the
defeated and vanquished. Above all, they could not go back to
the people who had just crowned the perfidy of the stab-in-the-
back by signing the Treaty of Versailles. Von Salomon describes
the impact which the news of Versailles had on his fellow *Baltikumers*:

One day . . . we were sitting in Lieutenant Wuth's log cabin . . .
smoking and talking quietly about the possibility of settling in this
land. Wuth was saying that he would get a farm and a saw mill even
though the Latvians still held his [*sic*] land. Then Lieutenant Kay
entered and announced to the smoke-filled room: "Germany has signed
the peace treaty!"
  For a moment everything was quiet — so quiet that you could hear
it. Then Schlageter jumped up. "So. So Germany has signed," he mut-
tered staring straight ahead, and when he spoke again, there was a
terrible note in his voice. "All right, what happens to us now?" He
slammed the door and was gone.
  We shivered . . . from the terrible cold of abandonment. We had
believed that our country would never betray us . . . that we were
one with it . . . that it felt our most secret desires and fulfilled them.
Now everything was over. The signing made us free.[106]

[105] The proclamation is signed by Siewert in the name of the Baltic Defense
Regiment, the Stever, Plehve, Brandis, Wildemann, Rieckhoff, and Von
Meden Free Corps and other volunteer formations. It is reprinted in the
official Wehrmacht history of the postwar military campaigns, *Darstellungen
aus den Nachkriegskämpfen deutscher Truppen und Freikorps*, III, Appendix I, 193–194.
[106] *Die Geächteten*, 109–110. The implication of the last sentences, namely
that the Freebooters were loyal to the government until the signing of the
"Dictate of Versailles," is repeated by von Oertzen: "Right up to these dra-

The most articulate of the Volunteers suggests another reason for wanting to stay in the Baltic. The very strangeness of this wild and inhospitable land was somehow congenial and compellingly attractive to the restless and turbulent soul of the Freebooter:

The dangerous strangeness of this land which held me in such a peculiar spell enticed me. Just to stand forever . . . on the treacherous bog-land was enough! It was a land which imparted to war something of its own turbulent and ever-changing character. This feeling had given the war up here its tumultuous character . . . This is perhaps what had given the Teutonic Knights that restless seeking which ever drove them, again and again, from their solid castles to new and dangerous adventures.[107]

VII. DEFEAT AND RETURN TO THE REICH

Bermondt's army of German Freebooters was disastrously defeated in brief campaigns during October and November 1919. Not the least of the reasons for the defeat was Bermondt himself. He had no conception of how to conduct a military campaign and his vaulting egotism would not allow him to take advice from anyone. Whatever slim chances he had for success depended, in large measure, on the extent of the native support he might win over. But Bermondt lacked the subtlety even of von der Goltz. One of his first acts was to issue a bombastic proclamation which announced that Latvia could henceforth consider itself a Russian province and would soon be placed under the Czar. In the meantime it would be ruled by the future Czar's representative, General Prince Awaloff-Bermondt.[108] His fantastic schemes for raising money did nothing to reassure the local population. When German industrialists failed to contribute as much as he had antici-

---

matic hours of June, 1919 every member of the Free Corps felt himself bound to carry out the orders of his superiors . . . but now they suddenly stood alone. It was as if the last tie that still bound the Free Corps to Germany had been, at this decisive moment, ripped asunder." (*Die deutschen Freikorps,* 82.) This interpretation, which seeks to heap further blame on the home government, is manifestly false. Actually the Free Corps began their revolt against the Republic long before the signing of the Versailles Treaty.

[107] Von Salomon, *Die Geächteten,* 115.

[108] F. W. Heinz, "Der deutsche Vorstoss in das Baltikum," in *Deutscher Aufstand,* 65.

pated, Bermondt issued his own currency and used the "Imperial Russian estates in the Baltic" (that is, lands now belonging to the Estonians and Latvians) as backing. When no one recognized his money, he hit upon another scheme. He said he would recruit local slave labor to operate sawmills which would ship paper pulp to Germany and Western Europe.[109]

The predictable result of these acts was that when Bermondt launched his ill-conceived offensive against Riga, he was met by the furious resistance of native forces. The Latvian army, now well equipped from British arsenals and aided by the bombardment from British naval guns,[110] threw back the attack on Riga and began a counteroffensive which pushed Bermondt's starving, ragged, dysentery-ridden Freebooter army relentlessly westward.

In their retreat, the Freebooters engaged in a wanton destruction of native property which is explicable only in psychological terms. They had been thwarted and frustrated and they found the realization of personal powerlessness unbearable. They therefore began to destroy all those objects which reminded them of their own lack of security. Notice the testimony of two of the defeated Free Corps fighters.[111] Friedrich Wilhelm Heinz writes:

[109] Wagener, *Von der Heimat geächtet*, 44–47. Bermondt apparently lacked neither enthusiasm nor ideas. After the complete defeat of his army and the return of all Free Corps to Germany, he burst into Noske's office in December 1919: "He opened a satchel crammed full of ideas of what should be done with the troops which had formerly been under his command . . . It seemed to him taken for granted that he could reorganize his men overnight and . . . continue the fight against the Bolshevists . . . the fact that he was completely without money did not bother him at all . . . he was a mixture of political foolishness and military megalomania . . ." (Noske, *Von Kiel bis Kapp*, 184.)

[110] General du Parquet calls the intervention of the British naval forces during the siege of Riga "decisive." (*L'Aventure Allemande en Lettonie*, 199.)

[111] Heinz, *Die Nation greift an*, 73; and von Salomon, *Die Geächteten*, 144–145. For a psychiatrist's discussion of the psychological reasons for destructiveness, see Erich Fromm, *Escape from Freedom* (New York, 1941), 179–181. The accounts of destruction given above are fully documented by Allied officers. See Du Parquet, *L'Aventure Allemande*, 204 ff; Vanlande, *Avec le Général Niessel en Prusse et en Lithuanie*, 97–102. It is admitted by German writers. Von Oertzen says, "Thus slandered and despised and called 'thieves and robbers' by the people of their native land . . . they adopted the formula: "So they think we are outlaws, eh? All right then, why the hell shouldn't we act like outlaws?' " (*Die deutschen Freikorps*, 102–103.) Erich Balla admits that during the retreat "every bond of discipline was dissolved

The soldiers of the Iron Division and the German Legion unloaded all their despair and fury in one wild power-blow against the Letts . . . Villages burst into flames, prisoners were trampled under foot . . . chaotic revenge and joy in destruction (*Vernichtungsfreude*). The leaders were powerless, or else they looked on with grim approval.

Or listen to von Salomon:

We roared our songs into the air and threw hand grenades after them . . . We saw red. We no longer had anything of human decency left in our hearts. The land where we had lived groaned with destruction. Where once peaceful villages stood, was now only soot, ashes and burning embers after we had passed. We kindled a funeral pyre and more than dead material burned there — there burned our hopes, our longings; there burned the *bürgerlich* tablets, the laws and values of the civilized world; there burned everything. . . . And so we came back swaggering, drunken, laden with plunder.

During the course of November, the Iron Division had been slowly pushed into a pocket near Thorensberg. Cut off from all supplies and communications, it would have been annihilated had it not been for the rescue work of the Rossbach Free Corps. Rossbach's march across Eastern Europe and his relief action at Thorensberg forms one of the sagas of the *Baltikum*. And justifiably so. For whatever one thinks of the man's character,[112] his gallant rescue of the Iron Division must remain one of the great feats of military history. Braving an early and unusually harsh Baltic winter, Rossbach led his badly equipped men over a twelve thousand mile trek from Berlin across Eastern Europe. They often marched forty miles a day.[113] As soon as they arrived at Thorens-

. . . several of the Leaders 'took off' in order to save their own skins . . . their men ran wild through the country side marauding in complete disorder." (*Landsknechte wurden wir: Abenteuer aus dem Baltikum,* 229.) Contrast these pictures with the version of the return given by von der Goltz: ". . . the last German soldiers to face the enemy re-crossed the German frontier in a model military manner with black-white-red flags waving . . ." (*Als politischer General im Osten,* 159.)

[112] Gerhart Rossbach was a sadistic murderer of the so-called *Fehmgericht* and the notorious homosexual who, according to his own testimony, perverted Ernst Röhm. For his later career and National Socialist activity, see below, pp. 191–194, 210 ff.

[113] One National Socialist account says that the men covered as much as ninety kilometers a day (Fritz Carl Roegels, *Der Marsch auf Berlin: Ein Buch vom Wehrwillen deutscher Jugend,* Berlin, 1932, 141). But Rossbach himself never claimed more than sixty-five kilometers. (Arnolt Bronnen, *Rossbach,* Berlin, 1930, 78.)

berg, the Rossbach Detachment attacked the Latvian army, cut a path through to the beleagured Iron Division, and held off the Latvians until Bischoff's men could escape.

Rossbach's march also illustrates the baselessness of the later Free Corps claim that the Supreme Command of the German Army meekly followed the orders of the Berlin government and left the gallant Volunteers in the lurch by "hermetically sealing the border" and stopping all reinforcements from reaching the Baltic.[114]

It is true that OHL lost its early enthusiasm for the Baltic project as soon as it saw the widespread reaction against the Baltic Free Corps which had set in after the fall of Riga. It is also true that it had no confidence in the harebrained schemes of Bermondt. But, as the official Wehrmacht history of the period has recently pointed out, this does not mean that the Army withdrew all its support from the Volunteers. It went through the motions of obeying the government's order and officially closed the frontier to reinforcements on October 6, 1919. It nevertheless continued to allow men and material to go to the Baltic throughout October and November.[115] The correspondent of the London *Times* was quite right when he cabled from Kovno on November 6: "There has been no attempt at evacuation. On the contrary, the Germans have received inforcements. The closing of the frontier is a farce . . ."[116]

Rossbach's experience with the Reichswehr general who was ordered to stop him at the border town of Tilsit is illustrative of the Army's attitude. The general went up to Rossbach and the following conversation took place:

"Lieutenant Rossbach, I order you in the name of the Government to turn around and go back."

"Excellency, I am sorry but I can not obey your order . . ."

The General forgot to be angry. These men were real soldiers and here was a real Leader. He smiled happily, stepped back and said, "I withdraw the order and wish you the best of luck." [117]

[114] See, for example, Bischoff's *Die letzte Front,* 209.

[115] *Darstellungen aus Nachkriegskämpfen deutscher Truppen und Freikorps,* III, 109–110.

[116] *Times,* November 11, 1919.

[117] The same story has slightly different versions. See Bronnen, *Rossbach,* 86–87, Bischoff, *Die letzte Front,* 192, and Kurt Bark, "Rossbach's Marsch ins Baltikum," in *Freikorpskämpfer,* 202 and 205.

Rossbach's case is only one of many examples. In spite of the fact that it had officially closed the border on October 6, the Army command authorized the sending of "several detachments of troops to the Baltic in the middle of October. The reasons for such a decision lay in the imminent reduction of the Army, the fear of unemployment and the excitement produced by the peace treaty." [118] The commander of the *Eiserne Schar Berthold* had no trouble transporting one thousand men from Munich to Mitau. His men were granted regular furloughs from the Reichswehr. The furloughs were marked: "Destination: Königsberg or Tilsit." [119]

The Free Corps found a number of reasons for the failure of their great Baltic adventure. Everyone had been their enemy. The Supreme Command had left them in the lurch; the ungrateful native population stupidly refused to believe that the Volunteers were only trying to save them from the perils of Bolshevism; the British had first supported and then betrayed them; Bermondt had been an incompetent leader; and even von der Goltz himself had turned traitor.[120]

But it was the home government which was made to appear the real villain of the piece. Von der Goltz looked back on the failure of his plans and complained bitterly:

I had to fight on four fronts: The Bolshevik army; the Soldiers Councils of Libau influenced by the German radicals . . . ; the Germanophobe, half-Bolshevist Latvian government and the Entente . . . *We could have easily done away with all these enemies . . . if the weak-kneed German Government had not allied itself as a fifth enemy with the other four. Germans can only be defeated by Germans . . .* [and again] The mission stimulated and enticed me. I never guessed at that time that a dull sword had been placed in my hands and that my worst enemy would be my own people and my own government.[121]

In short, it was contended, that what had happened to these front fighters of the Baltic Volunteers was exactly what had hap-

[118] *Darstellungen,* III, 109.

[119] Gengler, *Kampfflieger Rudolf Berthold,* 161.

[120] Major Bischoff complains that "von der Goltz was a soldier of the old tradition . . . [who] unfortunately was never satisfied to choose one path and go its entire length . . . I have recently learned with amazement that Count von der Goltz himself . . . discouraged reinforcements from going to the Baltic." (*Die letzte Front,* 50 and 235.)

[121] *Als politischer General,* 86–87 (italics are in the original); and *Meine Sendung,* 123.

pened to them in 1918: once again they had been stabbed in the
back by the "November Traitors": "The anniversary of the dis-
graceful revolt of 1918 brought the realization that once again
the fighting troops of the German field army had been betrayed
and stabbed in the back by the cowardly and traitorous
Etappe." [122]

Specifically the Volunteers claimed that they had not been paid
or equipped by the home government; that the government had
not permitted the recruitment of Free Corps within the Reich and
that its officials and their "Jewish-Bolshevist press" had consistently vilified and slandered them.

Actually the government officials were not only remarkably tol-
erant of the Freebooters, but in the press and in the National
Assembly, they defended them against the criticism of the extreme Left. For example, even after the Freebooters had defiantly
and openly disobeyed the Government's order to return home, the
Foreign Minister of the Republic in a speech to the National Assembly expressed the opinion that the Baltic Volunteers were
sincere and much maligned patriots and concluded, "I must say
that I have received a very good general impression of these
troops." [123]

Nor is it true that the government failed to supply the Baltic
volunteers. In July, during a heated debate over the Baltic question, the Foreign Minister had assured the Assembly that "complete evacuation of the Baltic area is in process." Haase, the
USPD delegate from Berlin, replied:

> Herr Minister Müller! The Baltic has not only not been evacuated;
> new troops are being sent there . . . The recruitment offices and the
> Volunteer Corps continue to function as before . . . If we do not want
> to have the charge made against us that we are playing a dishonorable
> game, then it is our duty to set aside the masquerade . . . Our army
> budget, as we heard yesterday, is just as high as it was during the war.
> No wonder! Look at how well the Volunteer Corps are supplied and
> paid.[124]

[122] Gengler, *op. cit.*, 177. Von der Goltz entitles one of the chapters of his
Als politischer General the "Dolchstoss."

[123] Müller in speech of October 9, 1919. (*Verhandlungen der verfassunggebenden deutschen Nationalversammlung*, Stenographische Berichte, 94
Sitzung, Vol. 330, 2968–2961.) And in the same session, Noske lauded the
sincerity and high patriotism of the *Baltikumers*. (*Loc. cit.*, 322.)

[124] Speech of July 26, 1919, *Verhandlungen der Nationalversammlung*, 67
Sitzung, 1964 and 1974.

It is important to notice that the Defense Minister did not deny
any of these charges in his blunt reply:

> Herr Haase has — I don't recall whether it's the second or the third
> time — spoken about conditions in the Baltic. They are in many re-
> spects extraordinarily unsatisfactory. The evacuation of the Baltic has
> been ordered — that I emphasize once again — and will be carried
> out. But there is only one railway line available for the evacuation.
> The troops can not live off the land. A considerable amount of pro-
> visions must be sent . . . I openly admit that there has been recruit-
> ment of volunteers for the Baltic in the last months. But they are
> not authorized. The recruitment is forbidden, but unfortunately many
> things have gone on in the last eight months that are forbidden . . .[125]

And in his memoirs, Noske shrugged his shoulders at the continued recruitment of Volunteers for Baltic service and wrote,
"While I was absorbed with my work at Dahlem, I could not
concern myself with all the little Wallensteins who recruited men
to go to the East. So it went on for months." [126] In an unguarded
moment, Herr von Oertzen admits, by inference, that the Free
Corps had been paid throughout the spring and summer of 1919.
In reporting von der Goltz's questions to the government after
receiving the Entente ultimatum of August 5, he says: "Count
von der Goltz asked . . . if the Russian formations [i.e., the German Volunteers in the Bermondt army] *would continue to be
paid and supplied by the Reich* through the month of September." [127]

The most responsible of the National Socialist historians is
guilty of flagrant and deliberate distortion of Noske's policy toward the Baltic Volunteers. Herr von Oertzen says that "in a
speech before the Reichstag [*sic*] during the first days of October"
the Defense Minister, who had first tacitly supported the adventure, now led the agitation against it and placed a "radical block-
ade along the German border." [128] Actually in the speech to which
von Oertzen refers, Noske repeated his earlier statement that he
was trying without success to get the Baltic Free Corps to return
home but that he had encountered great difficulties. He then

[125] *Loc. cit.*, 67 Sitzung, 1974.
[126] *Von Kiel bis Kapp*, 177–178.
[127] *Baltenland*, 323 (italics are mine).
[128] Von Oertzen, *Die deutschen Freikorps*, 104, 105–106. See also his *Baltenland*, 326.

turned to the Independent Socialist critics of the Volunteers and
said:

> You are complicating Germany's position abroad by malicious and
> unjust criticism of the military administration . . . You are licking the
> boots of the British and French [disarmament] commissioners in Ber-
> lin . . . I have been advised to place an immediate blockade on all
> supplies [going to the Baltic] but in consideration of the Latvian prov-
> ince, I deem that such stringent action is not desirable at this time.
> The immediate blockade of supplies would naturally result in plunder-
> ing by the troops.[129]

The conclusion would seem to be that the Baltic Volunteers
were not shamefully vilified and stabbed in the back by the German government. But here again — as we have had occasion to
notice before — the important point is not what happened but
what the Free Corps *thought* had happened. The returning Freebooters were completely convinced that they had been betrayed
by the home government. They were now more than ever determined to march on Berlin and settle accounts with the "November
Criminals."

Here our attention is called to a peculiarity of the Freebooter
mind. It is a mind devoid of both sense of logic and sense of
humor. The men who complain most bitterly of their betrayal
by the treacherous government are the same men who admit that
they had planned to use the Baltic as a base from which they
would march on Berlin and overthrow this government. Von der
Goltz had long planned such a putsch.[130] And Bischoff, in closing
his memoirs, first expresses his surprise at the treachery of the
government and then records an illuminating interview he had
had with a Reichswehr general. Major Bischoff, it will be recalled,

---

[129] Speech of October 9, 1919, *Verhandlungen der Nationalversammlung*,
94 Sitzung, Vol. 330, 2957. The speech was greeted by cries of "Very true!"
and "Very right!" by the Democrats and Social Democrats.

[130] Von der Goltz says that his work in organizing Bermondt's army took up
so much of his time that "As a result . . . the special secret plans to march
against Berlin had to be postponed for the moment." (*Als politischer General*,
145.) And, after the failure of the Bermondt Project he writes: "The idea
that I might still play the last trump . . . march on Berlin and with the aid
of the Free Corps within Germany overthrow the Ebert Government won no
support from the troops in spite of all my propaganda. They wanted to stay
. . ." (*Ibid.*, 166–167.) See also his article, "Baltikum," in *Deutscher Aufstand*, at page 100.

had led the revolt against the Army's official order to return to Germany. He was nevertheless welcomed back into the Republican army. In December, he called on His Excellency General von Estorff, the Commander of Defense District I (East Prussia):

I had known him and admired him since my trooping days in German East Africa. He greeted me with the words: "Oh, I know, my dear Bischoff, that you would like to march on Berlin. I can't stop you because half of my troops would join you, and the other half would not shoot. But don't do it — there is no point in doing it." . . . It was hard for me to give up the thoughts which I had held uninterruptedly since November 9, 1918, — thoughts which had led to the East and determined my every thought and action and to let the instrument of their execution [*i.e.*, his Free Corps] fall from my hands.[131]

Bischoff and other *Freikorpsführer* never lost sight of their ultimate goal. A main reason for delaying the return of their troops as long as possible had been to keep their men together so that they might stage such a putsch.[132] And this was the reason that the Leaders did everything in their power to prevent the dissolution of their Corps after the final return to the Reich in December 1919.

Quite typically, the former commander of the German Legion complains bitterly that the ungrateful Republic refused to pension his Freebooters. He then describes some of the methods used to keep "the Leaders and those led steadfastly together" so that they might one day seize the government.[133] The most popular technique was to establish military "Labor Associations" (*Arbeitsgemeinshaften*) of all sorts. Bischoff's officers, for example, organized their men into groups of "agricultural laborers" (*Landarbeitsgemeinschaften*), who were welcomed to the estates of members of the Prussian and Pomeranian *Landbund*.[134] Noske

---

[131] Bischoff, *Die letzte Front*, 243–244.

[132] In an unguarded moment, a member of the staff of General Eberhardt, the man who relieved von der Goltz of his command, said as much to General Niessel's chief of staff. Niessel was the president of the Inter-Allied Commission charged with evacuating the Germans from the Baltic. (See Jacob, *Das neue deutsche Heer und seine Führer*, 8.) General Niessel tends to agree. See his memoirs, *L'Evacuation des Pays Baltique par les Allemands* (Paris, 1935), 240.

[133] Wagener, *Von der Heimat geächtet*, 162–164.

[134] Bischoff, *Die letzte Front*, 245.

himself authorized and helped set up these outfits apparently
because he hoped that by dispersing the dangerous *Baltikumers*
he was lessening the threat of their attack on the government.[135]
Other Free Corps tried to establish coöperative settlement colo-
nies in East Prussia and Mecklenburg. These attempts, such as
those of a Captain Wiese,[136] often failed, but they set a precedent
for the later Nazi "Labor Service." Some of the Free Corps commanders took their men to work in the coal mines of Upper
Silesia. Here they met and joined such well-established Volunteer formations as those of Ehrhardt and Loewenfeld.[137] These
"Labor Associations" later played a part in the Kapp Putsch and
in the Korfanty rebellion of 1921. One of the Leaders took all his
men and opened a large peat-processing plant, others established
sawmills, and cycle shops.[138]

Thus though the Baltic formations themselves were destroyed,
something of them remained, for the men who had built them
were still there. "They lived and with them and in them lived the
indestructible Free Corps spirit. They were only a few thousand
now. But those thousands were anything but broken. They had
seen and experienced too much to be able now to change over
into a safe and comfortable civilian life. They remained *Freikorpskämpfer* . . ." [139]

The Baltic adventure of the German Free Corps had ended in
defeat, frustration, and bitter disillusionment. But the leading
German historian of the movement, in closing his chapter on "The
Baltic Tragedy," insists that it had not been a failure; for in defeat
the Freebooters had learned two valuable lessons: first, that their
greatest enemy was republican Germany; second, that the Volun-

---

[135] Noske, *Von Kiel bis Kapp,* 182. Schultze-Pfaelzer, who describes the
system, writes, "Noske was clever enough to look for a peaceful solution.
The Germans were scattered throughout the countryside as "Labor Associations" . . ." (Gerhard Schultze-Pfaelzer, *Von Spa nach Weimar, die
Geschichte der deutschen Zeitwende* (Leipzig, 1929), 326.

[136] See Franz Wiemers-Borchelhof, "Freikorps, Arbeitsdienst, Siedlung:
Das Schicksal eines Vorkämpfers der Freikorpssiedler," in *Freikorpskämpfer,*
407 ff. See below, pp. 189 ff.

[137] Von Oertzen, *Kamerad, reich mir die Hände,* 140; and Rudolf Mann,
Mit Ehrhardt durch Deutschland, 125.

[138] Wagener, *op. cit.,* 162–163.

[139] Von Oertzen, *Die deutschen Freikorps,* 114–115.

teers themselves would have to form their own "higher and more intense political purposes." Von Oertzen concludes: "to sum up: military politics against the politicians. That was what they brought home with them from their great life of comradeship in the Baltic." [140]

We are about to see those lessons applied by the Freebooters in the Kapp-Lüttwitz Putsch and during the rest of their activity in the Reich.

[140] *Ibid.*, 116.

VI

IN THE SERVICE OF REACTION:
THE KAPP PUTSCH

Everything that the Free Corps experienced in the bloody spring of 1920 may be considered the preparation of the soil for the seed which was planted by National Socialism and harvested under Adolf Hitler.

— Von Oertzen

I. THE MARCH ON BERLIN

It was about twenty miles from Camp Döberitz to Berlin and the men of the Ehrhardt Brigade were thoroughly enjoying the march. A light rain had fallen during the morning of March 12, 1920, and had cleared the air. The soft breezes of a false-spring evening fluttered the black-white-red standards of the troop and the large swastikas painted on their helmets were clearly visible in the clear, moonlit night. The men were in good spirits. Earlier in the evening they had "bucked-up" their newly issued equipment, shaved, and had a good sleep. The boredom and restlessness of a month in the barracks wore off under the jarring cadence of hobnailed boots on the asphalt road. As they marched they sang their Ehrhardt Lied. The verses were sung to a catchy old English melody. In the days that lay ahead, the song would be equally popular in Biergarten and children's playground:

> Comrade, give me your hand
> Steadfast we'll stand together.
> Let those fight us who will
> Our spirit marches forever.
>
> Swastika on helmet,
> Colors of Red, White, Black

The Ehrhardt Brigade
Is marching to attack! [1]

The men were in no hurry. They had practiced the march to
Berlin many times and knew exactly how long it would take. They
were not due there until seven o'clock the next morning; for in
an ill-advised moment Captain Ehrhardt had promised the government's representatives that he would not seize the government
until hearing its answer to his ultimatum.[2] His men would await
the answer in the Tiergarten. Since there was plenty of time, the
march was halted at the Pickelsdorfer Bridge. Field kitchens were
drawn up and the men sat around drinking steaming mugs of
coffee, smoking, and looking forward to Der Tag. After a short
break, the march was resumed.

As they entered Berlin, the soldiers tensed and unslung their
rifles as a group of the Berlin *Einwohnerwehr* approached. But
the only challenge was a friendly greeting: the Civil Guards
called out, "Good morning and good luck!" and went home to put
on their old field gray. The Brigade halted in the Tiergarten and
watched the sun come up over the sleeping city. A couple of civilians approached. One was *Generallandschaftsdirektor* Wolfgang
Kapp. The other was General Ludendorff, military and impressive
even in mufti. He had just happened by — he said later — while
out for a morning walk. The General saluted the Freebooters,
complimented them on their military bearing,[3] and wished them
Godspeed. Promptly at 7:00 the Ehrhardt Brigade marched
through the Brandenburger Tor and down the Wilhelmstrasse.[4]

It was all over in a few hours. By noon, the Freebooters were
the masters of the capital of Germany. The empty government
buildings were occupied; machine guns were placed at strategic
street intersections and detachments of soldiers patrolled the

[1] When men of the Ehrhardt Brigade joined Hitler, they took their song
with them and simply substituted "Sturmabteilung Hitler" for "Die Brigade
Ehrhardt" in the chorus.

[2] See below, p. 154.

[3] Dr. Heinrich Brüning told me that the Ehrhardt Brigade was the
finest military troop that he had ever seen.

[4] The details for the march on Berlin as described here are taken from
the memoirs of participants: Mann, *Mit Ehrhardt durch Deutschland*, 147–
152, and Ehrhardt, *Kapitän Ehrhardt, Abenteuer und Schicksale*, 166–167,
172–180.

quiet streets. But the machine guns were never used and the street patrols did not touch the safety catches on their Mausers. Berlin had fallen without a shot being fired.[5] The self-styled liberators were given a cold reception by the Berliners. "The absolute vacuum of moral support in which the invading troops moved," says a British witness, "could be felt within the first few hours of their capture of the city."[6]

Shortly after noon, one of Ehrhardt's adjutants stopped to talk to the commander of the patrol that was watching the Chancellery. "You see," he said, "there was nothing to it! Kapp is already up there in his office working."[7]

The Freebooters had lived up to their part of the bargain. They had seized the seat of Germany's government. It was now up to the politicians to make their new government work. .

II. BACKGROUND OF THE PUTSCH

The Kapp-Lüttwitz Putsch, like other events in history, may be attributed to causes of two different kinds. The underlying cause was the violent reaction among nationalist-military circles to the signing of the "Diktat" of Versailles. The immediate cause — the catalytic agency — was the attempt of the government to demobilize a part of its Volunteer army in accordance with the provisions of the peace treaty.

The most important immediate result of the signing of the Versailles Treaty was that the precarious and temporary alliance between the Free Corps and the civilian government was now finally and irreparably shattered. The Volunteers' attitude can be stated briefly. Once again, they said, the government which relied for its very existence upon their support had traitorously stabbed them in the back by accepting this "Treaty of Shame." And what would they have done had they been in power? The answer is simple. They would have coldly refused to sign the Treaty of Versailles; then they would have declared war on the Allies. The

[5] A director of the Bibliothèque et Musée de la Guerre, Guy Charles Cros, was particularly impressed with the cold, military efficiency of the occupation. See his detailed account, "Le Coup d'État de Kapp," in *Les Archives de la Grande Guerre*, No. 28 (November 1921), 560 ff.

[6] "An Eye-Witness in Berlin," in *The New Europe*, April 1, 1920, 274.

[7] Mann, *Mit Ehrhardt durch Deutschland*, 152.

simple fact that they were not in power was, of course, of inesti-
mable advantage because, secure in their lack of responsibility,
they could later claim full credit for having been the true defenders of the German Faith and the champions of a program
which — had it only been adopted — would have been the salvation of Germany. When one considers the relative military
strength of Germany and the Allies in the spring of 1919, one is
not impressed with the feasibility of their program of war. But
the Volunteers and their historians insist that, given the unfath-
omable resources of the Freebooter spirit, such a war would
certainly have ended in a glorious victory. But once again victory
was torn from their grasp by the cowardly politicians. Von Oertzen's argument here is typical of a dozen others:

> The responsibility for the fate [of Germany] lay with the officers and
> soldiers of the Free Corps. They were not only soldiers but at the same
> time the first bearers of the political will of a new Germany which
> would never have bowed to the yoke of the Versailles Diktat . . . All
> that was needed was the creation of a military supreme command
> . . . In a few weeks the bayonets of the Free Corps would have added
> the whole of Poland with its invaluable industries . . . to a German
> Eastern State . . . Everything was thus ready to take up the Great
> War anew.
> The morale of the troops was glowing. Old Freebooters, as well as
> young Volunteers were overjoyed at the prospect of fighting again. The
> preparations became more and more intensive . . . Then one day
> from Könisberg came the report that the *Politiker* considered the en-
> tire undertaking unfeasible. All the brilliant prospects were dashed
> to the ground . . . The officers were thunderstruck . . . They knew
> that they could have made quick work of the Poles . . . And now the
> politicians came along and said that everything was impossible. Cold
> fury mixed with despair gripped officers and men of all the Free Corps.
> Once again, as at the end of the previous year, they had been con-
> fronted with betrayal. No one . . . knows the depth of their depres-
> sion . . . They now stood suddenly and completely alone . . .[8]

Even those who realized that to reopen hostilities would mean
only the further ruin of Germany insisted that it was far better
that Germany be ruined than Germanic honor sullied. This is only
a slightly different way of saying that in 1919 — as in 1923 and

[8] Von Oertzen, *Kamerad, reich mir die Hände: Freikorps und Grenzschutz*, 120–121; and *Die deutschen Freikorps*, 77, 80–81.

the *Götterdämmerung* of 1945 — the so-called patriots were more concerned with saving their pride than in saving their Fatherland. General Groener, one of the more capable Army leaders, said as much in his official report of May 1919. He then demonstrated the total impossibility of resuming hostilities and concluded: "It is our duty to think not of ourselves but of Germany. A new war would mean foreign troops right up to the capital . . . *Finis Germaniae*. Germany would be forever wiped from the tablet which contains the names of the great nations of the earth." [9] For holding this opinion, Groener was unanimously denounced by the extremists as a miserable pacifist and a "half-German." [10]

After the Ebert government — acting, it should be noted, on the advice of the Army — signed the Treaty, a group of army officers began to agitate for the establishment of a dictatorship which would overthrow the Weimar constitution. They distributed pamphlets to their regiments entitled "Reflections on Dictatorship" [11] and bombarded Noske with demands that he desert his colleagues and join them in a putsch. The Defense Minister flatly refused all these overtures on the grounds that "any attempt to govern against the will of the broad masses of the people would lead, as certain as death, to catastrophe." [12] But the officers kept up the pressure.

The most insistent agitator for dictatorship was Captain Pabst, the general staff officer who had organized the Volunteer formation, the Division of Horse Guards. Pabst despised the Republic[13] and had repeatedly urged Noske to join the officers in overthrowing it. On July 5, 1919, he again called on the Defense Minister

[9] For Groener's report of May 21, 1919, on the feasibility of going to war, see Caro and Oehme, *Schleichers Aufstieg*, 79.

[10] Von Oertzen, *Die deutschen Freikorps*, 75–77. See also General Walther, Freiherr von Lüttwitz, *Im Kampf gegen die November-Revolution* (Berlin, 1933), 69–70. Ehrhardt calls Groener an outright traitor. (*Kapitän Ehrhardt*, 145.)

[11] One of the pamphlet's chapters, "The Person," suggests that Gustav Noske was the strong man needed. (Caro and Oehme, *op. cit.*, 89.)

[12] Noske, *Von Kiel bis Kapp*, 196; see also his *Erlebtes*, 110–112.

[13] See his savage indictment of the "November Traitors" in *Deutscher Aufstand, Die Revolution des Nachkriegs*, edited by Curt Hotzel (Stuttgart, 1934), 28 ff.

and repeated his demands. When Noske again refused to listen to him, Pabst became angry:

Pabst: It would be unfortunate, Herr Minister, if you did not find yourself on the side of the officers when the national uprising occurs.

Noske: Is that a threat? I have always suspected that some day you might arrest me along with the entire government.

Pabst: You, Herr Minister? Under no conditions!

Noske: That remark, Herr Captain, shows that there is a considerable difference between us. I will give you no guarantee that I won't arrest you one of these days.[14]

Two days later, Noske ordered that the Division of Horse Guards should begin to demobilize and had Pabst dismissed without promoting him to his majority.

Noske lived to regret that he had not carried out his threat of July 5, for the infuriated Pabst now organized and became the driving spirit behind a political club, the *Nationale Vereinigung*, whose avowed purpose was the overthrow of the Republic. To this society belonged Major Stephani, the commander of the Potsdam Free Corps, Wolfgang Kapp, Colonel Bauer, a former section chief of the OHL, Generals Ludendorff and von Lüttwitz, Hugo Stinnes, and other reactionary industrialists, the journalist "Doctor Schnitzler," [15] and the renegade pseudo-intellectual Trebitsch-Lincoln.[16]

[14] Noske, *Von Kiel bis Kapp*, 200, and Volkmann, *Revolution über Deutschland*, 325. Von Oertzen says that the incident has been misinterpreted and that Noske was only joking when he made his counterthreat. (*Deutsche Freikorps*, 357.) Noske admits that he said it in a half-joking way but concludes: ". . . there was a serious undertone. I had given a warning."

[15] Schnitzler's real name was Handke. He was a dentist from Ingolstadt who had received his degree from a correspondence school. He made it a point to cultivate and impress old East Elbian landowners, Westphalian industrialists, and retired Army colonels. After serving as "Press Chief" to Colonel Bauer and chief adviser to the Kapp government, he became Ehrhardt's "political adviser." He subsequently double-crossed Ehrhardt and made his living by blackmail and extortion. A competent writer has called him "a self-styled political expert, a bleary-eyed Bohemian who was chronically in debt." (Schultze-Pfaelzer, *Von Spa nach Weimar*, 328.) Members of the Free Corps agree. (See F. W. Heinz, *Sprengstoff*, Berlin, 1930, 224 f.)

[16] Trebitsch-Lincoln (or Lincoln-Trebitsch) was a Hungarian Jew who went to England and became an evangelist preacher, a member of Parliament for the Liberal Party, and a German spy. Indicted for espionage, he fled to the United States. He returned to Germany after the Armistice.

For years *Generallandschaftsdirektor Geheimrat* Wolfgang
Kapp had been a relatively obscure, hard-working civil servant
in charge of the East Prussian land office. There was nothing in
his record or personality to disassociate him from hundreds of
other Prussian bureaucrats until the spring of 1916. At that time
he gained national recognition as one of the leaders of the opposition to Chancellor Bethman-Hollweg and the founder of the
Fatherland Party which was largely instrumental in removing
Bethman from office.[17] When the Revolution broke out, Kapp
was, of course, horrified. He was also determined to do something
about it. He managed to salvage something from the wreckage of
the Fatherland Party by changing its name to the "Bureau for
National Union" and helping to maintain its offices at the old
Schellingstrasse address.[18] But the Bureau was a rather moribund affair until Captain Pabst arrived in July and reorganized
it as the *Nationale Vereinigung*. The energetic young Freebooter
captain and his friends infused some of their own enthusiasm into
the tired, old civil servant. Kapp set out at once on an indefatigable — if ill-organized and inconclusive — campaign to win
support for the counterrevolution.

Geheimrat Kapp had been a Prussian bureaucrat for too long
to have any delusions of personal power. He knew both his limitations and his place and he never thought of himself as the strong
man of Germany. Quite naturally, he believed that that role
should be played by an Imperial general. "It was Kapp's wish
and hope," his biographer tells us, "that General Ludendorff
should be our savior." [19] But the people — "in rank ingratitude"

His long prison record did not stop Kapp from making him the Director
of Press Affairs in his government. (See *Fünf Tage Militärdiktatur: Dokumente zur Gegenrevolution*, edited by Karl Brammer, Berlin, 1920, 32.)

[17] Kapp and his friends charged that the Chancellor was guilty of pacifism
and of a "non-German" attitude. Specifically, he had opposed ruthless
submarine warfare and had said that Belgium should be returned to the
Belgians after the war. Admiral von Tirpitz is usually given credit for
founding the party but Tirpitz himself gave all the credit to Kapp and
called him ". . . the founder of the Deutschen Vaterlandspartei." His letter
is quoted in Ludwig Schemann, *Wolfgang Kapp und die Märzunternehmung
vom Jahre 1920* (Munich and Berlin, 1937), 105 f.

[18] "Junius Alter" (Franz Sontag), *Nationalisten, Deutschlands nationales
Führertum der Nachkriegszeit* (Leipzig, 1932), 30.

[19] Schemann, *op. cit.*, 126–127.

— had turned against the ruthless dictator of the war years. He was much too unpopular to lead the national uprising that Kapp had envisaged. So General von der Goltz was approached. But Count Goltz, made cautious by the recent Baltic fiasco, felt that "the time is not yet ripe"; besides, he was not on friendly terms with the highly influential von Seeckt.

Finally Kapp thought of General Freiherr von Lüttwitz. The commander of the Free Corps around Berlin was his last choice and, as it proved, not a very happy one, for the two conspirators never reached agreement either on the correct policy to pursue or on the date of its execution. Kapp's careful, bureaucratic mind saw the necessity of quietly and methodically preparing the ground for the putsch. Lüttwitz's arrogant little brain persisted in thinking that the politicians could be forced to accept a dictatorship and thereby abandon the Republic which they had established. To further his plans, Lüttwitz called on a great variety of politicians and in long, noisy conferences managed only to convince them that he was their worst enemy.[20] Kapp repeatedly warned his colleague against tipping his hand to the opposition and warned him of the utter futility of negotiating with the politicians. But General Baron von Lüttwitz was not the person to take advice from a civil servant. He continued his activity. The exasperated Kapp was quite right when he exclaimed to a friend, "For God's sake, Lüttwitz even hands them the calling card of the counterrevolution!"[21]

Nor was Lüttwitz successful in winning his fellow generals to his cause. Maercker was opposed from the beginning.[22] Von der Goltz was cool and von Seeckt — a key man in the army even in 1919 — considered Lüttwitz a fool. He pointed out quite rightly that Lüttwitz was not even able to control his own son-in-law and chief of staff, Baron von Hammerstein, let alone the Officers' Corps.[23]

[20] Lüttwitz, *Im Kampf gegen die November-Revolution,* 98–102, and *passim,* and Alter, *Nationalisten,* 38–39. Although his memoirs have considerable competition, they are perhaps the most patently unreliable, twisted and confused products of any of the revolutionary figures.

[21] Alter, *op. cit.,* 39.

[22] Volkmann, *Revolution über Deutschland,* 326.

[23] See the able biography, General Friedrich von Rabenau, *Seeckt, Aus seinem Leben 1918–1936* (Leipzig, 1940), II, 219 and *passim.* Rabenau,

Throughout the summer of 1919, the *Nationale Vereinigung* increased its agitation against the Republic. Its activity, apart from unrewarding negotiations for support, took two forms. First, it tried systematically to embarrass and discredit the government by making demands which it knew the government could not possibly fulfill. Lüttwitz, for example, writes with great indignation that the "Weimar incompetents" were unable to satisfy his demands. He includes some of them in his memoirs: (1) immediate and full employment; (2) absolute prohibition of all labor disputes; (3) rigorous suppression of the press and the end of its "vituperative attack on the Army"; (4) continuation of the special military courts; and (5) no changes in the army uniforms or the Imperial flag. These "suggestions" are given as the *sine qua non* of continued army support of the Republic. He closes his demands with the warning: ". . . if these measures are not undertaken, anti-government and anti-parliament sentiments will be produced in the army." [24]

Meanwhile, the National Unity Society was doing all it could to produce exactly those sentiments. It distributed pamphlets to the soldiers which said, among other things, that their government had sold Germany out to the Bolshevists, that it was totally incompetent, that it had betrayed Germany, and that it despised the soldiers and would sit back and let them starve to death. [25]

But on the whole, the counterrevolutionaries had little to show for their machinations by the end of the year. And time was working against them. Public anger over Versailles cooled perceptibly as the weeks passed. Furthermore the Government stole much of their thunder and silenced their criticism by demonstrating that it was capable of handling the domestic economic situation which had been made chaotic by a series of Communist strikes. In the middle of January, Ebert put Noske in charge of a commission

---

however, qualifies Lüttwitz's charge that Seeckt was the "soul of the opposition to my plans" (Lüttwitz, *op. cit.*, 123). It is not true, Rabenau insists, that his hero worked actively against Lüttwitz; but it is true that his indirect influence was definitely against the type of putsch Lüttwitz was trying to conduct. (Rabenau, *op. cit.*, II, 219 and 225–226.)

[24] Lüttwitz quotes his letter of September 1, 1919, to Noske in his *Kampf gegen die November-Revolution*, 90–93.

[25] Noske, *Von Kiel bis Kapp*, 197–198.

composed of generals and civilian experts. Using as their slogan the ancient admonition, "if a man shall not work, neither shall he eat," the commission cracked down on the crippling strikes, helped to restore production, reduced unemployment, and in general showed the German public that the Ebert Government was capable of effective action. "It began to appear," says Volkmann, "that a strong government under the leadership of Ebert and Noske was taking the initiative and was beginning to make the road clear for national stability." [26]

The patriots of the *Nationale Vereinigung* were seriously alarmed at such a prospect. They were afraid — like Hitler after them — that Germany might recover before they had a chance to seize power and save it for themselves. Furthermore, their dwindling chances for staging a militarist putsch were further dimmed by the government announcement of February that within a few weeks the army would be reduced to 100,000 men in accordance with the Treaty of Versailles. Ehrhardt's elite 2nd Marine Brigade was to be the first to go.

In the problem of demobilizing the Free Corps, the now desperate conspirators recognized their last chance of seizing the government. For the Volunteers, furious at what they considered the final betrayal by the government, were talking openly of marching on Berlin. The counterrevolutionaries grabbed at the opportunity. It took little effort to encourage Freebooter discontent and enroll them in the service of reaction. Thus it came about that General Baron von Lüttwitz, rebuffed by members of his own caste, turned to Ehrhardt, the Freebooter captain, and used his men to seize the government of Germany.

III. THE IDES OF MARCH, 1920

In revolutionary Wilhelmshaven, during the January days of 1919, *Korvettenkapitän* Hermann Ehrhardt gathered a small group of his fellow naval officers about him to fight the Republic of Soviets which had recently been proclaimed by the Spartacists. The little Storm Troop performed so ably that Gustav Noske authorized Ehrhardt to organize a large Volunteer formation. On March 1, 1919, Ehrhardt established headquarters in the

[26] *Revolution über Deutschland,* 335–336.

Thousand Man Barracks in Wilhelmshaven and sent out a call
for recruits. The response was so overwhelming that he could
choose his men carefully. The result was that he established the
best organized and best trained Free Corps in postwar Germany.
The nucleus of his Brigade was composed of officers and noncommissioned officers of the Imperial Navy, and the "fine looking
students who streamed to his colors" first underwent a rigorous
six-weeks training program before being admitted to the elite
formation.[27]

The Brigade received its baptism of fire in the Brunswick
campaign of April 1919. After spearheading the attack on Munich
in May, it moved to Upper Silesia to fight the extreme nationalist
Polish formations, the P.O.W. (*Polska Organizacja Wajskowa*).
While in Upper Silesia, the Brigade absorbed hundreds of the
ruthless, battle-hardened, veterans of the returning Baltic Free
Corps. This fact has caused the widespread and erroneous belief
that both Ehrhardt and his original Brigade had fought in the
Baltic.[28] Though this was not the case, it is nonetheless true that
the influx of *Baltikumers* and their savage nihilism did have a
profound effect on the spirit of the Brigade.[29]

Suddenly one day during the winter of 1919, the men of the
Ehrhardt Brigade stopped their looting of the Silesian population and set off, some five thousand strong,[30] for Berlin. Noske's
orders had come through: the Freebooters found them highly
amusing — they were to defend the government from anticipated
Communist unrest![31] The government treated them well. The
excellent barracks at Döberitz were ideally situated, just an hour's
bus ride from the capital; they were given garrison rations and

[27] For the organization and training of the Ehrhardt Brigade, see K.
Helmerich, "Von der 1000 Mann-Kaserne zur Marinebrigade Ehrhardt," in
Das Buch vom deutschen Freikorpskämpfer; Ernst von Salomon, "Die Bri-
gade Ehrhardt," in *Deutsche Soldaten,* 120–121; Mann, *Mit Ehrhardt durch
Deutschland,* 37 ff.; and Ehrhardt, *Kapitän Ehrhardt,* 87–94.

[28] See, for example, Otto Braun, *Vom Weimar zu Hitler* (Europa Verlag,
New York, 1940), 85–86, and more recently, Fischer, *Stalin and German
Communism,* 122.

[29] Mann, *op. cit.,* 125; and Ehrhardt, *op. cit.,* 157.

[30] Von Salomon, "Die Brigade Ehrhardt," in *Deutsche Soldaten,* 120.

[31] "Junius Alter," *Nationalisten,* 81; Mann, *op. cit.,* 130; and Ehrhardt,
op. cit., 157.

issued new equipment. They had little to complain about except lack of activity.

Then as suddenly as the call away from their happy hunting in Upper Silesia, came the call for the Brigade to disband. Ehrhardt sought out General Lüttwitz, angrily disclosed that his men were on the verge of marching on Berlin, and asked him what he should do about it. This was all good news to the general:

Lüttwitz: Don't do a thing and keep quiet. I will not permit the troops to be disbanded.
Ehrhardt: But the order has already gone out.
Lüttwitz: That is my worry.

Ehrhardt hurried back to camp, and when the Freebooters gathered around him to ask about the dissolution, he grinned and said, "Shut up and get back to duty." The director of the *Reichsarchiv*, who records the conversations, reports that "the men were as happy as children." [32]

On March 1, 1920, Lüttwitz made public his earlier assurances to Ehrhardt. On that day the Second Marine Brigade celebrated the first anniversary of its formal founding by holding a parade at Camp Döberitz. Lüttwitz reviewed the troops. Amid the cheers of the Freebooters, he announced: "I will never permit such an elite troop to be taken away from me in such tempestuous times." [33]

Two days later, the two leaders of the Rightist opposition parties, Hergt, of the German Nationalist People's Party, and Heintze, of the German People's Party, called on Lüttwitz. They told the general that they were alarmed over the widespread rumor that he was about to seize the government. They asked him to deny the rumor because it was ruining their chances of pushing through a proposal they were about to make to the National Assembly. Within the next few days, they said, they were going to propose that the Assembly dissolve, that new elections be held, that a President be elected by plebiscite, and that a new ministry composed of experts (*Fachminister*) be formed. When Lüttwitz told them bluntly that he had no confidence in politicians — "I

[32] Volkmann, *Revolution über Deutschland*, 336–337. No date is given for this conversation, but it probably occurred toward the end of February.
[33] Quoted by Ehrhardt, *Kapitän Ehrhardt*, 170.

prefer to rely on my battalions" — they replied with equal candor that they would never support his militarist putsch.[34]

Thus on the eve of the event, Baron von Lüttwitz had alienated or failed to win the support of precisely those forces whose help was absolutely essential to the success of any counterrevolutionary coup — the leadership of the German Army and the dissatisfied parties of the Right. He nevertheless went ahead with his plans. It is just possible that it was more than mere stubborn arrogancy that urged him on. The open declaration of March 1 had so encouraged the Free Corps that it is doubtful if Lüttwitz could have backed out of the putsch even if he had wanted to do so. "We had decided to march whatever happened," says von Salomon, "without Lüttwitz and without Kapp. Perhaps even against them." [35]

Noske, of course, was aware of the increased activity going on in the offices of the *Nationale Vereinigung* on Schellingstrasse; but he saw no particular cause for alarm. He knew definitely that the key figures in the Army, General Reinhardt, the Chief of the Army leadership, and General von Seeckt, the Chief of the General Staff (now called for the Allies' benefit the *Chef des Truppen-amtes*), were opposed to the putsch. And he suspected, quite rightly, that the Rightist parties were not interested in Lüttwitz's program. Besides, the conspirators lacked leadership. Hindenburg himself might conceivably have pushed through a coup, but his name was never associated with the National Union Society. One could not sweep the country with names like Pabst, Kapp, Bauer, and Lüttwitz. Nevertheless, Noske felt that some action should be taken. He ordered that a complete report on the activity of the *Vereinigung* be drawn up. But he did not read the report until March 10, and then the only security measure he took was to remove the Ehrhardt Brigade from the command of Lüttwitz and place it under Admiral von Trotha for purposes of dissolution.[36]

Events moved rapidly after that. On the same day, Lüttwitz

[34] Volkmann, *op. cit.*, 340–341, and von Oertzen, *Freikorps*, 365.

[35] Von Salomon, *Die Geächteten*, 157.

[36] Noske, *Von Kiel bis Kapp*, 204–206. Noske himself regretfully admits that "in my blind confidence, I did not heed the warning [of State Commissioner von Berger's report]."

stormed into the Chancellery and delivered another "calling card of the counterrevolution." He demanded that the order for the dissolution of the Free Corps be rescinded, that General Reinhardt be replaced by a "harder" man, and that the Ehrhardt Brigade remain under his command. When Ebert and Noske sarcastically asked if he had any political program to suggest, the humorless general, taking them seriously, was hard pressed for an answer. The only answer he could think of was the one Hergst and Heintze had suggested to him on March 3: new elections, a new President elected by plebiscite, and a ministry of experts. When he was ushered unceremoniously to the door, he said angrily that he had only wanted to warn them before it was too late.[37]

Even then, Noske waited twenty-four hours before dismissing Lüttwitz and issuing the order for the arrest of Kapp, Bauer, and Pabst. It was too late. The three conspirators had been warned — probably through a leak in the police office. When the officials arrived at the Schellingstrasse address, they found the offices of the *Nationale Vereinigung* empty.

Informed of increasing activity in Camp Döberitz, Noske sent Admiral von Trotha to investigate on the afternoon of March 12. When Trotha arrived, he found the camp completely quiet; he reported back to Noske that there was no cause for alarm. It is not surprising that Trotha found no activity when he arrived: before setting out, he had telephoned and warned Ehrhardt that he was coming! [38]

Later that same evening, General von Oven, the man who had taken over Lüttwitz's command, and another Reichswehr general went to Camp Döberitz. They told Ehrhardt that they had come to negotiate with him and begged him not to march on Berlin that night because if he did, the Reichswehr would fire on his men. Ehrhardt replied brusquely that he would accept orders

[37] The conference scene is described in Lüttwitz, *Im Kampf gegen die Revolution,* 112–113; Noske, *Von Kiel bis Kapp,* 207; and Volkmann, *op. cit.,* 346–348.
[38] Chancellor Bauer in a speech to the National Assembly, March 18, 1919 (*Verhandlungen der verfassunggebenden deutschen Nationalversammlung,* Stenographische Berichte, 157 Sitzung, Vol. 332, p. 4901). When the putsch came, Trotha immediately entered the service of the new government. He is listed on page 497 of the Nazi *Führerlexikon* for 1934.

only from his commanding officer and the only commander he
recognized was General von Lüttwitz. But he recoiled from the
thought of firing on old wartime comrades. He therefore promised to wait in the Tiergarten until 7:00 A.M. If by that time
the Government accepted his conditions, he would not continue
the march. Asked what his conditions were, Ehrhardt simply
repeated the Lüttwitz demands of March 10. The generals returned to Berlin to report the conversation to Noske.[39]

As the singing Ehrhardt Brigade approached the city, Noske
called a hurried conference of military leaders. That meeting
held at 1:00 A.M. in the Chancellery was to be one of the most
decisive conferences in the history of the Weimar Republic. The
issue was crystal clear: would the Republican Army defend the
Republic or would it not? Noske looked at the assembled generals
and asked them point-blank to order the Reichswehr to fire on
the approaching revolutionaries. It was a memorable moment.
In the heavy silence that followed his request, Noske turned
first to General Reinhardt, the Chief of the Army Leadership.
Reinhardt had always supported the Republic and he did not
desert it now: "In such a situation, there can be no neutrality for
the Reichswehr. The quicker we act, the quicker the spark will be
put out."

Then all eyes turned to the man who was known as "The
Sphinx with a Monocle," Colonel General Hans von Seeckt. He
was sitting in the shadows of the room and the reflected light from
his monocle acted as a partial mask. One ice-cold blue eye looked
slowly from one general to the next and then fixed on Noske.
When he finally spoke, his deceptively soft voice had issued a
command:

[39] The scene at Döberitz on the night of March 12 is probably unique in
the history of the relationship between German generals and their junior
officers. Imperial German generals simply did not make it a practice to plead
and negotiate with their inferiors. The reception Generals von Oven and
Oldershaufen received was also unusual. Ehrhardt had been sleeping. When
the generals entered his room, the Freebooter captain jumped up, grabbed
his pistol, and told the astonished generals to keep their hands up. (See
"Junius Alter," *Nationalisten*, 41.) When Noske asked them why they had
not put a bullet through Ehrhardt's head, they shrugged their shoulders in
reply. (Noske, *Von Kiel bis Kapp*, 209.)

Troops do not fire on troops. Do you perhaps intend, Herr Minister, that a battle be fought before the Brandenburger Tor between troops who have fought side by side against the common enemy? . . . When Reichswehr fires on Reichswehr, then all comradeship within the Officers Corps has vanished.

Gustav Noske was not easily shaken, but he was shaken now. In desperation he threatened to call out the workers of Germany in a general strike against the putschists. Seeckt only smiled. "Then I'll mobilize the police!" said Noske. Again the Sphinx smiled and said softly that he was sorry, but that he would have to disappoint the Minister here too. The police were making common cause with the putschists. "Seeckt," his most recent biographer tells us, "thoroughly enjoyed his triumph." [40]

Deserted by the army of the Republic, Noske threw in the sponge. He ordered all loyal troops to stay in their barracks,[41] and got into an automobile to join the procession which was taking the government ministers to Dresden. As he sat down in the back seat, he felt a hard, uncomfortable object. It was a live hand grenade. The Defense Minister closes his memoirs with the rueful comment: "I had been sitting on a hand grenade that might have gone off at any minute all during the course of the last year and a half during the long, painful trip from Kiel to Kapp!" [42]

[40] General Rabenau, *Seeckt, Aus seinem Leben,* II, 222. The description of the conference of March 13, 1920, as given above is drawn from Rabenau's detailed study of Seeckt; Volkmann, *op. cit.,* 356–359; and Caro and Oehme, *Schleichers Aufstieg,* 96–98. As Mr. Clark has pointed out (R. T. Clark, *The Fall of the German Republic,* London, 1935, 89), what Seeckt really meant when he said that the Reichswehr could not fire on their former comrades was that they would not fire on militantly nationalist comrades. As we shall see, they could and did fire on the Red Guards, among whom were great numbers of front soldiers and former members of the first Free Corps. (See below, page 176, note 20.)

[41] Cros, "Le Coup d'État de Kapp," in *Les Archives de la Grande Guerre,* No. 28 (November, 1921), 550.

[42] Noske, *Von Kiel bis Kapp,* 211. Noske resigned as Minister of Defense shortly after the return of the legal government. He became Minister-President of the province of Hanover, a position he held until the Nazis forced him to resign in 1933. During World War II he was arrested twice by the Nazis; the second time in connection with the General's revolt of July 1944, at which time he was indicted for high treason and held in Moabit Prison. He was freed by United States troops. He died on November 30, 1946, at the age of seventy-eight, as the result of a stroke.

The fleeing officials of the Weimar government arrived in Dresden about noon of the same day (March 13, 1920). They were met at once by General Maercker, who informed them that he had orders from General von Lüttwitz to place them all under arrest. Noske told Maercker that his orders proceeded from illegally constituted authority and hence were not valid. The commander of the Volunteer Rifles then made the remarkable declaration that he would interpret his orders in such a way as to do everything in his power to support the Ebert government.[43] Ebert and Noske were grateful but confused by this ambivalent statement. They thought it safer to proceed to Stuttgart, where the Reichswehr commander, General von Bergmann, had told his troops unambiguously that he would "support and protect the legally constituted government."[44] In the meantime Ehrhardt's men occupied Berlin.

IV. THE FAILURE OF THE KAPP PUTSCH

Seldom in history has the leader of a revolutionary movement been less prepared to assume office than was Wolfgang Kapp on March 13, 1920. During the time that Lüttwitz was planning the march on Berlin, Kapp had been in East Prussia talking to August Winnig and trying to drum up support for the counterrevolution. He and his friends had set no definite timetable, but they thought that the preparations might be ready by April or perhaps July, 1920.[45] Kapp did not even know that Lüttwitz had

[43] *Fünf Tage Militärdiktatur,* edited by Karl Brammer, 13. The charge that Maercker was a bitter enemy of the Republic and a supporter of the Kapp putsch made by such recent writers as Hans Fried (see above, p. 34 at note 2), and by Ruth Fischer, who calls him "one of the leaders of the Kapp putsch" (*Stalin and German Communism,* 97), is not borne out by his action at Dresden. Nationalist writers are correct, at this point, when they agree that Maercker was opposed to Kapp from the start and that by allowing the government to escape, he contributed greatly to the failure of the putsch. See, among others, "Junius Alter," *Nationalisten,* 42; Schemann, *Wolfgang Kapp,* 148–149; and von Oertzen, *Die deutschen Freikorps,* 372.

[44] His order of the day is quoted in von Oertzen, *Freikorps,* 372–373.

[45] His biographer gives the earlier date (Schemann, *Wolfgang Kapp,* 142). A member of the inner circle of the *Nationale Vereinigung* arrived in Berlin on March 8, 1920, and was amazed to hear that the putsch was to be held within the week. He had understood that it was not to take place until July. See "Les Dessous de la Politique Réactionaire en Europe Centrale

ordered Ehrhardt to march on Berlin. As a matter of fact, he first learned that such was the case when he bumped into Ehrhardt and Lüttwitz about six o'clock on the morning of March 13, at the corner of the Charlottenburger Chaussee and the Siegesallee.[46]

Nor were the Free Corps any better prepared for the putsch. The Volunteers had always hated the Republic and since their return from the Baltic had talked openly of overthrowing it. This, as we have seen,[47] was the main reason for the commanders' attempt to keep the formations intact. But no definite plans had been made. Each leader insisted that his own formation should be the nucleus for the national revival and concocted his own schemes for attaining that end. No one leader was big enough to coördinate the Free Corps into one great anti-Republican movement. Captain Pabst tried to play the role of coördinator without much success. One of his letters to Berthold of the *Eiserne Schar* indicates the type of difficulty he encountered. He urges Berthold to coöperate with the Berlin conspirators and entreats him not to assemble any more new formations in Bavaria: "There are already far too many separate organizations there . . . we will have great difficulty in bringing them all under one roof." [48]

---

et ses Dangers pour la France," a series of three anonymous articles written by a close friend of Kapp, Bauer, Pabst, and Stephani, and appearing in the periodical *L'Europe Nouvelle* for April 1921. This writer suspects that either Trebitsch-Lincoln or Schnitzler is the author.

[46] Schemann, *op. cit.*, 146–147. Lüttwitz, in his anxiety to pin the blame for the failure of the putsch on anyone but himself, blames Kapp for failing to make adequate preparations and flatly denies that he did not inform his partner: "During the critical time, I had conversations with him on February 23 and 28, on March 3, 4, and 8 and, obviously, on the eve of the undertaking, on March 10, 11 and 12 . . . In short, he could not have been surprised . . . and had a time period of 14 days to complete his preparations." (Lüttwitz, *Gegen den November-Revolution*, 119–120.) Schemann rather charitably comments on the "forgetfulness" of Lüttwitz and says that while Kapp did indeed talk to Lüttwitz on some of the days in question, Kapp had argued for postponement and certainly had no idea that Lüttwitz had already planned to seize the government (Schemann, *op. cit.*, 142–143). Schemann is supported here by August Winnig. See Winnig's *Heimkehr*, 3rd ed. (Hamburg, 1935), 288–302.

[47] See above, pp. 136 ff.

[48] The letter written on *Nationale Vereinigung* stationery and dated January 17, 1920, is reprinted in E. J. Gumbel, *Verschwörer: Beiträge zur Geschichte und Soziologie der deutschen Nationalistischen Geheimbünde seit 1918* (Vienna, 1924), 17.

But Berthold, his biographer tells us,[49] was too conscious of his own charismatic qualities to place himself under a lesser *Führer*. He went ahead with his own plans and was not informed of the putsch until the morning it took place. He then sulked but finally called his men together and told them that they might as well join the other marchers. The speech did nothing to inspire confidence in the undertaking:

He said that the present action would be a putsch to overthrow the present government but . . . that the putsch would fail, that the gentlemen in Berlin were acting eight days too early and that he did not know why because he no longer had any connection with them.[50]

This lack of preparation and coördination of the Free Corps must be considered an essential cause of the failure of the coup. Two or three more examples must suffice. The members of the Free Corps von Hindenburg had been more or less drunk during the entire period prior to the putsch. Lieutenant Schmidt, their ordnance officer, recalls:

We had celebrated the anniversary of our founding on March 10, 1920. The Field Marshal had visited us . . . Celebration followed celebration. They were so strenuous that officers and men had not gone to bed until early in the morning of March 13. The telephone suddenly interrupted my most beautiful dream: "Herr Leutnant, come to my office at once!" It was 4:00 A.M. . . . Yesterday for the first time, vague reports had reached us that there was to be a *coup d'état* in Berlin. We had no clear picture of what was going on.[51]

Ernst Röhm bitterly regrets the lack of preparation and illustrates the type of response the Berlin putsch had in Bavaria.

General von Lüttwitz . . . simply *assumed* that the Bavarian Reichswehr would automatically join in the movement. . . . Naturally we "rash" young officers jubilantly welcomed the liberation act in Ber-

[49] Gengler, *Kampfflieger Rudolf Berthold,* 188–190.

[50] Georg Seitz, "Die Eiserne Schar Berthold in Harburg," in *Freikorpskämpfer,* 353. The Nazis later adopted Berthold as one of the proto-Nazi fighters for the "national revival." They are fond of describing his exploits in the Baltic and his death at the hands of Harburg workers who were combating the Kapp putsch. After 1933, monuments were erected to his memory and the name of the school where he died was changed to the Berthold School. After their leader's death, many of his men joined Löwenfeld's Third Marine Brigade.

[51] Oberleutnant Schmidt, "Einsatz in Hannover," in *Freikorpskämpfer,* 376.

lin. My completely "rash" ordnance officer immediately unfurled the black-white-red flag on receiving the news from Berlin . . . But they [the Bavarians] left their comrades in Berlin in the lurch.[52]

Not even Rossbach, a personal friend of Ehrhardt, had been informed that the blow was about to fall until the actual night of the march on Berlin.[53] Indeed, Ehrhardt himself did not know what Kapp was planning to do! [54]

It is not necessary here to follow the narrative of the Kapp government in any detail. From the start, it showed its total incapacity for governing Germany. Kapp began his five-day rule by making the interesting promise, "We will not govern according to any theory." [55] He then proceeded to demonstrate that he had also neglected to make any practical arrangements for carrying on the government. All those details had been left to the bogus doctor and free-lance journalist, Schnitzler. But when the great day came, "Doctor Schnitzler" was nowhere to be found. The new rulers of Germany were, quite understandably, alarmed at the sight of their portly *Führer* running through the halls of the Chancellery and shouting anxiously, "Where is Schnitzler? Where is Schnitzler? I can not govern without Schnitzler!" [56]

Apart from the total inadequacy of its preparation and leadership, there are a number of other reasons for the failure of the counterrevolutionary *coup d'état* of March 1920. The overwhelming majority of the German people saw no need for another revolution and showed no inclination to exchange their as yet untried Republic for a dictatorship. And, as we have pointed out, the attempt lacked the support of vitally important sections of the Army leadership. But the most telling single cause for the

[52] Röhm, *Die Geschichte eines Hochverräters*, 7th ed. (Munich, 1934), 117. The adjutant of the Munich *Einwohnerwehr* reports that his men — an excellent potential support of a Rightist putsch — had absolutely no idea that a coup was being staged in Berlin. Rudolf Kanzler, *Bayerns Kampf gegen den Bolschwismus: Geschichte der bayerischen Einwohnerwehren* (Munich, 1931), 55.

[53] Arnoldt Bronnen, *Rossbach* (Berlin, 1930), 99 and 101.

[54] *Kapitän Ehrhardt*, 138.

[55] Kapp's proclamation of March 13, 1920, is given in *Deutsche Reichsgeschichte in Dokumenten 1849–1934: Urkunden und Aktenstücke zur innern und äusseren Politik des deutschen Reiches*, edited by Johannes Hohlfeld (Berlin, 1934), II, 793–794.

[56] Volkmann, *op. cit.*, 363, and von Oertzen, *op. cit.*, 366.

failure of the Kapp-Lüttwitz putsch was the concerted way in which the workers of Germany responded to the summons for a general strike which the Social Democrats had issued as they fled the capital in the early morning hours of March 13.[57]

Seldom in history has a general strike been so comprehensive, and never has one been so effective in blocking the functions of government. The strike spread its paralysis throughout the Reich, but it was particularly effective in Berlin. Chancellor Kapp stood by and watched helplessly as the heart of a great city seemed to hesitate and then cease to beat. There was no water, no lights, no gas, no municipal transportation, no garbage removal. And all the time hostility and anger mounted against the new government.[58]

[57] For a discussion of the responsibility for calling the general strike, see below, pp. 174–176. The frustrated and humiliated conspirators thought up a number of other reasons to explain their failure. General Lüttwitz, with total disregard for consistency, lists some of them: (1) The army leaders on whom he had relied, deserted him at the last moment. (2) He had intended to march on Berlin on the 12th, but Ehrhardt's negotiations with the generals postponed the entry until March 13 and thus lost the element of surprise and permitted the government to escape. (3) Kapp had failed to make adequate preparations. Finally the putschist complains that the government was itself at fault for not supporting his efforts to overthrow it! In an amazing passage, Lüttwitz writes: "By fleeing, the government had rejected our support. This was very unfortunate for it meant that we could not work with them directly. To me, it was immediately clear that as a result our undertaking would now be more difficult . . ." (*Im Kampf gegen die Revolution,* 121.) It hardly needs to be repeated that from the very beginning, Seeckt and other key military figures had told Lüttwitz that they would not support him; that Lüttwitz had not kept Kapp posted on his plans and had systematically refused to listen to his advice; and that there never existed the slightest chance of the government coöperating with him. As early as June 1919, Noske had told him flatly that the Majority Socialists would not support any dictatorship (Volkmann, *op. cit.,* 315–316, and Noske, *op. cit.,* 196). Indeed, in August, Lüttwitz himself had said that any thought of coöperation was "absurd" (*Im Kampf,* 98). In addition to blaming Lüttwitz, Maercker, and Ehrhardt, Kapp found still another reason for his defeat. He had counted on the support of the bureaucracy but they turned traitor and deserted him. His biographer writes: ". . . the same men [the bureaucrats] who took their oath to the Emperor as lightly as a feather after November 9, 1918, now regarded their oath to the Usurpers and their constitution as heavy as a hundred-weight." (Schemann, *Wolfgang Kapp,* 154.)

[58] See Cros, "Le Coup d'État de Kapp," *Les Archives de la Grande Guerre,* November 1921, 570 ff.

If Kapp lacked ideas and the ability to handle the impasse, the Freebooters had an easy solution: "Everything would still have been all right," says Lieutenant Mann, "if we had just shot more people." [59] Lieutenant Heinz agreed. "Blood is the cement of Revolution. Whoever shrinks from letting it flow . . . is no revolutionary, he is only a *Bürger* gone mad." [60] But the Freebooters would have to wait for several years before they had a chance to put their type of revolution into practice. To the disgust of the Volunteers, Kapp and Lüttwitz ordered that there should be no general shooting of the civilian population.[61] The strike continued.

As one after another of their erstwhile supporters deserted them, the conspirators met in an all-night session the night of March 16, They could think of no constructive program, so they engaged in angry self-justification and mutual incrimination. Since Lüttwitz was not there to defend himself, his comrades therefore unanimously agreed that the failure was all his fault. Bauer, "crying like a child," and supported by Ehrhardt, demanded that Lüttwitz be replaced with Ludendorff, but the wily Ludendorff refused the honor. Bauer was then dispatched to give the command to Seeckt, but the Sphinx saw through the chronic little conspirator and coldly declined his offer.[62]

On the morning of March 17, it was reported to Kapp that even the Berlin Security Police had lost all confidence in him and had asked for his resignation. Kapp capitulated and left the Chancellery at noon. Lüttwitz resigned soon after. That night, Schnitzler, Bauer, Stephani, Ludendorff, and Pabst put on civilian clothes, changed their names (Ludendorff became "Herr Lange"), and

[59] *Mit Ehrhardt durch Deutschland*, 189.

[60] Friedrich Wilhelm Heinz, *Die Nation greift an: Geschichte und Kritik des soldatischen Nationalismus* (Berlin, 1932), 91.

[61] General von der Goltz — a man who had had considerable experience with putschs and in dealing with recalcitrant civilian populations — was perfectly willing to handle the situation in a way that would have satisfied the Volunteers. He had been appointed commander of the defense area of Berlin by the Kapp government. As soon as the strike broke out, he issued orders that all strike leaders be shot immediately. But Lüttwitz rescinded the order. (Benoist-Méchin, *Historie de L'Armée Allemande*, II, 102–103.)

[62] The conference is described in the article "Les Dessous de la Politique Réactionaire," *L'Europe Nouvelle*, April 9, 1921, 475–477.

fled to Munich. They dissolved the National Union Society but not their hopes of overthrowing the government.

The punishment given to participants in the Kapp-Lüttwitz putsch underscores the validity of Franz Neumann's thesis that an essential reason for the failure of the Republic lay in the refusal of its courts to punish anti-Republican nationalists.[63] We shall have occasion to comment on the vagaries of Republican justice when we discuss the notorious Feme murder trials of the middle twenties, but the point is also illustrated here. Some fifteen months after the actual putsch (May 21, 1921), the Reich Minister of Justice announced officially that a total of 705 men charged with high treason against the state had been examined. Of them, 412 were amnestied in accordance with the law of August 4, 1920 — despite the fact that that law specifically denied amnesty to putschists; 108 cases were dismissed due to death or "other reasons"; 11 cases had not yet been reviewed.[64] Of the leaders of the putsch, only one, the former Police President of Berlin, von Jagow, was ever actually sentenced. He received five years honorary confinement. When the Prussian state withdrew his pension, the federal court reviewed the case and ordered the pension restored. Kapp and Lüttwitz were acquitted of all charges and the rest of the defendants either fled the country or were simply not brought to trial.[65] Jagow's five-year sentence represents the sum total of years served by all the participants in the putsch.

A comparison of the five-year figure with the total number of years given to the adherents of the Bavarian Soviet Government of 1919, is a dramatic illustration of the vastly different way in which the Republic dispensed justice to its Leftist opponents. The Bavarian Leftists were sentenced to a total of 615 years and 2 months in prison.[66]

On the afternoon of March 17, the Ehrhardt Brigade had been

[63] Neumann, *Behemoth: The Structure and Practice of National Socialism* (New York, 1942), 20 ff.

[64] *Ibid.*, 22.

[65] Major Pabst went to Austria and was naturalized under the name of Peters. He became the leader of the Tyrolean *Heimatbund* and the Austrian *Heimwehr*. Colonel Bauer spent some time in Hungary before returning to Germany. (See Gumbel, *Verschwörer*, 33.)

[66] Professor Gumbel lists the sentences of each *coup d'état* government in parallel columns in his *Verschwörer*, 99–107.

ordered to leave Berlin. A crowd of citizens lined the Unter den Linden and watched the retreat in hostile silence. The Free-booters were in an ugly mood. From the shadow of their helmets, eyes flashed hatred at the civilians who had thwarted them. This time there was no band music and no singing. The oppressive silence was broken only by the jarring thud of marching boots. Suddenly the tension was snapped by the laughter of a small boy. Two Freebooters broke ranks, knocked the towhead down, beat him with the butts of their rifles, and kicked his curled-up little body until it lay quite still. The crowd made no move to inter-fere, but someone did have the courage to hiss. An officer barked a command — the only word intelligible to a British witness was the word *rücksichtslos* — and machine guns opened fire on the crowd. Then the Brigade formed ranks and marched in impec-cable order through the Brandenburger Tor.[67]

V. FREE CORPS REACTION TO THE PUTSCH

Shortly after the putsch, one of the British officers attached to the staff of the Inter-Allied Military Commission of Control asked Ehrhardt why his men had marched on Berlin. The astonished Freebooter captain replied, "Why? Because I told them to! Wasn't that enough?"[68]

It was almost that simple. Here, as elsewhere, the men of the Free Corps acted instinctively and angrily. There was some justification for their belief that they had been betrayed by the Republic. Recruitment officers had given them formal guarantees that their formations would not be dissolved.[69] Noske himself, in order to counteract the anti-Republican agitation being dissemi-nated by the *Nationale Vereinigung,* had assured the Volunteers, both verbally and in the pages of the *Vorwärts,* that he would not desert his troops. One of the Volunteers comments:

[67] Brigadier General John H. Morgan, a member of the Inter-Allied Mili-tary Commission of Control, was present at the scene. See his *Assize of Arms: The Disarmament of Germany and Her Rearmament, 1919–1939* (New York, 1946), 92. Compare Mann, *Mit Ehrhardt durch Deutschland,* 196–201.

[68] General John H. Morgan, "The Disarmament of Germany and After," *Quarterly Review,* CCXLII (October 1924), 425.

[69] Leo Wulfsohn, "The Enforced Demobilization of the German Army," in *The New Europe,* XII (August 21, 1919), 133.

Now this minister. This Noske. We had gone through thick and thin with him . . . and he had looked us in the eye at the parade in Wünsdorf and had said, "You are my most loyal men. You came to my help in the darkest hour. You have brought order back to our dear Fatherland . . . I will never forget. I will take care of you." But now he wanted to dissolve us and send us out into the streets.[70]

The Freebooters marched at the side of the counterrevolution not because they believed in the philosophy of political reaction but simply because the reactionaries provided them with the opportunity to smash the Republic. Theirs was a simple logic:

The soldiers unloaded their complaints in their "bull sessions." . . . This government won't do anything for us. O.K. then, we would be better off with a different one. Yes. We will get another one . . . It will not have any assemblies and it will not pass any resolutions and if that doesn't help we will let the guns do the talking.[71]

That is a representative statement of Freebooter sentiment and it shows the extent of their thinking on political matters. The conclusion reached by their best historian is not expressed in academic language, but it is, nonetheless, a valid conclusion. "These men," says von Oertzen, "knew damned little about complicated [political] matters . . . they were soldiers and comrades and wanted to be nothing more." [72]

Thus any questions as to their specific political objectives in March 1920 must be answered negatively. Did they want the return of Imperial Germany? "Nobody ever spoke of the Kaiser," says one of the marchers, "No, Nobody." [73] Another recalls a revealing incident of the occupation of Berlin. An old Berliner came up to one of Ehrhardt's street patrols and asked with shining eyes if the soldiers were going to bring back his beloved Kaiser. A confused Freebooter stammered, "N-no, no. Not that, not that . . ." What was the sense of it all then? The question embarrassed the *Freikorpskämpfer*. He repeated it to himself and decided: "The sense? The sense? There is sense only in danger. Marching into uncertainty is sense enough for us, because it answers the demands of our blood." [74]

[70] Mann, *Mit Ehrhardt durch Deutschland*, 134.
[71] *Ibid.*, 136–137.
[72] Von Oertzen, *Die deutschen Freikorps*, 362.
[73] Mann, *op. cit.*, 143.
[74] Von Salomon, *Die Geächteten*, 162–163.

Nor did they want a military dictatorship under General Freiherr von Lüttwitz. A social and psychological chasm separated
the Generation of the Uprooted and Disinherited from this Prussian baron. Besides, Lüttwitz was "too complicated" — that is,
he meddled too much in politics. They liked Captain Ehrhardt
much better; not only because he was one of them, but because he
was as ignorant of politics as they were. He, too, was a "primitive
man." [75] One of his admirers explains the secret of his success:

In the Primitiveness (*Primitivität*) and simplicity of his attitude,
he did not encumber himself with any sort of political or philosophical
convictions. On the contrary, the reason for his success undoubtedly
lay in the fact that his stoic soldierly instinct showed him what was
necessary; hence, at the same time, what was right.[76]

They certainly had no interest in a conservative government
under Wolfgang Kapp. "We had never heard of the name Kapp
before. But that did not make any difference. Our soldierly *Führer*
were fighting fools (*knarsche Kerle*) who knew what they wanted.
We had absolute confidence in them." [77]

But did the "fighting fools" who led the putschist army really
know what they wanted? As they marched in the early morning
hours of March 13, men of the Hindenburg Free Corps asked
their leader if they were going to fight for Kapp or against Kapp.
Their leader told them that he was not sure.[78]

The Freebooters were not depressed after the failure of the
putsch. They were fond of writing doggerel verse and singing it

[75] Although Ehrhardt's memoirs are shot through with monarchist sympathies (he married into the Hohenzollern family), he makes no clear
statement of his political thinking. In fact, he displays an almost complete
lack of interest in the political aspects of the putsch. He supported Kapp
although Kapp gave him absolutely no indication of what his plans were
(p. 138); and notes that while "penetrating conversations" were held
among the chief conspirators, "I myself did not take part in these discussions." The reason why he did not participate in them is given in the
familiar refrain: "I was a soldier and wanted only to remain a soldier."
(*Kapitän Ehrhardt*, 171.)

[76] "Junius Alter," *Nationalisten*, 80. Salomon's only comment on Lüttwitz
is: "He, too, is an old General. I salute Ehrhardt and nobody else." (*Die
Geächteten*, 159.)

[77] Manfred von Killinger, *Das waren Kerle!* (Munich, 1944), 96. Similar
statements are repeated in virtually all the memoirs.

[78] Oberleutnant Schmidt, "Einsatz in Hannover," in *Freikorpskämpfer*, 376.

to the tune of old battle songs. The one they composed after they arrived in their barracks at Camp Döberitz is highly indicative of their attitude:

> Why should we cry when a putsch goes wrong?
> There's another one coming before very long.
> So say good by — but remember, men,
> In a couple of weeks we will try it again! [79]

They had to wait longer than two weeks, however, because, as we shall see in the next chapter, the government they had just overthrown hired them back to defend it from the Communists!

Although they laughed off the failure of the Kapp-Lüttwitz putsch, the thinking of the Volunteers was seriously affected by it. The men had always distrusted "civilian governments," but after they had seen the ludicrous, fainthearted attempts of Wolfgang Kapp and his fellow politicians to lead the national revival, they made up their minds. Politicians of the traditional type had forfeited forever their chance to govern Germany because they had shown that they lacked what the Freebooters considered the one primary essential of the new government: ruthless action. "The Kapp government shrank from putting even a half dozen generals, under secretaries of state, and parliamentarians to the wall," one of them writes disgustedly, "Instead . . . it occupied a few rooms and held fruitless discussions. Blood is the cement of revolution . . ." [80]

When the real German revival came, it would not be led by the timid politicians. It would be ruthless and it would be led by military men with the spirit of the front soldiers. But it would be led by the captains and the lieutenants and not by the generals. For Ernst Röhm, Friedrich Heinz, Ernst von Salomon, Rudolf Mann, Peter von Heydebrech, Albert Leo Schlageter, Friedrich Glombowski, and — it can be assumed — hundreds of their less articulate comrades had now decided that the generals too had proven unequal to the task. One of these junior officers looked back at the Kapp-Lüttwitz putsch and wrote bitterly:

[79] Quoted in Gerhard Günther, *Deutsches Kriegertum im Wandel der Geschichte* (Hamburg, 1934), 202. A slightly different version may be found in Killinger, *Das waren Kerle!*, 64.

[80] Heinz, *Die Nation grieft an*, 91.

What did the generals do? They just tried to preserve the spirit of the old officers. It is their fault [that we failed] . . . The hearts of these soldiers-playing-politics were not made hard enough by the war. They had seen war all right, but they had not felt it to the core.

They were afraid: afraid of losing their skins; afraid of losing their bread and butter [i.e., afraid that the junior officers would come to power with Kapp]. I can still hear them: "No shooting! I forbid any show of force!" But things would have been a lot better if there had been some shooting . . .

Conceited. Cautious. And, again, cautious. These are hard words, but they were often repeated by the boys who went to Ehrhardt's school. I can give no other report [of their attitude]. It is the truth.[81]

The political education of those who attended Ehrhardt's school was progressing. The counterrevolutionary coup of March 1920 had taught them one important lesson, albeit a negative one: old-line conservatism would not lead them to the new Germany. They did not know what would; nor, apart from the obvious fact that it would have to be congenial to the "primitive Freebooter spirit," did they yet know what the government of the new Germany would be like. But they had begun to think about it and they were open to suggestions. The *Freikorpskämpfer* had not yet become "political soldiers" in the fullest sense of that Nazi phrase, but they were moving in that direction.

Writing well before Hitler came to power — and hence before the time when it was expedient for a writer to read back National Socialism into Free Corps thinking — the Volunteers' most reliable spokesman was impressed by the fact that after the Kapp putsch, his comrades began to think about politics. "Its collapse," he writes, "meant that for the first time the road was now completely open to the young men's own political thinking. The second bid for power in November, 1923 [Hitler's Beer Hall Putsch], is not conceivable without this development in their political thinking." [82]

[81] Mann, *Mit Ehrhardt durch Deutschland*, 188–189. For other examples of the same attitude, see Röhm, *Geschichte eines Hochverräters*, 117; Heinz, *Die Nation greift an*, 83, 90–91, and *passim;* Glombowski, *Organisation Heinz (O.H.): das Schicksal der Kameraden Schlageters* (Berlin, 1934), *passim;* and Peter Heydebreck, *Wir Wehrwölfe, Erinnerungen eines Freikorpsführers* (Leipzig, 1931), *passim.*

[82] Ernst von Salomon, "Der verlorene Haufe," in *Krieg und Krieger,* edited by Ernst Jünger (Berlin, 1930), 115.

VII

IN THE SERVICE OF THE REPUBLIC:
THE KAPP AFTERMATH

> We might have known what would happen: once more we would
> have to haul the chestnuts out of the fire . . . for the government
> that had abandoned us.
> — Manfred von Killinger

I. THE EBERT-SEECKT CONVERSATIONS

A decision of crucial importance to the future of the Weimar
Republic was made in 1920 by the Ebert government. Ever since
its founding, the Republic had been seriously handicapped by its
dependence on the Army leadership and the Free Corps system.
The Kapp-Lüttwitz Putsch and von Seeckt's refusal to defend the
legal government gave final and dramatic proof of the unreliabil-
ity of that support; and the total collapse of the putsch gave the
Ebert government its first real opportunity to rid itself of so faithless and dangerous an ally.

A wave of antimilitarist feeling swept the country during those
March days. The broad masses of the German people were thoroughly fed up with "the group of irresponsible tyrants" who had
"tried to stab the homeland in the back" [1] by imposing a military
dictatorship on Germany. The Ebert government might well have
profited by this sentiment, started afresh, and created a truly

[1] This quotation from the *Berliner Tageblatt* of March 24, 1920, is indicative of an important shift in attitude on the part of the moderate press.
Until the putsch — indeed on the morning of the putsch — the *Tageblatt*
had supported the Free Corps against their Leftist critics and described
von Lüttwitz as "the man who has saved Germany from chaos." (March
13, 1920, morning edition.) The Leftist press was, of course, more violently
antimilitarist than ever.

republican military force upon which it could rely in the uncertain and difficult years which lay ahead. The editor of *Vorwärts* urged the government to do so,[2] but his advice went unheeded. Instead, the Ebert government actually hired back the very formations which had so recently overthrown it. This amazing development needs to be looked at rather closely.

It will be recalled that the last act performed by the fleeing members of the government was to call forth a general strike. Thus, in its extremity, the government authorized the use of the chief weapon of the extreme Left — the weapon that had been a constant threat to the existence of the Ebert government and from fear of which the Free Corps had originally been organized. Except for the names which appeared at the bottom, the incendiary proclamation of March 13, 1920, was not very different from those previously issued by the Communists:

WORKERS! PARTY COMRADES!

The military putsch is here. The Baltic Freebooters who were afraid that they would be dissolved have made an attempt to overthrow the Republic and establish a dictatorial government with Lüttwitz and Kapp at its head.

WORKERS, COMRADES!

We did not make a revolution only to have it overthrown by a bloody Freebooter regiment. We will not negotiate with the Baltic criminals.

Workers, Comrades!

The work of an entire year will fall into ruins. Your freedom, bought at such a heavy price, will be destroyed. This goes for everybody. Therefore the most drastic counter measures are required. No factory dare operate as long as the military dictatorship of Ludendorffe [*sic*, a reminder of the war years] prevails.

---

[2] See Richard Bernstein's intelligent and moderate account, *Der Kapp-Putsch und seine Lehren*, Revolutions-Bibliothek Nr. 10 (Berlin, 1920), 11–12. A contemporary Communist pamphlet admits that the government had a good chance of winning Leftist support if it had acted against the militarists. (M. J. Braun, *Die Lehren des Kapp Putsches*, "Internationale" Flugschrift Nr. 23, Leipzig, 1920,. 85.) The same position is taken by such Leftist writers as Georg Bernhard, *Die deutsche Tragödie: Der Selbstmord einer Republik* (Prague, 1933), 140–141; and Rosenberg, *Geschichte der deutschen Republik*, 88–89, 112. See also Fischer, *Stalin and German Communism*, 127–134.

THEREFORE QUIT WORK! STRIKE!

Throttle the reactionary clique! Fight with every means for the maintenance of the Republic. Lay aside all petty discord. There is only one way to prevent the return of William II:

> Paralyze all economic activity!
> No hand dare move!
> No proletarian dare help the military dictatorship!
> General strike all down the line!

PROLETARIANS UNITE! DOWN WITH
THE COUNTER-REVOLUTION!

(The Social Democratic Members of the Government: Ebert, Bauer, Noske, Schlicke, Schmidt, David, Müller. The party leadership of the Social Democratic Party, Otto Wels.[3]

The ensuing strike was far more successful than the government leaders had bargained for. Throughout the country — and especially in the Ruhr — the Communists took full advantage of the unexpected windfall. They systematically fomented unrest and made hurried plans for seizing the government. Alarmed by this turn of events, the Ebert government called off the strike on March 16, and its spokesman denied that it had had anything to do with the whole affair.[4] But it was too late. The Communists pressed their advantage; unrest and disorder continued.

President Ebert could think of only one way out of his distress. Once again, as on the night of November 9, 1918, he picked up his telephone and put through a call for help to the Army. This time the call went to General von Seeckt. The man who five days previously had flatly and defiantly refused to protect the Republic, was now made Commander in Chief of its military forces (*Militäroberbefehlshaber*). He immediately ordered all Free Corps commanders to reënter the service of the government. Thus it came about that exactly those "Baltic criminals and Freebooters" who had just overthrown the Republic were now called upon to defend it. By this time, the Free Corps had become accustomed

[3] Reprinted in Hans Spethmann, *Zwölf Jahre Ruhrbergbau, 1914 bis 1925: Aus seiner Geschichte von Kriegsanfang bis zum Französenabmarsch* (Berlin, 1928), II, 77–78. The proclamation was made too early to reach the Berlin newspapers. It was spread throughout the country by telephone.

[4] See below, page 174, note 18.

to the routine. "Their officers and men smiled ironically and a little disgustedly; for once again, though hated and despised, they were still needed." [5]

The Freebooters really did not mind their new assignment. They liked to fight and the Ebert government gave them that opportunity. When Ehrhardt told his men that the whole putsch had failed — due to the "cowardly *Bürgertum*" — and that they must now fight for the government against the Communists, he was greeted by three rousing cheers.[6] "We were in a black mood, an excited and irritable condition," one of them recalls, "and we needed to turn open a valve . . . and let off a lot of steam. Here was an enemy that suited our needs." [7]

The Weimar Republic cannot be accused of mistreating its enemies — at least not those in the Rightist camp. The Kapp government had promised the three thousand soldiers of the Ehrhardt Brigade a bonus of sixteen thousand gold marks if they succeeded in overthrowing Ebert. The Ebert government kept the promises of its predecessor. It paid the bonus. It also granted amnesty to all those who had participated in the putsch. Ehrhardt, like all *Freikorpsführer,* wanted to keep his men together so that they might one day succeed in overthrowing the government. Here too the government came to his assistance. It passed another decree which charged any Freebooter with desertion if he left the Ehrhardt Brigade without permission.[8] The men of the Brigade were satisfied with these arrangements:

We went there [Camp Döberitz] at the orders of the government . . . It was not bad at all: The Kapp pay of 7 marks per man per day . . . was agreed to [by the government] and the Reichsbank willingly furnished us with whatever money was necessary. The soldiers were happy and said that everything would still turn out for the best . . . The government showed us the best of good will and even strengthened us. The 3rd Courland Infantry Regiment . . . entered our Brigade as

[5] Von Oertzen, *Die deutschen Freikorps,* 384.

[6] Schultze-Pfaelzer, *Von Spa nach Weimar,* 339.

[7] Mann, *Mit Ehrhardt durch Deutschland,* 207.

[8] See Professor E. J. Gumbel's bitter article, "Le Capitaine Ehrhardt et L'Organisation C," in *L'Europe Nouvelle,* VI (August 25, 1923), p. 1078. His facts are verified by the memoirists and by Schultze-Pfaelzer, *op. cit.,* 341–342.

a unit . . . so the official number in our Brigade was increased to its highest point: 5,000 men.[9]

Ehrhardt's men were first used to crush the Berlin Communists, but they went about their work with such brutality that von Seeckt transferred them to the area around Münster.[10] The Iron Division was probably the most hated Free Corps in Germany. But now its men were hired to fight for the government in the Berlin suburb of Henningsdorf. Their commander comments wryly: "The Berlin press celebrated 'the great victory of the Reichswehr'; of course the general public never learned that it was the outlawed *Baltikumers* who fought that day." [11] Similarly throughout the Reich,[12] the Volunteers were used to put down the Communist rebellions which the government-endorsed strike had precipitated. The most important action of the "government troops," however, took place in the Ruhr. This was to be the last officially authorized intervention of the Free Corps in the postwar period.

II. THE RUHR INTERVENTION

For months the Ruhr Communists had made plans for seizing power if ever the opportunity presented itself. Detailed plans for the organization of a Red Army were drawn up in May 1919,[13] and in December of that year Party headquarters in Düsseldorf issued instructions to local leaders and outlined the tasks they were to perform in the event that a nationwide general strike were called: ". . . hostages will be taken immediately . . . Public buildings such as banks, postoffices, railway stations will be seized . . . railways will be blown up . . . A Republic of Soviets will be proclaimed at once . . ." [14]

[9] Mann, *op. cit.*, 206–207. See also Ehrhardt, *op. cit.*, 182–192.

[10] Here, in May 1920, the Ehrhardt Brigade was theoretically dissolved. We shall follow their subsequent career in a later chapter.

[11] Bischoff, *Die letzte Front*, 246.

[12] For a general account of these interventions, see von Oertzen and von Schmidt-Pauli. Personal reminiscences of the "battles" may be found in *Das Buch vom deutschen Freikorpskämpfer.*

[13] The Secret memorandum entitled "Organization of the Red Army" is reprinted in Spethmann, *Zwölf Jahre Ruhrbergau*, II, Appendix I, 330–331.

[14] Reprinted in Hans Spethmann, *Die Rote Armee an Ruhr und Rhein: Aus den Kapptagen, 1920* (Berlin, 1930), 11. For other preparations see Paul

Now, on March 13, 1920, the same day and virtually the same hour that the strike was announced by the fleeing government, the Communists called out their followers in the Ruhr:

WORKERS! COMRADES!

The Ebert-Noske regime has fallen. The bourgeoisie, on whom this government depended, have thrown their tool to the devil. The military camarilla that forced us into the war and then lost it so shamefully has come to power.

Workers! Comrades! Now is the time to act. Now is the time to seize power . . . We do not fight for the Ebert-Noske Government. Down with the betrayers of Socialism. Down with the tools of the bourgeoisie! On to the Dictatorship of the Proletariat!

Workers! Comrades! To arms!

Communist Party of Germany
(*Spartakusbund*)[15]

In calling the general strike, the Ebert government not only supplied the Communists with their long-awaited opportunity, but also supplied them with weapons to carry out their plans. For in its determination to defeat the militarists, the government actually opened its arsenals not only to loyal Social Democratic trade unions, but to the Communists as well.[16]

General von Watter, the commander of Defense District VI, had drawn up plans for a military campaign in the event that the Ruhr Communists staged a general strike. But he was embarrassed by the report that the government itself had authorized the strike. He therefore took no action until he heard from Defense Minister Noske. Noske called from Stuttgart on March 16 and assured the general that the government had neither promulgated nor approved the general strike. That afternoon General von Watter issued the following order to his troops:

Wentzcke, *Ruhrkampf: Einbruch und Abwehr im Rheinisch-Westfälischen Industriegebiet,* 2nd ed. (Berlin, 1930), I, 33 ff.

[15] A facsimile poster is reprinted in *Freikorpskämpfer,* 365. See also Spethmann, *Rote Armee,* 23–24.

[16] This fact is admitted by Social Democratic members of the government. See the memoirs of the Minister President of Prussia, Otto Braun, *Von Weimar zu Hitler* (New York, Europa Verlag, 1940), 95, and the memoirs of Reichskommisar for Westphalia, Carl Severing, *1919–1920 im Wetter und Watterwinkel* (Bielefeld, 1927), 145.

TO MY TROOPS!

. . . After National Defense Minister Noske definitely assured me
today (16. 3. 20) over the telephone that the old government did not
issue the fateful proclamation for the general strike, but on the contrary condemns it as much as we do and will do everything possible
to put it down, I have placed myself under the old government.[17]

The degree of responsibility shared by Noske and other government members in issuing the strike order of March 13 is open to
debate.[18] But there can be no doubt about the results. The strike

---

[17] The order of the day is quoted in Spethmann, *Zwölf Jahre Ruhrbergbau*,
II, 95.

[18] Strictly speaking — and only strictly speaking — Noske told General
von Watter the truth when he said that the government had not issued the
strike order. The proclamation was endorsed by Ebert, Bauer, Noske, and
the others as private members of the Social Democratic Party and not in their
capacity as government officials. But this pedantic argument does not absolve
the Ebert government from responsibility. The men whose names appeared
on the strike proclamation were not just private citizens. They were, respec-
tively, the President, the Chancellor, and the Defense Minister of Germany.
And their names attached to a public proclamation had the effect of giving
that proclamation official government approval. This was certainly the impression received by contemporaries. The Berlin correspondent of the *Times*,
for example, simply cabled: "The government has issued a proclamation calling upon the workers from all over Germany to defeat the revolutionists by
engaging in a general strike." (The London *Times*, March 15, 1920.) Statements made by some of the members of the government did nothing to con-
tradict this interpretation. On March 17, Chancellor Bauer sent the following
telegram to the Reichskommissar for Westphalia: "Traitors Kapp and Lüttwitz have capitulated. General strike can be called off . . ." (quoted in
Severing, *1919–1920 im Wetter und Watterwinkel*, 169). And in the National Assembly he spoke proudly of the "defensive measures" taken by the
government and their success in thwarting the militarists. (Speech of March
29, 1920, *Verhandlungen der verfassunggebenden deutschen Nationalversammlung*, Stenographische Berichte, 157 Sitzung, Vol. 332, pp. 4932–4933.)
Minister of the Interior Koch's speech is also worth quoting: "But, Ladies and
Gentlemen, I must declare most emphatically here that even a general strike
had become necessary. ('Very true!' by the Democrats.) Much has been said
about whether the national government proclaimed the general strike or
whether it did not. That is completely immaterial. (Call from the Rightist
deputies: 'No! It is a decisively important question!') . . . Mr. Düringer
(a representative of the Nationalist party) has said that the general strike
is an instrument of war. Certainly it is — but we are engaged in war which
was declared by the people of the Right and in such a war *any available
means must be used*. ('Very right!' by the members of the majority parties.)"
(Speech of March 30, *Verhandlungen*, 158 Sitzung, Vol. 332, pp. 4997–
4998.) In Dresden, however, members of the government told General

plunged western Germany into the most widespread revolt of
the postwar period.

Maercker a different story. "I was definitely informed," the general writes,
"that the names of the Socialist members of the national government had
been affixed to the general strike order without their approval." (General
Maercker, *Vom Kaiserheer zur Reichswehr*, 354.) According to this version
of the story, Otto Wels, the chairman of the Social Democratic Party, and
Ulrich Rauscher, the highly influential Ministerial Director of the Chancellery, had written the proclamation and had signed the names of the government leaders without their authorization. (Otto Braun, *Von Weimar zu
Hitler*, 94, and Richard Bernstein, *Der Kapp-Putsch und seine Lehren*, 9.)
Noske's position in the whole affair is not easy to evaluate. On two separate
occasions he had threatened to call just such a strike to defeat a militarist
putsch. On March 10, 1920, he told Lüttwitz, "if you use force, we shall pro-
claim a general strike." Quoted in H. G. Daniels, *The Rise of the German
Republic* (New York, 1928), 133. General Lüttwitz agrees with this state-
ment in his memoirs, *Im Kampf gegen die November-Revolution*, 113.)
Noske repeated the threat in the crucial cabinet meeting of March 13.
(Rabenau, *Seeckt: Aus seinem Leben*, II, 222, and Volkmann, *Revolution über
Deutschland*, 359.) In his memoirs published at the time of the general strike,
Noske is silent about the government's part in the proclamation. There is
absolutely no mention of it in his *Von Kiel bis Kapp*. In his autobiography
published posthumously, he repeats the story of the added names. He says
that Rauscher had drawn up a rough draft of the proclamation, had added
the names of government officials who might be counted upon to endorse
it, and had shown the document to Noske. Noske then makes this important
statement: "An approval of the draft did not take place in my presence."
(Gustav Noske, *Erlebtes aus Aufstieg und Niedergang einer Demokratie*,
(Offenbach-Main, 1947, 160.) Noske's denial of all responsibility to both
General Maercker and again to General von Watter is quite understandable.
The strike had gotten out of hand and Noske needed Free Corps assistance
to cope with the situation. To get it, it was necessary to deny that he had
anything whatever to do with the strike. If Noske did not approve of the
strike, why did he not tell Rauscher so at the time that Rauscher showed him
the copy of the proposed proclamation? He did not do so. Instead, he gave,
in effect, his tacit approval of the project by refusing to take any definite
stand. If his name were added to the actual proclamation against his wishes,
why did he wait until March 16 before protesting his innocence? And why
did he not expose the fraud in his memoirs written at the time of the general
strike? The answer would seem to be that he was perfectly willing to endorse
the strike as long as it was directed against the Kapp government, but as soon
as it got out of hand and threatened his own government as well, he denied
responsibility. It is conceivable that the story of the forged signatures may
have been invented by Noske in Dresden after he saw that the general strike
had reached dangerous proportions and when he saw that he needed Free
Corps help to combat it. Recent secondary accounts confuse the issue of responsibility by implying that neither the government nor its members had
anything to do with the strike. Thus Mr. Scheele says simply that the working
class itself called out the strike. (Godfrey Scheele, *The Weimar Republic*,

On the night of March 14, the "Red Army of the Ruhr," now some 50,000 strong[19] — and including in its ranks many former *Freikorpskämpfer*[20] — began its offensive against the still disorganized Free Corps. At Wetter-on-Ruhr, the Hasenclever battery of the Lichtschlag Corps was attacked and decimated in a much-remembered massacre.[21] In the days that followed, one after another of the industrial cities of the Ruhr fell to the Red Army. Remscheid, Dortmund, and Hagen were occupied on March 18; Düsseldorf and Essen on the 19th. The Essen watertower was the scene of a gallant defense made by the Weissenstein Volunteers. Forty of the men were killed and their leader shot with the white flag of surrender in his hand. The National Social-

---

Overture to the Third Reich, London, 1945, 84.) Miss Fischer says that the strike was called by the German Federation of Labor. (*Stalin and German Communism,* 123.) It is true that the support given the strike by the Federation was of decisive importance to its success and that the Federation's Carl Legien was the chief organizer of the resistance. But the initiative for first calling the strike was taken by members of the government.

[19] Free Corps historians follow their usual practice and exaggerate the strength of an enemy in order to emphasize the brilliance of a Volunteer victory. Thus von Oertzen sets the figure at 80,000 men. (*Deutsche Freikorps,* 404.) Reichswehr officials at the time estimated that there were about 100,000 men in the Red Army. A representative of the Allied Military Commission of Control suggests a reason for this figure. The army leaders wanted to impress the Allies with the extent of the "Red Peril" and thus secure surplus armament from the Commision. (General John H. Morgan, *Assize of Arms,* 439.) Nationalist accounts such as Spethmann's *Rote Armee an Ruhr und Rhein* also grossly exaggerate the power and the threat of the Red Army. It is nonetheless true, however, that it was a force of considerable size and armament. Carl Severing speaks of "50,000 workers well armed and standing ready." (*1919–1920 im Wetter und Watterwinkel,* 173.) A communist pamphlet of the period agrees with this figure. (M. J. Braun, *Die Lehren des Kapp Putsches,* Leipzig, 1920, Appendix I.)

[20] This is admitted by Schmidt-Pauli: "Embittered and despondent over the state of affairs and having nothing else to do . . . men from the ranks of the Free Corps, especially the *Baltikumer,* took up common cause with the insurgents. The Freebooter temperament does not make the worst soldiers." (*Geschichte der Freikorps,* 250.)

[21] Here again in the Ruhr, as in all their activity, each separate skirmish in which the Volunteers participated is discussed with the greatest detail by Free Corps historians and participants. For the massacre of the Hasenclever battery see, in addition to von Schmidt-Pauli and von Oertzen, the accounts given by the adjutant of the Lichtschlag Free Corps, Heinrich Mahnken, "Freikorps im Westen, 1918–1920" in *Deutscher Aufstand,* edited by Curt Hotzel, and the same writer's "Der Kampf der Batterie Hasenclever," in *Deutsche Soldaten,* edited by Hans Roden.

ists later converted the watertower into a Nazi shrine and preserved the non-Aryan name of Weissenstein as a symbol of the spirit of the proto-Nazi *Freikorpskämpfer*.[22]

By March 20 the Reds dominated the entire area east of Düsseldorf and Muhlheim, and the leader of the Dortmund Communists could write: "The Ruhr is in the hands of the proletariat. . . . When one reads in the history of the world about the revolutionary struggle of the proletariat, . . . the victory of the Ruhr will stand next to the Russian triumph." [23] The remarkable ease and rapidity of their victories[24] prompted the Ruhr Communists to expand their aspirations. Thus, on March 20, the *Ruhr Echo* set a new goal for the victorious Red Army: "There can be only one salvation for the German people. The red flag must wave victoriously over the whole of Germany. Germany must become a Republic of Soviets and, in union with Russia, the springboard for the coming victory of the World Revolution and World Socialism." [25]

III. THE SEVERING NEGOTIATIONS

This and other declarations of the Communist press thoroughly alarmed the Ebert government. Karl Severing, since 1919 the Reichskommissar for Westphalia, was charged with the difficult task of bringing peace to western Germany, and he tried to do so by negotiating peace treaties between the Free Corps and the Red Army. The single fact that the government found it necessary to

[22] For this, and other pictures, see *Das Buch vom deutschen Freikorpskämpfer*, 397 and *passim*.

[23] Quoted in Spethmann, *Die Rote Armee an Ruhr und Rhein*, 84.

[24] The whole question of the "Red Army of the Ruhr" needs further examination. General Morgan draws on the reports made by an Allied intelligence agent, one Graff, to show that a Red Army of the type suggested by Spethmann and other German nationalist writers simply did not exist. Morgan further maintains that the German Army deliberately fomented the Communist unrest in the Ruhr through the use of *agents provocateurs*, and that the "Red Army" was able to occupy the Ruhr cities with such surprising speed because the German Army leaders ordered all Free Corps units stationed in them to withdraw. The whole episode is thus, for Morgan, a gigantic hoax perpetrated by the German Army in an attempt to impress the Allies with the "Communist Peril" and thus to force them to slacken the arms clauses of the Versailles Treaty. (Morgan, *Assize of Arms*, 184–192.)

[25] Quoted in Spethmann, *Zwölf Jahre Ruhrbergbau*, II, 133–134.

negotiate with the Free Corps is eloquent testimony of the lack
of the government's control over those Freebooter forces which
were theoretically under its command. On March 24, 1920, Severing negotiated the Bielefeld Agreement. It was a compromise
which called for the cessation of Communist activities, the dissolution of certain Free Corps formations, and the surrender of all
arms by both contestants within ten days.[26] The ten-day truce
period resulted only in an armament race in which both sides participated. The Red Army utilized the armistice to requisition supplies, increase its membership, and deploy its troops to points of
better strategic advantage.[27] Meanwhile, thousands of Volunteers
were pouring into the Ruhr from all parts of the Reich in open
defiance of the peace agreement.[28]

Severing's first effort to reach agreement by arbitration failed.
He tried again and the so-called Peace of Münster was signed. Its
terms simply repeated those of Bielefeld and extended the truce
period to noon of April 2. It also produced the same result: both
sides used the armistice to increase and consolidate their forces.
Finally on the morning of April 3, Severing permitted his deputy
to issue the order which allowed the Free Corps to attack the
Communists.

Severing's mission had failed for a very good reason. He had
tried to arbitrate between the Free Corps and the Red Army, but

[26] The full text of the accord together with the names of those who signed
it is given in Severing's memoirs, *1919–1920 im Wetter und Watterwinkel,*
178–180.

[27] The National Socialist writers are corroborated here by the leading authority on the period. Spethmann reprints a series of Red Army orders which
are flagrant violations of the terms of the Bielefeld Agreement. (*Zwölf Jahre
Ruhrbergbau,* II, 169–176.)

[28] This fact is admitted by virtually all participants. See, as examples, the
testimony of Georg Gilardone, "36 Soldatenjahre," in *Franz Ritter von Epp,
Ein Leben für Deutschland,* edited by J. H. Krumbach (Munich, 1939), 71;
and Vice-Admiral von Loewenfeld, "Das Freikorps von Loewenfeld," in
Deutsche Soldaten, 155–156. Von Oertzen, with habitual disregard for consistency, accuses the Reds of first violating the peace terms (p. 410), then
gives a long list of the Free Corps who had arrived in the Ruhr during the
truce period and comments, "Free Corps who, according to the meaning and
contents of the Bielefeld and Münster agreements, should have been immediately disbanded and whose intervention on behalf of the Berlin government
. . . was certainly grotesque." (*Deutsche Freikorps,* 416.)

neither of the contestants felt bound by his arbitration because neither had been invited to participate in the negotiations, and an examination of the twenty names affixed to the Bielefeld Agreement shows that no representative of either of the enemies had signed it. Four of the signers were Independent Socialists; three were Majority Socialists; two represented the Center; four spoke for industrial groups; two were city mayors; two were government officials; one was a Democrat; and two were Communists. The two Communists who signed the agreement (Fritz Charpentier and O. Triebel) did not represent the Red Army. Indeed they were not even from the Ruhr area.[29]

Severing distorts the facts when he says that representatives from the Volunteer army participated in the negotiations and implies that they were in general agreement with the terms of the Bielefeld settlement.[30] It is difficult to believe that the Volunteers would have agreed to any proposal which sought to negotiate with an enemy; it is impossible to believe that they agreed to this particular proposal which demanded the dissolution of Free Corps formations. It is true that two Volunteer officers put in a brief appearance at the afternoon session of March 21; but they had come because General von Watter had ordered them to, and not because Severing had invited them. They did not participate in the negotiations, they did not sign the agreement, and they had absolutely no intention of abiding by its terms.[31]

Carl Severing was neither a traitor nor a Bolshevist, as National Socialist writers have maintained. He was a sincere patriot who tried to arbitrate a situation which required the use of force. His greatest mistake, however, was to insist on postponing a decision which he realized was inevitable. He knew, almost from the start, that ultimately the Free Corps would have to be called into the Ruhr to fight the Communists, but he shrank from making that

[29] Severing gives the party affiliations in another connection. (Severing, op. cit., 177.)

[30] Severing, op. cit., 177.

[31] Spethmann, *Zwölf Jahre*, II, 150; von Schmidt-Pauli, *Geschichte der Freikorps*, 260, and von Oertzen, op. cit., 410. For a Freebooter's attitude to the negotiations, see Ernst von Salomon's account, *Nahe Geschichte, Ein Ueberblick* (Berlin, 1936), 88.

decision.[32] His one desire was to avoid further bloodshed. Yet his policy of procrastination could have only one result: by giving each side time to strengthen its forces, it only served to increase the cost in lives of the final battle.

IV. FREE CORPS VICTORY

The last phase of the Ruhr intervention began when General Freiherr von Watter, in command of all Free Corps formations, gave the order for a "surging attack" and launched a full-scale military offensive on April 3, 1920. Before the order was given, the Volunteers had already taken up their positions around the Ruhr in three main groups:

I. The area between Wesel and Münster was occupied by Loewenfeld's Third Marine Brigade. The Wesel Division composed of the Free Corps Schulz, Düsseldorf, and Libau; and Free Corps under Rossbach, Faupel, Khüne, Lützow and Aulock.

II. The area east of Münster and Dortmund was assigned to the Münster Division composed of the Von Pfeffer Free Corps (ostensibly dissolved after the Ulmanis putsch in the Baltic), the Westphalian Rifles, the Free Corps Severin, Von Hindenburg, Gabcke and student formations from Hannover, Göttingen and Münster; and the Haas Division.

III. The front south of Remscheid and Düsseldorf was held by the Epp Division, composed of the Leupold Regiment, the Oberland

[32] As early as March 19, after the Reds took Essen and sixteen days before Severing ordered the Free Corps to enter, he writes: "The events of Dortmund and Essen showed any impartial person that . . . order could be reestablished by the intervention of an extraordinary strong military force. Nonetheless, in those days I used all my influence to prevent the sending of troops to the towns of the Ruhr districts . . . After three more days, it was obvious that neither the representatives of the political parties nor those from the workers were capable of halting . . . the tide which swept from one village to the next." (*1919–1920 im Wetter und Watterwinkel*, 166–167.) He then answers charges of procrastination by saying that General von Watter's ultimatum (March 29) was "absolutely the only cause of further hesitation" (*Ibid.*, 202.) After it was rejected by the Communist, he nevertheless tried to attain peace by negotiating the Peace of Münster, although "negotiations seemed hopeless." And after it too was violated by both parties, he says regretfully, "it was now completely clear to me that I could no longer hesitate in sending for the troops." (*Ibid.*, 191.) He nevertheless waited for three more days before calling for the Free Corps. And then he had his deputy, one Mehlich, sign the order.

Free Corps and various "Emergency Volunteer" (*Zeitfreiwillige*)
formations; the Von Oven Corps, and other smaller groups.[33]

The Ruhr campaign will not be followed here in any detail.
On April 3, Von Aulock's Free Corps took Gelsenkirchen. And,
Schmidt-Pauli assures us, "the thanks of the liberated people
knew no bounds." [34] Bottrop fell to Loewenfeld's Marine Brigade
on the same day. The Wesel Division entered Mühlheim on April
5. Dortmund was "liberated" by Colonel von Epp's men on the
6th. Essen fell the next day, and by April 8 the entire area was
in the hands of the Freebooters.

One of the more moderate historians of the early years of the
Weimar Republic gives an honest picture of the activity of these
government troops in their last officially sponsored intervention
on behalf of "law and order":

The putsch and battle fever swept through the whole of Germany. No
province, no area was left unscathed . . . Dead everywhere, often an
insane raging against the proletariat, a terrible death toll. Here ten,
there twenty-two; here fifteen, there eighteen dead, and so it went . . .
Historical truth requires that these scenes of horror must not be allowed
to rest in the comfortable obscurity which official Germany . . . has
assigned them. The study of charges and counter-charges unfortunately
shows that they [atrocities] are not mere bloody legends of Communist
propaganda. Certainly the Red Guardists too were guilty of atrocities
. . . But the Volunteer bands were the first to set the example and the
first to make those methods of domestic strife popular.[35]

In the Ruhr, hundreds of Free Corps prisoners were rounded up
and shot "while attempting to escape," and once again, as in
Munich and the Baltic, dozens of citizens were sentenced to death
by illegal Freebooter "courts-martial." [36]

[33] Details for the deployment and strength of each formation may be found
in Mahnken's article in *Deutsche Soldaten*, 130–131. See also the military
map in *Freikorpskämpfer*, 365, and von Schmidt-Pauli, *op. cit.*, 268 ff.
[34] *Geschichte der Freikorps*, 273.
[35] Schultze-Pfaelzer, *Von Spa nach Weimar, die Geschichte der deutschen
Zeitwende*, 235 and 334.
[36] Severing calls his chapter on the Free Corps occupation, "*Inter arma silent leges!*" and writes: "In the Recklinghaus district alone, in a few days,
33 death sentences were issued by a local court-martial." The Ebert government issued an order making such informal courts-martial illegal. But as
Severing says, "Most of the troop leaders were indignant over this order . . .

182 VANGUARD OF NAZISM

Protestations made by National Socialist writers to the effect that the Freebooters "felt a deep hurt at having to bear arms against German workers," [37] are not borne out either by available statistics of the casualties suffered by the working class[38] or by the spirit of Free Corps participants. A part of that spirit is caught in a letter written by a young member of the Von Epp Free Corps. The letter is addressed to the boy's family. He writes:

Wischerhöfen, 2 April 1920

I have finally joined my company . . . Yesterday at 1 o'clock in the afternoon we staged our first attack. If I were to tell you everything, you would say I was lying to you. No pardon is given. We shoot even the wounded (*Selbst die Verwundeten erschiessen wir noch*) . . .

The enthusiasm is terrific — unbelievable. Our battalion has had two deaths; the Reds 200–300. Anyone who falls into our hands first gets the rifle butt and then is finished off with a bullet . . . We even shot 10 Red Cross nurses (*Rote-Kreuz-Schwestern*) on sight because they were carrying pistols. We shot those little ladies with pleasure — how they cried and pleaded with us to save their lives. Nothing doing! Anybody with a gun is our enemy . . .

My address is Oberjäger Max Zeller, Student, Company 11, Von Epp Brigade, Rokow, Westphalia.[39]

After the Ruhr revolt had been crushed, the Ebert government felt that it could dispense with the services of the Volunteers. Their formations were dissolved during the early summer of 1920. The history of the German Free Corps movement does not end here, however; it only enters a different phase. We now turn to the fascinating story of their underground activity during the "War in Darkness" — that is, during the period after their dissolution had theoretically taken place.

---

they declared that the prohibition of the courts-martial would make their work much more difficult." The *Standgerichte* therefore continued to function. (Severing, *op. cit.*, 216–217.)

[37] Von Oertzen, *op. cit.*, 421.

[38] The total casualties will probably never be known, but von Oertzen admits that in the first two days of fighting alone, over one thousand workers were either killed or wounded. (*Die deutschen Freikorps*, 419.)

[39] The letter is reprinted in a book with the suggestive title, *Blut und Ehre*, edited by Maximilian Scheer (Paris, 1937), 43. Volunteer students were at least as "reckless" as the older Freebooters. Schultze-Pfaelzer reports, for instance, that near Mechterstädt, students of the Marburg Free Corps killed a number of workers, because, as one student put it, " 'We needed cadavers for our anatomy class.' " (*Op. cit.*, 346.)

VIII

THE FREE CORPS UNDERGROUND: "THE WAR IN DARKNESS"

The men gave up their outward organizational form quite easily. But not their way of life and not their existence. Their readiness for action remained the same as before only under different forms and in the shadows of illegality . . . Naturally only a part of the Free Corps remained, but this part formed the active nucleus and even if the rest of the men were scattered to the four winds, they could collect themselves at the distress signal of their leaders and stand once more as a Corps.

— Ernst von Salomon, Nahe Geschichte

I. FREEBOOTERS AND THE 100,000 MEN ARMY

As soon as he assumed command of the Republic's Army after the Kapp-Lüttwitz Putsch, General Hans von Seeckt began the slow task of reconstructing the military strength of Germany. His long-range program called for converting the 100,000 men allotted him by the Versailles Treaty into what he liked to call his *Führerheer* — that is, an army of 100,000 carefully selected, beautifully trained, and rigidly disciplined officers. Such an army obviously had no room for the wild Freebooters of the Free Corps system. Seeckt was not unmindful of "the imperishable service" the Volunteers had rendered the Fatherland, but he felt that they had outlived their usefulness. "A new building," he observes, "requires very solid foundations and must be constructed according to a definite plan. The Free Corps had neither the plan nor the construction; . . . they were simply not suited for the work of peace." [1]

Apart from the fact that they lacked the type of discipline and

[1] Generaloberst Hans von Seeckt, *Die Reichswehr* (Leipzig, 1933), 14–15.

organization he required, Seeckt by-passed the Freebooters for
another reason: they were too fond of overthrowing governments.
General von Seeckt did not like the Republic either,[2] but he was
willing to put up with it because he needed time and he needed
relative political stability in order to accomplish a thorough military reconstruction. He therefore insisted that the Army was, and
must remain, above politics. This did not mean, as Seeckt is careful to point out, that the Army was not interested in the functions
of the state. On the contrary, it meant that the Army should control the state. But it could perform that legitimate and traditional
function only if it remained unencumbered by irresponsible
putschist elements and unweakened by the strife of party politics. The General is quite clear about this:

And now to conclude. I have tried to treat my theme from a purely
political point of view. In the sense in which I understand the word,
the Army must be "political" — i.e., it must grasp the concept of the
state. But it certainly must not be "political" in the sense of party politics. "Hands off the Army!" is my cry to *all* parties. The Army serves the
state and only the state because the Army is the state.[3]

Given his attitude and his program, it is not surprising that in
his first official proclamation as commander of the army, the
"Gneisenau of the Republic" aimed a shaft directly at the men
who had recently tried to seize the German government:

The Officers' Corps of the Reichswehr stands in its most fateful hour.
Its conduct in the days to come will decide whether or not it will retain
the leadership of the young army . . .
    I see from many signs that the situation produced by the event of
March is not yet clear to many members of the army [or] . . . that we
must all bear the consequences of that treasonous act of political short-

[2] In addition to Seeckt's own writings, see General Rabenau's *Seeckt, Aus
seinem Leben, 1918–1936* (Leipzig, 1940), II, 237 and *passim;* Herbert
Rosinski, "Rebuilding the Reichswehr," *Atlantic Monthly* CLXXIII, No. 2
(February, 1944), 98. Heinz Brauweiler has a difficult time trying to show
that Seeckt was a main pillar of the Republic, *Generäle in der deutschen
Republik: Groener, Schleicher, Seeckt* (Berlin, 1932).
[3] Generaloberst Hans von Seeckt, *Gedanken eines Soldaten* (Berlin, 1929),
116. It is interesting, but not surprising, that the sentence " 'Hände weg vom
Heer!' rufe ich *allen* Parteien zu," is omitted from the enlarged edition of
the book published after the Nazis came to power. (Erweiterte Ausgabe,
Leipzig, 1935.)

sightedness. I have no intention of either tolerating or overlooking such activity. The Reichswehr has no room for soldiers who violate the honor of soldiers.

It can not be expected that everyone, in his heart, welcomes these changed times. Nevertheless, everyone must be permeated with the fundamental realization that the path to a brighter future is open only when the soldier is loyal to his constitutional duty.[4]

The distrust which von Seeckt felt for the Freebooters was reciprocated. They felt that he had betrayed them by refusing to let "the old fighters" dominate the new Army; they did not understand his constitutional approach. Nor, indeed, did they understand anything about General von Seeckt. "We were antagonized by his cold and formal bearing," one of them writes. He then adds an interesting indictment which in itself is illustrative of the Freebooter mentality. "His spirit was without imagination . . . He always acted intelligently."[5] In short, they simply did not like "the Sphinx with the Monocle" — indeed, several of them tried to kill him[6] — and most of the "true Freebooter type" did not enter his army.

It is true that many of the larger, better disciplined, and better organized Free Corps such as Maercker's Volunteer Rifles, the Reinhard Free Corps, and the Von Epp Brigade entered the Reichswehr almost without change. Both the Volunteers themselves and their historians, however, insist that these groups were

[4] Quoted in Brauweiler, *op. cit.*, 60. Brauweiler, von Oertzen, Volkmann, and Benoist-Méchin all incorrectly date the proclamation March 18, 1920. Although Ebert gave Seeckt actual command of the Army on that day, he was not officially installed as Chef der Heeresleitung until April 18, 1920. It was on that day that he issued his proclamation to the Officers' Corps. (See Rabenau, *Seeckt*, II, 239, at note 1.)

[5] Friedrich Wilhelm Heinz, *Die Nation greift an: Geschichte und Kritik des soldatischen Nationalismus* (Berlin, 1932), 83.

[6] In January 1924, men who had been connected variously with the Rossbach Free Corps, the Ehrhardt Brigade, the Schutz und Trutzbund, the Viking Bund, and the NSDAP attempted to shoot Seeckt because he had ordered the Reichswehr to fire on their comrades during Hitler's abortive Beer Hall Putsch. They were convinced, as one of them testified, that "Seeckt is the enemy of the National Revival and as much of a national menace as the Jews." Reports of the trial, which was later hushed up by the Nazis, may be found in the *Berliner Tageblatt*, May 26 ff, 1924; and *Vorwärts*, May 26 ff, 1924.

not typical. They lacked that "primitive Freebooter spirit" which characterized the other corps; they were not, to use von Salomon's expression, "real Free Corps" (*eigentlichen Freikorps*).[7]

Even these atypical formations, after entering the *Reichswehr*, attempted to maintain some of the traditions of the Free Corps system. Maercker, for example, did his best to preserve that independent spirit which had been a hallmark of the Volunteers. "I was determined," he writes, "to keep the name as long as possible, for I knew what a lift the word 'Landesjäger' gave the troops. It was therefore agreed that the name should always appear before the number designation: *Freiwilligen Landesjägerkorps* (Reichswehr Brigade, 16)."[8] He also founded a special newspaper in which, on one occasion at least, he assailed the government for its base ingratitude to the noble, patriotic *Freikorpskämpfer*.[9] In later years, he kept the spirit of his Rifles alive by organizing the *Landesjäger Bund*, an affiliate of the *Stahlhelm*.

Other *Freikorpsführer* continued to recruit men long after the formations which bore their names were absorbed into von Seeckt's army. In the spring of 1920, Colonel Reinhard's Corps joined the national army as the Fifteenth Reichswehr Brigade. But their commander retired to his estate in West Prussia and proceeded to recruit and organize another "Reinhard Free Corps." In 1921 he was able to send four companies of well-equipped men to fight in Upper Silesia.[10] Some of the results of the activity of this former Free Corps commander and Reichswehr officer who

---

[7] Von Salomon, *Nahe Geschichte*, 94–95 and *passim*. The expression also occurs throughout his *Die Geächteten*. See also Mann, *Mit Ehrhardt durch Deutschland*, 38–39; von Schmidt-Pauli, *Freikorps*, 278; von Oertzen, *Die deutschen Freikorps*, 360–361; and Noske, *Erlebtes*, 267.

[8] General Ludwig R. von Maercker, *Vom Kaiserheer zur Reichswehr, Geschichte des freiwilligen Landesjägerkorps*, 3rd ed. (Leipzig, 1922), 225.

[9] *Landesjäger-Zeitung*, Sunday, July 10, 1921. Other Free Corps commanders followed Maercker's lead and established their own newspapers in an effort to maintain the cohesiveness of their corps. *Das Buch vom deutschen Freikorpskämpfer* reprints representative mastheads: *Deutsche Zukunft* (organ of the Association of Former Members of the Schlichtingsheim Volunteer Storm Battalion); *Die Möwe, Wochenszeitschrift des Freikorps Dohna; Das Blatt der Schwarzen Garde; Der Vormarsche* (organ of the Ehrhardt Brigade), and *Der Reiter gen Osten; Organ der Baltikumkämpfer*.

[10] Colonel Wilhelm Reinhard, *1918–1919: Die Wehen der Republik* (Berlin, 1933), 132–133. For the Upper Silesian campaign, see below, pp. 227 ff.

was to become a SS Oberführer under Hitler are suggested by an entry in the official Who's Who of the National Socialist Party. The terse biographical sketch is of one Wolfgang Zarnach:

Birth: July 9, 1902, in Eberswalde, son of a veterinarian . . . Military experience: March, 1919, to the end of 1921 [sic] a member of the Reinhard Free Corps . . . and the German Racial Fellowship Society (cover name for the Reinhard Free Corps) . . . Professional career: . . . entered the NSDAP on May 11, 1923 . . . after the dissolution of the Party, returned to Berlin and was again active in the camouflaged Reinhard Free Corps which was later united with the Stahlhelm as Gau I, Reinhard Group . . . In 1930, an SA leader . . . Since April, 1933, member of the executive committee of the NSDAP and of the Academy of German Law . . .[11]

Other examples could be given, but one more must suffice. The Von Epp Brigade joined the Reichswehr as the Twenty-first Defense Regiment. But Colonel von Epp, through his intermediary, the notorious Ernst Röhm, continued to recruit men and to channelize Reichswehr funds and equipment into the various anti-Republican military and semimilitary Volunteer formations he sponsored. Captain Röhm and other Freebooters who entered the Reichswehr were often reproached by their former comrades for swearing allegiance to the Republic they all hated and for serving the government of the "November Criminals." Röhm admits that "because service in the Army is, and will remain for all time, the most beautiful profession (*schönste Beruf*)," he and "other officers of character could not bring themselves to leave the service."[12] He vehemently denies, however, that he ever took his oath seriously[13] and shows to anyone's satisfaction that he consistently worked for the overthrow of the Republic. Röhm and his comrades found no ethical inconsistency in conspiring against the Republic while ostensibly serving it

---

[11] *Das deutsche Führerlexikon, 1934–1935* (Munich, 1934), 540–541.

[12] Ernst Röhm, *Die Geschichte eines Hochverräters*, 7th ed. (Munich, 1934), 202.

[13] "The oath to the constitution, that is to a *thing* is something unnatural. An oath is something that can be given only from one man to another — not to an impersonal *thing*." (*Ibid.*, 295.) Hitler was less subtle. In 1923, in speaking to the cadets of the Munich War Academy, he said: "The highest duty that you have to your oath to the [Republican] flag, Gentlemen, is to break it . . ." Quoted in Arnolt Bronnen, *Rossbach* (Berlin, 1930), 144.

because, to the mind of the German nationalist, there is a vast difference between "patriotic treason and non-patriotic treason" (*Unterschied zwischen vaterlandstreuem und vaterlandsfiend- lichem Hochverrat*).[14]

Captain Röhm, the self-styled "Archtraitor," complains bitterly of the persecution he suffered at the hands of Republican officials. He then gives a revealing example of the extent to which the Weimar Republic persecuted its Rightist enemies. On one occa- sion, he says, a Bavarian deputy maligned him and betrayed the cause of national revival by reporting his anti-Republican activity to Dr. Otto Gessler, the Minister of Defense who had succeeded Noske. The deputy demanded that Röhm be dismissed from the army. Röhm was incensed at the punishment he received as a result of this "cowardly betrayal." It consisted of being transferred from Colonel von Epp's staff — "I was cut off from my beloved commander" — and being promoted to the general staff of the Seventh Division of the regular army.[15]

If Ernst von Salomon is right when he insists that "from the beginning the overwhelming majority of the [real] Free Corps would have nothing whatever to do with their transfer into the Reichswehr," [16] what happened to them? It is a difficult question and the available source material gives only a partial answer. In general, two methods were used by the Free Corps commanders to keep their men together after their formations had been officially dissolved: either they refused to disband their men, or else they allowed them to return to civilian jobs but maintained contact with them by establishing special newspapers,[17] "Sports Societies," and a bewildering variety of Bund organizations. Both of these methods were considered only "a compromise with

[14] Ludwig Schemann, *Wolfgang Kapp und die Märzunternehmen vom Jahre 1920: Ein Wort der Sühne* (Munich and Berlin, 1937), 154.
[15] When his dismissal was again demanded, Röhm was again transferred, this time to the 7th Artillery Regiment of the official Reichswehr. (Röhm, *op. cit.*, 156, 201–202.)
[16] *Nahe Geschichte*, 95. I tend to agree with von Salomon, but I have the definite impression that more Volunteers entered the 100,000 Men Army than von Salomon and other Free Corps historians care to admit. Some indication of the disposition of representative Free Corps is given in Appendix A of the doctoral thesis. See the note in the appendix of this book.
[17] For examples, see above, p. 186 at note 9.

bürgerlich life,[18] but they helped to preserve the spirit of the Freebooters until the expected Leader would arrive to make compromise unnecessary.

II. IN THE SHADOWS OF ILLEGALITY

Free Corps commanders, wanting to keep the nucleus of their Corps intact, covered up their activity by organizing business concerns the operation of which required large groups of strong young men — trucking companies, bicycle renting agencies, road gangs, private detective bureaus, and traveling circuses. But the most popular subterfuge was to disguise their men as members of large labor camps. Here the Free Corps reverted to the experience of their youth in the *Wandervogel* and the labor camps it had established.[19] More important, they set a precedent for the future: the so-called *Arbeitskommando*[20] of the Black Reichswehr period and the *Arbeitsdienst* of the National Socialists were both patterned directly after the Free Corps labor camps.

Since it will be necessary to break the chronological sequence of the narrative throughout this chapter, let us glance now at one of the labor camps founded in 1931 by a famous Free Corps leader. The organizer of the camp was Heinz Oskar Hauenstein, the youthful leader of the Heinz Storm Battalion, called after its dissolution the "Organization Heinz" or OH. A National Socialist publication gives Heinz credit for being "the first to put the concept of *Arbeitsdienst* into practice in Dresden" and for establishing "*the first Leadership School for Camp Leaders.*" [21] The Dresden camp and its school for *Lagerführer* is described by one of Heinz's lieutenants. The author had become embittered by "the hard fate" of having to adjust to a quiet civilian life.

A telegram brought me to my feet: "Course for labor camp leaders begins Saturday. Expect you Labor Camp Dresden. Hauenstein." I had a hard time getting money for the fare — Hauenstein never thought of such matters . . . I arrived at the former Artillery Depot . . . In the yard some hundred men were answering the call. They

[18] The phrase is von Salomon's, *Nahe Geschichte*, 99.
[19] Howard Becker, *German Youth: Bond or Free?* (London, 1946), 90–91.
[20] See below, pp. 240–247.
[21] *Die Geschichte des deutschen Unteroffiziers*, edited by Ferdinand Freiherr von Ledebur and others (Berlin, 1939), 499. Italics are in the original.

didn't look at all bad. The men, mostly young, were in uniform and drawn up in military formation, platoon commanders and section leaders front and center . . . Hauenstein realized that the question of leadership was basic to the whole idea of labor service. The Leader School opened the next day. The first class was composed almost entirely of old comrades of the Free Corps . . . We had set our hands to pioneer work. That was in accordance with our tradition . . .

Months later I took charge of a labor camp near Leipzig. It is hard for me to describe the physical and spiritual change which I had undergone during these months. Little by little, I ceased to be the human slag-heap I had become during the long years of inactivity . . . In Leipzig we constructed a big dam . . . At Gelsenkirchen we cultivated a stretch of waste land . . . Above the camp fluttered the large black flag which bore our Free Corps insignia . . . Comrades were there to receive us. Familiar faces — faces that brought back memories . . .[22]

During the early twenties, similar *Arbeitslager* or *Arbeitsgemeinschaften* were established in various places throughout the Reich. They were most prevalent in eastern Germany, especially in Pomerania and Brandenburg, where they were sponsored by the Pomeranian *Landbund* and located on the estates belonging to its conservative members.[23] Here they formed the type of half-military, half-agricultural communities that General von der Goltz had hoped to establish in the Baltic.[24]

Peter von Heydebreck, for example, took his *Wehrwölfe* to Count Brühl's estate and established his headquarters in an old castle. His men interspersed their work in the fields with military drill and maneuvers. At night they sat about the great fire in the hall of the castle and discussed ways and means of overthrowing the Republic. For a time Heydebreck was happy. "For the first time," he says, "my rough Freebooter life experienced months of

[22] Friedrich Glombowski, *Organisation Heinz (O.H.): Das Schicksal der Kameraden Schlageters* (Berlin, 1934), 235–239. Detailed descriptions of other labor camps founded in pre-Hitler Germany may be found in F. W. Heinz, *Kameraden der Arbeit, Deutsche Arbeitslager: Stand, Aufgabe und Zukunft* (Berlin, 1933).

[23] See the report of the *Landbund's* affiliation with the *Arbeitsgemeinschaft* drawn up by Karl Severing, Prussian Minister of the Interior, and presented to the Reichstag investigating committee. Quoted in Gumbel, "*Verräter verfallen der Feme!" Opfer, Mörder, Richter, 1919–1920* (Berlin, 1929), 143–144.

[24] See above, pp. 98–99, 137–138.

uninterrupted peace after long years of war and postwar fighting." [25] But his restless Freebooter spirit soon grew tired of the peaceful life — "desire for action seized me like a fever" — and he was delighted when trouble broke out in Upper Silesia. Once again he had the chance to lead his men into battle. [26] Other fighters of the Free Corps shared Heydebreck's desire for action and some of them felt strongly that peace was ruining not only the morale but the moral fibre of their comrades. In May 1921, one of them made the following entry in his diary:

The qualities that had stood out strongly at the front: vanity, self-assertion, independence and so forth, now became in the inactivity of peace almost overbearing in some of the comrades . . . If these men are to be considered a cross-section of our present youth, then one can really no longer believe in the resurrection of Germany. I have never in my life seen such depravity, brutality and moral degeneracy. Some people still think that they can find here in the Free Corps "the noblest youth of Germany." Oh, what a disappointment is in store for them! [27]

It would, of course, be impossible to discuss the underground activity of all Free Corps formations. A brief outline of the career of the Rossbach *Sturmabteilung* will serve to indicate the lengths taken by some of the Free Corps leaders to keep their men together after their formations had been officially dissolved. When he returned from the Baltic in December 1919, [28] Rossbach received orders from the Reichswehr to disband his men. He simply refused. Subsidies from various nationalistic quarters such as the National Union enabled him to preserve his organization. [29] After participating in the Kapp Putsch, his men were incorporated into the Reichswehr as *Jägerbataillon 37*. As such, his

[25] Peter von Heydebreck, *Wir Wehrwölfe: Erinnerungen eines Freikorps-führers* (Leipzig, 1931), 82–83.

[26] *Ibid.*, 85 ff.

[27] Carsten Curator, *Putsche, Staat und Wir!* (Karlsruhe, 1931), 139. Curator had been a member of the Ehrhardt Brigade. He was dropped from one of its successor organizations, the Viking Bund, for refusing to take part in the Beer Hall Putsch.

[28] For his activity in the Baltic, see above, pp. 131 ff.

[29] J. Benoist-Méchin, *Histoire de L'Armée Allemande* (Paris, 1938), II, 153.

men helped to crush the general strike of March 13–16, 1920.[30] However, when General von Seeckt assumed command of the Army and began to reorganize it according to his rigid specifications, Rossbach again received orders to dismiss his men. Again he refused. Supported by the Pomeranian *Landbund* — and with at least the tacit approval of Reichswehr officials[31] — Rossbach organized his men into *Arbeitsgemeinschaften* and scattered them on several of the great estates in Pomerania and West Prussia. The arms and munitions he had cached near Güstrow after receiving von Seeckt's order to disband his formation were shipped to his men as "machine tools." Rossbach then opened a night club in Berlin at 18 Hohenzollern Strasse and staffed it with his men. The "Tiergarten Club" served both as his Berlin headquarters and as a front for collecting arms and munitions.[32] A steady stream of "machine tools" were thus shipped to the various estates where his men were working. In addition to collecting and storing guns, a main part of the work of the *Arbeitsgemeinschaft* was to discourage "communist" activity, that is, to crush the bona fide agricultural laborers who were agitating against the sorry labor conditions which existed on the estates belonging to members of the *Landbund*. When complaints were made, Rossbach would dispatch a Storm Section, arrest the workers, and bring them before the "Judicial Section" of the *Arbeitsgemeinschaft*. The sentence was usually death.[33]

[30] Reichswehr officials later flatly denied that Rossbach's men had been associated with the Reichswehr. But at his trial in Stettin in April 1928, evidence was introduced which showed that Rossbach had received orders directly from the Army. The orders were dated March 16, 1920, addressed to the "Rossbach Detachment" and signed by a Reichswehr brigade commander. The trial is reported in *Vossische Zeitung*, April 28, 1928.

[31] The commander of the Defense District II (Stettin), Lieutenant General von Weber, was certainly cognizant of Rossbach's activity and did nothing to stop it. See Gumbel, *Verräter*, 142.

[32] Arnolt Bronnen, *Rossbach* (Berlin, 1930), 97.

[33] During the course of his trial at Stettin in April 1928, Rossbach jocularly testified that he had personally killed "a number of Mecklenburg laborers and Spartacist sympathizers." He was acquitted of all charges. (*Berliner Tageblatt*, April 25, 1928.) Lieutenant Heines was another of the judges of the Rossbach Judiciary Section. Eight years after murdering one Willi Schmidt as a "communist traitor," he too was brought to trial and acquitted in spite of the fact that he boasted openly that he had committed the crime. In the meantime he had joined the NSDAP and in 1932 was elected to the

Rossbach organized and outfitted his men so effectively that within forty-eight hours after the outbreak of the Third Polish Revolt, he was able to send some four thousand men to join Heydebreck's *Wehrwölfe* and other "dissolved" formations in Upper Silesia.[34] At the conclusion of the Silesian campaign, orders were again issued to dissolve all Free Corps formations, but the Rossbachers greased their guns, buried them, escaped to Pomerania, and resumed work as "agricultural laborers." The arms followed within a few weeks. Toward the end of November 1921, however, the *Arbeitgemeinschaften* — forbidden from the first by the Versailles treaty — were finally declared illegal by the Republic.[35]

But Rossbach was resourceful. He transformed a part of his men into "Detective Bureaus." "Thus," says an admirer, "a *bürgerlich* form was found and the police could not interfere . . ."[36] Most of his men, however, entered an organization with the innocuous name, "Savings Society" (*Sparvereinigung*). When the Prussian Minister of Interior outlawed that group, the indefatigable *Freikorpsführer* demonstrated the truth of his boast, "I can organize new outfits faster than they [the authorities] can dissolve them";[37] He changed its name to the "Union for Agri-

---

Reichstag as deputy for Breslau. (*Die Braunhemden im Reichstag: Die Nationalsozialistische Reichstagsfraktion, 1932*, Munich, 1932.) In later years he became the sadistic SA commander of Silesia. A notorious homosexual, he was the lover of both Rossbach and Röhm. In light of the fact that he was murdered by orders of Hitler on the night of June 30, 1934, the following entry in Baldur von Schirach's *Die Pioniere des Dritten Reiches* (Essen, 1933[?]) is not without interest: "This soldier of Adolf Hitler was not broken by the shameless trial [for the murder of Willi Schmidt]. On the contrary it only spurred him on to fight all the harder for Germany. The confidence of our Führer in Edmund Heines is great. How great is shown by the fact that in 1931 he was made commander of the SA in Silesia . . . his example inspires his subordinates." (Pp. 87–88.)

[34] Benoist-Méchin, *Histoire*, II, 154.

[35] The law of November 24 is given in *Reichsgesetzblatt* (Zweiter Halbjahr, 1921) Number 8383. The half-apologetic decree reads in part: ". . . as a result of the Allied governments' ultimatum of May 5, 1921, the organizations Rossbach, Aulock, Heydebreck . . . are herewith declared dissolved."

[36] Fritz Carl Roegels, *Der Marsch auf Berlin: Ein Buch vom Wehrwillen deutscher Jugend* (Berlin, 1932), 144.

[37] Quoted in Benoist-Méchin, *op. cit.*, II, 155.

cultural Instruction" (*Verein für Landwirtschaftliche Berufs-bildung*). All of these disguises were pretty transparent. It seems apparent that if the national government had made a really serious effort to ferret out and crush the Free Corps underground, it could have done so without undue difficulty. But while it feared and distrusted the Freebooters, the Republic was not sure that it could get along without them. It was still impressed by the threat of Bolshevism; it was afraid — not without cause — that the Poles might attack its Eastern frontier; it could not afford to wait for Seeckt to organize his army. Government officials there-fore closed at least one eye to illegal Free Corps activity. Some of them even encouraged it. Thus, after the Silesian campaign, Gradnauer, the Reich Minister of the Interior, gave the following advice to Rossbach: "Disband your men — but stand ready." (*Lösen Sie sich auf, aber bestehen Sie weiter.*)[38]

Since the government — after May 1920 — no longer paid the Free Corps, money had to be sought elsewhere. Free Corps historians like to leave the impression that no one financed the Volunteers and that these forgotten, impoverished, and hounded patriots had to struggle on alone for the good of the Fatherland.[39] The memoirists are also reticent about discussing financial de-tails. Von Salomon's only comment is, "finances proved difficult, but never an insoluble problem," [40] and von Killinger, in speak-ing of an underground leader says, "He got his money. Just don't ask me how!" [41]

Actually, there was nothing particularly mysterious about the sources of their financial support. We have already seen that the *Landbund* sponsored them. Heavy industry also made gener-ous contributions.[42] Then, too, there was considerable profit in

[38] Quoted in Edgar von Schmidt-Pauli, *General von Seeckt: Lebensbild eines deutschen Soldaten* (Berlin, 1937), 115. See also Roegels, *op. cit.*, 142–143.

[39] See, for example, von Oertzen's pathetic picture of ragged Volunteers begging cigarettes on the street corners of German cities. (*Freikorps*, 435–436.)

[40] Von Salomon, *Nahe Geschichte*, 99.

[41] Manfred von Killinger, *Ernstes und Heiteres aus dem Putschleben*, 6th ed. (Munich, 1934), 30.

[42] Arthur Rosenberg, *Geschichte der deutschen Republik* (Karlsbad, 1935), 131; Georg Bernhard, *Die deutsche Tragödie, Der Selbstmord einer Republik* (Prague, 1933), 54; and Ambroise Got, *La Contre-Révolution Allemande*

stealing and selling contraband arms. The government itself had inadvertently provided the Freebooters with this source of revenue. In order to meet the demands of the Allied Commission of Control, the Republic passed a law which dissolved the Free Corps and provided that "compensation will be made for the surrender of all arms which have been legitimately acquired." [43] Since the officials did not tend to investigate the legitimacy of the acquisitions, the Free Corps were able to steal arms from the government and surrender them for a profit. Arms were also sold to the enemies of the Republic. Rossbach's biographer, for example, describes what he considers a "somewhat humorous but nevertheless effective means" of raising money. Rossbach would sell German machine guns to the Poles, then a section of his Storm Troops would "liberate" the arms and resell them to other Polish groups. The process was then repeated. "They did a booming business." [44]

Early in November 1922, Rossbach was arrested and charged with conspiring to overthrow the Republic.[45] The authorities were kind enough to release him, however, in time for him to join his men in Munich for the celebration of the fourth anniversary of the founding of the Rossbach Free Corps on November 22, 1922. Two *Hundertschaften* of Hitler's newly formed SA and most of the former *Baltikumers* now living in Bavaria — including twelve Reichswehr soldiers in the uniform of the Republic — helped him

(Strasbourg, 1920[?]), 46. Schlageter testified at his trial that "Every one of our men received a daily pay of 18,000 [inflated] marks besides traveling expenses. The money came from Berlin from heavy industry." Quoted in an anonymous article, *Naziführer sehen Dich an! 33 Biographien aus dem Dritten Reich* (Paris, 1934), 173. Eduard Stadtler, the founder of the Rightist Anti-Bolshevik League, reports that at a meeting in which he harangued industrialists about the Red Peril, Hugo Stinnes approached him with the suggestion that an "Anti-Bolshevik Fund" of some 500,000,000 marks be raised. The fund was distributed to various nationalist organizations including the Free Corps. See Stadtler's memoirs, *Als Antibolshewist 1918– 1919* (Düsseldorf, 1935), 48–49. Paul Frölich, the Communist, gives a list — for what it is worth — of the major industries of Germany and their contributions to Free Corps and post-Free Corps organizations. *Wider den Weissen Mord*, 2nd ed. (Berlin and Leipzig, n.d.), 46 ff.

[43] *Reichsgesetzblatt* (Jahrgang 1920) Nr. 7719, "Gesetz über die Entwaffnung der Bevölkerung vom 7 August 1920," p. 1553.

[44] Bronnen, *Rossbach*, 61–62; see also Roegels, *op. cit.*, 136–137.

[45] *Berliner Tageblatt*, November 14, 1922.

celebrate. During the festivities Rossbach made one of his rare speeches. He said:

We have now been dissolved for a year [*sic*] and yet we still exist. I can promise you that we will soon create little Bavarias in the darkest parts [of the Reich] . . . Out of the mess of innumerable, separate and competing national groups and societies a great unified Power Organization must be founded which will end this present nonsense [that is, the Weimar Republic] forever. To accomplish that, we must clear the way with blackjacks and bayonets . . . In Bavaria, you will soon have the opportunity to act. It is to be hoped that we will soon have the same chance in Prussia . . .[46]

While in Munich, Rossbach joined the NSDAP and was sent to Mecklenburg as their chief representative. During this time he was active in organizing youth groups.[47] Arrested for a second time in the summer of 1923, he was again released and, like so many other *Freikorpskämpfer*, found refuge in Munich. He and his men marched with Hitler during the Beer Hall Putsch; after its failure he fled to Salzburg where he was again active in the youth movement. Hermann Goering found him there and brought him back to Munich on Hitler's orders, to help organize the scattered SA.[48]

The Rossbach Free Corps was at long last officially — and permanently — dissolved on November 9, 1933, on the tenth anniversary of the march on the Feldherrnhalle. At that time the Nazis staged an elaborate "Flag Surrender" ceremony during which the former Free Corps commanders made emotional speeches lauding the Third Reich and handed over their battle-scarred flags to an honor guard of SA and SS troops. The standard

---

[46] *Münchener Post*, quoted by E. J. Gumbel, *Verschwörer: Beiträge zur Geschichte und Soziologie der deutschen Nationalistischen Geheimbünde seit 1918* (Vienna, 1924), 91.

[47] For the contributions made by Rossbach and other Free Corps leaders to the postwar youth movement, see below, pp. 207 ff.

[48] Rossbach claims: "I assumed the leadership of all National Socialist *Sturmabteilungen* in the Reich and in Austria." Quoted in Bronnen, *Rossbach*, 171. Actually Franz von Pfeffer, the former Baltic fighter, was the leader of the SA from the period after the Beer Hall Putsch until Röhm took over in 1930. (Konrad Heiden, *Geschichte des Nationalsozialismus: Die Karriere einer Idee*, Berlin, 1932.) Rossbach was nevertheless an important factor in the reorganization of the Storm Troopers and, among other things, designed the official SA uniform. Scheer, *Blut und Ehre*, 64.

of the Rossbachers (a golden *R* on a black field transversed by two horizontal silver stripes) was placed beside the flags of Ehrhardt, von Epp, Hauenstein, and the rest. It was preserved with the others in the Hall of Honor of the Brown House "for all eternity" [49] — at any rate until the American invading forces found it there in the summer of 1945. Rossbach barely escaped the blood purge of 1934 and was not politically active during the Third Reich. He survived both Hitler and the war to become an insurance broker in Hamburg. He died in 1967.[50]

As will be seen in a later chapter, not all Free Corps entered the Nazi movement as directly as did Rossbach's; and not all of them were as successful in maintaining their separate identity. The activity of those who left their formations to submit to the rigors of civilian life must be considered next.

III. "COMPROMISING WITH BURGERLICH ACTIVITY"

The Volunteers who returned to civilian jobs after years in the Army and in the Free Corps maintained contact with their comrades by joining one or more of the half-legal, half-military Bund organizations which abounded in Germany during the twenties. One of the chief of these was the "Civil Guards" (*Einwohnerwehr*).

At the time of the November Revolution, these formations had been established with Noske's blessing throughout the Reich. As we have seen,[51] General Maercker modified the Free Corps system by forming Civil Guard units in Halle and Brunswick. Franz Seldte organized the *Selbsthilfe* of Magdeburg — a group which was to form the nucleus of his famous *Stahlhelm*.[52] Similar

[49] The ceremony is described in the special issue of the *Völkischer Beobachter* for November 9–10, 1933. The actual flag surrendered by Rossbach was not his original standard. That had been burned in a steel helmet upon his return from the Baltic so that "it would not be defiled by entering Marxist-Prussian lands." The ashes of the original flag rested for years in the Schlageter Museum in Berlin. (*Völkischer Beobachter*, August 2, 1933.)

[50] *Der Spiegel*, September 4, 1967. Kurt G. W. Ludecke incorrectly reported him as being shot on Goering's orders June 30, 1934. (*I Knew Hitler: The Story of a Nazi Who Escaped the Blood Purge*, New York, 1938, 775.) During 1961, Rossbach sought to sue William L. Shirer who, on the basis of this present study, had quite correctly called Rossbach a homosexual. (*Rise and Fall of the Third Reich*, New York, 1960, 66.) After his lawyers examined the evidence, Rossbach wisely decided to drop the case.

[51] See above, p. 68.

[52] Wilhelm Kleinau, *Franz Seldte, ein Lebensbericht* (Berlin, 1933), 44.

formations were organized in Berlin, Hamburg, Augsburg, and other key German cities. The stronghold of the *Einwohnerwehr* movement, however, was in Munich.

Under the able leadership of Major Doctor Forstrat Escherich[53] and his adjutant, Obergeometer Rudolf Kanzler,[54] the Bavarian *Einwohnerwehr* soon began to play a dominant role in the political life of Bavaria. In 1919, for example, an order emanating from the Bavarian Department of the Interior reads: "The attitude of the authorities of the internal administration toward the *Einwohnerwehr* will not be that of commanders, but of advisers and supporters." [55]

Escherich's success in Bavaria recommended him to *Einwohnerwehr* leaders of the North and they asked him to organize their various groups into one national movement. The basis for coöperation between north and south Germany was laid in a series of meetings at Regensburg during May 1920 which resulted in the formation of the nation-wide "Orgesch" (*Organisation Escherich*).[56] "Thus before the dissolution of the Free Corps had taken place," writes Heinz, "Escherich had united almost all German *Einwohnerwehr* under his leadership." [57]

German officials always insisted that the *Einwohnerwehr* was

[53] As late as 1928, the indefatigable Escherich was organizing nationalist defense organizations. This activity prompted the *Völkischer Beobachter* to write an editorial which asserted that men such as Escherich had long since served their purpose. It warned him against carrying on his nationalist activity in competition with the NSDAP. (*Völkischer Beobachter,* December 5, 1928.) And when Baron Müffling listed Escherich as one of the "pathfinders and champions" of the Third Reich, the Nazis placed his book in their closed archives. (Wilhelm Freiherr von Müffling, *Wegbereiter und Vorkämpfer für das neue Deutschland,* Munich, 1933, 31.)

[54] Kanzler's memoirs, *Bayerns Kampf gegen den Bolshewismus: Geschichte der bayerischen Einwohnerwehren* (Munich, 1931) are a valuable source for the period. Kanzler later split with Escherich and founded the "Orka" (Organization Kanzler) which absorbed many of the nationalist groups of the Tirol, Austria, and Carinthia. Major Pabst of the Division of Horse Guards and the Kapp Putsch served as Kanzler's adjutant in forming the Austrian *Heimwehr.*

[55] G. Axhausen, *Organisation Escherich* (Leipzig, 1921), quoted in Ernst H. Posse, *Die politischen Kampfbünde Deutschlands,* 2nd enlarged edition, in *Fachschriften zur politik und staatsbürgerlichen Erziehung,* Ernst von Hippel, general editor (Berlin, 1931), 13.

[56] Kanzler, *op. cit.,* 80.

[57] *Die Nation greift an,* 115.

a purely civilian organization with no military importance whatsoever. Dr. von Kahr, for instance, informed the British ambassador that the *Einwohnerwehr* was more like a fire brigade or a private club than a regiment, that the formations did not even engage in military drill, and concluded, "There is no militarism in the idea." [58] Actually it was a military force of considerable size which was designed to serve as a reserve for the Free Corps system; it was armed, instructed, and drilled regularly by Reichswehr officers.[59] For the benefit of the Allied Military Control Commission, however, no military titles or terms were used. Thus, in terminology that anticipated Hitler, the country was divided into military areas called *Gaue* and *Kreise;* the formations were called *Hundertschaften* and *Gruppen* and the commanders addressed as *Gauleiter, Gruppenführer,* and so forth. Two circular letters issued by government offices and addressed to *Einwohnerwehr* leaders best illustrate the nature and real function of the Civil Guards and the efforts of Republican officials to disguise that function from the Allies. Circular number 156016 of the Minister of the Interior dated July 1, 1919, reads in part:

The Minister of Defense calls attention to the instructions of the Reichswehr Minister of May 25, 1919 (No. 4188) by virtue of which the members of the *Einwohnerwehr* units . . . are to be treated exactly like the combatant Reichswehr . . . In case of an emergency, the *Einwohnerwehr* will be incorporated into the Reichswehr.[60]

When Allied officials became suspicious of the military character of the Guards, Noske sent the following directive (Reichswehr ministry circular VIII 2844 L 2) to *Einwohnerwehr* leaders:

[58] Quoted by Viscount Edgar Vincent D'Abernon, *An Ambassador of Peace,* 3 vols. (London, 1929–1930), I, 94–95.

[59] The best discussion of the military aspects of the *Einwohnerwehr* and the difficulties it presented to the Inter-Allied Commission of Control is given in the memoirs of the Commission's president, General Charles M. E. Nollet, *Une Expérience de Désarmament: Cinque Ans de Contrôle Militaire en Allemagne* (Paris, 1932), 118 ff. A former member of the Ehrhardt Brigade who entered the *Einwohnerwehr* gives an account of his training and activity and concludes: "Militarily outfitted, instructed by Reichswehr officers, Sunday field maneuvers — naturally everything disguised." Curator, *Putsche, Staat und Wir!,* 80.

[60] Quoted in the memoirs of the French military attaché, Ambroise Got, *La Contre-Révolution Allemande* (Strasbourg, 1920[?]), 186.

The further existence of the home defense units [*Einwohnerwehren*] is threatened by the peace conditions. By Article 177 [of the peace of Versailles] organization of home defense units is forbidden without question. In order to be able to retain home defense units with the consent of the Entente they must be deprived of every military character at once. The civil authorities must take over their command . . .

[However] even after complete demilitarization of the home defense units it will be very desirable for military officers to help the civil authorities with their advice. Arms, registers, supplies, &c., for the home defense units are to be delivered to the civil authorities . . .

All further measures will be agreed on orally. Oral reports will be made on special problems that may arise.

(signed) Noske[61]

Official: von Stockhausen,
          Major, General Staff

Thus supported by the German government, *Einwohnerwehr* leaders retained their Guard organizations and continued to arm. Arms came from two main sources: the Free Corps, who had never surrendered their weapons, contributed a great deal, but the bulk of the armament came from the official German Army. In Bavaria, for instance, the cofounder of the *Orgesch* reports that Colonel von Epp, now commander of the Twenty-first Reichswehr Brigade, "gave us more support than anyone had dared to hope for . . . Transport after transport of [Reichswehr] arms was delivered to trustworthy people, . . . so that every man had a model '98 rifle with 50 rounds of ammunition; each *ortswehr* had machine guns; every *gau* had two artillery batteries; and, in the cities, each man had hand grenades, steel helmets, cartridge belts, and side-arms besides his rifle." [62]

On October 12, 1920, the President of the Inter-Allied Military Commission of Control, sent one of his many[63] demands to the

[61] This letter dated July 5, 1919, was discovered by a member of the United States Army headquarters at Coblenz and sent to the *New York Times* by their correspondent in Coblenz. (*Current History, A Monthly Magazine of the New York Times,* Vol. X, No. 3 (September, 1919), 430–431.) "Home Defense Units" is the American correspondent's translation of *Einwohnerwehren*. In the French translation of the same letter, the term is left in the original: *Einwohnerwehren*. See Got, *La Contre-Révolution,* 187. Noske gave similar instructions to Escherich in a letter dated July 30, 1919 (Kanzler, *op. cit.,* 46–47).

[62] Kanzler, *op. cit.,* 174–176.

[63] For the repeated demands made by General Nollet that the Guards dissolve and the repeated evasive refusals made by the German government, see

German government insisting that the *Einwohnerwehr* be disbanded. The *Orgesch* leaders consequently decided to give in a
little. Escherich and Kanzler announced officially that their organization was disarming, and ostentatiously delivered up some
179,000 rifles; but since the total number of rifles belonging to the
Bavarian guards alone amounted to over 400,000 in 1920, they
still had well over 220,000 hidden in secret depots.[64]

Even though the *Einwohnerwehr* was a great deal more militarist and nationalist than its leaders cared to admit to the Allies,
it was not nearly extreme enough to suit the Freebooters. They
sneered at "the *bürgerlich* mentality" which, they said, characterized it; and they flatly opposed its bylaws which promised — at
least for public consumption — to protect the Weimar constitution, to defend law and order, and "to thwart every putsch
whether from the Left or the Right." [65] One of the leaders of
the *Einwohnerwehr* movement is quite right when he says that
"the members of the Free Corps . . . formed the backbone of the
local *wehren*," [66] but the men of the Free Corps joined only because the Guards gave them the arms and the opportunity to
transform the individual *wehren* into organizations which were
more congenial to their activist temperament. "The men who lived
National Socialism before it was organized," says Heinz, "formed
their own *Wehrbunde* and detached themselves from the *Orgesch*
. . . Sometimes sabotaged by the *Orgesch*, they carried forward

---

Deutsche Geschichtskalender, edited by Friedrich Purlitz (Leipzig, 1920),
July–December, 1920, Band II, 31; 42–44; 67–68; 70–72. Finally, after the
Allies met in London and delivered the so-called London Ultimatum of May
5, 1921, the *Einwohnerwehr* was officially disbanded on May 24, 1921.
(*Geschichtskalender,* January–June, 1921, Band I, 423–424.)

[64] P. Dreyfus and Paul Mayer, *Recht und Politik im Fall Fechenbach*
(Berlin, 1925), 407.

[65] The bylaws are quoted in Posse, *Die politischen Kampfbünde,* 12, and
Kanzler, *op. cit.,* 80–81. According to Kanzler, the founding fathers had a
further purpose in mind: "Apart from the official purpose for which the *Einwohnerwehr* was established, Escherich and I had envisaged other goals . . .
we wanted, among other things, to keep the people vigilant in respect to
. . . their defense duties (*Wehrpflichten*) . . . further, we wanted to en-
thuse the German Volk, which threatened to submerge itself in crass materialism, with an *Ideal* of comradeship, sacrifice, community and, if necessary, to
fight for the holy estate of the *Volk.*" (*Ibid.,* 42.)

[66] *Ibid.,* 173.

the tradition of the Free Corps and its battles . . . against the spirit and the letter of the Weimar Constitution and hence (*damit*) against the spirit and the letter of the *Orgesch* . . ." [67]

Apart from their activity in the *Orgesch*, the men of the Free Corps founded or joined one or more of the literally dozens[68] of nationalist societies which flourished in Germany during the twenties. It is extraordinarily difficult to get a clear picture of these associations. They often changed their names in order to confuse the authorities — and subsequently the historian — and it is impossible to estimate their membership with any degree of accuracy. If one combines the totals of each group, one reaches a figure of well over a million members. This, however, is not accurate; for, as the leading authority on the subject has pointed out, the same people were often members of a half dozen or more similar groups. The total membership was probably not more than 200,000 men.[69] It would be impossible, as well as unrewarding, to discuss these associations here in any detail. Our purpose is simply to show their importance to the preservation of the Freebooter spirit and to suggest their influence on the growth of proto-Nazi thinking. Whatever their form or name, the secret[70] nationalist societies had a common purpose: the overthrow of the Weimar Republic and the dissemination of militant, racist nationalism. A few typical examples will serve as illustrations.

Immediately after the Kapp-Lüttwitz Putsch, Major Stephani, former commander of the Potsdam Free Corps and member of

[67] Friedrich Wilhelm Heinz, *Die Nation greift an,* 114 and 117. For Freebooter attitude to the *Einwohnerwehr* see, in addition to Heinz, Curator, *Putsche, Staat und Wir!,* 79–80, 148–149; and Mann, *Mit Ehrhardt durch Deutschland,* 83–84.

[68] A comprehensive list of the names of these associations is given in E. J. Gumbel, *Verschwörer: Beiträge zur Geschichte und Soziologie der deutschen Nationalistischen Geheimbünde seit 1918* (Vienna, 1924), 64 ff; and in Paul Frölich, *Wider den Weissen Mord,* 2nd ed. (Berlin, n.d.), 24 ff.

[69] Gumbel, *Verschwörer,* 64.

[70] Heinrich von Treitschke's insistence that the open honesty of the German mind makes it recoil from secret societies of all sorts (*History of Germany in the Nineteenth Century,* translated by Eden and Cedar Paul, New York, 1915, I, 352–353) is illustrated by neither the *Burschenschaften* of the period with which he is concerned nor by the twentieth century societies. All of these latter groups had secret passwords, handshakes, and ritual and at least one of them, "The Ring of the Nibelungen," developed its own secret language.

the *Nationale Vereinigung*, together with officers of the Ehrhardt Brigade, organized the Association of Nationally Minded Soldiers (*Verband Nationalgesinnter Soldaten*, commonly abbreviated the VNS). This association, one of its members writes with a good deal of pride, "collecting unto itself 150,000 soldiers of the Free Corps, threatened the state." [71] It was closely associated with other groups which bore such suggestive names as "the Activists," "the Intransigents," "The Association of Baltic Fighters," [72] "the Defenders of the Eastern Frontiers," and the "Young German Order." [73] Forbidden by the government authorities in 1922, and ostensibly dissolved, the VNS continued to function as the *Völkischer Soldatenbund*.

As we have seen, after helping to crush the Communist revolt which followed the Kapp Putsch, the Ehrhardt Brigade was dissolved by orders of General von Seeckt. To circumvent the order, Ehrhardt's men immediately organized the "Association of Former Ehrhardt Officers" (*Bund ehemaliger Ehrhardtoffiziere*). "This was a patriotic organization," one of its admirers tells us, "which carried on the spirit of Fatherland love and militarism, and led the battle against the Versailles Treaty, the un-German Weimar Constitution, and Marxism. It fostered the racist Idea . . ." [74] It was from this group that the O.C. murder association, which we shall deal with later,[75] developed. After members of the O.C. murdered Walther Rathenau, the name was changed to the Viking Bund, which was, in turn, closely associated with the "Olym-

---

[71] Heinz, *Die Nation greift an*, 119. Gumbel agrees with his figures and notes that in Berlin alone the VNS numbered over 3,000 members. (*Verschwörer*, 65.)

[72] General von der Goltz and Baron Manteuffel were the founders of this group.

[73] The *Jungdeutsche Orden*, or the "*Jungdo*" is particularly interesting. Originally founded as a Free Corps, it fought in the area around Kassel and in Upper Silesia. When the Free Corps were dissolved, the *Jungdo* kept its personnel and became a Bund organization which was affiliated with the *Orgesch*. It soon broke with Escherich, however, because it felt that the very size of his organization was destroying the Free Corps ideal of allegiance to the individual leader, in this case, Lieutenant Mahraum. Under Mahraum, the *Jungdo* developed a separate, well-articulated organization with *gaue*, *gruppen*, *gauleiter*, and *gruppenführer*. (See Posse, *op. cit.*, 52–54.)

[74] Roegel, *Der Marsch auf Berlin*, 156.

[75] See below, pp. 213 ff.

pia Sports Association." [76] The "Vikings" were considered the elite of all the secret militarist societies and rated a salute from the members of other groups.[77] "Our political program," so runs the bylaws of the Viking Bund, "is the program of the National Socialist German Workers Party." [78]

In 1926 the Prussian Minister of the Interior ordered the dissolution of the Viking Bund on the understandable grounds that it was an illegal military organization dangerous to the Republic. Not only did the Bund refuse to disband, but also it refused to accept the legality of the dissolution order. A year after the order was issued, it brought court action against the government. During the course of the trial, members of the Bund testified that their organization wanted to overthrow the Republic and institute "a national, racist dictatorship" (*nationale, völkische Diktatur*).[79] In light of this testimony the very fact that the Bund itself initiated the legal action indicates the really tremendous gall of the Freebooters. It also shows that the confidence they had learned to place in the law courts of Germany was warranted.

The trial itself is interesting. In his opening statement the presiding officer, Herr Niedner, suggested that since "much of the evidence is of importance to the security of the state" it could not be presented in open court.[80] On the third day of the trial, the Bund's attorneys made their main argument: the Viking Bund had as much right to exist as did the Republican *Reichsbanner,* "which is also an armed military organization." [81] They did not, of course, point out that there was a considerable difference between the

[76] The *Sportverein Olympia,* which also included hundreds of former members of the Reinhard Free Corps, was only one of dozens of sports groups, gymnastic societies, and hiking clubs which were founded by former Free Corps leaders. Members of the Rossbach Free Corps, for instance, founded the *Turnerschaft Ulrich von Hutten,* which, like the Olympia, was "only a clever camouflage [for the Free Corps]." (Ludwig Freiwald, *Der Weg der braunen Kämpfer: Ein Frontbuch von 1918–1933,* Munich, 1934, 170–172.)

[77] Testimony given in the Viking Bund trial, *Deutsche Allgemeine Zeitung,* April 27, 1927.

[78] *Münchener Post,* December 27, 1922, quoted in Gumbel, *Verschwörer,* 82.

[79] Testimony of April 24, 1927, *Deutsche Allgemeine Zeitung,* April 25, 1927.

[80] *Loc. cit.,* April 22, 1927.

[81] *Loc. cit.,* April 24, 1927.

two groups, namely that the *Reichsbanner* was organized to defend the Weimar Constitution, the Viking Bund to overthrow it.

Ehrhardt at first simply refused to attend the trial. When he finally appeared, on the fourth day, the states attorney agreed that "even though Captain Ehrhardt is the leader of the Viking Bund, it will not be necessary for him to testify." [82] Although, in this case, the court upheld the Prussian Minister of the Interior's decision and recommended that the Bund be dissolved, it continued to function unmolested for another year. It was not until the end of April 1928 that the Bund was dissolved and then it was done on the initiative of Ehrhardt himself. At that time he made a public declaration which suggests that the post-Free Corps societies — exactly like Hitler[83] — suffered acutely from the relative peace and prosperity of the late twenties. On April 27, 1928, Ehrhardt published the following statement: "Captain Ehrhardt has dissolved the Viking Bund throughout the Reich. The reason is that he is convinced that there is no future in power politics (*keine machtpolitische Zukunft*). Captain Ehrhardt intends to enter pure politics." [84]

One example is enough to suggest Ehrhardt's ubiquitous influence on the secret societies. The stronghold of his movement, as indeed of all extremist national groups, was in Munich, but the *Wehrkraft Hamburg* states in its bylaws: "The *Wehrkraft* is a society which is organized on a military basis and is built on nationalist foundations. It carries the spirit of Ehrhardt in its heart." [85]

Although some of the Freebooters entered the *Stahlhelm*,[86]

---

[82] *Loc. cit.*, April 25, 1927.

[83] As Konrad Heiden has pointed out, National Socialism served as a pretty reliable negative barometer of national well-being. Hitler and his movement went through their worst agonies when it seemed possible that the Fatherland might recover without them; they took a new lease on life whenever the country was in serious difficulty. (*Der Fuehrer,* 164, 167, 248–250, 416 and *passim*.)

[84] The *Vossische Zeitung* published the statement in its issue of April 28, 1929, and commented, "This communique by the leader of the Kapp Putsch is really very remarkable. Captain Ehrhardt has long been an element of unrest . . . we wonder what is meant by his use of the term 'pure politics.'"

[85] Quoted in Gumbel, *Verschwörer,* 70.

[86] Ehrhardt was associated with the *Stahlhelm* for a time, as was Reinhard's *Kyffhaüserbund*.

the majority considered it too stuffy and conservative. The younger Volunteers were never admitted to its elite corps, the *Kernstahlhelm,* because its entrance requirements specified that all members must have served at least six months at the front during the war. The Steel Helmets will therefore be by-passed here in favor of the secret society which was, by all odds, the most popular[87] among former Free Corps fighters: "The German Racist League for Defense and Attack" (*Deutschvölkischer Schutz-und-Trutzbund* — commonly abbreviated, S-u-T). From this Society the Volunteers, along with thousands of their countrymen, were indoctrinated with the savage anti-Semitism which prepared them for National Socialism.

The *Schutz-und-Trutzbund* was organized in October 1919 by Alfred Roth, a man who had been active in prewar racist groups such as the *Reichshammer-Bund.* The purpose of the S-u-T is stated in its constitution:

> The Bund fights for the moral rebirth of the German *Volk* . . . It considers the pernicious and destructive influence of Jewry to be the main cause of the defeat [in World War I] and the removal of this influence to be necessary for the political and economic recovery of Germany, and for the salvation of German *Kultur.*[88]

Well before Hitler became a dominating influence in the struggling little German Workers Party, the *Schutz-und-Trutzbund* had established its own printing presses and was flooding the country with the most violent and scurrilous anti-Semitic propaganda. "In the year 1920 alone," declares its founder, "we distributed over 7,642,000 pieces [of propaganda material]." [89] The Bund had its own newspaper, the *Deutschvölkischen Blätter,* and its own pseudoscientific magazine, the *Politische-Anthropologische Monatschrift;* both publications carried the swastika on their mastheads. This was long before Hitler adopted the crooked

[87] Almost without exception, the leading figures of the Free Corps movement had been members of the S-u-T at one time or another. (In addition to the memoirs, see the biographical sketches in *Das deutsche Führerlexikon.*) Ernst von Salomon is a notable exception. In his memoirs he notes ruefully that that anti-Semitic organization was no longer interested in him after he told its leader his name.

[88] Alfred Roth, *Aus der Kampfzeit des Deutschvölkischen Schutz-und-Trutzbundes* (Hamburg, 1939), 15.

[89] *Ibid.,* 20.

cross as the symbol of mystic Aryan racism and the official sign of his party.[90] Before it was ostensibly dissolved in January 1923, the Bund had a total membership of almost a quarter of a million men.[91]

The *Schutz-und-Trutzbund* did important work in preparing Germany for Nazi racism, but it made a more specific contribution than that. A list of only its more distinguished graduates who figured prominently in Nazi Germany would include the following: Julius Streicher, Gauleiter of Nuremberg, editor of the unspeakable *Stürmer;* Dietrich Eckart, with Alfred Rosenberg co-editor of the *Völkischer Beobachter,* also a charter member of the Thule Society; Reinhard Heydrich, SS Grupenführer, Chief of the Security Service of the Gestapo; the Duke of Saxe-Coberg-Gotha, President of the German Red Cross; Wilhelm Murr, Federal Governor of Würtemberg; Walter Buch, Reichsleiter and President of the Party Court; and Fritz Sauckel, Federal Governor of Thuringia, notorious Chief Administrator of the Labor Draft Law.[92]

IV. THE FREEBOOTERS AS LEADERS OF YOUTH

A German educator has given the following description of the psychological tone of Germany's postwar youth:

The state? All one could see was ruins. Faith? All one could hear was the hate-filled wrangling over who was "guilty" for the lost war. Fatherland? All one could feel was insulting disgrace at the sight of silent guns and humiliation at the acceptance of Versailles . . . To be

[90] Most authorities say that Hitler first picked up the idea of using the swastika from the Ehrhardt Brigade in 1920. (Thus, Heiden, *Der Fuehrer,* 143.) But two organizations that were Hitler's immediate predecessors in spreading the doctrine of Aryan supremacy, the Thule Society and the S-u-T, had popularized its use as a racist symbol in 1919. And before them, the racist *Reichshammer Bundes* had used it as its "battle sign" as early as 1912. (Photographs of early editions of newspapers and pamphlets which bear the crooked cross are given in Roth, *op. cit., passim.*) The Nazis did not like to be reminded that they had precursors. The memoirs of the founders of both the S-u-T and the *Thule Gesellschaft* (Sebottendorff's *Bevor Hitler Kam*) were placed in the closed archives of the NSDAP and stamped with the "V" sign. Ehrhardt himself says that in January 1920 his men began to bear the swastika for the first time and comments, "I can not determine how this happened." *Kapitän Ehrhardt,* 164–165.)

[91] Roth, *op. cit.,* 7. Gumbel agrees with this estimate, *Verschwörer,* 67.

[92] *Das deutsche Führerlexikon, passim.*

sure there was a state, but party politics seemed to dominate it completely. Besides it completely lacked the visible brilliancy which is so essential to winning the hearts of youth . . . A wave of pessimism engulfed the youth . . . God, State, Work — everything profaned, defiled and cynically discussed . . . "The Decline of the West!" [93]

It is not at all surprising that, given this attitude, thousands of young people concluded with Günther Gründel that "radicalism is trumps" [94] and turned to extremist organizations to lead them out of their own — and their country's — impasse.

Although dozens of competing organizations[95] vied for the allegiance of postwar youth, the main issue was drawn between Leftist internationalism and folkish nationalism.[96] Former commanders of the Free Corps were in no small way responsible for the fact that in the ensuing years the camp of the extreme Left fought a losing battle against the militant forces of the far Right. We have already seen that the *Freikorpsführer* welcomed students into the ranks of their fighting formations. The leaders of the dissolved formations now became active in the youth movement.

Their work was made easy by the fact that their romantic exploits had already won the hearts of teen-age boys. "Former Free Corps leaders," Ernst von Salomon writes without exaggeration, "had an almost legendary reputation . . . Youth of all provinces gathered around them, enticed by the magic of their names . . ." [97] The youthful hero of a postwar novel, for instance, idolized a Free Corps fighter, tried to ape his "manly conduct," and even copied his little personal mannerisms.[98] One student was

[93] Wilhelm Hedemann, "Die geistigen Strömungen in der heutigen deutschen Studentenschaft," in *Akademisches Deutschland*, edited by Michael Doeberl, Otto Scheel and others, 4 vols. (Berlin, 1930–1931), III, 387–388.

[94] See above, p. 42.

[95] Some 157 separate youth associations are listed and discussed by the contributors to *Die deutschen Jugendverbände: Ihre Ziele, ihre Organisation sowie ihre neuere Entwicklung und Tätigkeit*, edited by Hertha Siemering (Berlin, 1931).

[96] This is the conclusion of a leading authority on the subject: Theodora Huber, *Die soziologische Seite der Jugendbewegung* (Inaugural dissertation, University of Munich, 1929), 15, 74–82.

[97] Von Salomon, *Nahe Geschichte*, 99.

[98] Ernst Ottwalt, *Ruhe und Ordnung: Roman aus dem Leben der national-gesinnten Jugend* (Berlin, 1929).

thrilled simply by seeing his hero, Captain Ehrhardt. He writes:

> I saw him for the first time in a local beer hall in Munich. For us students the Captain was not only the very epitome of military loyalty and honor. He was more than that. He was the very type and model of a soldierly dare-devil (*Draufgänger*) — the man who could form and direct all our youthful enthusiasm and young passions . . . He was our Captain. There can only be one Captain Ehrhardt.[99]

With the exception of Ehrhardt, Gerhard Rossbach, sadist, murderer, and homosexual, was the most admired hero of nationalist German youth. "In Ehrhardt, but also in Rossbach," says a popular book on the youth movement, "we see the Führer of our youth. These men have become the Ideal Man, idolized (*Vergöttert*) and honored as can only happen in a time when the personality of an individual counts for more than anything else." [100]

Freebooter commanders were not unmindful of the trust placed in them by German youth. They were well aware of the valuable role youth could play in the cause of resurgent, racist nationalism. Ernst Röhm, who enrolled hundreds of them in his SA, pays them high tribute:

> Next to the racist officers, it was primarily the aggressiveness and loyalty of the students that strengthened us. Under the spiritual influence of the War the young student . . . of 1923 bore within him the same spirit as the founders of the *Burschenschaften* 110 years before them — a spirit which had led them into the Free Corps of 1919.[101]

The Association of Former Ehrhardt Officers sponsored at least two youth groups, the Count Strachwitz Storm Company[102] and the *Knappenschaft*.[103] Von der Goltz later claimed that his work in the Young German Order had helped to imbue youth with "those spiritual values" which were, he felt, a prerequisite for the "spiritual revolution" which came in 1933.[104] Lieutenant Georg

[99] "Begegnung mit dem Kapitän," anonymous article in *Kampf: Lebensdokumente deutscher Jugend von 1914–1934*, compiled and edited by Bert Roth (Leipzig, 1934), 63–64.

[100] Roegels, *op. cit.*, 192.

[101] Röhm, *Geschichte eines Hochverräters*, 264.

[102] Roegels, *op. cit.*, 157.

[103] Gumbel, *Verschwörer*, 74. The name means, literally, the novitiate of a knight.

[104] Count Rudiger von der Goltz, "Die deutsche Revolution," in *Deutschlands Erneuerung*, XVII Jahrgang (June 1933), 335.

Mumme, after an active career in the Gerstenberg Free Corps, founded the Academic Homeland Service (*Akademischer Heimatsdienst*) which supplied reinforcements for the Eastern Free Corps and the Black Reichswehr.[105]

The list of former *Freikorpsführer* who became youth leaders could be continued at length, but it must terminate with the most important single contributor to the pre-Hitler youth movement — Gerhard Rossbach. He, along with Werner Lass,[106] founded the *Schilljugend*,[107] which became one of the largest youth organizations of the days preceding Baldur von Schirach and the Hitler Youth. Rossbach has left the following statement of the purpose and importance of the Schill Youth:

> I organized the *Schilljugend* . . . in order to carry on the tradition of the Free Corps directly. The youth of Germany had to be rebuilt anew and constructed, in the words of Ernst Jünger, on "nationalistic, socialistic, authoritative and militaristic" lines. This the *Schilljugend* would do . . . The existence of the *Schilljugend* helped to purify the whole German youth movement. We purged from the old established youth movement all purely intellectual elements and attracted all the most activistic elements around us.[108]

In addition to "purging all purely intellectual elements" from the youth of Germany, the volunteers made more specific contributions to the Nazi youth movement. The concept of organizing youth groups as "feeders" for the Party is at least inchoate in such groups as Ehrhardt's *Knappenschaft,* Rossbach's *Schilljugend,* Mumme's Academic Homeland Service and the Young German Order in which Rossbach and von der Goltz were particularly active.

[105] Mumme later became Gauführer of the Association of National Socialist German Jurists and Deputy Section Leader of the Party's legal section. *Führerlexikon,* 324.

[106] Lass had founded the *Sturmvolk, Bund deutscher Jugend* in Riedau in 1923. In 1926 when it was absorbed by Rossbach's *Schilljugend,* Lass collaborated with Ernst Jünger in editing the *Schill's* newspaper, *Der Vormarsch.* (Ernst Gronau, "Freischar Schill," in *Die deutschen Jugendverbände,* 93–94.)

[107] The name Schill was chosen to remind German youth of another "War of Liberation." A famous painting depicts the shooting of a row of young German officers by members of Napoleon's army. Schill is the last man standing. He is trying to hold up a mortally wounded comrade while gesturing defiantly at the enemy.

[108] Quoted in Bronnen, *Rossbach,* 172.

The Strength-through-Joy slogan of the Hitler Youth has a direct predecessor in such half-military groups as the Olympia Sports Society and the work camps founded by such former *Freikorpsführer* as Heinz Hauenstein, Friedrich Glombowski, and Gerhard Rossbach.[109] For the labor camps had a twofold purpose: they helped to keep the personnel of the Free Corps together, and, more importantly, they enrolled hundreds of German children, who were imbued with racist nationalism, and thus prepared for a war of revenge against the western democracies. Thus at a typical camp, actual labor was limited to five or six hours a day. The rest of the time was spent in military drill, target practice, "defensive exercises," and listening to "cultural lectures" delivered by battle-tough *Freikorpskämpfer* in front of signs which reminded the children that *"Versailles muss fallen!"* [110] In their capacities as advisers and leaders of such youth groups as the Young German Order and the Eagle and the Falcon (*Adler und Falken, Bund deutscher Jugendwanderer*), former Volunteer commanders saw to it that their charges established similar labor camps. In 1924, for instance, the Eagle and Falcon, a group which covered 24 *gauen* and had a membership of some 3,390,[111] sent out a call for "voluntary-compulsory labor service" (*freiwilligen Arbeitsdienstpflicht*) to drive the Polish summer laborers off the trans-Elbian estates. The response to the summons was gratifying:

The call awakened a loud echo in the *völkisch* youth. From the *Treubund* to the *Jungdo*, German youth responded . . . From the estates of five of the leading landowners in Saxony and Mecklenburg, complete Eastland squads were enrolled, each anxious to be the first to drive out the Polish summer workers. On April 13, 1924 on the Junker estate of Limbach near Wildsruf, Saxony, the solemn consecration [of one of the squads] . . . took place . . . The sacred swastika greets us from the black-white-red field of the Limbach Section

[109] See above, pp. 189 ff.

[110] For descriptions of these camps and pictures of their activity see Heinz, *Kameraden der Arbeit*, 33–37, 53, 96–98 and *passim*. Rossbach organized a "work and play" group, the *Spielschar Rossbach*, which had its headquarters within the labor camp he had established for his men on the estate belonging to one Herr von Viereck in Mecklenburg. Here the boys and girls he enrolled had ample opportunity to hear the experiences and imbibe the *Weltanschauung* of the Rossbachers. See Bronnen, *Rossbach*, 174.

[111] Hans Leme, "Adler und Falken, Bund deutscher Jugend," in *Die deutschen Jugendverbände*, 88.

flag. The inscription on the flag calls us: "To the Eastland we will ride!" [112]

To conclude, the Volunteers were at least partially responsible for the fact that by 1931 between 250,000 and 400,000 [113] German boys and girls were participating in the type of activity which later characterized Hitler's Strength-through-Joy and *Arbeitsdienst* programs.

In January 1933, the labor camps held impressive ceremonies to welcome the great Leader they had been told to expect. Glombowski describes a ceremony which took place at his camp in the Ems Valley. After a parade in honor of *Der Führer*, the flag-lowering rites were performed:

The columns gathered around the flagpole in a great square. I spoke. I told them of our battles: "Battles on the frontiers, battles inside Germany. The comrade-circle around Schlageter alone lost 53 comrades and we were only a small part of the grand conspiracy (*Verschwörung*) against the system of Weimar. But we threw ourselves into the battle with enthusiasm . . . Today has brought us the fulfillment of our battles . . . Attention, eyes right!"

Slowly our old black flag with its Free Corps insignia [a wreathed anchor on inverted chevrons] fluttered to the ground. I could not hold back a few tears . . . Around me like iron stood the youth of Germany, their eyes flashed as they watched the flag of the Third Reich climb the mast. The Horst Wessel Song resounded over the valley and ended with a Heil to the *Führer*.[114]

v. "TRAITORS FALL TO THE FEME!"

The original *Femgericht* (or *Vehmgericht*), readers of historical romances will recall, had been established in medieval Germany as a kind of vigilante society which dispensed crude but effective justice at a time when there was no efficient judicial

[112] Erich F. Berendt, *Soldaten der Freiheit* (Berlin, 1935), 149–150. "Nach Ostland wollen wir fahren!," it will be recalled, was the battle cry of the Baltic-bound Freebooters of 1919.

[113] F. W. Heinz gives the first figure in his *Kamerad der Arbeit*, 63. The larger estimate is given in Fritz Wilung, "Die Jungenpflege und Jugendbewegung im Arbeitersport," in *Die deutschen Jugendverbände*, 21. See also Theo Herrle, *Die deutsche Jugendbewegung in ihren wirtschaftlichen und gesellschaftlichen Zusammenhängen*, second enlarged edition (Stuttgart, 1922), 69–77.

[114] Glombowski, *Organisation Heinz (O.H.): Das Schicksal der Kameraden Schlageters*, 239–240.

system. During the period of their dissolution, the Freebooters revived the idea of the Feme and in its name meted out their "folkish justice" to all those people they loosely classified as traitors. The chief resemblance between the medieval *Femgericht* and its twentieth century namesake was this: the only sentence handed down by the "court" was death.

While the Feme was used by virtually all the post-Free Corps organizations, it is chiefly associated with Captain Hermann Ehrhardt's mysterious "O.C." — the Organization Consul, of which Ehrhardt was the "Consul" — for it was the former commander of the Second Marine Brigade who organized the Feme into a system for dispensing sudden death. In the days following the Kapp Putsch, Ehrhardt and a group of his most trusted lieutenants fled to Bavaria and established themselves as agricultural laborers on the great estates in the vicinity of Munich. Here, in the spring of 1921, the O.C. was formed. Pöhner, the chief of the Bavarian police, was the chief patron of the organization.[115] In addition to channeling police funds into Ehrhardt's coffers, he supplied false passports to members who had committed murders (that is, to those who had "carried out the stern justice of the *Femgericht*"). Such people, understandably, found it advisable to leave the country for a few weeks.[116]

One incident will illustrate the attitude of Police President Pöhner. "One day," Ernst Röhm recalls, "an alarmed statesman went up to the Police President and whispered in his ear, 'Herr President, political murder organizations exist in this country!' Pöhner replied, 'I know — but there are too few of them!'"[117]

The bylaws of the O.C. include the following statements of purpose:

[115] It was at Pöhner's invitation that Ehrhardt went to Bavaria. See E. J. Gumbel's article, "Le Capitaine Ehrhardt et L'Organisation C," in *L'Europe Nouvelle,* VI (August 25, 1923), 1073.
[116] Between 1919 and 1921 alone, the Munich police provided some twenty-five such passports. Gumbel, *"Verräter verfallen der Feme!,"* 131. Donations from heavy industry were also generous but insufficient. Ehrhardt therefore organized his own bank and later a "Wood Products Corporation." See Gumbel, *loc. cit.,* 1074.
[117] "So, So, aber zu wenig!" The story is told in Röhm's *Geschichte eines Hochverräters,* 131.

VANGUARD OF NAZISM

214

Spiritual (geistig) aims:

The cultivation and dissemination of nationalist thinking; warfare against all anti-nationalists and internationalists; warfare against Jewry, Social Democracy and Leftist-radicalism; fomentation of internal unrest in order to attain the overthrow of the anti-nationalist Weimar constitution . . .

Material aims:

The organization of determined, nationalist-minded men . . . local shock troops for breaking up meetings of an anti-nationalist nature; maintenance of arms and the preservation of military ability; the education of youth in the use of arms.

Notice:

Only those men who have determination, who obey unconditionally and who are without scruples (*keinen Anstand nehmen*) will be accepted . . . The organization is a secret organization. All members will swear the following oath: "I swear unconditional obedience to the Supreme Leader of the organization . . . I swear that I will remain absolutely silent in regard to all activities of the organization . . ." Membership is dissolved: (a) by death. (b) by expulsion as the result of dishonorable activity. (c) by disobedience. (d) by voluntary resignation. All members falling under categories (b) and (c) and all traitors will fall to the Feme! [118]

The Republic waited until 1924 before investigating the O.C. and bringing it to trial. And then, in spite of the fact that the bylaws were introduced as evidence, the *Reichsgericht* trying the case decided that the O.C. was not a secret society; that it did not possess arms; and finally that its political purpose was "to modify the constitution by political means." [119] In a word, that

[118] Accounts of the bylaws vary slightly. The statement given above is drawn from direct quotations given in the following sources: The statement read by Dr. Rosenfeld, SPD deputy in the Reichstag, in a speech of July 24, 1925; *Verhandlungen des Reichstags* (Stenographische Berichte) 101 Sitzung, 3486–3487; the statement in the Baden Diet made by Dr. Trunk, the Bavarian President, quoted in Gumbel, *Verschwörer*, 77–78; and the *Münchener Post*, December 27, 1922, quoted in Fried, *Guilt of the German Army*, 197.

[119] See Dr. Rosenfeld's bitter Reichstag speech, *Verhandlungen, loc. cit.*, 3485–3486. Rosenfeld quotes the court's decision, and comments, "If one reads the indictment of the state's attorneys against the 26 members of the Organization Consul, one might think that he is reading not an indictment at all but a defense plea . . ." (3485).

no murder organization known as the Organization Consul ever, in fact, existed. Captain Ehrhardt used this decision to silence criticism of his methods. Thus in 1929 he wrote to the Berlin Police President: "The O.C. never existed. It is only a phantasy of the press. For proof, I refer you to the court's decision." [120] Other members of the O.C. found the decision highly amusing. Heinz, who had been a member for years, writes:

In order to make the mockery complete, a Federal Court officially decided that the O.C. never existed. Now since the *Reichsgericht* is the highest court of appeal in the land, and since it is incapable of error, the author is also forced to recognize its decision and conclude that his activity in the years 1920 to 1923 was only a part of his dream life (*Traumerlebnis*).[121]

In another place, this same Heinz indicates the scope of Ehrhardt's murder organization:

Every new local group that Tillessen [the member of the O.C. who was directly involved in the murder of Erzberger and Rathenau] and Georg [an alias for Heinz] founded, formed a knot which drew the net closer together . . . In every city, in every village where the conspirators set their feet they found a few trustworthy men, unconditionally capable fanatics — [*Fanatiker*. As with the Nazis, a term of approbation] soldiers of the Great War in whom the fire of battle still burned, Freebooters who had fought under Maercker in Saxony, under Awaloff-Bermondt in Courland . . . These were the men who formed the nucleus . . . In the beginning of March [1921?] Tillessen took over the whole of South Germany . . . So it went throughout the Reich: in Berlin, in Hanover, in Dresden, in Munich, in Hamburg. Almost all the leaders knew each other . . . Ehrhardt finally gave me an entire district — the whole of Western Germany.[122]

[120] *Berlin am Morgen,* September 13, 1929, quoted in Scheer, *Blut und Ehre,* 46.

[121] Friedrich Wilhelm Heinz, "Politische Attentate in Deutschland," in *Deutscher Aufstand: Die Revolution des Nachkriegs,* edited by Curt Hotzel, 207.

[122] Heinz, *Sprengstoff* (Berlin, 1930), 87, 96, 167. It is easy to be misled by other statements made by members of the O.C. Von Salomon, for instance, in one place says flatly that the Organization Consul never existed. (*Die Geächteten,* 257.) In his later book, however, the same writer takes its existence for granted and discusses its work (*Nahe Geschichte,* 100–101). Heinz himself in his *Die Nation greift an,* writes, "The O.C. as an organization never existed" (p. 135). What these statements apparently mean is that contemporary newspapers exaggerated the scope and activity of the O.C. Röhm, among others, simply assumes its existence when he writes, "Nu-

According to the rather conservative estimate of the National Minister of Justice, 354 political murders were committed in the name of "folkish justice" and the Feme during the period from 1919 to the death of Walther Rathenau in June 1922.[123] The victims usually fell into one of three main categories: either they were leading members of the government, or civilians who had betrayed the activists by disclosing the existence of arms caches to the authorities, or else they were former comrades who had had a falling out with their Freebooter friends. We shall use case histories to illustrate each of these types.

The murder of distinguished republican leaders was not conceived by the Freebooters to be an end in itself. It was a means to the larger end of creating chaos. The idea was succinctly expressed by von Salomon when he told Heinz that if they were able to kill enough of the Weimar leaders, the Bolsheviks might come to power and in the accompanying chaos, the Freebooters would take over. "Yes," he concluded, "we have got to kill Scheidemann, Rathenau, Zeigner, Lipinski, Cohn, Ebert, and all the rest of the men of November, one after another." [124] And at the Scheidemann trial, one of the defendants testified: "About

---

merous national groups refused to disband. The O.C., from whose circle came the men who shot Rathenau, carried on . . . [and again] ". . . the O.C., whose leader, Captain Ehrhardt . . ." (*Hochverräter*, 141, 150–151.) That there was indeed such an organization would seem to be indicated by the fact that members of the Nazi party later listed membership in the O.C. among their other qualifications for leadership of the German people. See the entries in *Die Braunhemden im Reichstag, Die Nationalsozialistische Reichstagsfraktion 1932* (Munich, 1933), and in *Das deutsche Führerlexikon, 1934–1935* (Munich, 1934). Ehrhardt himself certainly admits that the Organization Consul existed and takes full credit for its activity. (*Kapitän Ehrhardt*, 214–215 and *passim*.)

[123] In 1923 at the request of the Reichstag, the National Minister of Justice drew up Reichstag Memorandum Number IV b. 2598 in which the estimates given above were made. The memorandum covers Bavaria only up to 1919, Mecklenburg only up to 1920, and Prussia up to 1921. The memorandum was never published. Professor Gumbel edited it and drew on its findings for his book, *Vier Jahre politischer Mord* (Berlin, 1922). The estimates are given on pages 144 and 145 of that book.

[124] Quoted in Heinz, *Sprengstoff*, 76. Von Salomon insists that the murders had a very definite purpose: "Every single one of our acts . . . might seem . . . to have had little practical result . . . But each act profoundly shook the foundations of the [Weimar] structure . . ." (*Die Geächteten*, 291.)

Christmas, 1921, we decided to remove republican leaders regardless of their policies." [125]

Germany's Minister of Finance, Matthias Erzberger, was the first to die. The Freebooters had hated him for years as the turncoat pacifist who was responsible for the peace resolution of 1917, the Armistice, and the acceptance of the Diktat of Versailles. When the Ehrhardt Brigade was doing guard duty in Upper Silesia in the fall of 1919, it used as password and countersign, "Erzberger! — Gravedigger!" [126]

On the afternoon of August 26, 1921, Erzberger was strolling through a light drizzle in the Black Forest near Griesbach. Years later, one of the assassins, Heinrich Schultz, sat in the comfort of his home on a Christmas Eve, sipped hot punch, and told a friend how the "act of liberation" was accomplished. He and his colleague of the O.C., Heinrich Tillessen, had stalked their prey through the mist and then called out, "Are you Erzberger?" The Minister's last word was a rather startled, "Yes!" The judges of the Feme drew their pistols. Erzberger thrust his umbrella in front of him as a shield in a pathetic gesture of self-defense. As he crumbled to the ground, the Freebooters reloaded and pumped a total of twelve shots into his head.[127]

Before joining the Organization Consul, the killers had been members, at one time or another, of the Ehrhardt Brigade, the Oberland Free Corps, and the *Schutz-und-Trutzbund*. After the assassination, they returned to O.C. headquarters in Munich, which were at that time the offices of the "Bavarian Wood Products Company." There they were given false passports by the

[125] *Politische Prozesse: Aktenmässige Darstellungen*, edited by Robert Breuer, Heft II, *Das Blausäure-Attentat auf Scheidemann* (Berlin, 1922–1924), 21. The same testimony was repeated by the defendants in the Rathenau trial. (*Loc. cit.*, Heft I, 25.)

[126] Ehrhardt gives the passwords in his memoirs and quite rightly notes that "A significant indication of the feeling of the troops is found in the passwords of the time." On the night of September 25/26: "Black-Red-Gold! — Incredible!"; September 28/29: "Forgotten! — Never!"; October 3/4: "Erzberger! — Gravedigger!"; October 5/6: "League of Nations — Nonsense!"; October 6/7: "Marine Brigade — Phoenix bird!"; October 7/8: "Poles — Smash them!" (*Kapitän Ehrhardt*, 158.)

[127] The story as told to Ludecke on a Christmas eve during the thirties (*I Knew Hitler*, 265) agrees with the accounts given by Heinz, Salomon, and Gumbel.

Bavarian police. They fled to Hungary where they were arrested
and subsequently released by orders of the Budapest police.[128]
The single sentence given in the Erzberger case was against
Franz Huber, the editor of the *Offenburger Tageblatt*. Because
he had published a part of the accusation against the defendants,
he was fined 1,000 marks.[129] Tillessen, the organizer of the attack,
was later imprisoned for his work in plotting other murders; but,
thanks largely to the intervention of Dr. Heinrich Brüning, he
was released after serving a few months' sentence.[130]

After killing Gareis, a USPD member of the Bavarian Diet, and
botching an attempt to blind Philip Scheidemann with prussic
acid,[131] the Feme moved on to its next main target, Walther
Rathenau, Foreign Minister of the Republic. Rathenau had long
been on the Feme's list of traitors. A year before his death, men
of the Organization Consul had included his name in one of their
doggerel verses sung to the tune of an old pirate song:

> You, brave hero, who shot Gareis down
> And thus wiped off our mournful frown
> Have brought us close to liberation
> From socialist dogs who hound our nation.

[128] *Berliner Tageblatt,* June 9, 1922.

[129] *Berliner Tageblatt,* August 17, 1922, cited in Gumbel, *Verräter,* 55–56.

[130] In an interview in Lowell House, Harvard University, March 12, 1948,
former Chancellor Brüning told me that Tillessen was "a decent sort of a
chap" and that he, Dr. Brüning, had spent considerable time and effort in
getting him released from prison. On November 25, 1946, Tillessen was
again tried before a German court for his twenty-five-year-old crime. He was
acquitted — largely because "the assassination had been motivated, in the
words of the court, by his exalted patriotic desire to lead Germany to a better
future." (Fischer, *Stalin and German Communism,* 285, citing the *Neue
Züricher Zeitung* of December 4, 1946.)

[131] On Sunday afternoon, June 4, 1922, Philip Scheidemann, the former
Chancellor of Germany and now Oberbürgermeister of Cassel, was out
walking with his daughter and granddaughter. Hustert, a member of the
O.C., following the orders of his superior, Tillessen, walked up to him, drew
a cheap rubber syringe from his pocket, and squirted a weak solution of
prussic acid in Scheidemann's eyes. Scheidemann was able to draw his pistol
and ward off further attack. The first congratulatory telegram the former
Chancellor received was from Walther Rathenau. An account of the attack
is given in Scheidemann's *Memoiren eines Sozialdemokraten,* 2 vols. (Dresden, 1928), II, 415–419. For the trial testimony, see *Politische Prozesse,* Heft
III, 7 ff. The defendants were given light sentences and then pardoned.

Then let us gladden, never dull,
Smash to pulp Herr Wirth's thick skull
Revenge will come to us some day
Hurrah! Hurrah! Hurrah!

Grab Herr Wirth by the scalp
Crack his skull 'til you hear him yelp
Knock off Walther Rathenau
The Goddamned dirty Jew! [132]

On the morning of June 24, 1923, Chancellor Wirth received a letter dated "On the Day of Rathenau's Murder!" The letter concluded: "You men of fulfillment mania will not listen to the voices of those who demand the end of your crazy politics (*Wahnsinnspolitik*). And so hard fate has taken its course in serving the Fatherland." [133] That same morning, about 11:00, a car driven by Ernst Werner Techow, the Berlin agent of the O.C., and two special agents, Erwin Kern and Hermann Fischer, overtook Rathenau's car as it slowed down to make the turn from the Königsallee to Wallotstrasse. Kern fired an automatic pistol at point blank range, Fischer hurled a hand grenade, and the second car speeded away.[134]

Thus died as a traitor the man who as Director of the Raw Material Department had made Germany's titanic war effort possible, thus died the cultivated philosopher, statesman, connoisseur of the arts, and the patriot who had written, "I am a German of Jewish descent. My people is the German people, my fatherland is Germany, my religion that Germanic faith which is above all religions." [135] There was added irony. During the early period, Rathenau had been an enthusiastic and generous supporter

[132] *Knallt ab den Walther Rathenau, Die Gottverfluchte Judensau!* The full text of the song is given in Paul Frölich, *Wider den Weissen Mord*, 2nd edition (Berlin and Leipzig, n.d.), 1.

[133] Speech of June 25, 1922 delivered in the Reichstag. *Verhandlungen* (Stenographische Berichte), 236 Sitzung, 8055–8056.

[134] Details of the planning and execution of the murder are given in Count Harry Kessler's biography, *Walther Rathenau: His Life and Work*, translated by W. D. Robson-Scott and Lawrence Hyde (New York, 1930). Kessler's account agrees, in all essentials, with the court testimony as reported in *Politische Prozesse*, Heft I, 25 ff.

[135] Walther Rathenau, *An Deutschlands Jugend* (Berlin, 1918), 9.

of the Free Corps. He had donated funds himself and had raised over $5,000,000 for their support.[136]

Kern and Fischer stayed one day too long in Berlin. When they reached the Baltic Sea, the pilot of the boat who had been hired to take them to Sweden had grown tired of waiting and had left. The fugitives fled to the south and were finally cornered in an old tower in a Thuringian village. The car sent from Munich to rescue them arrived just as the police authorities closed in. Kern ran to the window of the tower, "laughed in the faces of the hyenas who attacked him," and shouted "We die for our ideals! Others will follow us!" Then a bullet hit his head. Fischer wiped the blood from his dead comrade's face, lay down beside him, and shot himself.[137]

The government of the Third Reich removed Techow's criminal record from the police files and erected a monument to the memory of Kern and Fischer. Members of the Ehrhardt Brigade and 5,000 SA and SS troops participated in the dedication ceremonies. A number of speeches were made. Ehrhardt said: "Here on July 17, 1922, our comrades Kern and Fischer died a hero's death for Germany." Before placing the official SS wreath, Heinrich Himmler commented, "As a sign of the loyal memory with which the 120,000 SS comrades feel spiritually united with you, I lay this wreath on your resting place." The main oration was given by Ernst Röhm, at that time commander of the SA and SS:

Germany is once more German. This Germany is the Germany of its vanguard (Vorkämpfer) who rest in this grave . . . Kern and Fischer, you gave your example to the SA and the SS and all the comrades who today fight shoulder to shoulder at the front in the battle for the New Germany. Your spirit, Kern and Fischer, is the spirit of the SS, Hitler's black soldiers . . .[138]

As one after another of the ablest leaders of the Republic was

[136] According to Dr. Brüning, interview with the author, March 12, 1948.
[137] This is the version of the deaths given by their friends, Heinz ("Politische Attentate in Deutschland," loc. cit., 209 ff), and von Salomon (Die Geächteten, 327 ff). According to Count Kessler, Kern first shot Fischer and then himself. (Op. cit., 350.) Techow found refuge on his uncle's estate but was later tried for murder. His fifteen-year sentence was commuted to seven years.
[138] The ceremony and the speeches are reported in the Völkischer Beobachter, July 18, 1933 (Berliner Ausgabe).

killed or threatened with death, Germans might well ask them-
selves the question which André Tardieu put to the French
Chamber of Deputies in commenting on Rathenau's murder:
"Est-ce qu'il faut mourir, pour prouver qu'on est sincère?" [139]

What might be called The Case of the Misguided Maid will
serve as one illustration of the measures taken by the Feme to
bring to justice "traitors" who had informed the authorities of
illegal Freebooter activity. While out walking with a friend, a
Munich domestic servant, one Marie Sandmayr, stumbled on a
cache of illegal arms. Since she took the law of the land [140] seriously, she reported her discovery to the authorized government
agency, the Disarmament Commission. The next day she was
found hanging from a tree in the Forstenreider Park. A note was
pinned to her chest: "You bitch, you betrayed your Fatherland,
so you die by the Black Hand." The actual "judge" in this very
typical Feme trial was a certain Schweighart. He was provided
with a false passport, probably by the Munich police department,
and fled to Austria. Apprehended, extradited, and brought to
trial, Schweighart was released because of "lack of evidence." [141]
Colonel von Epp was jubilant over the verdict:

I deem it to be an act of self defense and a moral right that patriotic
circles take action against the betrayers of arms . . . The murder of
Waffenverräter . . . is approved by all patriotic circles . . . There
is no difference whatever between those who betray arms to the Entente and those who betray them to the Leftist-radicals who comprise
the Disarmament Commission.[142]

[139] Quoted in Wheeler-Bennett, *Wooden Titan,* 246.
[140] The law of August 7, 1920 ("Gesetz über die Entwaffnung der Bevölkerung") required that all citizens who knew of the existence of illegal arms
depots must report them to the Disarmament Commission which the same
law established. *Reichsgesetzblatt* (Jahrgang 1920), paragraphs 1 and 6.
[141] The case is discussed by Otto Landsberg, "Die Münchener Feme" in
Deutsche Republik, edited by former Chancellor Josef Wirth, Heft III
(Erster Jahrgang, 1926), 29 ff. The practice of pinning notes to the chest of
their victims before hanging them in a tree — the usual procedure in the
medieval Feme — was common among the Freebooters. Thus the two men
who allegedly informed Deputy Gareis of arms caches were found in the
Forstenreider Wald with the note: "I'm a rat who betrayed by Fatherland,
so I die by my own hand." (Heinz, *Die Nation greift an,* 129.)
[142] Quoted in Landsberg, "Die Münchener Feme," in *Deutsche Republik,*
30.

Since a great many, perhaps a majority, of all the judgments of the *Femgericht* were rendered against people who disclosed, or threatened to disclose, the existence of illegal arms, it is worth noting the reason for hiding and guarding arms so sedulously. It was not so much that the arms themselves had any real military value — most of them were in a bad state of disrepair. It was rather for a psychological reason. Arms are a symbol of power and, lacking power themselves, the men of the post-Free Corps groups clung all the more tenaciously to that symbol. The men expressed the idea differently. To them, weapons were "sacred things," [143] or, more commonly, "honor." Thus Heinz ends his discussion of a typical Feme murder by writing a paragraph which contains the single sentence, "Arms are honor." [144] And again: "Arms are an indispensable condition of national honor . . . Colonial people are disarmed and therefore dishonorable." [145] The National Socialists used the same terminology. In the official secret handbook of the NSDAP, the side arms of the political leaders are not called automatics, they are invariably referred to as "Ehrenwaffe." [146]

The Feme was often directed against former comrades of post-Free Corps organizations. The very multiplicity of Bunds and secret societies led to competition, quarreling, and death. Since each society tried to grow at the expense of the others, there were constant brawls over recruits and periodic purges of traitors who had deserted and disclosed the secrets and the arms depots to their new formations.[147] Competition and conflict was intensified by the fact that many of the Freebooters were homosexuals

[143] ("Die Waffe, das Heiligtum des Soldaten,") Major Pabst writing in *Deutscher Aufstand*, 34.

[144] *Die Nation greift an*, 129.

[145] *Ibid.*, 111.

[146] *Organisationsbuch der NSDAP*, published by the Reichsorganisationleiter der NSDAP (Munich, 1940). The preface states: "Written or verbal dissemination of the contents . . . is strictly forbidden."

[147] *Vorwärts* reported the swamp of intrigue, betrayal, double-cross, and murder that accompanied one such case under the ironic headline, *"Ich hatt' einen Kameraden."* (Morning edition, May 27, 1924.) Ehrhardt insists that his men were uniquely virtuous. He writes, "In contrast . . . to other Bunds, among us there was never any betrayal of a comrade . . ." (*Kapitän Ehrhardt*, 219.)

and hence prone to jealousy and "lovers' quarrels." The Mayer-Hermann case will serve as an example.

Oberleutnant Mayer was *Kreisleiter* of the "Arbeitsgemeinschaft Rossbach." He was also, as the court testimony euphemistically put it, "an enemy of women," as was his Leader, Gerhard Rossbach. In 1921 Mayer broke off relations with Rossbach and, supported by a wealthy tobacconist, one Kurt Hermann, he founded his own "Arbeitsgemeinschaft Mayer." But Oberleutnant Mayer soon became jealous of a certain Gebauer, a former Baltic fighter, who was also courting Herr Hermann. Mayer charged Gebauer with treason and sent two of his men to Hermann's home. They found the traitor in bed with Herr Hermann — Frau Hermann was away at the time — and carried out the sentence of the Feme.[148]

A responsible leader of the Weimar Republic comments on the almost criminal leniency with which the courts of the Republic handled the cases of the Feme murderers and concludes that the whole business forms "a very black page in German history." [149] In this he is quite right. Of the 354 murders committed by post-Free Corps groups, only the defendants in the Rathenau case received heavy sentences — then they were amnestied. All the rest were given a few weeks in prison or fined a few inflated marks.[150] Even so, the Freebooters were incensed at the injustices they claimed to have suffered at the hands of republican courts

[148] In this instance, the Feme was only partially successful. Hermann was smothered in his bedclothes and clubbed to death but Gebauer managed to escape to the police. In addition to newspaper reports of the trial which was held on October 9, 1924, see the summary of this and similar cases given in Gumbel, *"Verräter verfallen der Feme!,"* 186–188, 107 ff and *passim.* Both Heinz and von Salomon were involved in a similar case. They had tried and failed to kill Wagner, a fellow member of the O.C. who had allegedly threatened to expose the Organization Consul to the authorities. Von Salomon served some time for his connection with the Rathenau case. Heinz was arrested in 1924 for activity in the Viking Bund but was released because, according to the court, he had been so active in the "interests of national defense." (*Vossische Zeitung,* March 27, 1927.)

[149] Otto Braun, *Von Weimar zu Hitler,* 206–207.

[150] See Gumbel, *Vier Jahre politischer Mord,* 147–148; and the same author's "La Psychologie du Meurte Politique en Allemagne," in *L'Europe Nouvelle,* V, No. 34 (August 26, 1922), 1066–1068. For statistical tables of the disposition of cases see Gumbel's *"Verräter verfallen der Feme!,"* 386–389.

and righteously indignant that real patriots like themselves should
have been forced to appear in court like common criminals. The
speech made by a defendant, one August Blum, is worth quoting
at some length:

> You say, Herr Staatsanwalt, that it has been clearly proved that I
> have committed a murder . . . You demand my head in the interest
> of "justice" — in the interest of justice of a state in whose name you
> speak. But this "state" is not our state; and its "justice" is not our jus-
> tice.
>   The man, our victim, of whose humanity you have said so much and
> for whose death you have demanded payment with so much fuss —
> that victim is a common traitor. He deserved to die. We aren't afraid
> of uttering the words that shock you. Yes! We killed him! . . .
>   You, Herr Staatsanwalt, and your children and every last German
> . . . should kiss our hand instead of prosecuting us for murder. You
> treat us like common murderers. Criminals! But I tell you that if any-
> one is "guilty" it is I and I alone for I gave the order to kill clearly
> and unmistakably. Orders! Troops! Soldiers! Laws of Warfare! . . .
> We are soldiers, not criminals! . . .
>   You should have been in all the border fights in the East and the
> West . . . If you had, you wouldn't stand here and mouth platitudes
> with false pathos about "freeing the people from dangerous adventur-
> ers," . . . "murderers," and "unprincipled ruffians" . . .
>   You can't bluff us with the verdict of your court. We are young. We
> have suffered much and we can suffer plenty more. We are only a part
> of the entire youth who are already gripped by our spirit and who also
> know that the time will come to attack this state — your state, Herr
> Staatsanwalt! [151]

After Hitler came to power, it was fashionable for Freebooters,
or their apologists, to exaggerate the extent of the persecution
they had suffered at the hands of Republican justice. Manfred
von Killinger, for instance, was imprisoned for a few weeks in
connection with his part in the Erzberger and Rathenau murders.
Killinger had been the Munich agent of the O.C. and the director
of its front, the "Bavarian Wood Products Company." As such,
he had plotted both the murders. His biographer paints a picture
of persecution and intimidation and concludes: "The martyrdom

---

[151] Quoted in *Kampf: Lebensdokumente deutscher Jugend von 1914–1934*,
edited by Bert Roth (Leipzig, 1934), 145–147. The defendant was acquitted.

of a nine months' investigation-arrest (*Untersuchungshaft*) ended in his acquittal." [152]

In passionate and inconsistent diatribes, the Freebooters argue hotly that no political murders were committed, or if they were, they were completely justified. The arguments and the mind that produced them are interesting:

In a vilifying book, *Acht [sic] Jahre politischer Mord,* the cowardly pacifist non-German Gumbel accuses German nationalism of organizing a "murder organization!" *This statement is a lie; besides it is unprovable.* Almost all the killings set forth by Gumbel resulted from open battle . . . *or else* they resulted from special cases in which the law of necessity gave the Nation no other course than the immediate physical neutralization of a man whose activity was a direct threat to national honor . . . Thus the so-called Feme murders took place. The liberal and humanitarian eras were inclined to overestimate the value of human life . . . The Feme murders had absolutely nothing whatever to do with "murder." They represented thoroughly conscientious deeds of political necessity . . . If mistakes were made . . . and innocent people killed, that is a question of secondary importance.[153]

In another place, the same writer argues the interesting thesis that since an immutable law of history — apparently applicable only in Germany — makes true patriots impervious to the bullets of any assassin, the very fact that a man died at the hands of the Feme proved that he was a traitor:

On German soil, all attacks, all catastrophes and all deliverances possess a deep historical meaning. For it is no accident when the bullet of an assassin reaches its mark or misses its mark. Just as it is no accident when statesmen or generals . . . remain alive or not. The statesmen or generals who are capable of being wounded (*verwundbar*) are never — that is, on German soil — of the highest rank. This

---

[152] Baldur von Schirach, *Die Pioniere des Dritten Reiches* (Essen, 1933[?]), 131. Killinger himself thought that the Republic's courts were too lenient. "If I were made investigation judge," he writes, "I would be as hard as a rock . . . After 3 months the prisoner would be ready to confess to twenty murders even if he had only swiped a few apples." Manfred von Killinger, *Ernstes und Heiteres aus dem Putschleben,* 110. Perhaps Hitler felt that this statement, in addition to Killinger's record as one of the judges of the *Femgericht,* was ample recommendation. At any rate, Der Führer made von Killinger judge of the Nazis' *Volksgericht* and later appointed him Minister President of Saxony.

[153] Heinz, *Die Nation greift an,* 127, 172–173. (Italics are mine.)

makes them, in the truest sense of the word *unverwundbar*. Frederick the Great, Bismarck and Wilhelm I had German problems to solve and they stayed alive even though bullets which were intended for them killed those standing nearest them . . . Wallenstein . . . and Franz Ferdinand [were killed] because they possessed no historical or metaphysical immunity.[154]

Finally, it was argued that the Feme was really a splendid system of justice because it did not make the victim go through the ordeal of a court trial. Thus, after calling Professor Gumbel a "liar" for exaggerating the number of murders committed by the Feme and asserting that the deaths only totaled eight, the author of an article in a book originally entitled *The Feme Lie*, writes:

All eight executions were accomplished without any cruelty. None of the victims was forced to undergo a death battle. They were either killed by an unexpected shot or a sudden blow. People have reproached the Feme for not instituting a sort of court. But [if that had been done] the victims would have had to undergo all the terror and anxiety of court deliberations.[155]

Such was the twentieth-century *Femgericht*. Some time has been spent discussing its purpose and methods because it was one of the prevailing manifestations of Freebooter activity during the period when the Free Corps as such had been officially dissolved. The Feme was used by the Black Reichswehr, in dealing with Palatinate separatism, and in combating the French occupation of the Ruhr. It was a predominate feature of Freebooter activity in Upper Silesia. During the period of the Silesian plebiscite, Heinz Oskar Hauenstein gathered former *Freikorpskämpfer* about him and organized them into small shock troop formations,[156] one of whose main functions was to "influence" German voters. Years later in a public trial Hauenstein guessed that his "Special Police" had killed "about 200 people" in Upper Silesia

---

[154] Heinz, "Politische Attentate in Deutschland," in *Deutscher Aufstand*, 190.

[155] Gerhard Kramer, "Greuelpropaganda und Wirklichkeit," in *Femgericht*, edited by Friedrich von Felgen (Munich, 1932), 93. Italics are in the original. This is the greatly enlarged fourth edition of the book which originally appeared under the title, *Die Femelüge*.

[156] The best source for the organization, training, and activity of the notorious *Spezialpolizei* is the memoir of one of Hauenstein's lieutenants, Friedrich Glombowski, *Organisation Heinz*, 40–42, 66 ff.

alone.[157] In fact it was in Upper Silesia that one of the better known Feme murderers learned what he considered to be the greatest lesson of his life — a lesson which "seared the heart like drops of molten lead: 'Traitors Fall to the Feme!' " ("*Verräter verfallen der Feme!*")[158]

We must now summarize briefly the remaining history of the Free Corps movement. It is a story of sporadic interventions, the most important of which is the Upper Silesian campaign of 1921.

VI. THE FREE CORPS IN UPPER SILESIA

As we have suggested in preceding chapters, men of the Free Corps had been active in Upper Silesia ever since the Armistice. It was not until the Third Polish Insurrection, however, that the Volunteers were once again called upon to play a decisive role in the history of postwar Germany.

The results of the plebiscite of March 20, 1921, had been bitterly disappointing to the Poles and to their highly sympathetic French friends. The leader of Polish nationalists, Wojciech Korfanty, was determined that Silesian lands would not go to Germany as the German victory in the plebiscite seemed to foreshadow. On May 3, a Polish fete day, Korfanty led a group of irregulars across the Silesian frontier with the intention of conquering the whole of Upper Silesia and presenting the Supreme Council at Paris with a *fait accompli*. His troops were regularly supplied from Polish sources and enjoyed the tacit support of the French government and the French troops stationed in Upper Silesia.[159] As the Polish irregulars swept unopposed through the

[157] Testimony given by Hauenstein at the trial of Lieutenant Heines, quoted in the *Berliner Tageblatt*, April 25, 1928, morning edition.

[158] Von Salomon, *Die Geächteten*, 252.

[159] This is, of course, the version of the highly controversial subject given by German writers. Of the more responsible German accounts, see Josef Albert Rittau, *Die Stellung Oberschlesiens nach dem Versailler Vertrage während der interallierten Besetzung* (Inaugural dissertation, University of Würzburg, 1928), 36–38 and *passim*. It is also supported by the author of the standard work on postwar plebiscites, Sarah Wambaugh, *Plebiscites since the World War*, 2 vols. (Washington, D.C., 1933). Miss Wambaugh writes, "As the insurgents advanced, the French troops retired . . ." (I, 254.) Lord D'Abernon shows that the French general in charge of the Allied plebiscite troops, General Le Rond, approved of the Korfanty attack. (*An Ambassador of Peace*, I, 313.) In a violently pro-Polish article, M. Noulens,

eastern part of the province, the Weimar government protested
vigorously to the Allies and offered to send in regular Reichswehr
troops to restore order. The Supreme Council, acting under pressure from France, flatly refused.[160] But when Korfanty's troops
showed signs of occupying the whole of Upper Silesia, the Prime
Minister of England rose in Commons on May 13, and delivered
the speech which was to give the Free Corps the opportunity of
participating in their last major intervention.

> Without waiting for discussion between governments, the Polish
> population under the leadership of Mr. Korfanty raised an insurrec-
> tion . . . and put us in the difficulty of having to deal with a *fait ac-
> compli.*
> That is the state of the case. It is a complete defiance of the Treaty
> of Versailles . . . It may be a bad treaty, it may be a harsh treaty,
> but the last country in Europe that has a right to complain is
> Poland . . .
> Either the Allies ought to insist upon the Treaty being respected, or
> they ought to allow the Germans to do it. Not merely to disarm Ger-
> many, but to say that such troops as she has got are not to be permitted
> to take part in restoring order in what, until the decision comes, is
> their own province — that is not fair. Fair play is what England stands
> for, and I hope she will stand for it to the end.[161]

This speech went far to encourage the German government in
supporting the Volunteers who were already arriving from all
parts of the Reich. Heydebreck's Wehrwolves, Rossbach's Storm
Sections, and Reinhard's Free Corps left their work as "agricultural laborers" on the estates of northeast Germany and set up
new headquarters in Upper Silesia during the first week of May.
The Oberland Free Corps and the nucleus of a dozen other formations soon followed. Former Baltic fighters were already on the
scene working as "mine laborers," [162] and student formations and

---

the French Ambassador and president of the "France-Pologne" Association,
does nothing to oppose the interpretation given above. "Le Point de Vue
Politique," in *Les Archives de la Grande Guerre,* July, 1921, No. 24 (a special edition devoted to the question of Upper Silesia). For a Polish interpretation of the Third Polish Insurrection, see Casimir Smogorzewski, "Le
Plebiscite et la Partage de la Haute-Silésie," in *La Silésie Polonaise,* Vol. II
of *Problems Politiques de la Pologne Contemporaine* (Paris, 1932), 330–332.
    [160] Wambaugh, *op. cit.,* I, 255.
    [161] *141 House of Commons Debates,* 5th Session, cols. 2382–2385.
    [162] See above, p. 138.

individual volunteers arrived by the hundreds. Von Salomon describes his trip across Germany and the gathering of the clans in Upper Silesia:

The train roared through the night . . . In Leipzig young men boarded who wore feathers in their hats, spoke Bavarian dialects, and carried no luggage . . . In Dresden a group of boys from the forestry school got on. The whole school with their teacher as their leader were off for Upper Silesia . . .

We got out at Namslau and a defense battalion was formed . . . The *Jungdeutsche* were there, the *Stahlhelm, Rossbachers, Baltikumers, Landesjäger, Kapp-Putschists* . . . It seemed to me that I knew about every third man from the battles of the German postwar period.[163]

The *Freikorpsführer* met at once and chose General Hoefer as their commander in chief.[164] On May 15 at a council of war, Hoefer outlined his strategy: the Free Corps would hold defensive positions, and wait for the decision of the Allies on the disposition of Upper Silesia. Hoefer's decision was greeted by a furious outcry from the Freebooters, who were itching for attack. Egged on by Heydebrech and the leaders of the Oberland Free Corps, Lieutenant General Bernhard von Hülsen, commander of Group South, countermanded his superior's orders and ordered his men to attack.[165]

The main objective of the Group South's offensive was the Annaberg, the ancient convent of St. Anna commanding the hills along the right bank of the Oder. At dawn on May 23, the Volunteers, spearheaded by the Free Corps Oberland, the Heinz Storm Battalion, and Heydebreck's Wehrwolves, began their assault. By noon the Annaberg was in the hands of the Freebooters and its name added to that of Riga and Munich as the symbols of Free Corps victories. "Oh, Annaberg!" goes a typical ode, "thou

[163] Von Salomon, *Die Geächteten*, 239–241.

[164] As Benoist-Méchin has pointed out, it is important to notice that "General Hoefer is neither the representative of the German government, nor of the Reichswehr command, but the choice of the central committee of the Free Corps leaders." *Histoire de L'Armée Allemande*, II, 191.

[165] For a discussion of the conflict between Hoefer and Hülsen and Hülsen's caustic comments on his superior's "weak-kneed attitude," see Hülsen's *Der Kampf um Oberschlesien: Oberschlesien und sein Selbstschutz* (Stuttgart, 1922), 21–22, and his article, "Freikorps im Osten," in *Deutsche Soldaten*, 114.

art a memorial to the German Volk! March! March! March!" [166]

On the twelfth anniversary of its fall, the Nazis — who made it a practice to claim Freebooter victories as their own — staged a great celebration and dedicated a memorial at the convent of St. Anna. The principal oration was delivered by SA Obergruppenführer Edmund Heines, a man who had stormed the Annaberg — and a man who was to fall a year later in the Blood Purge. "Your soul, SA men," he said, "is the same as that of the men who twelve years ago . . . stormed the Annaberg." [167]

May 23, 1921, was a proud day for the reassembled Free Corps. That night as the jubilant Freebooters sat about their camp fires singing their *Landknechtslieder,* they laid plans for the conquest of the whole of Upper Silesia.[168] The next day they were stunned by the news that the President of Germany, drawing upon powers vested in Article 48 of the Weimar Constitution, had issued a decree outlawing all Volunteer formations. Imprisonment and fines would be given to anyone joining or participating in such formations.[169]

The decree was forced on Ebert by the Allies, but to the Volunteers it seemed that the home government itself had once again stabbed them in the back at the very moment of their greatest triumph for the Fatherland. In their fury and frustration they became convinced that the government was solely responsible for their failure, that it had given them absolutely no support during the entire campaign, that as altruistic patriots they had fought and died to save two-thirds of Upper Silesia, and that they would have conquered the rest of it if only the Ebert government had not betrayed them. Their attitude is completely understandable, and there is more than the usual modicum of truth in their assertions.

---

[166] Erich F. Berendt, *Soldaten der Freiheit: Ein Parolebuch des Nationalsozialismus, 1918–1925* (Berlin, 1935), 92.

[167] The dedication ceremonies are reported in the *Völkischer Beobachter,* May 25–26, 1933.

[168] See von Oertzen, *Kamerad, reich mir die Hände,* 237–239. Von Hülsen was also convinced that his Volunteers could have conquered the whole of Upper Silesia. *Kampf um Oberschlesien,* 52–55.

[169] "Verordnung des Reichspräsidenten über das Verbot militärischer Verbände vom 24 Mai 1921," *Reichsgesetzblatt* (Erstes Halbjahr, 1921), 711–712.

While it is manifestly untrue that the government did not support them,[170] and it is very doubtful indeed if the Allies would have permitted them to seize the whole of the province, it is indubitably true that their intervention helped to save that part of Upper Silesia which later went to Germany. It must also be said that in the Upper Silesian campaign of 1921 — more than in any of the other postwar interventions — sincere and unselfish patriotism was the prevailing motivation of the Volunteers.

Their experience in the Third Polish Insurrection thus confirmed the Volunteer's hatred of the November Criminals. "We had hoped," one of them writes, "that perhaps the German *Volk-seele* would boil over and force the Fulfillment Government to stumble into resistance. But nothing boiled over . . . For God's sake all that happened was peace and business as usual." [171] And another of the men who stormed the Annaberg concluded: "In the hearts of the Free Corps fighters and the stormers of the Annaberg, the realization became increasingly clear that any great German War of Liberation presupposed the overthrow of

[170] Because they did not wish to provoke the Allies, and particularly France, government officials at the time denied that they were sending aid to the Volunteers in Upper Silesia. Thus, in 1921, Chancellor Wirth simply said that the frontier was officially closed. But in 1926 in a Reichstag speech he admitted that the government had sent supplies and equipment throughout the period (Speech of December 16, 1926, *Verhandlungen*, 252 Sitzung, 8589); and in 1931, according to the *Schlesische Volkszeitung*, Wirth said that "it was by virtue of his own instruction and recommendations that the volunteers had been organized, armed and equipped." (Quoted in *La Silésie Polonaise, loc. cit.*, 353.) Perhaps the best evidence of government support is given in the memoirs of Major Buchrucker, the man who staged the Kustrine Putsch of 1923. Buchrucker admits: "The Reichswehr had been barred from the disputed area by virtue of the Treaty of Versailles; the government therefore allowed the Volunteers to carry on the struggle. It gave money, arms and equipment. Otherwise the battle would not have been possible. Naturally the government officials denied having anything to do with the matter and represented it as an action undertaken by the local population itself." Major Bruno Ernst Buchrucker, *Im Shatten Seeckts: Die Geschichte der "Schwarzen Reichswehr"* (Berlin, 1928), 5. General von Seeckt, while officially denying any connection with the Free Corps of Upper Silesia, secretly sent them arms, munitions, and supplies and even dispatched staff officers in civilian clothes to advise them. "It can be calmly asserted," his biographer writes, "that Seeckt's activity made it possible to achieve . . . as much as was achieved." Rabenau, *Seeckt, Aus seinem Leben*, II, 300.

[171] Manfred von Killinger, *Kampf um Oberschlesien, 1921*, 2nd edition (Leipzig, 1934), 33–34.

western parliamentarianism and the whole Liberal-Marxist system." [172]

To attain that end, the Free Corps once more determined to defy the government's dissolution order and to keep their formations intact. Heydebreck took his Wehrwolves underground as forest laborers in the neighborhood of Kandrzin. "Here," their leader assures us, "my wild and foolhardy wolves met terror with terror." [173] Other groups also stayed in Upper Silesia. Von Aulock's Free Corps became forest laborers near the Riesengebirge, and the Free Corps Oberland was assigned to the great estates near Neustadt, Neuse, and Glatz. [174] The Rossbachers remained for a time and then returned to their work as *Arbeitsgemeinschaften* in Pomerania. They were joined by hundreds of unattached Freebooters whose formations had been dissolved. Carsten Curator was one of them:

> Rifles and machine guns were heavily greased . . . packed away in crates and buried near the border of Upper Silesia — just in case of an accident . . . We became "agricultural laborers." There was really no pressing need for us, for the little farmers could easily do their own work and the great estates had plenty of workers of their own. So we led the life of Riley (*Faulenzerleben*) . . . [175]

On the whole, however, the Free Corps were not as successful in maintaining their cohesiveness as they had been after they were "dissolved" in 1920. As the months passed, financial difficulties, inactivity, and inter-Free Corps feuds claimed many of their members. By the autumn of 1922 only a few scattered remnants of their formations remained intact. As we shall see in the next chapter, it was from these stubborn nuclei that the Black Reichswehr of 1923 was to grow.

[172] F. W. Heinz, "Die Freikorps retten Oberschlesien," in *Deutscher Aufstand*, 88.

[173] Heydebreck, *Wir Wehrwölfe*, 133.

[174] The Oberland withdrew its last troops from Upper Silesia early in 1922 and returned to Bavaria. There it changed its name to the Oberland Bund. Its newspaper was called *Das Dritte Reich*. Under the leadership of Dr. Friedrich Weber, the Bund joined Hitler and marched in the Beer Hall Putsch. It is only one of the lesser ironies of recent German history that the Oberland's insignia, the edelweiss, that little mountain flower which is the traditional symbol of freedom, should become the symbol and name of the largest anti-Hitler movement of the period from 1942 to 1945.

[175] Curator, *Putsche, Staat und Wir!*, 131.

VII. THE FRENCH OCCUPATION OF THE RUHR;
ALBERT LEO SCHLAGETER

National Socialist historians of the Free Corps movement have grossly exaggerated the part played by their heroes during the French occupation of the Ruhr. They like to think that the despised and outlawed Volunteers once more gathered at the Fatherland's call of distress and, singlehanded, crushed the French-endorsed separatist movement which sought to create independent governments along the Rhine.[176] And it was the Free Corps, they say, who first kindled the fire of passive resistance and then kept it alive by the gallant example they set by their *Krieg im Dunkeln*.[177]

Actually the separatist movement failed for three main reasons,

---

[176] President Poincaré officially denied that his government had any direct connection with the separatist agitation in the Rhineland and the Palatinate, and Paul Tirard, the High Commissioner of the Allied occupation, insists in his memoirs that it was a purely autonomous and spontaneous movement (*La France sur le Rhin: Douze Années d'Occupation Rhénane*, 5th edition, Paris, 1930, 71, 287, 403–405). Nevertheless, there can be no doubt that France was directly involved. A long report from the French representative in Wiesbaden, the Marquis de Lillers, addressed to Tirard, marked "strictly confidential," and dated April 16, 1923, shows, among other things: that as early as May 1921 the Marquis had been given instructions to cultivate and advise separatist leaders; that Tirard himself had supplied Dr. Dorten and other separatist leaders with a great deal of financial aid; that the French railway system was placed at the disposal of the separatists; and that while all nationalist German forces were outlawed, the French occupation forces supplied the separatists with arms, instructed them in maneuvers, and helped them to stage demonstrations. The full report is reprinted in Max Springer, *Loslösungsbestrebungen am Rhein 1918–1924* (Berlin, 1924), Appendix II, 150–165. The report is fully substantiated by neutral observers. See especially the account written by G. E. R. Gedye (a former member of the British Army Intelligence service and special correspondent of the *Times*), *The Revolver Republic: France's Bid for the Rhine* (London, 1930) and the memoirs of the commanding American General Henry T. Allen, *The Rhineland Occupation* (Indianapolis, 1927), 192–196. General Mordoque, commander of the Thirtieth Corps of the French Army, shows Tirard's complicity but castigates him for not going far enough: "We should have supported their insurrections by every means at the disposal of those who are the masters of a province." General Henri Mordacq, *La Mentalité Allemande: Cinq Ans de Commandement sur le Rhin*, 9th ed. (Paris, 1926), 197, 216–217.

[177] Von Oertzen, *Die deutschen Freikorps*, 438 ff, 500; von Schmidt-Pauli, *Geschichte der Freikorps*, 277, 331 ff.

none of which is directly connected with the Free Corps: First, the British government opposed it from the start.[178] Second, the assorted group of criminals[179] chosen by the French to lead the movement were totally unreliable. Finally, the embattled farmers and miners of the Rhenish provinces defeated and routed the separatists in open battle. In the Battle of Siebengebirge it was not the men of Rossbach, Heinz, and Steinacher who won the victory. The farmers and miners who fought that day were led by obscure and humble patriots like the miner, Hermann Schneider; the blacksmith, Peter Staffel; Kraus Wiegard; and Philipp Schmitz.[180]

In fact, the only direct contribution made by the Freebooters to the overthrow of separatism was made by five members of the Organization Consul who assassinated Heinz-Orbis, the "President of the Autonomous Republic of the Palatinate." One of the

[178] See, for example, Bonar Law's outspoken attack on French policy in Commons, 160 House of Commons Debates, cols. 39–41; and the British Consul's report on separatism and the accompanying debates, 169 H.C. Debates, cols. 154, 485–486.

[179] Gedye drew up a list of leading separatist officials and checked their criminal records against old police files. He found that the Chief of Police had served three sentences, one for highway robbery; the Minister for Religion and Education was a brothel keeper with 22 convictions; the Minister of Art and Culture, 13 convictions, the Minister of Health, 12 convictions, and so forth. One of the leaders told Gedye: "I am a professional leader of putsches, I am not a politician. I am no German but a French citizen of Polish descent . . . I was brought to the Rhineland three weeks ago to force through the Rhenish Republic . . . This is my trade. One of my finest achievements was the organization of the Putsch for the French and Poles in Upper Silesia . . . My men will fight for anyone in the world who will feed and pay them." (Gedye, Revolver Republic, 198–199 and 203.) Mr. Clark does not exaggerate when he speaks of the "utter despicability of the tools selected by the French authorities." (The Fall of the German Republic, 95.) For an unconvincing defense of the leaders he chose and endorsed, see Tirard's La France sur le Rhin, 287. Former Chancellor Brüning told me that he knew of several separatist leaders who later became SA leaders in 1933.

[180] It is important to notice that German historians of the separatist movement who wrote before Hitler came to power, make no mention of Free Corps participation. The fullest account is given in Friedrich Grimm, Vom Ruhrkrieg zur Rheinlandräumung: Erinnerungen eines deutschen Verteidigers vor französischen und belgischen Kriegsgerichten (Hamburg, 1930), 81–111; see also Spethmann, Zwölf Jahre Ruhrbergbau, IV, 85, 285, 360 and passim.

leaders of the Palatinate resistance movement and a member of the *Bund Oberland,* had appealed to Captain Ehrhardt for help. "The Consul" dispatched Gunther Muthmann and four other former *Freikorpskämpfer* to the Palatinate. There, at the Wittelsbacher Hotel in Speyer, Heinz-Orbis sat eating his supper. Muthmann ordered his comrades to guard the hotel doors. He then entered the dining room and shot his victim in the back. Having accomplished "the glorious deed of liberation," Muthmann and his friends returned to O.C. headquarters in Munich.[181]

Nor can it be argued (as Herr von Oertzen argues) that the Free Corps were mainly responsible for the passive resistance to the French occupation of the Ruhr.[182] That was primarily the work of the Free and the Christian Trade Unions. The Freebooters never understood the use of the adjective "passive" to describe resistance. They therefore organized little Shock Troops of saboteurs who went about indiscriminately blowing up railway bridges, coal transports, and French troop trains. In the opinion of one of the leaders of the Christian Trade Unions, passive resistance was seriously handicapped by these individual acts of terrorism, for they provoked the type of reprisals which the resistance leaders had wanted to avoid.[183]

The Ruhr episode nevertheless forms an important chapter in the history of the German Free Corps movement. It provided the Volunteers with a martyr of national stature and the National Socialists with a powerful propaganda weapon. For, fortunately

[181] Seldom has a political assassination been so well documented. Muthmann himself has left a swaggering account of his work in the article, "Der Tod von Speyer, das Strafgericht an den separatistischen Verrätern," in *Reiter gen Osten* (November 1934), reprinted in *Freikorpskämpfer,* 459 ff. Gedye, the correspondent of the London *Times,* was eating supper at the Wittelsbacher Hotel when the assassination took place. His eyewitness account agrees with Muthmann's. *The Revolver Republic,* 218 ff.)

[182] Von Oertzen, *Die deutschen Freikorps,* 438 and 500. See also Dr. Reckhaus, "Krieg im Dunkeln: gegen die französische Besetzung in Essen," in *Freikorpskämpfer,* 422–423, and von Salomon, *Nahe Geschichte,* 104–105.

[183] Dr. Brüning in interview of March 12, 1948. Rosenberg also notes that "the positive effects of this active resistance were slight." (*Geschichte,* 156.) The organization and activity of the Ruhr Shock Troops is best described in Glombowski's *Organisation Heinz* (O.H.): *das Schicksal der Kameraden Schlageters,* 132 ff.

for the Nazis, Albert Leo Schlageter had joined the NSDAP during the course of his restless life. He was therefore hailed by the Party as the symbol of all those "pure-souled warriors" who had died fighting for the Third Reich.

In many ways Schlageter's career[184] parallels that of thousands of his generation. Like so many of his comrades, he was the son of a respected middle-class family, and like them he interrupted his education to volunteer for service in the War. He was decorated with the Iron Cross first and second class and was commissioned in the field. After the Armistice he tried for a time to adjust to student life at the University of Freiburg. But he was restless. He joined his old artillery battery and set off for the Baltic, where he entered the Von Medem Free Corps. He participated in the victorious siege of Riga and, after the mutiny of August 1919, joined the German Legion to fight for Awaloff-Bermondt. As a member of the 3rd Marine Brigade he took part in the Kapp Putsch and was then hired by the government to fight against the Communists. When the Third Polish Insurrection broke out, he hurried to Upper Silesia and joined the Heinz Storm Battalion in time to storm the Annaberg. "Riga and Annaberg," says a close friend and admirer, "the two most brilliant battles of the German postwar period, are inseparably linked with the name of Schlageter." [185] After the campaign, he and a group of Rossbachers accompanied Heinz Hauenstein to Munich. There at dinner[186] in November 1922, he heard *Der Führer* speak for the first time. Converted at once to the cause, he, Rossbach, and Hauenstein were sent to Prussia to organize the NSDAP there. But the French invasion of the Ruhr interrupted their work. Schlageter and Hauenstein set off at once for the Ruhr and organized squads of saboteurs to fight the "Battle in the Dark."

[184] Of literally dozens of biographies and memorial essays, see the sentimental encomium written by Martin Freitag, *Albert Leo Schlageter: ein deutscher Held* (n.p., n.d.); and von Salomon's "Albert Leo Schlageter," in *Freikorpskämpfer*.

[185] Von Salomon, "Albert Leo Schlageter," *loc. cit.*, 485.

[186] Under the National Socialists, the Reichsarchivs carefully preserved the menu upon which Hitler scribbled the notes of his speech. Schlageter was Number 61, Hauenstein Number 62, on the membership list of the NSDAP Ortsgruppe Berlin.

On March 15, 1923, Schlageter blew up the railway bridge near Calkum. Betrayed by his friends[187] to the French, he was arrested and tried by a French military court. During the course of the trial he disclosed the identity of several of his comrades.[188] On May 26, 1923, he was led to his place of execution on Golzheimer Heide and shot by a French firing squad.

Overnight Schlageter became a national hero and a martyr to the cause of German liberation. When his body was removed for burial to Elberfeld in the unoccupied zone, at every station en route, a British observer noted, "worshipping crowds assembled to pay a last tribute . . . his grave became for many months a place of pilgrimage at which to register vows of vengeance against the French." [189] The National Socialists were quick to capitalize on the propaganda possibilities presented by the former *Freikorpskämpfer's* death and the national adoration it had occasioned. Hitler sent 70,000 SA troops and a like number of the Hitler Youth to march by the casket, and five of the six honorary pallbearers were SA men who subsequently became big wheels in the Nazi machine.[190]

On May 24, 1933, on the tenth anniversary of his death, the Nazis unveiled the Schlageter monument on Golzheimer Heide.

[187] National Socialists always insisted that Schlageter was betrayed by the Prussian police and by Karl Severing, who was, they say, in league with the French. See Hans zur Megede's article in the *Nationalsozialistischen Schulungsbriefen*, quoted in von Oertzen, *Die deutschen Freikorps*, 453–454. One of his closest friends, however, admits that Schlageter was delivered over to the *Service de Sureté* by two of his former comrades of the Rossbach Free Corps, Götzte and Schneider. See Glombowski, *op. cit.*, 148, 213.

[188] Here again, the National Socialists insist that the tight-lipped German hero, though tortured by the French, refused to divulge any information about the Shock Troops. But the court testimony shows that the Nazi hero gave the French officials the names of the organizations, their personnel, the sources of their money and weapons, and a detailed description of how each group operated. Records of the trial are reprinted in an anonymous book, *Naziführer sehen Dich an! 33 Biographien aus dem Dritten Reich* (Paris, 1924), 170–176.

[189] Gedye, *op. cit.*, 138.

[190] Karl Kaufmann, the future Reichstaathalter of Hamburg; Erich Koch, Oberpräsident and Gauleiter of East Prussia; Viktor Lutze, Oberpräsident of Hannover and, after Röhm's death, chief of staff of the SA; Hein, SA Gruppenführer of Saxony, and SA Storm Leaders Jürgens and Hügenell. See the *Völkischer Beobachter*, May 24–May 27, 1923, Norddeutsche Ausgabe.

The choice of design was deliberate, and it would have shocked the devout and simple soul [191] of the hero it honored. The memorial was an exact copy of the Cross that stood on Golgotha. The analogy was obvious. Here, too, was a leader of his people, despised and rejected by them and betrayed to a foreign army of occupation for trial and execution. The Christian cross is the symbol of resurrection. And so was Schlageter's. "The cross on Golzheimer Heide," so concludes a typical Nazi account, "stands on Holy Ground as the symbol of eternal life . . . Eternal Germany!" [192]

[191] A devout Catholic, Schlageter had seriously considered entering the priesthood. His simple, pious letters to his old professor of theology are reprinted in the collection, *Deutschland muss leben: Gesammelte Briefe von Albert Leo Schlageter,* edited by Friedrich Bubendey (Berlin, 1934), 7 ff.

[192] Berendt, *Soldaten der Freiheit,* 128. In the foreword approving Glombowski's book, Heinz Oskar Hauenstein also points up the resemblance — and the contrast — between the two messiahs: "Cross and steel helmet; crown of thorns and laurel wreath." And one of the better biographies notes that at Schlageter's trial the French judge, like Pilate, hesitated to condemn so honorable a man but the crowd howled for his death. (Freitag, *Schlageter,* 85.) The dedication of the memorial is reported in the *Völkischer Beobachter* for May 25–May 27, 1933. The titles of the articles in this Nazi organ are suggestive of the party line: "Schlageter, First Soldier of the Third Reich"; "Schlageter's Spirit is the Spirit of the SA"; "Schlageter is Ransomed and Redeemed"; and so on. There was precedent in German history for the blasphemy of Schlageter's cross and "Golgotha." Karl Sand, a Volunteer fighter of the original "War of Liberation" against Napoleon and a member of the 1817 *Burschenschaften,* was executed for the murder of the Russian publicist, Kotzebue. Comrades of the *Burschenschaften* rushed to the scaffold and dipped flags in his "martyr's blood." The spot where Sand's head had fallen became known as Ascension Meadow.

IX

DER TAG, 1923

With feverish longing we awaited the Day that would bring liberation . . . Every morning when we got up, we heard the ever more
urgent question asked by the liberation-fighters: "Will today finally
bring the decision?"
— Ernst Röhm

I. THE BLACK REICHSWEHR

As early as November 1922, the French cabinet had completed
plans for a military occupation of the Ruhr, to go into effect as
soon as the German government provided the necessary excuse
by defaulting on reparations payments. In the first week of January 1923, Germany failed to deliver 140,000 telegraph poles on
schedule, and Poincaré seized this opportunity to put his plan
into effect. On January 11, 1923, French and Belgian troops
marched into the Ruhr.

A wave of excitement bordering on hysteria swept through
Germany. The activists clamored for war and even the usually
imperturbable Seeckt was excited. His eyes flashed and his voice
trembled when he told the British ambassador that "the road
from Dortmund to Berlin is not very long, but it passes through
streams of blood." [1] He began to prepare for the war he felt was
inevitable.

---

[1] General Friedrich von Rabenau, *Seeckt, Aus seinem Leben 1918–1936*
(Leipzig, 1940), II, 324. See also Hans Henning Grote, *Seeckt: der wunderbare Weg eines Heeres* (Stuttgart, 1938[?]), 83–85. Rabenau criticizes his
hero for losing his perspective in thinking that a war against France was
feasible in 1923 and dutifully quotes *Mein Kampf* to prove that it was out
of the question. Actually Hitler's position was extremely ambivalent. Since
he realized that a successful war would ruin his movement, he demanded
peace. But he did not want to lose the activist elements who were supporting

Members of the Weimar government were equally alarmed, and not without due cause. The Poles began at once to demand a "rectification" of their frontier at Germany's expense, and, shortly after the French invasion, Lithuania seized the city of Memel by force. The Republic was faced with the realization that it was unable to protect itself from its weakest neighbors. Once again, as so often in the past, the Ebert government turned to its most bitter enemy and asked for help. It invited the now dispersed Free Corps to reassemble.

In a series of secret conferences ending on February 7, 1923, an agreement known as the "Seeckt-Severing Accord" was signed by Ebert, Seeckt, Severing, Braun, and Cuno. Since both government and Reichswehr officials agreed that the contents of the accord should not be divulged and that no record of future conferences should be put into writing,[2] it is difficult to get a clear picture of the agreement. The main outlines, however, are clear enough. The understanding was that a reserve army which would greatly exceed the limits set by the Versailles Treaty should be created; that this army would be composed primarily of the post-Free Corps "Labor Associations" and "Sports Societies" and other half-legal, half-military formations. In order to circumvent opposition from the Left and from the Allies, it was further agreed that this reserve army would be called "Labor Troops" (*Arbeitstruppen*).[3] Thus was born that illegal, secret army famous in recent German history as the "Black Reichswehr."

---

his party. He therefore blamed the Weimar pacifists for not declaring war. Thus after noting that war would have been "injurious" to the movement (p. 813) and saying that "only a mad man" would have advised such a course (p. 982), he insists that the Weimar government could have raised an army of "80 or 100 divisions" and won a smashing victory. *Mein Kampf*, Reynal and Hitchcock edition (New York, 1940).

[2] Colonel von Schleicher of the General Staff made the following testimony to the Reichstag investigating committee: "Conversations took place between the War Ministry and the Prussian Ministry of Interior and between the War Ministry and the District Defense Commanders . . . but I must emphasize that nothing was put in writing . . . Minister Severing warned that nothing in writing should exist concerning these negotiations: neither from us to him nor from his office to our offices." Quoted in von Oertzen, *Deutsche Freikorps*, 465–466.

[3] Both Leftist and Rightist authors agree on the general contents of the Accord: Caro and Oehme, *Schleichers Aufstieg*, 156–169; Rabenau, *Seeckt*,

Criticism of the government's program of calling back the Free Corps was not lacking in Germany, but it went begging. Dr. Erich Zeigner, the Social-Democratic Minister President of Saxony, for instance, repeatedly warned the national government of the dangers it would face if it persisted in encouraging the Freebooters. When the Seeckt-Severing Accord was in the offing, Zeigner threatened to disclose the nature of the Republic's allies. The Chancellor of the Republic warned him against so doing and then threatened him with "countermeasures." Zeigner concluded a bitter speech before the Landtag of Saxony:

> It is certainly a grotesque state of affairs that on one hand the organizations which are patently enemies of the state are dissolved and prosecuted by the state and yet on the other hand, the members of these very organizations are encouraged to enlist in the [Black] Reichswehr.[4]

The Black Reichswehr, in the narrow meaning of the term,[5] stemmed directly from the *Arbeitsgemeinschaften,* which the Free Corps leaders had established during the days of their dissolution. The name was only slightly changed in 1923. They now became known as the *Arbeitskommandos* or, more commonly, simply as the AK. The leadership of these formations was vested in the Chief of Staff of the Third Reichswehr Division, Lieutenant

---

II, 328; Röhm, *Geschichte eines Hochverräters,* 181; Edgar von Schmidt-Pauli, *General von Seeckt: Lebensbild eines deutschen Soldaten* (Berlin, 1937), 116; and Gumbel, *"Verräter verfallen der Feme!,"* 254–256. In later years, former government officials either denied that such an agreement had ever been made or avoided mentioning it. Thus former Chancellor Brüning told me flatly that no such agreement ever existed. Otto Braun, the able Minister President of Prussia, skirts the issue by saying nothing about the February accord. He stresses his friend Severing's agitation against the Free Corps during the *preceding* year and says that *prior* to February, 1923 he, like Severing, had also "fought against . . . any association of the Reichswehr with any illegal groups or organizations." Braun, *Von Weimar zu Hitler,* 265.

[4] Speech of October 18, 1923, *Verhandlungen des Sächsischen Landtages* (Stenographische Berichte), 60 Sitzung, Vol. II, 1678–1681.

[5] Some writers include in the Black Reichswehr the government sponsored sabotage squads of the Ruhr, Hitler's SA, Ehrhardt's O.C., Heydebreck's Wehrwolves, and similar groups. Thus, Paul Wentzcke, *Rheinkampf,* 2 vols. (Berlin, 1925), I, 434, 439, 441–444. Normally, however, it refers only to those formations which grew out of the "Labor Associations" of West Prussia, Pomerania, Brandenburg and Upper Silesia.

Colonel von Bock. But the actual work of organization was entrusted to Major Buchrucker and Lieutenant Paul Schulz, both
of whom had been active as Free Corps Commanders in Upper
Silesia. Rossbach, Hauenstein, Heydebreck, and other *Freikorpsführer* were also active recruiters and organizers of the AK. And
so was Konstantin Hierl. It was no accident that when Adolf
Hitler looked about him for the leader of his *Arbeitsdienst,* he
should choose this former commander of the Hierl Detachment
of the Augsburg Free Corps and the organizer and trainer of
"labor commandos" of the Black Reichswehr.[6]

In addition to enrolling thousands of former Free Corps fighters
— the backbone of the illegal army — the Black Reichswehr
sought recruits among the student youth of Germany. Supported
by the rectors of such universities as Berlin, Jena, Leipzig, and
Halle,[7] the recruitment of students was so successful that it became a standing joke among student circles to answer questions
regarding academic careers by saying, "Next semester I'm taking
the [Black] Reichswehr." [8]

The Black Reichswehr was drilled and trained by former Free
Corps and Reichswehr officers; it was financed by army funds
and the generous contributions of heavy industry and conservative landed interests.[9] Thus the work of organizing and training
an illegal army progressed nicely through the summer of 1923.
By September, the total number enrolled was in the neighborhood
of between 50,000 and 80,000 men.[10]

[6] *Das deutsche Führerlexikon, 1934,* 193, and Baldur von Schirach, *Die
Pioniere des Dritten Reiches,* 97.

[7] E. J. Gumbel, Jacob Berthold, and others, *Weisbuch über die Schwarze
Reichswehr* (Berlin, 1925), 23.

[8] Gumbel, *Verschwörer,* 109; see also Curator, *Putsche, Staat und Wir!,* 43.
We have already noted that former Free Corps commanders such as Mumme
founded military student organizations to serve as feeders for the Black
Reichswehr. (See above, p. 210.)

[9] The best source of an account of the organizing and training of the
Black Reichswehr is the memoirs of Major Buchrucker, *Im Schatten Seeckts:
Die Geschichte der "Schwarzen Reichswehr"* (Berlin, 1928), 9 ff.

[10] Buchrucker says his men numbered only 18,000, but he is speaking of
the *Arbeitskommando* under his immediate command at Kustrine. (*Ibid.,*
32.) Wentzcke gives the larger estimate, *op. cit.,* I, 435. This is probably a
conservative figure. The Allied Commission of Control never received satisfactory figures because, as General Morgan has pointed out, the Commission
was never allowed to inspect recruitment returns. John H. Morgan, "The

USPD members of the Reichstag were alarmed at both the size and the personnel of this illegal army. They bombarded Dr. Otto Gessler, Noske's successor as the Minister of National Defense, with questions concerning it. Gessler answered by warning his opponents that anyone who discussed German armament might be considered guilty of high treason.[11] He parried all specific questions by saying that the whole subject would be aired by a special investigating committee of the Reichstag.[12] The memorandum submitted by Gessler to the committee is a deliberate and flagrant misrepresentation of the purpose and activity of the so-called "Labor Troops." In it Gessler admitted that Reichswehr and government officials had agreed to organize *Arbeitstruppen* but said flatly that "these troops had nothing whatever to do with any so-called Black Reichswehr," and that their sole purpose was to do the "heavy work of removing, sorting, and destroying (*Aufräumung, Aussonderung, und Zerstörung*) arms . . . Because of the very nature of their work, it was necessary for them to be instructed in the military use of each weapon, at least in broad outlines." Again he repeated, "it should be emphasized that the use of these bands of common laborers had nothing to do with the building of a so-called 'Black Reichswehr' . . . To call these bands of laborers 'regiments' and 'battalions' . . . and their overseers 'commanders' . . . is a ludicrous exaggeration." [13]

Disarmament of Germany and After," in *Quarterly Review*, CCXLII (October, 1924), 446.

[11] *Verhandlungen des Reichstags* (Stenographische Berichte), 168 Sitzung, May 28, 1925, Vol. 385, 2136. Throughout the 1920's, Gessler was an enthusiastic supporter of German-Russian military collaboration. Ulrich von Hassell links him with Seeckt, Beck, and Fritsch as one of the four architects of the post-Versailles Wehrmacht. During World War II he joined in the General's Plot against Hitler. At that time he argued in favor of a return of the monarchy. His candidate was Rupprecht of Wittelsbach. Hitler had him interned in the Dachau concentration camp in 1944. Released by the Allies, he was living quietly in Bavaria in 1947. (Cf. *Von Hassell Diaries*, 50, 143 and *passim*).

[12] *Loc. cit.*, 169 Sitzung, March 3, 1926, Vol. 389, 5911.

[13] The Reichstag investigating committee met during 1926–1927. It was never permitted to publish its findings. Gessler's memorandum of March 2, 1926, is quoted in Caro and Oehme, *Schleichers Aufstieg*, 147–148, and Gumbel, *Verräter*, 240, 244. Gessler repeated the gist of his report in an article published in the *Berliner Tageblatt*, October 31, 1926.

Gessler's testimony is refuted by every other available source: by both Leftist and Rightist accounts; by his colleagues in the government and, above all, by the men who organized and participated in the Black Reichswehr. Buchrucker knew more about the *Arbeitskommandos* than anyone else and his testimony to the investigating committee was substantiated by its investigations. His reply to Gessler is worth recording here:

It was supposed to look as if we were "removing, sorting and destroying arms" and that we were only laborers — hence the name *Arbeitskommandos*. This cloak was used to cover what really happened: the creation of a reserve army! Not destruction of armament, but conservation and preservation of arms! Not civilian laborers, but soldiers! . . . In August 1926 Gessler told a friend of mine that by my lack of discretion [the putsch at Kustrine] I had destroyed the "carefully built up Eastern defense system" . . . Dr. Gessler here stated clearly the real purpose of the Black Reichswehr . . . Laborers? I will only say that throughout 1923 we were not looking for laborers. We recruited volunteer soldiers . . . The regular soldiers addressed them not as "overseers" or "laborers" but with their correct military titles.[14]

The former Chancellor of Germany, Josef Wirth, also contradicts Gessler's testimony. In a passionate speech delivered before the Reichstag in 1926, Wirth insisted that he was never a pacifist, likened the Germany of 1923 to the besieged Germany of Frederick the Great, and disclosed the measures taken by his government in 1923 to meet the emergency:

I have been silent [about these measures] . . . because it was the patriotic duty of the government of which I was a member to be silent . . . [But] in those fateful hours, the government of the time . . . did its patriotic duty by making the necessary preparations on the Eastern Frontier . . . We organized the defense and created a volunteer frontier guard (*Grenzschutz*) . . .[15]

A contributor to a leading moderate republican magazine also refuted both the spirit and the letter of Gessler's memorandum. He defended the creation of the Black Reichswehr and "even the use of Lützow's wild, dare-devil Rifles" in order to defend

[14] Quoted in Gumbel, *Verräter,* 247–251. Buchrucker repeated the substance of this statement in his memoirs, *Im Schatten Seeckts,* 6–7, 62, and in an interview recorded in the *Vossische Zeitung,* April 28, 1928.

[15] Speech of December 16, 1926, *Verhandlungen* (Stenographische Berichte), 252 Sitzung, Vol. 391, 8589–8590.

the Fatherland. The author regretted, however, the inevitable result of relying once again on "those ruthless men who dreamed of action and thought only of putsches." In conclusion he expressed a wish that was to remain unfulfilled: "We can only hope that this passionate chapter of the Black Reichswehr and the Feme murders has finally ended . . ." [16]

Reichswehr officials joined Gessler in denying that there was any connection between the "Labor commandos" and the regular Army. Thus Colonel von Schleicher of the General Staff made the following sworn testimony to the Reichstag investigating committee:

What concerns us here especially is the relationship of the Reichswehr as such to the *Arbeitskommandos,* the "Black Reichswehr" and so forth . . . How little the Army knew of these matters is shown by the fact . . . that I knew neither Herr [*sic*] Buchrucker — I never saw the man — nor Herr Schulz, nor Herr Klapproth nor any of the others, whatever their names are. I had no idea that these men ever existed . . . That alone is evidence of how little was actually known by the War Ministry . . . That is absolutely all that I can say in regard to specific cases.[17]

The old Freebooters and the young students of the Black Army were enraged by the denials of Gessler and Schleicher. They were particularly furious that their proudest possession — the title of soldier — was taken away from them and that they should be insulted by being called not only civilians but civilian laborers. They insisted that they were in fact soldiers and that they were directly associated with the regular army. In both these assertions they were quite right. "The 'labor troops' were really soldiers," says their commander, Major Buchrucker, "they not only considered themselves soldiers but were so considered by the Reichswehr." [18] They were billeted in Reichswehr barracks,

[16] Robert Breuer, "Die Schwarze Reichswehr," in *Deutsche Republik,* Heft XXII (1926), 11–12. Another writer in the same publication admits the fact of an illegal army and regretted that Dr. Gessler had shielded the use of the "dark societies" which composed it. "Herr Defense Minister," the article concludes, "by shielding certain people and organizations . . . you have lost the confidence of the people." Karl Spiecker, "Geheimfonds der Reichswehr?" in *Deutsche Republik,* Heft VI (1926), 11–12.

[17] Quoted in von Oertzen, *Deutsche Freikorps,* 467 and in Caro and Oehme, *Schleichers Aufstieg,* 141.

[18] Quoted in the *Vossische Zeitung,* April 28, 1928.

dressed like soldiers, fed, armed, and trained like soldiers. The Reichswehr itself sent "retired" officers to help the veteran Free Corps commanders drill and supervise the Army maneuvers staged by the *Arbeitskommandos*.[19] The men who Dr. Gessler was pleased to call "common laborers" of Section K of the *Arbeitskommando* at Kustrine, attended a regulation Noncommissioned Officers School in the barracks at Kustrine and were there instructed by officers of the General Staff.[20] Corporals and privates of the illegal reserve army occasionally stood guard before the Reichspräsidentum.[21]

One must refuse to believe that the German Army was as ignorant of this activity as Schleicher maintained. The offices of Buchrucker and Schultz were located in the same building as those of the Wehrkreiskommando of the Berlin area, at 63 Kurfürstenstrasse.[22] One of the many official directives sent from the Reichswehr to the *Arbeitskommandos* (also known as the *Erfassungs Abteilungen* or E.A.) is sufficient in itself to refute the statements made by both Gessler and Schleicher. These officials swore that there was absolutely no connection between the "Labor Troops" and the regular Army. The duty directive (*Dienstanweisung*) is addressed "to all Erfassungs-Abteilungen (E.A.)," signed by Lieutenant Colonel Held, adjutant of Wehrkreiskommando III (Berlin), and dated January 31, 1923:

Purpose and duty of the E.A.: The purpose and duty of the E.A. is the acquisition, maintenance and distribution of all materials that are necessary for the strengthening of the state and the Army . . .

Working Districts: The W. Kr. Kdo. [Wehrkreiskommando] will assign each E.A. to its working district.

Strength and Organization: A leader, preferably an officer, will command each E.A. The commander is responsible directly to the W. Kr. Kdo. for the general functioning and condition of each E.A. The activity of each E.A. is to be recorded in day books . . .

[19] See the documents cited in the *Weissbuch über die Schwarze Reichswehr*, edited by Gumbel, 20–23.

[20] Friedrich von Felgen, "Die Schwarze Reichswehr und Oberleutnant Schultz," in *Femgericht*, edited by Friedrich von Felgen (4th ed., Munich, 1933), 42.

[21] *Vossische Zeitung*, April 28, 1928.

[22] Friedrich Grimm, *Oberleutnant Schulz, Femeprozesse und Schwarze Reichswehr* (Munich, 1929[?]), 7.

[which] are to be kept secret. It is forbidden to copy, to take extracts or to allow anyone to look at them . . . They will be kept in an iron safe in the commandant's office . . . The aforementioned commandant will regulate matters pertaining to provisions, clothing, garrisons, furloughs and pay according to the orders of the Wehrkreiskommando.[23]

After 1933, Army spokesmen were no longer reticent about discussing the illegal army of 1923. An official Wehrmacht historian of the postwar period not only admits the existence of the Black Reichswehr, he emphasizes its importance, shows its continuity, and considers it the direct predecessor of the great "people's army" of Hitler:

In spite of all this [the work of the Inter-Allied Commission of Military Control] it was possible to withhold not inconsiderable stocks of munitions from the enemy's grasp and thus to create the first basis for the never-surrendered purpose of all the labor: the creation of a great, new people's army (*Volksheer*) . . . In the first years the work was more or less without plan . . . It was only in 1923 that system was introduced . . . At first Reich funds were not available through the Reichstag . . . [hence] agriculture and industry supplied the money . . .

From 1925 on, the Reichswehr ministry organized and coördinated the entire field of these "black" jobs and expanded it to all *Wehrkreise* under the title of "*Landesschütz*"; a uniformly constructed and well directed organization was built up. Its job was the concealment of arms and munitions and especially the preparations and training of troops . . .

Thus when Adolf Hitler had fashioned the political principles and undertook the first strengthening of the Army, . . . arms, munitions and men were already available in sufficient quantities and the first beginnings of his supplementary army organization (*Wehrersatzorganisation*) had already been made.[24]

II. THE KUSTRINE PUTSCH

The French invasion of the Ruhr and the subsequent Seeckt-Severing Accord of February 1923 gave the moribund, discour-

[23] The directive was presented as evidence at the *Weltbühne* trial, April 17, 1928. It is quoted in full in Felgen, *loc cit.*, 16–18, and in part in Gumbel, *Verräter*, 216–217.

[24] Gerhard Thomée, Major im Oberkommando der Wehrmacht, *Der Wiederaufstieg des deutschen Heeres 1918–1938* (Verlag, "Die Wehrmacht," Berlin, 1939), 72–76.

aged, and disunited Free Corps a new lease on life. The Free-booters had always thrived on chaos. The plummeting mark, the increasing Leftist agitation, and the presence of foreign troops on the Eastern and Western soil of Germany now renewed their strength and their hopes. They were confident that 1923 would bring the great "Day of Decision" that they had been awaiting so long. Seeckt and Severing may have planned to use the Black Reichswehr as a reserve in the event of a defensive war,[25] but the Freebooter, anti-Republican elements which predominated in the illegal army[26] had no such purpose in mind. Their first objective was, and remained, the overthrow of the hated government of "November Criminals." The Black Reichswehr gave them that opportunity. Heydebreck's reaction to the Seeckt-Severing Accord which revitalized his Wehrwolves is typical. He was not interested in taking part in a war to defend the Republic. On first hearing of the agreement, his only comment was this: "We clenched our fists and said, 'The Republic is only dead weight. This state has no soul. Our day will come! And on that day . . .' " [27] He did not finish the sentence.

Men at Kustrine under the command of Major Buchrucker were the first to try to seize the Government of Germany. This Kustrine Putsch will be discussed in some detail here because the story has not heretofore been told in English and because it is important to the history of the Free Corps.

[25] Leftist and antimilitarist writers have insisted that the regular Army supported the Black Reichswehr not because it wanted a military reserve but because Seeckt and the other generals wanted to use it as their tool to overthrow the Republic. Thus, Caro and Oehme, *op. cit.*, 132–134 and *passim;* and the *Weissbuch über die Schwarze Reichswehr,* 27–35. General Rabenau admits that "It cannot be denied that many of the immediate circle around Seeckt raised the question of whether it was not the duty of the Wehrmacht to fight the system directly . . . Seeckt, however, rejected such ideas [in 1923] . . . The time was not yet ripe." *Seeckt, Aus seinem Leben,* II, 329.

[26] Gessler's statement that the *Arbeitskommando* was not composed of anti-Republican or Rightist elements (*Verhandlungen des Reichstags,* 300 Sitzung, March 30, 1927, Vol. 393, 10146) is not borne out by Buchrucker's testimony at the trial of one of the Feme murderers of the Black Reichswehr: "Only those elements who declared themselves to be enemies of the existing state . . . were considered "safe" and admitted into the A.K." (Quoted in Gumbel, *Verräter,* 221.)

[27] *Wir Wehrwölfe,* 154. Similar attitudes may be found in Heinz, *Die Nation greift an,* 170–171, and Röhm, *op. cit.,* 230–231.

Major Buchrucker, quite typically, was enthusiastic about the results of the French invasion of the Ruhr. It gave him the chance to revitalize the volunteer army, and seemed to provide him with the opportunity to lead a great national movement to shake off the shackles of Versailles and the Weimar system. He assured one of his friends that the situation in 1923 was very different from what it had been in 1920 at the time of the Kapp Putsch. The German people, distraught with fear of invasion and made miserable by inflation, were now ready for any radical program. "We'll carry on the Ruhr war!" he told Heinz, "Mobilize the people for the War of Liberation against France and Poland! England considers the Versailles Treaty broken [by France]. She will do nothing to stop me! The French army is honeycombed with mutiny. Poland is not yet ready for war!" [28] Like his colleagues in the Black Reichswehr, Buchrucker had no confidence in the Cuno government's policy of passive resistance. But at least it was resistance. He only decided to act when he heard that the government was about to give up even that cowardly and unsoldierly type of opposition to France.

His plan was simple and remarkably stupid. The four battalions of Black Reichswehr troops under his immediate command at Kustrine would quietly mobilize, march to Berlin, and seize the government. This act would be the signal for all the other post-Free Corps groups scattered throughout the Reich to rise and proclaim the new War of Liberation. Buchrucker later maintained that he had no intention of overthrowing the Ebert government. He just wanted Ebert to form a war cabinet with Seeckt and Gessler. This cabinet would immediately strengthen the power of the Army, incorporate his Black Reichswehr into the regular Army, and declare war on France. He was sure that Seeckt and Ebert would welcome this act of daring. Or else they would be shot on the spot.[29]

[28] Friedrich Wilhelm Heinz, *Sprengstoff* (Berlin, 1930), 218–219. Buchrucker's satisfaction with the domestic situation is also expressed in his memoirs, *Im Schatten Seeckts*, 22–23, 30.
[29] Heinz, *Die Nation greift an*, 178. Buchrucker maintains that he "considered an overthrow of the constitution not only unnecessary but also harmful [*schädlich*] for internal and especially for external political reasons." He says that it was necessary for Germany to remain a republic "with a govern-

"In the middle of September, 1923," the conspirator writes, "I suspected that the Ruhr resistance would be given up by the end of September . . . On September 15, I ordered the beginning of the mobilization of the [four] battalions . . . so that they would be prepared for action the night of the 29–30th. It was later shown that the estimate was accurate. The Ruhr resistance ended on September 26; the date chosen was the first Saturday night after that date." [30] He was convinced that the Reichswehr would support him — or at least give their tacit approval. He was led to believe that such was the case when the regular army did not object to the mobilization of the *Arbeitskommando* which took place after September 15th. He was further encouraged by the fact that on September 22, Colonel Held, the General Staff officer and adjutant of *Wehrkreiskommando* III, asked him if his men would secretly occupy the Brandenburg Reichswehr barracks while the regular army was putting down the Leftist disturbance in Saxony and Thuringia. [31] Since the occupation of the barracks could not remain unnoticed for more than a few days at most, Buchrucker concluded that Held's proposal implied that the Reichswehr intended that the occupation should remain secret

ment as socially democratic as possible" so that her former enemies would not have the excuse of liberating the German people from the "tyranny of the militarists." Furthermore, the constitution itself was useful. "A clever and dexterous President" (*kluger und geschickter Reichspräsident*) could use Article 48 to create the type of military dictatorship he wanted. Even the Social Democratic majority in the Reichstag was of great advantage, he argues, because ever since voting the war credits in 1914 they had shown their willingness to support "necessary measures." He concludes: "It was only necessary to bring the Reichspräsident and the Reichstag into a position in which they would be forced to do what was necessary." (Buchrucker, *op. cit.*, 24–25.) Buchrucker may have been naïve enough to believe that Fritz Ebert was the "clever and dexterous" leader his plan required. Buchrucker may even have been simple enough to believe he could enlist Majority Socialist support — presumably even after he had shot Ebert, Seeckt, Gessler and, it may be assumed, a score of others. But his men never thought in any other terms than those of overthrowing the entire government of Germany. "They wanted to fight," their commander admits, "and they felt that the War of Liberation . . . was only possible after first overthrowing the constitution." (*Ibid.*, 28–29.)

[30] *Ibid.*, 35. Like Caesar, Buchrucker modestly writes in the third person. But in order to avoid confusion, I have taken the liberty of changing his personal pronouns in translating his memoirs.

[31] See below, p. 257.

only until Buchrucker had marched on Berlin. "I therefore saw in Held's question a new indication that the *Wehrkreis* knew of my intentions and approved of them." [32]

Buchrucker's plans were completely ruined by the decision made by the Reich cabinet in an all-night session of September 26–27. In order to counter von Kahr's declaration of an "Exceptional State" in Bavaria and the threat of Bavarian separation from the Reich, Ebert drew on the powers of Article 48 of the Weimar constitution and proclaimed a state of siege throughout the Reich (*Ausnahmezustand*). This made von Seeckt virtual dictator of Germany.[33] It the Reichswehr had ever tacitly approved Buchrucker's plans, it no longer had any reason to do so. It now acquired the power — legally — which might otherwise have been gained only by a putsch. Buchrucker had lost his *raison d'être*. "It was now clear," he writes, "that [the regular Army] would no longer support my independent action . . . and since my plan envisaged not an overthrow of the government but the strengthening of the existing Reichswehr, . . . I realized that I must give up my plan — difficult as that was for me." [34] He ordered his troops to be dissolved.

Buchrucker had reckoned without the Freebooters. He discovered — like Ebert before him and Hitler after him — that it was a great deal easier to stir up the Volunteers than it was to dismiss them. The men refused to disband. They were tired of the dirty work of collecting and storing munitions. They were sick and tired of being called "common laborers." The despised and rejected Volunteers had been led to believe that the incorporation of the Black Reichswehr into the regular Army would mean for them high positions in a militarist state. This close to success, they brooked no thwarting. Captain Stennes, the veteran *Freikorpsführer* in command of the Fourth Battalion of the Black

[32] *Ibid.*, 37.

[33] The word dictator was carefully avoided in the proclamation. The Minister of the Reichswehr received "vollziehende Gewalt." But everyone realized that the real holder of power in Germany during the emergency was General von Seeckt. National Socialists had a ready explanation of the reason why Seeckt could not exploit his chance to become dictator in fact. He lacked the necessary prerequisite. "Hans von Seeckt was simply not primitive enough." Quoted in Rabenau, *Seeckt*, II, 375.

[34] Buchrucker, *op. cit.*, 38–39.

Reichswehr, started the rebellion. The men chose a former Ehrhardt officer, Major Günther, to lead them. After telephoning to
Ehrhardt in Munich and getting his approval,[35] Günther announced that he was ready to carry out the *coup d'état*.

In the meantime, on September 30, the Reichswehr ordered the
arrest of Buchrucker for not carrying out the demobilization of
his Black Reichswehr. At this point Major Buchrucker either "lost
his head" [36] — or else he kept it. According to his story, he realized
that there was now absolutely no chance of a successful putsch;
he also realized that his men were going to try one and would
probably be shot down by the regular Army. He therefore decided to stage a sham putsch (*Scheinunternehmung*) to make the
men think that he was carrying out his plan. But he planned to
conduct it in such a way that it would fail quickly and without
bloodshed. He chose the 550 men of the battalion stationed at
Kustrine under Major Herzen to carry out the token putsch. Herzen was chosen because he was considered "less primitive and
foolhardy" than the other commanders and because his battalion
lay farthest from Berlin. On the night of September 30, Buchrucker went to Kustrine and told Herzen's men that the putsch
would be carried out and that they had been chosen to spearhead
the attack. On the next day they would seize the Kustrine barracks and armory and lead the march on Berlin. Kustrine, Buchrucker concluded, would be the signal for the great War of Liberation. "I said that to bring the troops to my side. If I had said
what I really wanted [their quiet dissolution] they would have
simply refused to obey." [37]

Early the next day, as Herzen's men advanced on the armory,
Buchrucker went unarmed to the commandant of the Fortress
of Kustrine, Colonel Gudowius, and informed him of his intentions. Gudowius immediately placed him under arrest and ordered his men to fire on the Black Reichswehr. Buchrucker at
once ordered his men to submit. The Kustrine Putsch collapsed
without a shot being fired. As a result of the surrender of Herzen's

[35] Heinz, *Die Nation greift an,* 182.
[36] Gumbel, *Verräter,* 233.
[37] Buchrucker, *op. cit.,* 49. The Major was probably right. First Lieutenant
Vogt, adjutant of Herzen's battalion, later testified that the men would indeed have mutinied and joined Günther.

battalion, the Freebooters under Major Günther realized the hopelessness of the situation and surrendered without a struggle.[38]

Buchrucker was sentenced to ten years fortress arrest for high treason. He profited by the Hindenburg Amnesty of 1927 and was released after serving less than four years. Herzen and other officers received sentences of a few months honorary confinement. The enlisted men were all acquitted because, in the opinion of the court, "they acted as soldiers in the execution of their duty." [39] The Black Reichswehr was officially declared dissolved. Actually a large part of it left Spandau and Döberitz fully armed under the eyes of the officials and found refuge in the great estates of Mecklenburg. There, as we have seen, it continued to function with the approval of the Reichswehr ministry.[40]

The Kustrine Putsch was quickly written off and forgotten as a ludicrous attempt on the part of the Freebooters to seize power in Germany. Forgotten, that is, by all but General von Seeckt and the Free Corps. The putsch marks a further breach between the regular Army and the irregular formations. In the future the Army would allow the Black Army to exist — it might be useful as a militia one day — but after Kustrine, Seeckt was more than ever convinced that only the legal way could lead to the reconstruction of Germany's military power. He would not tolerate Freebooter interference in either the Army or in politics.

[38] The facts are confirmed by both Gumbel and Heinz, but they interpret them differently. They contend that Buchrucker simply lost his head and that "with childish naïveté" (Heinz) he was really convinced that the putsch would succeed even after the Reichswehr had told him that they would oppose it. I see no reason for doubting Buchrucker's version. He had already recognized the futility of his cause when the state of emergency was proclaimed and he had made a serious effort to dissolve his men. (See Benoist-Méchin, *Histoire de L'Armée Allemande*, II, 272.) He may well have been naïve in thinking that Seeckt, Ebert, and the Social Democrats would support his original plan. But the way in which his hurried, revised plan of September 30 was executed is explicable only if one accepts Buchrucker's statement that he had intended that it should fail for the reasons he gives. He was indeed politically naïve. But as a former General Staff officer, he was not stupid enough to believe that he could capture the government of Germany with the 550 men of the Kustrine battalion when the German Army was determined to stop him.

[39] Heinz, who records the sentences, is nevertheless furious with the courts for persecuting the patriots and for bringing them to trial. *Die Nation greift an,* 184–185.

[40] See above, pp. 170–172.

For their part, the Freebooters felt that once again, as in March 1920, they had been betrayed by the Reichswehr. Since Seeckt had deserted them, they turned to Hitler. Many of the leaders of the Black Reichswehr went directly to Munich and joined the ranks of the NSDAP and the SA. Those who remained behind helped to forward the cause of National Socialism in northern Germany in the years which lay ahead.[41]

III. THE BEER HALL PUTSCH

The Volunteers had been attracted to Munich ever since they conquered the city in May 1919. Ironically enough, it was Adolf Hoffmann, the restored Social Democrat Minister President of Bavaria, who first encouraged their activity.[42] It was not until the

[41] Buchrucker joined the Party shortly after his release from Gollnow Fortress. He left it, however, to join Otto Strasser's opposition group, the *Kampfgemeinschaft Revolutionärer Nationalsozialisten* — the so-called "Black Front." The Nazis put him in a concentration camp in 1934 but released him, probably because the Army intervened on his behalf. Stennes became supreme SA commander in Silesia. In 1931, egged on by Dr. Goebbels (who was at that point in opposition to the Führer), he led the shortlived "Stennes Putsch" against Hitler. Goebbels deserted him and the revolt was quickly crushed by Lieutenant Paul Schulz, another former leader of the Black Reichswehr who had become an SA leader under the Nazis. Stennes later bragged publicly that he had beaten Dr. Goebbels to a pulp for his defection. He left the Party and joined the Black Front. We have already noted the National Socialist activity of Rossbach, Hauenstein, Mumme, and Hierle. Former commanders of the Black Reichswehr who became SA leaders in the North included Hayn in Saxony, Heydebreck in Pomerania, and Ernst in Berlin. The last three men were killed at Hitler's orders during the Blood Purge. (*Völkischer Beobachter,* July 14, 1934.)

[42] One of Hoffmann's first acts after returning from Bamberg was to announce that in the future, in order to avoid "the embarrassment of having to rely on Prussian troops," Bavaria would form its own army. It would be built on "the already existing Free Corps"; it would recruit new Volunteer formations and it would encourage the development of the *Einwohnerwehr* system started by Dr. Escherich. Hoffmann's choice of leader for what he hoped would be "a young, democratic, socialist army," was strange. He turned to Colonel von Epp, the future Nazi Reichstatthalter of Bavaria and even then a sworn enemy of republican government. "Colonel von Epp," the proclamation concludes, "has rendered great service by forming his corps . . . he does not merit the distrust which has confronted him from many sides . . . Citizens of Munich! A new day is dawning! The people have turned their backs to the old militarism." The government proclamation of May 5, 1919, is reprinted in the memoirs of a former member of Hoffmann's cabinet, Josef Karl, *Die Schreckensherrschaft in München und Spartakus im bayr. Oberland* (Munich, 1919[?]), 292–294.

advent of Gustav von Kahr as virtual dictator of Bavaria, however, that the Freebooters began to have a dominant influence on Bavarian politics.

The Kapp-Lüttwitz Putsch proved a fiasco in the rest of the Reich, but in Bavaria it produced important and lasting results. In a stormy cabinet meeting held at 6:00 A.M. on March 14, 1920, Ernst Müller-Meiningen, the leader of the Democrats, supported by Escherich, General von Mohl, and Police President Pöhner, urged that a strong man was needed to meet the alleged Communist peril. He suggested that Gustav von Kahr, the governor of Upper Bavaria, be made Civil Commissar.[43] Hoffmann resigned, and on March 16 the Diet elected Kahr Minister President of Bavaria. From that day forward, Munich was the haven and the headquarters of all Freebooter activity.

No effort will be made here to disentangle the snarled web of petty intrigue and mutual double cross which characterized the history of the dozens of competing militarist formations which flourished in Bavaria during Kahr's regime.[44] Amid the constant shifting of allegiances and alliances one can note a general movement: the post-Free Corps groups tended to gravitate either to Kahr and his program of Wittelsbach restoration or to Hitler and his superracist nationalism.

When, in May 1921, Escherich resigned his leadership over the Bavarian *Einwohnerwehr*,[45] Kahr and Hitler began at once to compete for its members. Supported by Kahr, Sanitätsrat Dr. Pittinger reorganized the *Wehr* into the *Bund Bayern und Reich*. Ernst Röhm, supported by Reichswehr funds, was able to split Pittinger's group and attract a large section of it to the Nazi-sponsored *Vaterländische Kampfverbände Bayerns*. But Hitler's triumph was short-lived. Important sections of the VKB deserted and went back to Kahr's camp. A directive sent out to all SA leaders by Hermann Goering, at that time supreme SA leader, is worth translating here for two reasons. It indicates the confusion

---

[43] Müller-Meiningen took the proceedings of the cabinet meeting down in shorthand. See his memoirs, *Aus Bayerns schwersten Tagen*, second edition (Berlin and Leipzig, 1924), 232 ff.

[44] The most detailed, if patently biased treatment, is given by Ernst Röhm, *Die Geschichte eines Hochverräters* (7th ed., Munich, 1934).

[45] See above, pp. 198 ff.

which existed among the various post-Free Corps groups. But, more important, it shows that contrary to later National Socialist claims, the Free Corps were not immediately and directly absorbed by the National Socialists:

Munich, July 4, 1923

To all SA District Leaders!

Many letters of a recent date show that there is not yet sufficient clarity in respect to the various patriotic groups . . .

It is obvious that competition between these groups is to be avoided at all costs. We are trying at this time to form connections with the local leaders of other groups . . .

The VVM [*Vereinigte Vaterländischen Verbände*] . . . is loosely connected with us. It is in the process of transformation . . . and will furnish a good Storm Battalion for [our] *Kampfverbände* . . . The Hermannsbund is also only loosely connected . . . but it is to be assumed that it will soon enter our ranks . . .

The Viking Bund [Ehrhardt's organization] wants to knock out the NSDAP. That is not good. The Viking Bund is in no way connected with the SA of the NSDAP. It is true that it was for a time related to the SA, but it has now declared war against the Party and the SA.

The Blücher Bund [an offshoot of the Free Corps Oberland] is a confused outfit . . . It is closely allied to the Viking Bund.

The *Bund Bayern und Reich:* The supreme commander of the SA [Goering] and the supreme leader of the VKP [Hitler] have nothing to do with this group . . . There is no point in trying to win them to our great cause because no activist, folkish-minded, great German men belong to it . . .

The Supreme Commander of the SA
and Chief of Staff: Göhring [*sic*] [46]

Adolf Hitler was very pleased with the condition of Germany in 1923. The Fatherland seemed to be tottering on the edge of chaos; his fellow Germans were stunned and shaken by the French invasion of the Ruhr; inflation was rampant; unemployment grew unchecked — everywhere there were signs of acute national distress. Conditions were never better! He thumbed his private horoscope[47] furiously. Yes, the stars in their courses seemed to be

[46] *Münchner Post,* August 20, 1923. Quoted in Gumbel, *Verschwörer,* 190–191.

[47] This, of course, was not the famous horoscope he had drawn up for him on January 30, 1933, which — along with Carlyle's *History of Frederick the Great* — he consulted so frantically during those last desperate days of April 1945 in his Berlin air-raid shelter.

working for him. Now was the time to act! He determined to
reorganize the various competing "battle associations" under his
banner and make a real bid for national power. On September 2,
1923, at Nuremberg — in what was to be the first of a long series
of "German Days" — he founded the *Deutscher Kampfbund* and
had himself elected its political leader. It was a great triumph
for Hitler. "The unification of all battle associations into one great
patriotic German Battle League," he screamed in his acceptance
speech, "absolutely guarantees the victory of our movement." [48]

Kahr was seriously alarmed at his rival's victory. Toward the
end of the month, he decided on a desperate measure to win the
Freebooters away from Hitler. The Bavarian Volunteers had long
clamored for a march on Berlin. But the timid little separatist
had never liked the idea — his one goal in life was to restore the
Wittelsbach dynasty to Bavaria. Now, however, Hitler's success
forced Kahr to support the activists. To win their support he,
too, must perform an act of daring. The political situation in
Saxony and Thuringia seemed to give him the opportunity. In
mid-October, Kahr told Ehrhardt to mobilize his men on the
Thuringian border. This was done ostensibly to protect Bavaria
from the "Red Peril" of the new Socialist-Communist governments of Saxony and Thuringia, but actually to march to the
North. As the well-armed troop of some 15,000 Freebooters including former Rossbachers, men of the Blücher Bund, the
Reichsflagge (not to be confused with Röhm's Nazi *Reichskriegsflagge*), the Viking Bund, and the Nürnberg *Wehrband* [49] gathered along the border, Chancellor Stresemann decided to act. On
October 29 he sent regular Reichswehr troops into Saxony and
Thuringia, removed the Leftist governments and, in so doing,
the Freebooters' excuse for intervention.[50] Kahr, quite probably,
heaved a sigh of relief and immediately called off the march.

[48] Quoted in Röhm, *op. cit.*, 213.
[49] See F. W. Heinz, *Sprengstoff*, 221 ff; Gumbel, *Verschwörer*, 203–204;
and Heiden, *Geschichte des Nationalsozialismus*, 138.
[50] Rosenberg calls Stresemann's action "an act of arbitrary brutality and an
open breach of the law." (*Geschichte der deutschen Republik*, 170.) And so
it was. It should be noticed, however, that the people of Saxony and Thuringia
suffered a good deal less from the Reichswehr occupation than they would
have under a Freebooter domination which was, as Rosenberg admits, a dis-
tinct possibility.

Ehrhardt hesitated for some time but finally complied with Kahr's order.[51]

Events now moved rapidly toward the climax of the Beer Hall Putsch. Both Hitler and Kahr found themselves being swept forward by a tide they had helped to release but could not control. Neither of them really wanted to march on Berlin, but neither could afford to admit it for fear of forfeiting Freebooter support.[52] About the first of November, Kahr invited the leading nationalists of Bavaria and the Reich to a meeting which was to be held on November 8, 1923. It is not clear what Kahr intended to accomplish at the meeting, but Hitler was afraid that his rival was about to make an important announcement — perhaps proclaim the restoration of the Wittelsbachs. At any rate the Nazi leader could not afford to let the initiative pass to Kahr. After sleepless nights of indecision, he finally decided that the time had come to act "decisively."

On the evening of November 8, 1923, Dr. von Kahr addressed the leading nationalists of Germany as they sat around the rough-hewn tables of the Bürgerbräu Keller drinking beer from great stone mugs. The awkward little peasant's son, his shoulders stooped and his great head bowed, was reading falteringly and badly from a prepared manuscript. As his voice droned on, the assembled dignitaries were startled by a commotion near the center of the hall. A ludicrous figure in an ill-fitting morning coat[53]

---

[51] According to one of his lieutenants, Ehrhardt toyed with the idea of marching on Berlin without Kahr's support. See Heinz, *Die Nation greift an,* 223–225.

[52] Hitler's SA were just as restless as Kahr's supporters. In a secret session of the Hitler trial, Wilhelm Brückner, then leader of the Munich SA and later Hitler's personal adjutant, testified: "I also personally told Hitler that the day was near when I could no longer restrain the men. If nothing happened now, the men would drift away from him." Quoted in Heiden, *Geschichte des Nationalsozialismus,* 143.

[53] Admiral von Hintze, the last Imperial Secretary of State for Foreign Affairs, was present at the beer hall on the night of November 8. In describing the scene, he also illustrates the hold which a uniform has on the German mind. He insists that things would have been very different if only Ludendorff had worn his Imperial general's uniform and concludes, "Hitler too — dressed in a morning coat, the most difficult of all garments to wear, let alone a badly cut morning coat, and let alone a man with as bad a figure as Hitler

had jumped to a table, fired two shots into the ceiling, and with blazing eyes announced that the national revolution had already taken place.

The rest of the scene in the beer hall and the march on the Feldherrnhalle is too well known to bear repetition here.[54] Hitler had sworn the sacred oath of a German soldier that he would either succeed or die. The next day, however, he decided that neither alternative was attractive. He wanted to call off the whole business, but Ludendorff ordered him to march with his men. As the Bavarian police fired their first shots at the advancing Nazis, *Der Führer* lay down to escape the gunfire. He then climbed into his waiting red Fiat and drove off. He was the first to leave. He sought refuge in the summer home belonging to one of Harvard University's less illustrious sons, "Putzi" Hanfstaengl. There, on Armistice Day, 1923, he was arrested by the authorities. *Der Tag* was over.

What was the Free Corps fighter's reaction to the Beer Hall Putsch and to its leader? The veteran of a dozen war and postwar campaigns spoke for hundreds of his comrades when he said, "Hitler led his men into battle with absolutely no protection. He had no idea what he wanted. Then when things got tough, Adolf the Swell-Head (*der grössenwahnsinnige Adolf*) took off . . . and left his men in the lurch. *Revolution mit dem Maul!* Did you expect that he'd do anything else?" [55]

IV. FAILURE IN 1923

It is generally conceded that the activists had an excellent chance to seize the government of Germany in 1923.[56] Why, then, did they fail? It was not because they lacked sufficient numbers or sufficient leaders. It was largely because there were far too

---

with his short legs and his long torso. When I saw him jump on the table in that ridiculous costume I thought, 'the poor little waiter!' " (*armes Kellnerlein!*). Quoted in Ludecke, *op. cit.*, 185.

[54] A satisfactory treatment is given in Heiden, *Der Fuehrer*, 185 ff. The official Nazi version is, of course, quite different. See *Der 9 November 1923, Die Wahrheit über die Münchner Vorgänge* (Munich, 1923[?]). The pamphlet has on its title page, "Preis 10 Pfg. Nachdruck erwünscht!"

[55] Heinz, *Sprengstoff*, 248.

[56] Rosenberg, *Geschichte*, 170.

many leaders, each conscious of his own charismatic qualities, each dominated by petty ambition, each jealous and suspicious of the other, each insistent that his solution was the only possible solution to Germany's problem. An editorial of September 11, 1923, appearing in Kahr's monarchist organ, *Das bayrische Vaterland,* accurately described the situation in Bavaria and, quite typically, insisted that the only way out of the impasse was Kahr's way:

> We have in Bavaria a half dozen parties . . . We have dozens of patriotic societies. We have — just to name a few — the *Bund Bayern und Reich,* the Munich League of Patriots, the Emergency Volunteers, the Viking Bund, the Blücher Bund, the VKV, which, in turn, consists of four bunds . . .
>
> Every one of these parties, every one of these tiny groups has its own leader, . . . each of these leaders intrigues and spins his web against the other. Dozens of Napoleons and just as many Bismarcks! Away with them all! One must be our Führer! And that one is our King . . .[57]

Loyalty to an immediate leader was not the primary reason for refusing to join forces with that leader's rival. One of Ehrhardt's men, Heinz, was approached by Major Buchrucker and asked if he would join in the Kustrine Putsch. Heinz, in effect, said that he would wait to see if Buchrucker succeeded. If he did, Heinz was perfectly willing to desert his commander and join Buchrucker: "I naturally can not place myself under your command, Herr Major," he said, "I am bound to Ehrhardt . . . But I promise that on the day the Black Reichswehr occupies Berlin, I will march into Marburg with at least 5,000 men." [58]

Ehrhardt himself, poised on the Thuringian border, was willing to let Buchrucker carry on the Kustrine Putsch alone because

---

[57] Quoted in Gumbel, *Verschwörer,* 196.

[58] Heinz, *Sprengstoff,* 218. Heinz's adjutant, Reichswehroberleutnant Rückmann — who was, it should be noted, "on furlough" from the Army of the Republic — later urged Heinz to support Buchrucker at once: " 'We must alert all our forces and start marching toward Kassel-Mannheim. Then by early morning we will have the first 2,000 men in Marburg. [My] Reichswehr battalion will join the movement if Berlin is definitely seized.' " But Heinz refused to act: "No! I'll go myself to Marburg. All the groups will be alerted but they will move only if Buchrucker really marches. Not a minute before!" (*Ibid.,* 232.)

he felt that whatever its outcome, he, Ehrhardt, would be the victor. If Buchrucker succeeded, Ehrhardt would reap the reward because, he told Heinz, "My name counts. Buchrucker is unknown. The men . . . who support him are either nonentities or else they stand by me. If he fails — and I expect that he will fail — then his men will all enter my formations." [59]

The gist of the trouble is seen in an interesting conversation which took place in September 1923 between Ehrhardt and one of his lieutenants:

Heinz: Buchrucker is near Berlin, the *Kampfbund* of Hitler, and Ludendorff sits in Munich; you, Herr Captain, hold power in Koburg, Chiemgau, and perhaps in Marburg. Kahr controls the Bavarian state. The *Bund Bayern und Reich* stands between the fronts . . . Would it not be possible to bring Ehrhardt, Ludendorff, Buchrucker, Hitler, and Kahr together, unite them, and direct them all toward a common goal?

Ehrhardt: Impossible! There can be no reconciliation with Ludendorff! [he had deserted Ehrhardt during the Kapp Putsch]. I reject Hitler completely! He failed miserably on the first of May and he will always fail. You yourself know what we think of Buchrucker . . . I alone am the strongest! [60]

In 1923 Hitler was also hesitant, suspicious, and jealous. And he refused to coöperate with the post-Free Corps associations which lay scattered throughout the Reich waiting impatiently for *Der Tag* to dawn. Heydebreck, the leader of the Wehrwolves, indubitably exaggerates when he says that he had organized "hundreds and thousands" of the Rightist extremists in the industrial cities of Silesia and that Rossbach, Heines, Ernst, and Hauenstein had been equally successful in Brandenburg, West Prussia, and Pomerania. But he is quite right in saying that northern and eastern Germany contained valuable support for Hitler. Yet when Heydebreck approached Goering and offered to place his men at the disposal of the National Socialists, he was rebuffed: "He [Goering] said that Munich was not interested in the groups that ran around in the North. Rossbach and others were already there. All he could say was that once Munich was brought to order, other provinces would be attended to . . . I was not the only one from the North who experienced similar rejections in Munich." [61]

Six days after the shooting before the Feldherrnhalle, the German mark was stabilized. During the coming months, unemployment dropped sharply, production increased, real wages rose, and Germany began to recover her strength. This was all bad news to the Freebooters. "The good weather for putschists seemed to have finally disappeared," one of them laments, "Life wasn't much fun any more. The Poles did nothing. The Communists did nothing. We were getting soft. The mark was stabilized — worse luck! (*Höchst fatal!*)" [62]

The men of the Free Corps had nothing to gain from the peace, order, and prosperity of the middle twenties. War and civil war had made them accustomed to a restless, aggressive life. Many of them found it impossible to demobilize psychologically. But more important, most of them had been recruited from the middle class; they were further uprooted by the great inflation of 1923. The captains and lieutenants who formed the backbone of the Free Corps system were particularly bitter. While the senior officers received extraordinarily high pensions, the junior officers received pensions which did not enable them, they felt, to maintain the social standards to which their rank seemed to entitle them. [63] While the senior officers entered lucrative positions in

[61] Heydebreck, *Wir Wehrwölfe,* 192.

[62] Manfred von Killinger, *Ernstes und Heiteres aus dem Putschleben,* 6th ed. (Munich, 1934), 101.

[63] The claim of nationalist and National Socialist writers that the Weimar Republic shamefully neglected its veterans simply does not bear examination. The Republic took far better care of its veterans than the Empire had ever done. The actual salaries of all public officials, for instance, lagged far behind the pensions of officers of comparable rank. True, the officers were badly hit by the inflation, but they were immeasurably better off than the rest of those who were living on fixed incomes. The important fact, however, is that the junior officers were dissatisfied and held the Republic responsible for their plight. On the question of pensions and the social position of the officers see Josef Nothaas, *Die Kriegsbeschädigtenfürsorge unter besondere Berücktsichtigung Bayerns* (Inaugural dissertation, University of Munich, 1922), 14–21, and the same writer's "Sozialer Auf- und Abstieg im Deutschen Volk" in *Beiträge zur Statistik Bayerns,* Heft 117 (Munich, 1930), 65–73. A part of the latter study was translated and mimeographed by the

trade and industry, the junior officers found that they had spent over nine years — the most decisive years of their lives — fighting, they said, for the society that now had nothing to give them in return. "If ever there was irony in history this is it!" says a leading apologist for the postwar battle societies. "The youth, to whose fighting intervention the maintenance of 'Order' is to be . . . attributed, rejected that order with an almost fanatical hatred." [64]

Writing in 1923, in the despair that would cause his suicide two years later, Moeller van den Bruck caught the despondency of the Generation of the Uprooted and Disinherited. *Der Tag* had dawned and passed away and it had left only shattered hopes:

Our history has gone astray. Nothing of ours is succeeding in the world. Nothing today; nothing yesterday. Nothing — if we think back — nothing for the last generation . . . Our cause was still-born from the start . . . Something has gone wrong with everything. And when we try to set anything aright, it breaks to pieces in our hands . . . An evil spell hangs over the Reich . . .[65]

Works Progress Administration, W. R. Dittmar, Supervisor, New York, 1937. See also the excellent discussion in Fried, *Guilt of the German Army*, 98–161.

[64] Posse, *Die politischen Kampfbünde Deutschlands*, 79.

[65] Moeller van den Bruck, *Das Dritte Reich*, 3rd ed. (Hamburg, 1931), 3, 7–8.

X

CONCLUSION

If one were to give a short, and hence rough, formula for the historical significance of the Free Corps . . . one could perhaps say that here for the first time in German history . . . was a new and completely novel political germinating force: namely, the first union of soldierly action with political activity . . . Here were the first political soldiers.

— Von Oertzen

Nazi historians of the German Free Corps Movement are not at all hesitant about making the most sweeping claims for the historical importance of their heroes. The fighters of the Free Corps emerge from their narratives as "the first soldiers of the Third Reich"[1] and the doughty warriors without whose help Hitler could not have built his New Order. Two main arguments are used in presenting their case. The first of these is that the Freebooters were political soldiers. The Nazis have here committed the original sin of Freshman history essays and have read back National Socialist ideology into Freebooter activity. By thus using past history for present purposes, the Volunteers of 1919 become the conscious champions of the Nazi creed: they too were anti-Communist, antidemocratic, antiliberal, and antireactionary. And as a result, they were, somehow, the bearers of a *positive* political program.

The second argument of the Nazis is like unto the first: as political soldiers, the Freebooters were only awaiting a great military-political leader. As soon as Adolf Hitler appeared, they

[1] The phrase was apparently first used by Hermann Goering in dedicating the Nazi shrine to Schlageter on May 24, 1933, the tenth anniversary of the Free Corps hero's death. (*Völkischer Beobachter,* May 25–26, 1933.) It is used by all subsequent Nazi histories of the movement.

recognized him as that leader and ran into his outstretched arms.

In concluding this history of the German Free Corps Movement it will prove fruitful to examine these interpretations and to reach our own conclusions. While the specific arguments used by the Nazi historians do not stand up under examination, the National Socialists are essentially correct in their insistence that the Freebooters played an important role in the formation of the Third Reich.

I. THE FREEBOOTERS AS POLITICAL SOLDIERS

One of the things that makes it difficult to discuss the concept of "the political soldier" is the fact that the Nazis are so much like Humpty Dumpty: when they use a word they are the masters. A word means just what they choose it to mean. "Political," for instance, would normally presuppose a more or less consistent set of beliefs centering on man's relationship to the state. But the writer who attempts to define the political theory of the Free Corps will be as embarrassed — and for the same reasons — as is the leading authority on the structure and practice of National Socialism: the Freebooters, like the Nazis, had no political theory.[2] And, lacking a political theory they — again, like the National Socialists — sought to cover up the deficiency by resorting to mysticism and bad metaphysics. Thus one of the more articulate of the Freebooters writes: "The state is an abstract concept of the consciousness. The men of the German postwar period who dedicated themselves to the state acted out of the basic essence of Being; not out of mere thought. In this way they removed the abstraction from the concept of the state. They themselves were the state . . ."[3] This, it will be recognized at once, is essen-

[2] "Every political system can be characterized by its political theory which expresses its structure and its aims. But if we were asked to define the political theory of National Socialism, we should be greatly embarrassed . . . National Socialism has no political or social theory . . . in a given situation, it will accept any theory that might prove useful and will abandon it as soon as the situation changes . . ." Franz Neumann, *Behemoth: The Structure and Practice of National Socialism* (New York, 1944), 459 and 437–438. See also pp. 462–463, 467.

[3] Ernst von Salomon, "Die Gestalt des deutschen Freikorpskämpfer," in *Freikorpskämpfer,* 14. The German reads: *Der Staat ist ein abstrakter Begriff des Bewusstseins. Die Männer des deutschen Nachkrieges, die sich ihm*

tially Alfred Rosenberg's appeal to "the innermost Essence of all things" — a concept which can be just as meaningfully rendered, "The Ultimate Whichness of the Whole Works."

The Nazis' antipathy toward defining their political or economic policies and their desire to free themselves completely from so crass and mundane a thing as any specific program,[4] is beautifully illustrated in the constitution of the Oberland Bund, which — years before Moeller van den Bruck — called for a *Führer* and the creation of the Third Reich. The Oberlanders deliberately eschewed any mention of a program for the reason suggested by one of their admirers:

Nothing is more characteristic of the associative spirit of the *Oberländer* than their Idea of the Third Reich . . . The men dreamed deep dreams of this Mystery — a mystery which would have been debased into a concrete political program as soon as one attempted to define it precisely.[5]

The Mystery is partially penetrated by the same writer: "Two motifs are constantly repeated in the recitals of the *Oberländer*: the sacredness of the *Volksboden* and the heroic *Führerschicht*, which must be accepted by the community as the force which will achieve the goal of the docile followship (*willige Gefolgheit*) of all."[6]

Or look at the term, "political soldiers," on another level — that of so-called practical politics. Here, again, appearances are deceiving; for the term does not mean that the Freebooters had any particular program to suggest when they became politicians. In fact, when they entered the political arena, the Free Corps fighters found it necessary to do one of three things: (1) proclaim that their political program was not really a political program; (2) apologize for entering politics; (3) insist that they were very unpolitical politicians. The program of the former commander of *Selbsthilfe* of Magdeburg and later of the *Stahlhelm* is recorded here not because of the delicacy of its language but because it is

---

verschrieben, handelten aus einem Sein, nicht aus einem Meinen. Dadurch nahmen sie dem Staat die Abstraktion. Sie selber waren der Staat. . . .

[4] See Neumann, *op. cit.*, 233 and *passim*.

[5] Posse, *Die politischen Kampfbünde Deutschlands*, 46–47.

[6] *Ibid.*, 48.

an honest reflection of the Freebooter mentality applying itself to politics:

We must fight to get the men into power who will depend on us front soldiers for support — men who will call upon us to smash once and for all these damned revolutionary rats and choke them by sticking their heads into their own shit (*Scheiss*).[7]

Ernst Röhm's description of himself as a political soldier is illuminating: "I am a political soldier . . . I wanted to serve a *Volk* of fighters, not a people of poets and dreamers. With this determination I entered . . . into political life." He then stresses the fact that "I was a terrible politician" and takes pride in pointing out that during his years in the Reichstag, "I made only one speech [May 28, 1924] . . . to demand that my comrade Lt. Colonel Kriebel be released from his arrest . . ."[8] Heydebreck, too, is careful to emphasize that though he became a member of the Reichstag, "only once during the whole time did I perform useful service in the high house of parliament."[9] One more example must suffice. Colonel von Epp ran for the Reichstag in 1928. He felt entitled to the voters' support because he assured them that he had none of the attributes of a statesman: "I have decided to become a parliamentarian," he said in an interesting campaign speech. "You will doubt that I have the requisite qualities for that position. I do not have those qualities. I will never have them; for nothing depends on those qualities." After he was elected, von Epp looked around at the assembled legislators and noted in his diary: "An attempt of the slime to govern. Church slime, bourgeois slime, military slime."[10]

The overwhelming majority of the Freebooters, however, did not enter politics directly. Glombowski speaks for thousands of his comrades: "Politics had no interest for us . . . We were sol-

[7] Quoted, with approval, by his biographer, Wilhelm Kleinau, *Franz Seldte, Ein Lebensbericht* (Berlin, 1933), 49. It should be remembered that most of the Freebooters rejected the *Stahlhelm* because they felt that its program was too moderate.

[8] *Geschichte eines Hochverräters,* 10, 176, 314.

[9] *Wir Wehrwölfe,* 175.

[10] His biographer, who quotes these passages, is careful to point out that what von Epp meant by military *Schleim* was Reichswehr officers like Groener. Walter Frank, *Franz Ritter von Epp: Der Weg eines deutschen Soldaten* (Hamburg, 1934), 141–142.

diers and said to hell with everything else . . . We were young guys without any political ideas — why should we bother ourselves with politics? . . . If Hauenstein was ready to give his support to this man [Hitler] that was good enough for me." [11] Far from barring them from the title of political soldiers, it was precisely this almost universal attitude which made the fighters of the Free Corps fit the National Socialist criteria of political soldiers: men who did not think for themselves; men who followed the Leader.

If nihilism, activism, and sheer opportunism are the essentials of National Socialist political thinking, then the Free Corps made a real contribution. This writer does not feel that Hermann Rauschning's "revolution of nihilism" [12] offers either an adequate explanation of the rise of Hitlerism or a sufficient analysis of its functioning. It is, however, an apt characterization of the political thinking of both the Free Corps Movement and the Freebooter element which formed so large a part of the New Order. It is important to notice that the National Socialist historians who insist throughout their narratives that the Freebooters were the first "bearers of the positive political Idea," rely on negatives in defining that idea. Thus, von Oertzen summarizes, "They sought their own form and philosophy of existence. Spiritually, they stemmed from the front officers and front soldiers of the Great War . . . [they were] *anti-bürgerlich* from their experience at the front; anti-November Republic from their natural tradition and from the force of political events . . . they [thus] developed a genuinely political outlook." [13] Von Schmidt-Pauli defines the positive political Idea in similar terms: "These men fought instinctively for the national good against everything that was putrid: . . . against the general *bürgerlich* helplessness and the threat of Bolshevism . . . They fought to accomplish something manly which would satisfy the needs which came from their own breasts . . ." [14]

[11] *Organisation Heinz (O.H.): Das Schicksal der Kameraden Schlageters,* 22–23, 127.

[12] *The Revolution of Nihilism: Warning to the West,* translated by E. W. Dickes (New York, 1939).

[13] *Die deutschen Freikorps,* xv.

[14] *Geschichte der Freikorps,* 347.

Since the Freebooters themselves felt strongly that "moderation is stupidity — no, it is worse than stupidity — it is a crime against one's *Volk* and state," [15] it followed that action was the only program worth following. This reliance on action for the sake of action itself is the *leitmotif* which runs through all the memoirs. In this the Free Corps were indeed the vanguard of that political system which has been defined as "action pure and simple, dynamics *in vacuo,* revolution at a variable tempo . . ." [16] A few excerpts from the writings of von Salomon, the recognized spokesman for the Freebooters, will serve to illustrate the point:

We could not answer the question that so often echoed from the other side of the gorge, "What do you really want?" We could not answer because we did not understand the question, and they could never have understood the answer . . . Over on the other side they wanted property and permanence . . . and we wanted no system, no order, no platitudes and no programs. We acted according to no plan, toward no established goal. Indeed, we did not act at all, something acted in us. (*Wir wirkten nicht, es wirkte in uns.*) And so the question seemed stupid and foolish to us . . .

"What do we believe in?" you ask. Nothing besides action. Nothing besides the possibility of action. Nothing besides the feasibility of action . . . We were a band of fighters drunk with all the passions of the world; full of lust, exultant in action. What we wanted, we did not know. And what we knew, we did not want! War and adventure, excitement and destruction. An indefinable, surging force welled up from every part of our being and flayed us onward . . .

Our job is to attack, not to govern. We often paraphrased Von Clausevitz's axiom: "Politics is the extension of war by other means." [17]

One more confession of faith in nihilism and action was given in a conversation between two "Old Fighters" of the Mannsfeld Free Corps and a student volunteer:

First fighter: I don't believe in anything: not in promises, not in a program of any kind. I only believe in one thing: in my machine gun — in the bullet! . . .

Student: But isn't the war over? Don't we still live under laws? How can we dare to take the law into our own hands?

---

[15] Von Killinger, *Ernstes und Heiteres aus dem Putschleben,* 21.
[16] Rauschning, *op. cit.,* 223.
[17] *Die Geächteten,* 72–73, 294, 307; *Nahe Geschichte,* 30; and "Der verlorene Haufe," in *Krieg und Krieger,* 116. A part of this quotation was used before. See above, p. 108.

Second fighter: Listen to me, youngster! . . . Get this through your
                head once and for all. There is no peace and there
                are no laws. You come with me and I'll show you . . .
                a power higher than all your laws! [18]

Some of the "Wanderers into a Void" [19] realized the limitations
of nihilism and the smash-it policy, but they seemed incapable of
doing anything about it. Thus Heinz, in a rather pathetic passage,
looks back on his life as a Freebooter and writes:

We stand between two eras waiting for the future without knowing
what the future will bring. Patience was never our virtue. We were always restlessly eager to attack; we were crazed with the desire to
smash and ruin. But our angry fist seemed only to strike at the empty
and shattered air. The great mistake was that we always called this
destruction "Erneuerung." [20]

But the realization of the futility of nihilism and destruction
did not turn them to other alternatives. Indeed, by increasing
their sense of futility, frustration, and powerlessness, it only
served further to exalt destruction. Thus Jünger epitomized the
attitude of the Generation of the Uprooted and Disinherited
when he wrote: "Order is the common enemy . . . Destruction is
the only possible program which fits the . . . requirements of the
Nationalists." [21]

[18] Edwin E. Dwinger, *Auf halben Wege* (Jena, 1939), 28–29. This historical novel based on the author's own experience in the Mannsfeld Free
Corps, is the sequel to his better known book, *Die letzten Reiter* (Jena,
1935).

[19] *Der Wanderer ins Nichts* is the title of a contemporary novel written by
Friedrich Freksa, the nationalist who edited Ehrhardt's memoirs and who
was a great admirer of Schlageter. The hero of the novel is a *Freikorpskämpfer* who died fighting the Communists. Karl Radek chose the expression
for the title of a speech made before the executive committee of the Communist International on June 20, 1923. Since Radek was the leading expo-
nent of National Bolshevism, his speech is highly sympathetic to Schlageter
and his comrades. It was made as a part of Radek's campaign to bring the
Freebooters into the Communist camp. It is quoted at length and with approval by Moeller van den Bruck, *Das Recht der jungen Völker,* edited by
Hans Schwartz (Berlin, 1932), 75–79. Von Salomon does not object to the
expression and admits that future historians will indeed seek in vain for any
set of political beliefs with which to associate the Freebooters. (*Nahe Geschichte,* 112–113.)

[20] Heinz, *Sprengstoff,* 8. For a similar statement, see Curator, *Putsche,
Staat und Wir!,* 50.

[21] Posse quotes the passage because, "At the end of our discussion, we can
give no better characterization of the spirit of the majority of the associated

To others of the generation, destruction was no longer enough. What was needed was all-consuming Wagnerian catastrophe. One of the spiritual fathers of the men who produced the *Götter-dämmerung* of 1945 longed for such a catastrophe in 1923: "The conservative rather believes in catastrophe, in the powerlessness of man to avoid it, in its necessity, and in the terrible disappointment of the seduced optimist." [22]

II. "WE BOLSHEVISTS OF THE RIGHT"

After 1933, it behooved the German historians of the Free Corps to follow the propaganda line dictated by their masters. They consequently insisted that their heroes, like the National Socialists, were fighting the good fight against the Communists and the Jews. Like so much of Nazi propaganda, the assertion is a half-truth. To say that the Freebooters were anti-Semitic is largely true. To imply that they were all anti-Communist is false. Nazi cant to the effect that the Free Corps fighters formed the vanguard of the great crusade to save the West from Communism, is well worth examining. First, it distorts the entire Freebooter *Weltanschauung*. Second, it insists that one form of totalitarianism (Hitler's National Socialism) is basically and in all respects different from another form of totalitarianism (Stalin's Communism). The latter point may take us beyond the chronological confines of this study. Yet, in this Year of Grace 1952, comment does not seem irrelevant.

Let it then be pointed out that the Freebooters fought Communism not because they hated Communism but primarily because they liked fighting and the "Red Peril" of the postwar period gave them an excuse to fight. These men were certainly not "instinctively anti-Communist." Quite to the contrary, the radical nature of the Freebooter mentality favored extremist doctrines. And consequently, it liked a lot of what it saw in Communism. The Free Corps fighters, it is worth repeating, did not often talk about political theory, but when they did, it was not

---

youth than that sentence written by Jünger . . ." (*Politischen Kampfbünde Deutschlands*, 79.)

[22] Moeller van den Bruck, *Das Dritte Reich*, 223–224. Erich Fromm quotes the sentence to illustrate his thesis that sado-masochism is a dominant characteristic of the German mind.

Communism but the moderate liberalism of the Weimar democracy which was the chief target of their attack. They like Communist extremism because it demanded action. Heinz writes with approval: "Russia . . . gave the example: . . . Attack! Attack with arms! Attack by terror and atrocities! Attack to the point of destruction!" [23] They liked it because it attacked the same things they attacked: liberalism, parliamentarianism, and the smug complacency of the *bürgerlich* mentality. They agreed with Moeller van den Bruck that the real enemy was not Marxism but the hypocritical sham of liberal democracy: "The whole system is a racket. Some are swindlers, others are swindled, but it is always the people who are the victims . . . Only the fighting parties, *whether of the Right or the Left,* have any convictions. Only they have power." [24]

The activists of the Right had two objections to Marxism: its materialism was not congenial to the misty idealism of the Teutonic soul;[25] more important, its internationalism was repugnant to their faith in the future of Germandom. It was for this latter reason, as Ruth Fischer has pointed out, that many of them were attracted to Karl Radek's "National Bolshevism." [26] Nor did the men of the Free Corps really despise either the "hated Jewish" leadership of the Communist party or its members. Schauwecker, for instance, calls Lenin "a great Führer," [27] and Heinz, while agreeing that it was necessary to kill Liebknecht and Luxemburg, contrasts them favorably with the weak-kneed moderates, Ebert

[23] *Die Nation greift an,* 206–207.
[24] *Das Dritte Reich,* 136. (Italics are mine.) For similar expressions, see von Salomon, *Nahe Geschichte,* 30, 32, 88; Heinz, *Die Nation greift an,* 37, 74, 199; Heydebreck, *Wir Wehrwölfe,* 189; Killinger, *Das waren Kerle!,* 61; Curator, *Putsche, Staat und Wir,* 176, and Franz Schauwecker, *So ist der Friede: Die Revolution der Zeit in 300 Bildern* (Berlin, 1928), 35 ff.
[25] See especially E. Günther Gründel, *Die Sendung der jungen Generation: Versuch einer umfassenden revolutionären Sinndeutung der Krise* (Munich, 1932), 260–265.
[26] For a discussion of National Bolshevism, see Ruth Fischer's *Stalin and German Communism* (Cambridge, Mass., 1948), 270–287. Heydebreck writes of a conversation he had with "a well-known person of their [the Communist] Party" and says that he was favorably impressed with the possibility of coöperating with "the best and most German-minded of the activist part of the Communists." *Wir Wehrwölfe,* 189.
[27] Schauwecker, *So ist der Friede,* 10.

CONCLUSION 273

and Scheidemann. He concludes: "Both of them . . . towered head and shoulders above the Majority Socialist pack."[28] Many of them admired their opposite numbers, the activists who fought for the Spartacists and, later, the Red Front Fighters' League. Indeed, hundreds of them joined the "brave young guys"[29] of the Communist camp. After the nominal dissolution of the Ehrhardt Brigade, for example, Manfred von Killinger — who liked to speak of his men as "we Bolshevists of the Right"[30] — took his Storm Company to Poland and fought side by side with the Soviet Army during the Russo-Polish War of 1920.[31] And, as we have already noticed, hundreds of Freebooters joined the Red Army of the Ruhr in its battle against their former comrades of the Free Corps.[32]

In their admiration for Communism, the Free Corps fighters anticipated the National Socialists. For Nazi totalitarianism displays great affinity for its Communist counterpart. That affinity is demonstrated by the record of their collaboration against the Weimar Republic, whether it was in the Reichstag, in the Prussian Diet, or in joint effort during the pre-Hitler transportation strike in Berlin. Adolf Hitler himself was the first to admit that National Socialism and Communism had much in common. "There is more that binds us to Bolshevism than separates us from it," he once said in a revealing conversation, "There is, above all, revolutionary feeling . . . I have always made allowance for this circumstance, and given orders that former Communists are to be admitted to the party at once. The *petit bourgeois* Social Democrat and the trade-union boss will never be a National Socialist, but the Communist always will."[33] Hitler, in this case at

[28] *Die Nation greift an,* 30. See also von Salomon, *Die Geächteten,* 47.
[29] Röhm, *Die Geschichte eines Hochverräters,* 88. Even General von der Goltz pays tribute to the bravery and élan of the Spartacist fighters. He notes that while he found it necessary to dismiss them from his Baltic Free Corps, it meant removing some of his bravest men. ("Baltikum," in *Deutsche Soldaten,* 98.)
[30] Killinger, *Kampf um Oberschlesien, 1921,* 34.
[31] Heinz, *Die Nation greift an,* 96.
[32] Killinger, *Ernstes und Heiteres,* 125. See also von Schmidt-Pauli, *Freikorps,* quoted above at p. 176.
[33] Quoted in Hermann Rauschning, *The Voice of Destruction* (New York, 1940), 131. Hitler's high opinion of Communist spirit and tactics is manifest throughout *Mein Kampf.*

least, was true to his word. After he seized power, he saw to it that thousands of Communists were enrolled in the NSDAP. They were particularly effective in the Gestapo and in the SA, where they formed perhaps a third of the total membership. Indeed, there were so many of them that they were given a special name. They were known popularly as the "Beefsteak Nazi" — Brown on the outside, Red on the inside.[34]

But the Thousand Year Reich — in its thirteenth year — crashed to its Wagnerian finale. The Communists immediately returned *Der Führer's* compliment and followed his example. Since 1945, hundreds of former Nazis have joined the Communist-controlled Social Unity Party of East Germany;[35] the so-called People's Police of the Soviet Zone are now officered by former commanders of the Wehrmacht;[36] and the Communist-directed *Freie Deutsche Jugend* who marched into Berlin in May 1950 were led by erstwhile commanders of the *Hitler Jugend*.[37]

While it is no doubt true that there are important differences between the two totalitarianisms, their striking similarities should not be forgotten. Both systems elevate the Party and the Leader to the heights of total infallibility. Both make free discussion the privilege of the ruling elite. For the rest, to end criticism and to stifle curiosity, there is the concentration camp, the secret police, the haunting fear of the unknown. Both use propaganda and thought-control to turn citizens into pliable, docile followers of a monolithic will. Both run on tension and fear. If tension and fear do not already exist, they must be created in order to maintain and increase the isolation of the individual, the power of the state. Domestic tension (whether it be Jewish capitalism or bourgeois thinking); foreign fear (whether it be the barbaric East or the predatory West) — these are essentials of both systems.

---

[34] Hans Bernd Gisevius, *To the Bitter End,* translated by Richard and Clara Winston (Boston, 1947), 105.

[35] At first this was done clandestinely, but recently it has become open. In July 1950, Otto Grotewohl, the Communist Minister President of East Germany, extended an open invitation to all Germans: "Our National Front is not limited to democratic elements . . . We want everyone including the former Nazis." (*Time,* July 31, 1950. See also The *New York Times,* July 25, 1950.)

[36] Drew Middleton in The *New York Times,* March 19, 1950.

[37] Joseph Alsop in *New York Herald-Tribune,* March 22, 1950.

Finally, there is miracle and mystery. They are found in the umbilical adoration of the *Volk;* in the genuflections at the shrine of Lenin; in the hysterical hails to the *Führer;* in the lighted candle before the picture of the Stalin icon, in the miraculous unfolding of Marxist teleology.

The essence of totalitarianism, past and present, lies in the Inquisitor General's reply to the returning Christ: "We too have a right to preach a mystery, and to teach them that it's not the free judgment of their hearts, not love that matters, but a mystery which they must follow blindly . . . So we have done. We have corrected Thy work and have founded it upon *miracle, mystery,* and *authority.* And men rejoiced that they were again led like sheep." [38]

III. FROM REACTION TO ACTION

Nazi historians complain that Leftist writers grossly malign and completely misinterpret the Freebooters by calling them "ultra-reactionary, monarchist, White Guardist formations." [39] Are the National Socialists correct when they insist that the Free Corps were not reactionary? I believe that they are correct and have pointed out that whatever desire the Freebooters may have had of returning to the Imperial Germany from which they had revolted in their prewar youth movements, was killed by the failure of the Kapp Putsch. [40] It is important to notice that such men as Heydebreck and Röhm — men who had been particularly sentimental about the Kaiser and the old regime — were then convinced that the solution did not lie in a return to the old. "I had lost my faith in reaction," says Heydebreck, " 'Give us back our old Germany' " we had beseeched them, . . . but they had failed us. We are satisfied to look out for ourselves." [41] Ernst Röhm is more emphatic: "Now we revolutionaries can say this: we will not be saved by returning to the old, to reaction. And not by depend-

---

[38] Fydor Dostoevsky, *The Brothers Karamazov,* translated by Constance Garnett (London, 1912), 271. (Italics are in the original.)

[39] For typical Leftist interpretations, see Caro and Oehme, *Schleichers Aufstieg,* 48–49, 136, 159; and Paul Frölich *Wider den Weissen Mord,* 2nd ed. (Berlin and Leipzig, n.d.), *passim.* See above, p. 64.

[40] See above, pp. 164–167.

[41] *Wir Wehrwölfe,* 121.

ing on the exhausted excellencies and generals. Only men of action . . . can help us — only the young and the front-fighters who are . . . filled with patriotism and fanaticism." [42]

If the Freebooters wanted neither international Communism, nor liberal democracy, nor a return of the monarchy, what did they want? Men who can hardly be held responsible for their actions can scarcely be expected to write responsibly about them. The clearest impression left on the reader of their memoirs is this: the men of the Free Corps simply did not know what they wanted. They sometimes used the term "New Nationalism." But they did not define it except by denying that it had anything to do with the old nationalism. Thus when Ernst Jünger was asked to discuss the term which he had helped to popularize, he said: "When someone asks what the New Nationalism demands, one must first establish the fact that it will have absolutely nothing to do with either monarchy, or conservatism, or *bürgerlich* reaction, or with the patriotism of the Wilhelmian period." [43]

The activists agreed with Moeller van den Bruck that the chief trouble with the reactionary is that he demands a definite political system and that he is a rationalist who insists on facing facts squarely.[44] The New Nationalism would avoid that pitfall, for it rested on no rational system of government. Its program was written on the *Volk* soul of the race. Or, put on a more scrutable level, it was written where Hermann Goering once said the program of National Socialism was written: on the faces of the marching Storm Troopers.

IV. FREEBOOTERS IN BROWN SHIRTS

We now turn, in conclusion, to the second main argument of the National Socialists: namely, that the men of the Free Corps at

[42] *Geschichte eines Hochverräters,* 280.

[43] Quoted, with approval, in Posse, *Politische Kampfbünde,* 77.

[44] In contrasting the reactionary to what he calls the true conservative, he writes: "The reactionary is a spurious type of conservative. The reactionary is a rationalist. He sticks to facts; . . . his interpretation of history is as superficial as the conservative's is profound. The reactionary looks at the world as it has been; the conservative looks at it as it has been and as it always will be. He distinguishes the transitory from the eternal." *Das Dritte Reich,* 217–218.

once recognized Adolf Hitler as their long awaited Leader and immediately became ardent Nazis.

It is quite true that the Wanderers into a Void had always longed for a great leader to direct them. The *Führerprinzip*, we have seen, was the very basis of both the Free Corps movement and its immediate predecessors, the prewar youth movements and the Storm Troops of World War I. In the despair produced by the failure of the Kapp Putsch, the Freebooters once again called for a great national leader. In 1920, a member of the Ehrhardt Brigade wrote a book, which is at once a reaffirmation of the leadership principle and a really remarkable prophecy. He called his book *1934: Germany's Resurrection.* In what at the time seemed to be the most fatuous sort of wishful thinking, the author predicted that a great leader would appear in the year 1934. He would come after a period of economic collapse and political turmoil. He would prepare the way to power by organizing a nationwide movement which would divide Germany into sections each of which would be entrusted to a former Free Corps fighter. On the decisive day, the Reichstag, already controlled by members of his party, would vote him an enabling act. Henceforth the Reichstag would be a mere rubber stamp for his omnipotent will. As soon as the enabling act was passed, all undesirable elements would be liquidated "without a twinge of conscience." And after transforming Germany into a haven for the Freebooter spirit, the Leader would launch a war of revenge against the West. Poland would fall in a blitzkrieg, France would fall in a few months.[45] A surprisingly accurate prophecy. Yet neither the author of the book[46] nor the vast majority of his comrades thought that Adolf Hitler would be that leader, and they did not join his movement without a struggle.

[45] F. E. Solf, *1934: Deutschlands Auferstehung,* 3rd edition (Naumberg, 1922). The first edition appeared in 1920. By 1922 it had sold over 25,000 copies. It is highly ironical that Professor Gumbel, writing in 1924, alluded to this book as an example of the "whole system of political fantasies" engaged in by the Free Corps. (*Verschwörer,* 80.)

[46] Solf does not name the leader. He follows the custom of the period and simply speaks of him as "The General." Similarly, Ludendorff was usually referred to as "The Dictator" by his colleagues in the National Unity Society. Ehrhardt was called "The Consul."

The picture of the period when Hitler made his first bid for power is not one which shows the Free Corps fighters rushing to the support of their future *Führer*. It is rather a confused picture of double cross and intrigue which shows Hitler as the head of only one of a dozen quarreling groups each engaged in savage competition with the others. It was only after 1933 that the men of the Free Corps found it expedient to jump on the band wagon and proclaim that they had always considered Hitler to be their great leader. Prior to that many of them considered him a miserable little politician and a petty demagogue who sought to stage revolutions with his mouth. As many more joined nationalist groups in direct and open opposition to the NSDAP.

Schmidt-Pauli ends his book with the assertion that the Third Reich was "the fulfillment of an old Free Corps dream." [47] And so, in great measure, it was. Yet many of the Freebooters, particularly those who belonged to Röhm's SA, expected a great deal more from the New Order than they received. The captains and the lieutenants were led to believe that they would become the colonels and generals of a Hitler-controlled Wehrmacht; the impoverished rank and file expected pensions and special concessions of all kinds; the men who had joined the NSDAP because they believed it stood for a type of true socialism — and there were many of them — expected that the "unalterable 25-point program" would be put into effect. The New Order started off well enough. One of its first acts was to grant special pensions to all the "Old Fighters" of the Free Corps.[48] But from that point on, the *Führer's* "eternal gratitude" began to pay off in less tangible dividends. Memorials were erected to the Free Corps dead, museums were built to hold their old battle flags, and special *Freikorpskämpfer* medals were struck. But the twenty-five point program did not materialize and the demands that the SA should become the commanders of the German Army were answered by the Blood Purge of 1934. For when the Officers Corps told Hitler to choose between them and the SA, Hitler did not hesitate. He sacrificed the "Old Fighters."

[47] *Geschichte der Freikorps*, 351.
[48] "Gesetz über die Versorgung der Kämpfer für die nationale Erhebung, February 27, 1933," *Reichsgesetzblatt*, Jahrgang 1934, Teil I, 133–134.

Nor did *Der Führer* welcome the Free Corps into his movement with the open-hearted enthusiasm described by the National Socialist writers. The pages of *Mein Kampf* are filled with bitter attacks on those men who, he says, were a detriment to the development of the Third Reich.[49] Indeed, as the American editors of the book have pointed out, if the trouble were taken to count the lines in *Mein Kampf* it would doubtless be found that more space is devoted to angry and jealous outbursts against his activist rivals than to attacking Marxism and democracy. Only the Jews draw more of his fire.[50] Hitler needed the Freebooters and without their help it is highly probable that the Nazi movement would not have come to power. Yet Hitler was never happy about his reliance on the Free Corps. Like Ebert, Noske, Lüttwitz, and Buchrucker before him, he soon discovered that they were difficult tools to handle. Appointed district leaders of the SA, they followed the best traditions of Free Corps atomism and persisted in running their districts as they had run their Corps — by cultivating the personal allegiance of their men and by totally disregarding central authority.

Furthermore, they embarrassed Hitler by taking the socialist part of his program seriously and alarmed him with their demands for a second revolution. A series of clashes between 1928 and 1931 came to a bloody head on June 30, 1934. On the "Night of the Long Knives," and on successive nights with less picturesque names, hundreds — perhaps thousands[51] — of "the first

[49] *Mein Kampf*, Reynal and Hitchcock edition (New York, 1940), 783, 789, 800 and *passim*.
[50] *Ibid.*, note at page 760.
[51] The numbers killed in the Blood Purge will probably never be known. The figure chosen by Hitler, seventy-seven, is meaningless. The official *Deutsche Führerlexikon*, which was printed before the purge and, as the editors say, "rectified" after it took place, contains over a hundred names which have been deleted by pasting strips of paper over them. And the *Führerlexikon*, of course, contains only those men whom the party hierarchy considered to be main leaders of the movement. Former Chancellor Brüning, who escaped the purge only because he was warned by a telephone call from his friend von Schleicher, told me that he had personally seen a list of over 5,000 names of the men who were killed. Some of the better-known Free Corps leaders who died during the purge included Röhm, Rossbach, Heines, Pabst, Heydebreck, Ernst, and Hayn. Ehrhardt and Killinger were also on the original execution list but Ehrhardt managed to escape across the Swiss

soldiers of the Third Reich" were shot down. Many of them died with "Heil Hitler!" on their lips, for it did not occur to them that they were being killed by Hitler's personal orders. They died believing that they were the victims of a plot led by Goebbels and Goering who, they believed, were trying to wrest power away from their beloved *Führer*.[52] Never was there better justification for the bitter complaint so often made by the Volunteers against the leaders of the Republic: that Ebert, Noske, and Seeckt had used them for their own selfish purposes and had then thrust them aside and abandoned them.

In his Reichstag speech in which he explained the necessity of the Blood Purge and played to the full his new role of *Adolf Légalité*, the defender of law, order, and decency, Hitler thundered against those men, living and dead, who had been so largely responsible for the success of his movement. In so doing, he gave a description that was as applicable to men of his own party as it was to the Freebooters:

[They are] permanent revolutionaries who in 1918 had been shaken in their former relation to the state and uprooted, and had thereby lost all inner contact with the human social order. Men who have no respect for any authority, . . . men who found their profession of faith in nihilism, . . . moral degenerates, . . . constant conspirators incapable of any real coöperation, ready to oppose any order, filled with hatred against all authority, their restless and excited minds find satisfaction only in incessant intellectual and conspiratorial activity

---

border in spite of his wife's efforts to detain him. He was later invited back to Germany by the Nazis, but never played a prominent role in the Party. Killinger was reprieved at the last minute by Hitler.

[52] All National Socialist accounts of the purge are based on Hitler's version made in his Reichstag speech of July 13, 1934, and printed in the *Völkischer Beobachter* in a special edition of July 14, 1934. The most reliable interpretation is given in an anonymous book entitled, *Hitler Rast: Die Bluttragödie des 30. Juni 1934, Ablauf, Vorgeschichte, und Hintergründe*, 3rd edition (Saarbrücken, 1934). The book was placed in the closed archives of the NSDAP and stamped with the "V" sign. A good brief account of the purge is given in Heiden's *Der Fuehrer*, 719 ff. See also the anonymous pamphlet, *Weissbuch über die Erschiessungen des 30 Juni 1934: Authentische Darstellung der deutschen Bartholomäusnacht*, 3rd edition (Paris, 1935), and Otto Strasser's *Die deutsche Bartholomäusnacht*, 7th edition (Prague, 1938). The last two accounts must be taken with the usual amount of salt, but they are certainly more trustworthy than the official Nazi version.

aimed at the destruction of all existing institutions . . . These pathological enemies of the state are the enemies of all authority . . .[53]

Throughout this study, it has been necessary to take serious
issue with National Socialist interpretation of the nature and importance of the German Free Corps Movement. Nevertheless, the
Nazis are right in their chief contention: the Free Corps did make
fundamental and direct contributions to Hitler's Germany.

They made a negative contribution of first-rate importance. The
Weimar Republic was indeed, as Scheidemann once said in a
brilliant metaphor, a candle burning at both ends. The Free Corps
and their successor organizations were largely responsible for the
fact that the flame at the Right end of the candle burned more
brightly and melted more wax than its competitor on the Left.

They made specific positive contributions. In spite of the toll
taken by the Blood Purge, hundreds of the Freebooters rose to
positions of power in the National Socialist regime.[54] They contributed a well-developed leadership principle, labor camps,
youth groups, violent racism, and the mystic adoration of the *Volk*
soul.

Yet the real importance of the movement lies in none of these
things. It lies in that brutality of spirit and in that exaltation of
power which the men of the Free Corps bequeathed to the Third
Reich.

[53] The speech is quoted in full in the *Völkischer Beobachter,* July 14, 1934.
Some ten years later, when the Reich was crumbling all about him, *Der
Führer* saw the Freebooters in a kindlier light. In a conference with his
army commanders in March 1945, he insisted that the Free Corps had done
great work in 1919, they had "raised an army of Liberation and for a time
saved Germany." In his extremity Hitler expressed the hope that leaders like
Pfeffer would again appear to save the Reich. But he then suggests that he
would treat them as he had treated them in 1934: "Pfeffer is a born organizer. I would let him organize something, and when it was finished, let him
go . . . I would have strung him up afterwards, but the Free Corps was
there . . . Anyway, those people managed to do it. I consider Kircheim as
suited for a job like that even today." Felix Gilbert, editor, *Hitler Directs
His War, The Secret Records of His Daily Military Conferences* (New York,
1950), 136.
[54] See Appendix.

APPENDIX

APPENDIX

APPENDIX

NOTE: The typescript of the doctoral thesis contains two Appendixes. The first lists forty representative Free Corps and gives the place of origin, name of the commander, number of men, type of armament, activity, and disposition of each Corps. The second Appendix gives brief biographical sketches of 250 men who figured prominently in both the Free Corps Movement and in National Socialism. Costs of publication necessitated omitting the first Appendix and reducing the size of the second. The list that appears here is only a representative sampling of the men discussed in Appendix B of the original manuscript. Each individual's Free Corps activity is listed first; then follows a paragraph (in italics) describing his National Socialist activity. Readers interested in fuller information are referred to the doctoral thesis in the archives of Widener Library, "The German Free Corps Movement, 1918–1923."

Albrecht, Herbert. Member of both the Halle Free Corps and the Anhalt Free Corps; an "agricultural laborer" in Black Reichswehr formations.

On the editorial staff of the Völkischer Beobachter; *one of the directors of the Labor Front; member of the Reichstag.*

Alpers, Friedrich. Member of the Maercker Free Corps.

SA Sturmführer, 1930; SS Standartenführer, 1931; State Minister for Justice and Finance in Brunswick, 1933.

Andreeson, Willy. A member of several volunteer formations active in the Baltic; a winner of the Baltic Cross; participated in the Kapp Putsch.

"Gauredner" for the NSDAP, Director of the Gau Leadership School, 1929; a director of the Strength Through Joy Movement.

Arent, Benno von. Machine gun officer in East Prussian Free Corps, adjutant of the Von der Heyde Corps.

SS Sturmführer (Berlin), 1932; member of the Battle Society for German Culture.

Aulock, Hubertus von. Founder and leader of the Von Aulock Free Corps and the "Aulock Labor Association."

Brigadeführer of the N.S.K.K. (National Socialist Motor Corps) of Greater Berlin.

Baumann, Hans. A battalion commander of the Von Epp Free Corps.

In 1919 member of German Workers Party which became the NSDAP in 1920; Gauarbeitsführer of Bavaria-Highland; member of Reichstag, 1933.

Belding, Robert. As member of Maltzahn Corps, fought in Baltic and Upper Silesia. After 1921 an "agricultural laborer" and member of Black Reichswehr.

Joined NSDAP in 1925; group leader of textile workers in the Arbeitsfront.

Bergmann, Robert. Ordnance officer of the Von Epp Free Corps.

SS Standartenführer, 1932; member of Reichstag; member of Supreme Leadership Group of the SA. Purged in 1934.

Beiber, Rudolf. Member of the Lichtschlag and Düsseldorf Free Corps and the Viking Bund; sabotage work in the Ruhr; district leader of Stahlhelm.

Entered NSDAP, 1929; SS Standartenführer and leader of SS Fliegerstaffel West 1931; adjutant of the German Air Sports Association.

Böchenhauer, Arthur. Active in various Free Corps; member of the "Blücher Gymnastic, Sports, and Wandervogel Society."

Bormann, Martin. Section leader of Rossbach Free Corps, participated in Feme murders.

Adjutant to Captain von Pfeffer in first organization of SA; member of Reichstag, 1936; Hitler's personal adjutant and bodyguard; a director of the Blood Purge; witness to Hitler's last will. Probably killed while attempting to escape from Hitler's bunker in Berlin, April 1945. Sentenced to death, in absentia, at Nuremberg, 1946.

Brückner, Helmuth. Member of Upper Silesian Free Corps.

A founder of NSDAP in Upper Silesia, 1925; editor of Schlesien Beobachter; member of Prussian Landtag and Reichstag; Oberpräsident of Silesia, 1932.

Busch, Karl. Free Corps leader in Berlin, Baltic, Upper Silesia, and East Prussia.

Joined NSDAP in 1923; contributor to Völkischer Beobachter,

Schlesischer Beobachter, *and* Der Deutsche; *director of the Office of Press and Propaganda of the Strength Through Joy Movement.*

Conti, Leonardo. Member of the Division of Horse Guards; co-founder of the Anti-Semitic Racist League (later absorbed by the Schutz und Trutzbund); a Berlin director of the O.C. murder organization.

Member of the NSDAP and SA, 1927; member of Prussian Landtag and Staatsrat, 1932; author of several books on racist medicine; a director of the German Red Cross.

Daluege, Kurt. Section leader of the Rossbach Free Corps and after its dissolution, leader of one of its "gymnastic societies."

Joined NSDAP in 1922; founder and organizer of the Berlin SA; member of Reichstag; Lieutenant General of the Prussian Landespolizei.

Dennler, Wilhelm. Member of Von Epp Free Corps; active in Munich, the Ruhr, and in Upper Silesia.

As member of Röhm's Reichskriegsflagge, marched on the Feldherrnhalle on November 9, 1923; member of Association of National Socialist German Jurists; a director of Bavarian Labor Office.

Eichinger, Friedrich. Member of the Lützow Rifles, then joined the Von Epp Free Corps.

Joined the NSDAP in 1921; SA Sturmbannführer, Munich; adjutant to Bavarian Minister of Interior.

Engel, Johannes. As Volunteer, fought against Berlin Spartacists and in Upper Silesia.

Joined Party in 1927; under Goebbel's tutelage became "Reichsredner" for NSDAP; District leader of Arbeitsfront.

Engelbrecht, Otto. Member of Von Epp Free Corps; an organizer of the Oberland Free Corps; member of Thule Society; "defendant in many political trials."

Marched on the Feldherrnhalle, 1923; Kreisleiter of the NSDAP, 1923; Special Representative of the Supreme SA Leadership, 1933.

Erdmann, Walter. Member of Oberland Free Corps and Oberland Bund; active in Black Reichswehr.

Joined Party in 1925, became a district leader and "Gauredner." Director of the NSDAP Farmers Association of Saxony.

Ernst, Karl. Member of the Rossbach Free Corps and its subsequent "labor organizations"; active in Black Reichswehr; member of several racist societies such as Rossbach's Ulrich von Hutten Bund.

SA Untergruppenführer for East Prussia; member of Reichstag, 1932; purged in 1934 because of his knowledge of the Reichstag fire.

Fichte, Werner von. Great-grandson of Johann Fichte, fought as Freebooter in Baltic and Poland; member of Ehrhardt Brigade and its successor, the Viking Bund.

Broke with Ehrhardt and joined NSDAP, 1928; made inspector of SA and SS in Westphalia, 1932; Police President of Erfurt, 1933; purged at Hitler's orders, 1934.

Frank, Hans. Member of Von Epp Free Corps.

In 1927, member of the Reichsleitung of NSDAP as director of its legal section; Bavarian Minister of Justice; Reichskommissar for Justice in 1933; editor of the periodical, Deutsches Recht.

Fritsch, Karl. Member of the Von Epp Free Corps.

SS Brigadeführer, Saxony; Minister of Interior, Saxony.

Gohdes, Otto. Member, variously, of Ehrhardt Brigade, Jungsturm, Schlageter Bund, and Organization Consul.

Entered NSDAP in 1923; SS Sturmbannführer; educational director of German Labor Front; a director of Strength Through Joy; editor of the Schulungsbrief.

Goltz, Graf Rudiger von der. Commander of all Free Corps in Baltic; active in Kapp Putsch; leader of VVVD (The United Patriotic German Associations).

In 1932, actively campaigned for Hitler's presidency; in 1934, made director of Reichsverbandes Deutsche Offiziere.

Gutsmeidl, Franz. Member of Loewenfeld Free Corps, Oberland Free Corps, Schutz und Trutzbund; winner of Silesian Eagle and Loewenfeld Cross.

Entered NSDAP in 1925; member of Reichstag; member of the Supreme Leadership of Political Organization of the Party; director of the Association of German Workers.

Hauenstein, Heinz Oskar. Member of Ehrhardt Brigade; organizer and leader of "Organization Heinz" and Storm Section Heinz; leader of a sabotage group in Ruhr; organizer of Free Corps work camps; judge in Femgericht; active in Black Reichswehr.

Joined NSDAP, 1922; subsequently dismissed and reinstated;

editor of National Socialist organ, Niederdeutschen Beobachter, *Hanover.*

Hayn, Hans. Member of several Free Corps active in Eastern Germany; member of Schlageter sabotage group in Ruhr; an organizer of Black Reichswehr; defendant in Feme trials; participated in Kustrine Putsch.

Joined NSDAP in 1923; Oberführer of SA Gausturm, Silesia; member of Reichstag, 1932; purged in 1934.

Heines, Edmund. As member of Rossbach Free Corps, active in Baltic and Upper Silesia; one of judges of Rossbach's Judicial Section; involved in Feme murder trials. Homosexual lover of Rossbach and Röhm.

Supreme SA Commander, Silesia; member of Reichstag, 1932; purged in 1934.

Heinz, Friedrich Wilhelm. Member of Ehrhardt Brigade and Organization Consul; active in Kapp Putsch, Upper Silesia, Black Reichswehr and in Ruhr; a judge of Femgericht.

Participated in the Beer Hall Putsch; sometime Supreme SA leader for Western Germany. Author of Die Nation greift an *and* Sprengstoff *and other proto-Nazi books. After 1933, one of the directors of the Reich Union of German Writers. Now a publisher in the American Zone, he prefers to forget his Free Corps and National Socialist activity and refuses to discuss it.*

Hess, Rudolf. Member of Von Epp Free Corps and the Thule Society.

Joined NSDAP in 1920; for years, Hitler's personal secretary and personal deputy. Pronounced insane at the Nuremberg trials and sentenced to life imprisonment.

Heydrich, Reinhard. Member of Maercker's Rifles and the Schutz und Trutzbund; cofounder of Deutschvölkische Jugenschar, Halle.

SS Brigadeführer, Chief of Security Section of RFSS; Himmler's deputy.

Hildebrandt, Friedrich. As member of Brandis Free Corps, active in Baltic; an "agricultural laborer," 1921–1924; an organizer of Black Reichswehr.

In 1925, Gauleiter of Mecklenburg-Lübeck; in 1932, member of Reichstag; in 1933, Reichstatthalter for Mecklenburg-Lübeck.

Hinkel, Hans. Member of Oberland Free Corps; engaged in sabotage work in Ruhr, 1923.

Joined NSDAP in 1921 (member No. 287); member of Reichstag; Prussian State Commissar for Economics, Art, and Education.

Hofmann, Hans Georg. Commander of the 3rd Battalion of Von Epp Free Corps; as member of regular Reichswehr, helped Röhm organize Einwohnerwehr and SA.

Leader of SA Gruppe Bavaria, in 1931; Inspector of SA and Police Chief of Regensberg, in 1932; member of Reichstag.

Jagow, Dietrich von. Member of Ehrhardt Brigade, and the Organization Consul.

In 1921, leader of Hitler's first SA company; in 1922, assigned by Hitler to organize student groups in Tübingen; SA Obergruppenführer; former Reichskommissar for Württenberg; member of Reichstag, 1932–1936.

Kaufmann, Karl. Member of Ehrhardt Brigade, Killinger's Storm Company, and the Organization Consul; saboteur and Feme murderer. "Only the devil and the Prussian authorities know how often Karl Kaufmann was arrested." (Schirach, *Pioniere*, 1924.)

Gauleiter and Reichstatthalter of Hamburg; member of Prussian Landtag and Reichstag.

Killinger, Manfred von. Member of Ehrhardt Brigade; participated in Kapp Putsch; leader of Storm Section Killinger; leader of the military section of the O.C. planned series of political murders including that of Erzberger and Rathenau; during investigation arrest organized troop and collected money for the support of the Irish Sinn Fein; after release, became leader of Viking Bund in Saxony.

SA Obergruppenführer; member of Reichstag; judge of Nazi Volksgericht; Minister-President of Saxony; sometime member of German legation in San Francisco; Nazi Minister to Slovakia, 1940; Minister to Rumania, 1941.

Klaiber, Alfred. Member of the Tübinger Student Volunteer Battalion.

Oberbürgermeister, Esslingen; legal adviser of the Party leadership in Esslingen; member of the Association of National Socialist German Jurists.

Klintsch, Johann Ulrich. Member of Ehrhardt Brigade and Organization Consul; an accomplice in Erzberger murder.

Assigned by Ehrhardt to help Hitler build his "Gymnastic and Sports Society" which became the SA on November 4, 1921.

Koch, Erich. As Volunteer, fought in Upper Silesia and in Ruhr; friend of Schlageter's and one of honor guard that brought his body back to unoccupied Germany.

Gauleiter and President of East Prussia; member of Reichstag and editor of the NSDAP organ, Preussische Zeitung.

Kolbow, Karl Friedrich. Fought in Baltic as member of Schneider Volunteer Battalion; in Upper Silesia as member of Oberland Free Corps.

Joined NSDAP in 1921 (membership number 2900); Obersturmbannführer of SA and Gauredner of NSDAP.

Kondeyne, Karl Walter. As member of Free Corps von Yorck, fought in Baltic; active in Kapp Putsch and Black Reichswehr.

Physician General of the Hitler Youth.

Krausser, Fritz Ritter von. Member of Von Epp Free Corps; a close friend of Röhm's; helped Röhm organize the SA.

SA Obergruppenführer and Chief of Section I of the "Osaf" (Supreme SA Leadership). Purged in 1934.

Lancelle, Otto. Section leader of an Upper Silesian Free Corps; member of Von Epp Free Corps; military adviser of racist youth groups.

On staff of "Osaf," 1931; Director of the Reichschule, 1933.

Lutze, Viktor. Member of the Organization Heinz; a founder of the Freischar Schill; friend of Schlageter and member of honor guard which brought his body back to Germany.

After Röhm's death, Chief of Staff of the SA.

Malsen-Ponickau, Johann von. Member of Von Epp Free Corps.

SS Brigadeführer; police president of Nürnberg-Fürth; on Himmler's personal staff; special interest: music.

Maurice, Emil. As Volunteer, active in the liberation of Munich and in Upper Silesia.

Feldherrnhalle, November 9, 1923; SS Standartenführer; member of Reichstag.

Meinberg, Wilhelm. As Volunteer, fought in Upper Silesia, East Prussia, and Ruhr; member of Schutz und Trutzbund.

Entered Party in 1929; in 1932 member of Prussian Landtag and Reichstag; Oberstürmbannführer of SS.

Moosbauer, Max. Member of Free Corps Oberland.

Kreisleiter of NSDAP; SS Sturmführer; Bürgermeister of Passau.

Mumme, Georg. Member of the Gerstenburg Free Corps and of

Maercker's Rifles; founder of the "Academic Homeland Service" which supplied the Black Reichswehr with student recruits.

In 1933, District leader of the Association of National Socialist Jurists; in 1934, Under Section Leader of the Reichsleitung's legal department.

Neubert, Reinhard. Member of the Division of Horse Guards; active in Kapp Putsch; member of the Olympia Sports Society.

President of Reich Chamber of Justice; member of directing council of the Association of National Socialist Jurists; legal adviser of the SA.

Nicolai, Helmut. Member of Ehrhardt Brigade, active in Kapp Putsch; member of Ehrhardt's O.C. and Viking Bund.

In 1931, leader of the Domestic Politics Department of the NSDAP; in 1933, Ministerial Director of the National Ministry of Interior; author of Rasse und Recht *and other party tracts.*

Pfeffer, Franz von. Founder and commander of the Von Pfeffer Free Corps; active in Baltic and Upper Silesia and leader of sabotage group in Ruhr; member of the O.C.

Chief of Staff of SA immediately preceding Röhm; involved in Stennes revolt, he was dismissed from SA and made a member of Reichstag.

Pitrof, Ritter von. The founder and leader of the Swabian Free Corps; active in the "liberation of Munich."

Member of the NSDAP, Gauführer for Upper Bavaria of the NSFKB (National Socialist League of Front Fighters). Author of Gegen Spartakus in München.

Radmann, Hans Joachim. Participated in Kapp Putsch; as member of Oberland Free Corps, helped storm the Annaberg; winner of St. Annaberg Cross.

President of Board of Industry and Trade in Upper Silesia.

Ramcke, Bernhard. Commander of a Storm Troop in World War I; fought in Baltic as an officer of the Brandis Free Corps.

Rose to the rank of Lieutenant General in Hitler's Wehrmacht. Commander of German paratroops, he directed the invasion of Crete in World War II. Author of Vom Schiffsjungen zum Fallschirmjägergeneral.

Ramshorn, Hans. Baltic volunteer; later joined Loewenfeld Marine Brigade; organized "Security Police" in Ruhr, 1920.

SA Brigadeführer for Upper Silesia; Police President of Gleiwitz. (Purged, 1934?.)

Reinhard, Wilhelm. Founder and leader of Reinhard Free Corps and its successor organizations; a commander of the Stahlhelm.

SS Oberführer, Berlin; member of Reichstag, general in Hitler's Wehrmacht, president of the Hitler-endorsed veterans association, the Kyffhaeuser Bund, 1934–1943. At time of dissolution, this Bund had a membership of 3,000,000 men. Reinhard, now eighty-three years old, is currently active in the effort to reconstitute the Kyffhaeuser Bund, and make it the single veterans association in West Germany.

Römer, Wilhelm. Member of Lichtschlag Free Corps and of the Münster Academic Defense Corps; active in Ruhr and Upper Silesia.

Member of Prussian Landtag and Reichstag; Gauführer of the Association of National Socialist Jurists.

Roosen, Berend. Officer of Reinhard Free Corps; organized Orgesch in Brandenburg; sabotage work in Ruhr, 1923.

Police President of Halle.

Rothenhäusler, Anton. Member of Württemberg Free Corps; active in Kapp Putsch, Upper Silesia, and Ruhr.

Member of the Political Organization of the Supreme NSDAP Leadership.

Ruberg, Berhard. Member of Berthold Free Corps; active in Orgesch.

Appointed leader of the NSDAP in the Cameroons, West Africa; foreign office of the NSDAP; Leader of the Verband Reichsdeutscher Vereine im Ausland.

Sauer, Hans. Member of Ehrhardt Brigade and Viking Bund.

President of the South Thuringian Chamber of Industry and Trade; founder and editor of the Beobachter für die Kreise Sonneberg und Hildburghausen.

Carl Eduard, Duke of Saxe-Coberg-Gotha. Staff officer of Franconian Volunteer Rifle Regiment; district leader in Thuringia of Ehrhardt Brigade and subsequently of the Organization Consul.

On staff of Supreme SA Leadership; President of German Red Cross; Senator of Kaiser Wilhelm Society.

Schemm, Hans. Member of Von Epp and the Bayreuth Free Corps.

Joined NSDAP in 1922; Gauleiter of Upper Franconia; Director of National Socialist Teachers Association; author of Gott-Rasse-Kultur (etc.); member of Reichstag.

Schlegel, August. Member of Engelhard Free Corps.

A director of the National Socialist Association of German Doctors; author of Die Kastration, Die Todesstrafe *(etc.).*

Schlumprecht, Karl. As member of Von Epp Free Corps, fought in Munich and in Ruhr, 1920.

Gauleiter, Oberbürgermeister of Bayreuth; Reichsredner; member of Reichstag.

Schneider, Eduard. Member, variously, of the Students' Volunteer Company, Von Epp Free Corps, and Oberland Free Corps.

Marched on the Feldherrnhalle; leader of Colonization Department of the NSDAP.

Schüler, Bruno. As member of the Maercker Rifles, active in Middle Germany; as member of Oberland Free Corps, stormed the Annaberg.

Oberbürgermeister of Dortmund; president of the Dortmund Chamber of Commerce and Industry.

Schulze-Wechsungen, Walther. Member of Frontier Defense Corps; active in East Prussia, Upper Silesia, and Ruhr.

Gauleiter of Enlightenment and Propaganda, Berlin; Reichsredner; member of Prussian Landtag and Reichstag.

Seidel, Martin. Officer in Ehrhardt Brigade and in its successor, the Viking Bund; active in Upper Silesia.

Kreisleiter of NSDAP for Southern Thuringia; Gau inspector for Thuringia; member of the Party Leadership; member of Reichstag.

Sommerfeldt, H. Martin. Baltic Volunteer, active in Kapp Putsch.

SA Sturmbannführer; member of Oberregierungsrat, Berlin; biographer of Hermann Goering.

Stable, Oskar. Member, variously, of Maercker's Rifles, Upper Silesian Volunteers, and Rossbach's Storm Troops.

National Leader of N.S.D.St.B. (National Socialist German Student Association). Purged, 1934.

Steinacher, Hans. Organizer of Carinthian Volunteers; under the name of "Bergmann" active in Ruhr, 1923–1924.

Reichsleiter of the VDA (League for Germans in Foreign Countries).

Stuckart, Wilhelm. Member of Von Epp Free Corps; active in sabotage work in Ruhr.

Entered NSDAP in 1922; Director of the Department for the

Defense Against Lies in Pomerania; Oberbürgermeister of Stettin; Director of the Prussian Ministry of Culture.

Tengelmann, Wilhelm. Member of Officers' Storm Company of the Ehrhardt Brigade; fought in Bremen, Thuringia, Munich, Berlin, and Upper Silesia.
SS Sturmbannführer; member of Prussian Ministry of Economics.

Thiele, Kurt. Member of Upper Silesian Free Corps; leader of various student volunteer formations.
Gauamtsleiter, Bremen; member of Reichstag; editor of Bremen NSDAP newspaper, "B.N.Z."

Tillessen, Karl. Member of Ehrhardt Brigade, and Organization Consul; defendant in Erzberger murder, sentenced to three years in prison for part in Rathenau murder.
Joined NSDAP in 1922 and helped organize Party in Hesse.

Wagener, Otto. Chief of staff then commander of German Legion in Baltic; also active in Upper Silesia and in Saxony.
SA Gruppenführer; member of Reichsleitung of the NSDAP; sometime Reichskommissar for Economics.

Wagner, Gerhard. Member of Von Epp Free Corps and of the Oberland Free Corps.
Cofounder and director of National Socialist Medical Association; adviser to Rudolf Hess on questions of national health.

Wantock-Rekowski, Heinrich von. Member of Maercker's Rifles.
Propaganda leader for Strength Through Joy.

Weiss, Wilhelm. Member of Von Epp Free Corps, helped Röhm organize German Battle League.
SA Gruppenführer; on staff of Völkischer Beobachter; member of Reichstag, 1936.

Winter, Hans Erich. Member of Bremen Free Corps.
Gauredner of NSDAP; member of State Chancellery of Saxony; member of the National Farmers' Council.

Wolff, Karl. Company commander in Hesse Free Corps, later adjutant to Von Epp.
SS Brigadeführer; Himmler's adjutant; member of Reichstag.

Zarnack, Wolfgang. Member of Reinhard Free Corps; Blücher Youth League; Defense and Attack League; League for German Racist Comradeship.
Obersturmführer on staff of Supreme SA Leadership.

Zengen, Hans Werner von. As Volunteer, active in Upper Silesia, Ruhr, and Palatinate; involved in Feme trials.

SA Sturmführer; on staff of Reichsstatthalter of Hesse.

Zunkel, Gustav. Member of Maercker's Rifles; established branch of Young German Order in Weimar.

SA Oberführer in Thuringia; on staff of Supreme SA Leadership; member of Reichstag and Thuringian State Council.

BIBLIOGRAPHY

BIBLIOGRAPHY

I. PRIMARY SOURCES

A. GOVERNMENT DOCUMENTS AND PUBLIC RECORDS

Germany

Allgemeiner Kongress der Arbeiter und Soldatenräte Deutschlands von 16 bis 21 December 1918, Stenographische Berichte (Berlin, 1919).

Amtliche Berichte über die Verhandlungen des Badischen Landtags (n.p., 1921).

Auswärtiges Amt: Der Aufstand im oberschlesischen Abstimmungsgebiet, August und September 1920 (Berlin, 1920).

Auswärtiges Amt: Denkschrift über den dritten Polen Aufstand Mai–Juni, 1921 im Kreis Hindenburg, O.S. (Berlin, 1921).

Reichsgesetzblatt, herausgegeben im Reichsministerium des Innern (Berlin, 1919–1934).

Reichstags Handbuch von 1936 (Munich, 1936).

Statistisches Jahrbuch für das deutsche Reich, herausgegeben vom statistischen Reichsamt (Berlin, 1918–1924).

Verhandlungen des Bayerischen Landtags, Stenographische Berichte (Munich, 1919–1924).

Verhandlungen des deutschen Reichstags, Stenographische Berichte (Berlin, 1907).

Verhandlungen des Reichstags, Stenographische Berichte (Berlin, 1920–1927).

Verhandlungen des Sächsischen Landtages (Dresden, 1920–1924).

Verhandlungen der verfassunggebenden deutschen Nationalversammlung, Stenographische Berichte (Berlin, 1919–1920).

Untersuchungsauschuss über die Weltkriegsverantwortlichkeit 4. Unterauschuss: Die Ursachen des deutschen Zusammenbruches im Jahre 1918. Unter Mitwirkung von Dr Eugen Fischer, Dr Walther Bloch, herausgegeben von Dr Albert Philipp, M.d.R., 12 vols. (Berlin, 1925–1929).

Great Britain

The Parliamentary Debates, Official Report, House of Commons
(London, 1918–1923).

United States of America

American Military Government of Occupied Germany: 1918–1920,
4 vols. (Washington, D.C., 1943).

Hearings before the Special Committee Investigating the Munitions Industry, United States Senate, 73rd Congress (Washington, D.C., 1934).

Senate Documents, 66th Congress, 1st Session, Vol. XV: Report of the Mission to Finland, Estonia, Latvia, and Lithuania on the Situation in the Baltic Provinces (Washington, D.C., 1919).

B. OFFICIAL, OR OFFICIALLY ENDORSED PARTY AND ARMY
   PUBLICATIONS *

Die Braunhemden im Reichstag: Die Nationalsozialistische Reichstagsfraktion 1932, VII Wahlperiod (November, 1932) (Munich, 1933).

Darstellungen aus den Nachkriegskämpfen deutscher Truppen und Freikorps. Im Auftrage des Oberkommandos des Heeres, bearbeitet und herausgegeben von der Kriegsgeschichtlichen Forschungsanstalt des Heeres, 7 vols. (Berlin, 1938–1939).

Das deutsche Führerlexikon: 1934–1935 (Berlin, 1934). The preface was originally written May 1, 1934. A postscript added after the Blood Purge reads: "As a consequence of a series of political events, we have rectified the already completed volume in all important respects in consideration of the events up to August 2 of this year. The further effect of these occurrences on the formation of the movement, state and *Volk* will be considered in a special supplement or in a second edition." The names and pictures of the men who were purged have been lifted from the forms or pasted over with strips of paper; in which case, the names of the

---

* Books written by private individuals, though stamped with the approval of the NSDAP, have been listed under the secondary sources. In a sense, anything published openly after 1933 may be considered officially sponsored by the Party.

purged are visible when the page is held up to a strong light.

Die deutsche Wehrmacht, 1914–1939: Rüchblick und Ausblick (Berlin, 1939).

Nationalsozialistisches Jahrbuch, herausgegeben unter Mitwirkung der Reichsleitung der N.S.D.A.P. (Munich and Berlin, 1932–1935).

Organisationsbuch der NSDAP (Munich, 1940). The official, secret handbook of the Nazi Party.

S.A. Blätter: Ein Volk! Ein Vaterland! Wie es geworden und was das ganze deutsche Volk wissen muss! (Leipzig, 1934). Specially prepared book for the enlightenment of SA troops. Grossly unreliable.

C. COLLECTIONS OF DOCUMENTS

Brammer, Karl, ed., *Fünf Tage Militärdiktatur: Dokumente zur Gegenrevolution* (Berlin, 1920). Documents relative to the Kapp Putsch and commentary by an opponent of the Kapp Government.

Breuer, Robert, ed., *Politische Prozesse: Aktenmässige Darstellungen.* Heft I: *Das politische Ergebnis des Rathenauprozesses.* Heft II: *Das Blausäure-Attentat auf Scheidemann,* 5 vols. (Berlin, 1922–1924). Prepared from official stenographic reports of the trials.

Buchner, Eberhard, ed., *Revolutionsdokumente: Die deutsche Revolution in der Darstellung der Zeitgenossischen Presse.* 2 vols. (Berlin, 1921).

Dokumente aus dem Befreiungskampf der Pfalz, collected and edited by the staff of the *Pfalzischen Rundschau* (Ludwigshafen, 1930).

Der Dolschstoss-Prozess in München October–November 1925 Eine Ehrenrettung des deutschen Volkes, Zeugen und Sachverständigen. Aussagen einer Sammlung von Dokumenten (Munich, 1926[?]).

Hohlfeld, Johannes, ed., *Deutsche Reichsgeschichte in Dokumenten 1849–1934: Urkunden und Aktenstücke zur innern und äusseren Politik des deutschen Reiches.* 4 vols. (Berlin, 1934).

Köhrer, Erich, ed., *Das wahre Gesicht des Bolschewismus! Tatsachen, Berichte, Bilder aus den baltischen Provinzen November 1918–Februar 1919* (Berlin, 1919).

Maier-Hartmann, Fritz, ed., *Dokumente der Zeitgeschichte*, 4th
    ed. (Munich, 1942). Officially approved by the NSDAP.
Purlitz, Friedrich, ed., *Deutscher Geschichtskalender* (Leipzig,
    1920–1923). Useful but not as valuable as Karl Wipper-
    mann's original *Geschichtskalender*.
*Reden an das neue Deutschland: Deutschlands Führer auf der
    Nationalversammlung in Weimar* (Berlin, n.d.).

D. MEMOIRS AND CONTEMPORARY ACCOUNTS

Allen, Henry T., *My Rhineland Journal* (Boston, 1923).
———, *The Rhineland Occupation* (Indianapolis, Ind., 1927).
    The memoirs of the commander of American occupation
    forces in the Rhineland. On the whole, sympathetic to Ger-
    many.
Ames, Knowlton L., *Berlin after the Armistice* (privately printed,
    n.p., 1919). Lt. Ames was a member of the American Pris-
    oner of War Mission to Berlin, 1918–1919.
Arnold, Alfred, "Freiwilligen-Detachment Tüllmann im Roten
    Lichtenberg," in *Das Buch vom deutschen Freikorpskämp-
    fer*, edited by Ernst von Salomon (Berlin, 1938).
Awaloff, General Fürst, *Im Kampf gegen den Bolshevismus*
    (Glückstadt and Hamburg, 1925). The rambling, senti-
    mental memoirs of the fantastic commander of the "White
    Russian Army of the West."
Baden, Prinz Max von, *Erinnerungen und Dokumente* (Stuttgart
    and Berlin, 1927).
Balla, Erich, *Landsknechte wurden wir: Abenteuer aus dem Bal-
    tikum* (Berlin, 1932). While in the form of a novel, this is
    actually the memoirs of one of the battalion commanders
    of the Iron Division. An accurate picture of the *Balti-
    kumers*.
Baltische Lande, edited by Alfred Brackmann, Vol. IV, "Der Bol-
    schewismus und die baltische Front" (Leipzig, 1939). A
    memorial volume which contains essays written by par-
    ticipants in the Baltic campaign of 1919.
*Die baltische Landeswehr im Befreiungskampf gegen den Bol-
    schewismus: ein Gedenkbuch herausgegeben vom bal-
    tischen Landeswehrverein* (Riga, 1929). Memorial essays
    written by members or admirers of the Baltic *Landeswehr*.
Bark, Kurt, "Rossbach's Marsch ins Baltikum," in *Das Buch vom*

deutschen Freikorpskämpfer, edited by Ernst von Salomon (Berlin, 1938).

Basedow, P. Ernst and Correns, Paul, editors, *Schicksalstunden: unvergessliches aus schweren Tagen in Posen und West-preussen* (Berlin, 1925). A series of personal reminiscences written by various citizens of Posen and West Prussia.

Bernhard, Georg, *Die deutsche Tragödie: Der Selbstmord einer Republik* (Prague, 1933). The interpretation of a Leftist. Undocumented.

Bernstein, Richard, *Der Kapp-Putsch und seine Lehren,* Revolutions-Bibliothek Nr. 10 (Berlin, 1920). A moderate, trustworthy account of the Kapp Putsch written by the editor of *Vorwärts.*

Bischoff, Major Josef, *Die letzte Front: Geschichte der Eisernen Division im Baltikum, 1919* (Berlin, 1935). The memoirs of the commander of the Iron Division. Honest, blunt, and chiefly concerned with minute details of military campaigns.

Blos, Wilhelm, *Von der Monarchie zum Volkstaat* (Stuttgart, 1923). Personal reminiscences of the Revolution; primarily concerned with Württemburg.

Braun, M. J., *Die Lehren des Kapp Putsches.* Pamphlet Number 23 of the "Internationale" (Leipzig, 1920).

Braun, Otto, *Von Weimar zu Hitler* (New York, Europa Verlag, 1940). Memoirs of the former Social-Democratic Minister President of Prussia. Written without access to diaries, notes, and papers which the police had taken from him.

Buchrucker, Major Bruno Ernst, *Im Schatten Seeckts: Die Geschichte der "Schwarzen Reichswehr"* (Berlin, 1928). An account written by the organizer of the Black Reichswehr and leader of the Kustrine Putsch.

Cros, Guy Charles, "Le Coup d'État de Kapp," in *Les Archives de la Grande Guerre* (November, 1921), No. 28 (Paris, 1921). An eyewitness account written by the director of the Bibliothéque et Musée de la Guerre.

Curator, Carsten, *Putsche, Staat und Wir!* (Karlsruhe, 1931). The memoirs of a former member of the Ehrhardt Brigade, the "Freischar Silesia" and various secret societies. A document of disillusionment.

D'Abernon, Viscount Edgar Vincent, *An Ambassador of Peace,* 3 vols. (London, 1929–1930). The reminiscences of the able, moderate British Ambassador to Germany 1920–1926. Sympathetic.

Dickhuth-Harrach, Gustav von, ed., *Im Felde unbesiegt. Der Weltkrieg in 28 Einzeldarstellungen* (Munich, 1920). Series of essays by Ludendorff, von Hindenburg, Schauwecker, and others, written to prove that Germany was stabbed in the back.

Du Parquet, Lieutenant-Général, *L'Aventure Allemande en Lettonie* (Paris, 1926). The impressions of the French representative of the Inter-Allied Military Commission.

Dwinger, Edwin Erich, *Die letzten Reiter* (Jena, 1935). A historical novel based on the author's own experiences in the Baltic as a member of the Mannsfeld Free Corps.

————, *Auf halben Wege* (Jena, 1939). The sequel to the above. Carries the story through the Kapp Putsch and the Ruhr fighting of 1920 in which the author participated.

Ebert, Friedrich, *Friedrich Ebert Kämpfe und Ziele, Mit einem Anhang: Erinnerungen von seinen Freunden* (Dresden, n.d.). A collection of some of Ebert's less known speeches. Also contains memorial essays written by his friends.

————, *Schriften, Aufzeichnungen, Reden*, 2 vols. (Dresden, 1926).

Ehrhardt, Hermann, *Kapitän Ehrhardt, Abenteuer und Schicksale*, edited by Friedrich Freksa (Berlin, 1924). Most of the book is written in the first person — apparently ghostwritten for Ehrhardt by Freksa. Portions of the narrative are filled in by members of the Ehrhardt Brigade, notably by Leutnant zur See Liedig. The copy of the book used in this study has been stamped, variously, "Pol. Vorschule Bamburg, Offiziers Bücherei"; "Heeres-Fachschule, Garmish"; and "Bücherei der 3. Heeresfachschule (V.W.) München." Each of these stamps has been stamped over with the word, "Ungültig."

Eichhorn, Emil, *Ueber die Januar-Ereignisse: Meine Tätigkeit im Berliner Polizeipräsidium und mein Anteil an den Januar-Ereignissen* (Berlin, 1919). A bitter attack on the Majority Socialists by a member of the Left wing of the USPAD.

Eisner, Kurt, *Die neue Zeit* (Munich, 1919). Eisner's speeches of November, 1919.

Engelhardt, Freiherr Eugen von, *Der Ritt nach Riga: Aus den Kämpfen der baltischen Landeswehr gegen die Rote Ar-*

mee, 1918–1920 (Berlin, 1938). The posthumous memoirs of Freiherr Wilhelm von Engelhardt edited and completed by his son, who was also an officer in the *Landeswehr*.

Escherich, Forstrat Dr., *Von Eisner bis Eglhofer: Die Münchener Revolution von November 1918 bis zum Zusammenbruch der Räteherrschaft* (Munich, 1922[?]). A collection of the *Escherich-Hefte* which covers the period noted in the title. Escherich was the founder of the Escherich Organization ("Orgesch").

Fabrizius, Wilhelm, "Der Aufstand des Bündischen Deutschland," in *Deutscher Aufstand*, edited by Curt Hotzel (Stuttgart, 1934).

Fletcher, Alfred, "Die baltische Landeswehr" in *Baltische Blätter*, 12. Jahrgang, No. 5 (March 1, 1929), 69–71.

———, "Das Wesen der baltischen Kämpfe vom Frühjahr 1919: Erinnerungen an die baltische Landeswehr" in *Baltische Lande*, edited by Alfred Brackmann, Vol. IV, "Der Bolschewismus und die baltische Front" (Leipzig, 1939). Fletcher was the commander of the Landeswehr.

Foerster, Friedrich Wilhelm, *Jugendseele, Jugendbewegung, Jugendziel* (Munich and Leipzig, 1923). An account written by the internationally known Christian pacificist and sponsor of the prewar German Youth Movement.

Foerster, Wolfgang, ed., *Wir Kämpfer im Weltkrieg: Feldzugsbriefe und Kriegstagebücher von Frontkämpfern aus dem Material des Reichsarchivs* (Berlin, 1929).

———, Linnebach, Karl and Volkmann, Erich Otto, editors, *Generaloberst von Seeckt: Ein Erinnerungsbuch* (Berlin, 1937). Memorial essays written by von Seeckt's friends.

Frölich, Paul, *Rosa Luxemburg: Gedanke und Tat* (Paris, 1939).

———, *Wider den Weissen Mord*, 2nd ed. (Berlin and Leipzig, n.d.).

———, *Zehn Jahre Krieg und Bürgerkrieg*, 2 vols. in one (Berlin, 1924).

———, *Die Bayrische Räterrepublik: Tatsachen und Kritik* (Petrograd, 1920). This pamphlet was written under the pen name of "Paul Werner."

Gedye, G. E. R., *The Revolver Republic: France's Bid for the Rhine* (London, 1930). A documented indictment of France's Rhine policy written by a former member of the British Army Intelligence Service during World War I and, during the Allied occupation, a special correspondent of the London *Times*.

Geisow, Hans, *So wurde ich Nationalsozialist* (Munich, 1931).

Gentizon, Paul, *L'Allemagne en République* (Paris, 1920).

——, *L'Armée Allemande depuis la Défaite* (Paris, 1920).

——, *La Révolution Allemande* (Paris, 1919). Gentizon was a special correspondent of the *Temps*. Valuable for eyewitness accounts of the Revolution in Berlin and in Munich.

Gerlach, Hellmut von, *Der Zusammenbruch der deutschen Polenpolitik,* Flugschriften des Bundes Neues Vaterland Nr. 14 (Berlin, 1919). A refreshingly honest and fair account written by the Under Secretary of State sent by Ebert to investigate conditions in Posen in 1918–1919. The book is based on his official report.

Gessler, Otto, "Der Aufbau der neuen Wehrmacht," in *Zehn Jahre deutsche Geschichte: 1918–1928* (Berlin, 1928).

——, "Schwarze Reichswehr, Arbeitskommandos und Zeitfreiwillige: zur Klärung der Begriffe," in *Berliner Tageblatt,* October 31, 1926. A clever defense of his policies written by the former National Minister of Defense.

Gilardone, Georg, "36 Soldatenjahre," in *Franz Ritter von Epp, Ein Leben für Deutschland,* edited by J. H. Krumbach (Munich, 1939).

Gisevius, Hans Bernd, *To the Bitter End,* translated by Richard and Clara Winston (Boston, 1947). The memoirs of the former member of the Gestapo and the Abwehr who figured prominently in the July Plot of 1944.

Glombowski, Friedrich, *Organisation Heinz (O.H.): Das Schicksal der Kameraden Schlageters* (Berlin, 1934). The memoirs of a member of the O.H. An expurgated English translation extols the book as "a vivid account of hair-raising adventures . . . courage, patriotism . . . [which] helps towards an understanding of the revolution [of 1933] that formed a new Germany." *Frontiers of Terror,* translated by Kenneth Kirkness (London, 1934). Page references are to the German edition.

Goltz, General Graf Rudiger von der, *Meine Sendung in Finnland und im Baltikum* (Leipzig, 1920). The frank and detailed memoirs of the commander of all German Free Corps in the Baltic.

——, *Als politischer General im Osten (Finnland und Balti-*

kum) 1918–1919 (Leipzig, 1936). The later version of von der Goltz's mission is an attempt to read back National Socialist motivation. Neither as complete nor as reliable as the first account.

——, "Die deutsche Revolution," in *Deutschlands Erneuerung,* Heft 6, XVII Jahrgang (June 1933), 332–338.

——, "Zum Frühjahrfeldzug im Baltikum, 1919," in *Baltische Blätter,* No. 5 (May 22, 1929), 7–11.

Got, Ambroise, *L'Allemagne après la Débâcle: Impressions d'un Attaché à la Mission Militaire Française à Berlin Mars–Juillet 1919* (Strasbourg, 1919[?]).

——, *La Contre-Révolution Allemande* (Strasbourg, 1920[?]).

——, *La Terreur en Bavière* (Paris, 1922).

Gronau, Ernst, "Freischar Schill," in *Die deutschen Jugendverbände,* edited by Hertha Siemering (Berlin, 1931).

Gründel, E. Günther, *Die Sendung der jungen Generation: Versuch einer umfassenden revolutionären Sinndeutung der Krise* (Munich, 1932). The efforts of a member of the Generation of Uprooted and Disinherited to find·his political soul.

Haas, Ludwig, "Der Kampf um die Reichswehr," in *Deutsche Republik,* Heft XIV, Erster Jahrgang (1926), 13–15. Moderate republican position in respect to the Army.

Hartmann, Georg Heinrich, "Aus den Erinnerungen eines Freiwilligen der baltischen Landeswehr," in *Deutsche Revue,* January bis März, 1921, 46 Jahrgang (Stuttgart, 1921).

Hassell, Ambassador Ulrich von, *The Von Hassell Diaries 1938–1944: The Story of the Forces against Hitler inside Germany as Recorded by Ambassador Ulrich von Hassell, a Leader of the Movement* (New York, 1947).

Heinz, Friedrich Wilhelm, *Kameraden der Arbeit, Deutsche Arbeitslager: Stand, Aufgabe und Zukunft* (Berlin, 1933).

——, *Die Nation greift an: Geschichte und Kritik des soldatischen Nationalismus* (Berlin, 1932).

——, *Sprengstoff* (Berlin, 1930).

——, "Die Freikorps retten Oberschlesien"; "Politische Attentate in Deutschland"; "Der deutsche Vorstoss in das Baltikum," a series of essays in *Deutscher Aufstand,* edited by Curt Hotzel (Stuttgart, 1934). Heinz was a leading member of the Free Corps movement. See Appendix.

Helmerich, K., "Von der 1000 Mann-Kaserne zur Marine Brigade

Ehrhardt" in *Das Buch vom deutschen Freikorpskämpfer* edited by Ernst von Salomon (Berlin, 1938).

Heydebreck, Peter von, *Wir Wehrwölfe: Erinnerungen eines Freikorpsführers* (Leipzig, 1931). The memoirs of the famous one-armed Free Corps leader who became a Nazi and was purged on June 30, 1934.

Hitler, Adolf, *Mein Kampf* (New York, 1940), Reynal and Hitchcock edition.

Hitler Directs His War, The Secret Records of His Daily Military Conferences, edited by Felix Gilbert (New York, 1950).

Hoffmann, Rudolf, ed., *Der deutsche Soldat: Briefe aus dem Weltkrieg: Vermächtnis* (Munich, 1937).

Hofmiller, Josef, *Revolutionstagebuch 1918–1919. Aus den Tagen der Münchener Revolution* (Leipzig, 1938).

Hotzel, Curt, ed., *Deutscher Aufstand: Die Revolution des Nachkriegs* (Stuttgart, 1934). A valuable group of essays written by participants in the Free Corps movement.

Hülsen, Generalleutnant Bernhard von, *Der Kampf um Oberschlesien: Oberschlesien und sein Selbstschutz* (Stuttgart, 1922).

——, "Freikorps im Osten," in *Deutsche Soldaten,* edited by Hans Roden (Leipzig, 1935). Hülsen was the commander of Group South in the Upper Silesian campaign of 1921.

Jünger, Ernst, *Der Kampf als inneres Erlebnis,* 5th ed., 40th thousand (Berlin, 1933).

——, *In Stahlgewittern: Ein Kriegstagebuch,* 16th ed., 125th thousand (Berlin, 1926).

——, *Das Wäldchen, 125: Eine Chronik aus den Grabenkämpfen 1918,* 6th ed. (Berlin, 1935). These are the war memoirs of a member and chief glorifier of the World War I Storm Troops.

——, editor, *Das Antlitz des Weltkrieges. Fronterlebnisse deutscher Soldaten* (Berlin, 1930).

——, editor, *Krieg und Krieger* (Berlin, 1930). A group of essays glorifying war as "The Father of All Things." Contributors include von Salomon, Werner Best, Albrecht Erich Günther, and Gerhard Günther.

Kanzler, Rudolf, *Bayerns Kampf gegen den Bolshewismus: Geschichte der bayerischen Einwohnerwehren* (Munich, 1931). The memoirs of the cofounder of the Organization

Escherich and founder of the Organization Kanzler ("Orka").

Karl, Josef, *Die Schreckensherrschaft in München und Spartakus im bayr. Oberland* (Munich, 1919[?]). The author, a Hoffmann democrat, draws from his diary and official decrees to give a detailed account of the period from Eisner to Hoffmann's return in May, 1919.

Killinger, Manfred von, *Das waren Kerle!* (Munich, 1944). Written by a prominent Free Corps fighter and leading Nazi (see Appendix) in an effort to boost the morale of World War II soldiers by reminding them of the spirit of the Freebooters.

——, *Ernstes und Heiteres aus dem Putschleben*, 6th ed. (Zentral verlag der NSDAP, Munich, 1934).

——, *Kampf um Oberschlesien, 1921*, 2nd ed. (Leipzig, 1934). Killinger was commander of the Killinger Storm Company operating in Upper Silesia.

Landsberg, Otto, "Die Münchener Feme," in *Deutsche Republik*, Heft III (Erster Jahrgang, 1926), 29–31.

Laubert, Manfred, *Die oberschlesische Volksbewegung: Beiträge zur Tätigkeit der Vereinigung Heimattreur Oberschlesier 1918–1921* (Breslau, 1938).

Lautenbacher, Friedrich, "Widerstand im Roten München," in *Das Buch vom deutschen Freikorpskämpfer*, edited by Ernst von Salomon (Berlin, 1938).

Leme, Hans, "Adler und Falken, Bund deutscher Jugend," in *Die deutschen Jugendverbände*, edited by Hertha Siemering (Berlin, 1931).

Lloyd George, David, *Memoirs of the Peace Conference*, 2 vols. (New Haven, 1939).

Loewenfeld, Vizeadmiral von, "Das Freikorps von Loewenfeld," in *Deutsche Soldaten*, edited by Hans Roden (Leipzig, 1935).

Ludecke, Kurt G. W., *I Knew Hitler: The Story of a Nazi Who Escaped the Blood Purge* (New York, 1938). The fascinating memoirs of a paranoid.

Lüttwitz, General Walther, Freiherr von, *Im Kampf gegen die November-Revolution* (Berlin, 1933). Subjective and unreliable reminiscences of the coauthor of the Kapp-Lüttwitz Putsch and commander of the Free Corps around Berlin.

————, "Einmarsch der Garde-Kavallerie-Schutzen Division in Berlin," in *Deutsche Soldaten*, edited by Hans Roden (Leipzig, 1935).

Maercker, General Ludwig R., *Vom Kaiserheer zur Reichswehr, Geschichte des freiwilligen Landesjägerkorps*, 3rd ed. (Leipzig, 1922). The memoirs of the moderate, able founder and commander of the "Maercker Rifles." Invaluable.

Mahnken, Heinrich, "Freikorps im Westen, 1918–1920," in *Deutscher Aufstand*, edited by Curt Hotzel (Stuttgart, 1934).

————, "Der Kampf der Batterie Hasenclever," in *Deutsche Soldaten*, edited by Hans Roden (Leipzig, 1935). The author of these memorial sketches was the adjutant of the Lichtschlag Free Corps.

Mann, Rudolf, *Mit Ehrhardt durch Deutschland: Erinnerungen eines Mitkämpfers von der 2. Marinebrigade* (Berlin, 1921). A valuable memoir not cited or used by the National Socialists. Was Mann killed in the Blood Purge?

Medem, Walter Eberhard Albert, Freiherr von, *Stürmer von Riga: die Geschichte eines Freikorps* (Berlin, 1935). The memoirs of the commander of the Von Medem Free Corps.

Mendelssohn-Bartholdy, Albrecht, "The War and German Society: The Testament of a Liberal," in *Economic and Social History of the War*, James T. Shotwell, general editor (New Haven, 1937).

Miller, David Hunter, *My Diary at the Conference of Paris, with Documents*, Vol. XVI (private printing, 1925).

Moeller van den Bruck, Artur, *Das Dritte Reich*, 3rd ed. (Hamburg, 1931). There is a slightly condensed, free translation into English, *Germany's Third Empire*, E. O. Lorimer, translator (London, 1923). Quotations in text are from the German edition.

————, *Das Recht der jungen Völker*, edited by Hans Schwartz (Berlin, 1932).

Mordacq, Général Henri, *La Mentalité Allemande: Cinq Ans de Commandement sur le Rhin*, 9th ed. (Paris, 1926). An indictment of the German people written by the commanding general of the 30th Army Corps, French Army of Occupation.

Morgan, John H., *Assize of Arms: The Disarmament of Germany and Her Rearmament, 1919–1939* (New York, 1946). A war book written by the former British representative on the Inter-Allied Military Commission of Control. This bitter attack on Germany totally lacks the moderation and perspective of his earlier accounts.

————, *The Present State of Germany* (Boston, 1924).

————, "The Disarmament of Germany and After," in *Quarterly Review*, CCXLII (October 1924), 415–457. A revealing, authoritative article based on the author's report to the British War Office.

Müller-Meiningen, Ernst, *Aus Bayerns schwersten Tagen: Erinnerungen und Betrachtungen aus der Revolutionzeit*, 2nd ed. (Berlin and Leipzig, 1924). The impressions of a member of the Bavarian Democratic Party who served as Minister of Justice in both the Hoffmann and Von Kahr governments.

Muthmann, Gunther, "Der Tod von Speyer, das Strafgericht an den separatistischen Verrätern," in *Reiter gen Osten* (November 1934), reprinted in *Das Buch vom deutschen Freikorpskämpfer*, edited by Ernst von Salomon (Berlin, 1938). The swaggering account of a murder written by the murderer.

Niessel, Général A., *L'Évacuation des Pays Baltiques par les Allemands* (Paris, 1935). The memoirs of the French patriot who was the President of the Inter-Allied Commission sent to the Baltic to supervise the evacuation of the Free Corps.

Nollet, Général Charles M. E., *Une Éxpérience Désarmament: Cinque Ans de Contrôle Militaire en Allemagne* (Paris, 1932). An account written by the President of the Inter-Allied Military Commission of Control, 1919–1924.

Noske, Gustav, *Von Kiel bis Kapp: Zur Geschichte der deutschen Revolution* (Berlin, 1920). The memoirs of the Minister of National Defense who organized the Free Corps system. Indispensable.

————, *Erlebtes aus Aufstieg und Niedergang einer Demokratie* (Offenbach-Main, 1947). Some bitter afterthoughts published posthumously. Not as valuable as his earlier book.

————, "Die Abwehr des Bolschewismus," in *Zehn Jahre deutsche Geschichte 1918–1928*, 2nd ed. (Berlin, 1928).

————, "Seine letzten Tage," in *Friedrich Ebert Kämpfe und Ziele, Mit einem Anhang: Erinnerungen von seinen Freunden* (Dresden, n.d.).

Noulens, J., "Le Point de Vue Politique" in *Les Archives de la Grande Guerre,* No. 24 (a special issue devoted to the question of Upper Silesia), Paris, July, 1921, 7–9. A pro-Polish account of the Upper Silesian question written by the French ambassador to Poland and President of the "France-Pologne Society."

Ottwalt, Ernst, *Ruhe und Ordnung: Roman aus dem Leben der nationalgesinnten Jugend* (Berlin, 1929). A novel which illustrates the problems of the postwar generation and idolizes the Free Corps fighters.

Pabst, Major W., "Spartakus," in *Deutscher Aufstand: die Revolution des Nachkriegs,* edited by Curt Hotzel (Stuttgart, 1934). The violent reaction of the adjutant of the Division of Horse Guards and an organizer of the Kapp-Lüttwitz Putsch.

Pitrof, Oberst der Landes-Polizei a. D., Ritter von, *Gegen Spartakus in München und im Allgau, Erinnerungsblätter des Freikorps Schwaben. Zusammengestellt vom ehemaligen Führer des Freikorps* (Munich, 1937).

Plehve, Karl von, *Im Kampf gegen die Bolschewisten: die Kämpfe des 2. Garde-Reserve-Regiments zum Schutz der Grenze Ostpreussens, Januar–November, 1919* (Berlin, 1926). The memoirs of the leader of the Von Plehve Free Corps.

Ramcke, Generalleutnant Bernhard, *Vom Schiffsjungen zum Fallschirmjägergeneral* (Berlin, 1943). The autobiography of a man who was one of the few commissioned in the field in World War I. Commander of paratroops in World War II. See Appendix.

Rathenau, Walther, *An Deutschlands Jugend* (Berlin, 1918).

Rauschning, Hermann, *The Revolution of Nihilism: Warning to the West,* translated by E. W. Dickes (New York, 1939). An interpretation of National Socialism written by the former Nazi president of the Senate of the Free City of Danzig.

————, *The Voice of Destruction* (New York, 1940).

Rautenfeld, Harald von, "Der 16. April, 1919" in *Baltische Blätter,* 12 Jahrgang, Nr. 5 (April 15, 1929), 118–121.

Reckhaus, Dr. (————), "Krieg im Dunkeln: gegen die fran-
    zösische Besetzung in Essen," in *Das Buch vom deutschen
    Freikorpskämpfer*, edited by Ernst von Salomon (Berlin,
    1938).
Reetz, Wilhelm, ed., *Eine ganze Welt gegen uns* (Berlin, 1934).
Reinhard, Colonel Wilhelm, *1918–1919: Die Wehen der Republik*
    (Berlin, 1933). The memoirs of the founder and leader of
    the Reinhard Brigade. See Appendix.
Roden, Hans, ed., *Deutsche Soldaten vom Frontheer und Frei-
    korps über die Reichswehr zur neuen Wehrmacht* (Leip-
    zig, 1935). A valuable collection of essays written by such
    prominent members of the Free Corps as von der Goltz,
    von Hülsen, von Salomon, von Loewenfeld, Reinhard and
    others.
Röhm, Ernst, *Die Geschichte eines Hochverräters*, 7th ed. (Mu-
    nich, 1934). The invaluable memoirs of the former Free
    Corps fighter who organized Hitler's SA and was purged
    in 1934.
Rose, A. W., "Sturm auf die Weserbrücken," in *Das Buch vom
    deutschen Freikorpskämpfer*, edited by Ernst von Salomon
    (Berlin, 1938).
Roth, Alfred, *Aus der Kampfzeit des Deutschvölkischen Schutz-
    und-Trutzbundes* (Hamburg, 1939). Roth was the founder
    and the leader of the proto-Nazi, racist S-u-T.
Roth, Bert, ed., *Kampf: Lebensdokumente deutscher Jugend von
    1914–1934* (Leipzig, 1934). A collection of reminiscences.
    Includes essays writen by von Salomon, F. W. Heinz, Ernst
    Werner Techow, and others. Approved by the NSDAP.
Salomon, Ernst von, *Die Geächteten* (Berlin, 1930). Indispensa-
    ble. The memoirs of the man who is recognized by both
    Rightist and Leftist writers as the most reliable spokesman
    of the Free Corps movement.
————, *Nahe Geschichte: Ein Ueberblick* (Berlin, 1936).
————, editor, *Das Buch vom deutschen Freikorpskämpfer* (Ber-
    lin, 1938). A valuable series of essays written by partic-
    ipants; contains a wealth of memorabilia: pictures of lead-
    ing Free Corps fighters, the insignia of the various Corps,
    recruitment posters, official proclamations, and so forth.
————, "Der verlorene Haufe," in Krieg und Krieger, edited by
    Ernst Jünger (Berlin, 1930).

————, *Fragebogen* (Hamburg, 1951). A recently published autobiographical sketch which reaffirms his faith in nationalism and his hatred of democracy.

Schauwecker, Franz, *Im Todesrachen, Die deutsche Seele im Weltkriege*, 1st edition (Halle, 1919). The memoirs of a member of the Storm Troops of World War I. Particularly valuable because each chapter was written at the front and mailed home.

————, *So war der Krieg: 200 Kampfaufnehmen aus der Front* (Berlin, 1937).

————, *So ist der Friede: Die Revolution der Zeit in 300 Bildern* (Berlin, 1928). A front soldier's bitter indictment of the Weimar pacifists. Sees only ray of hope, not in Hitler, but in the Stahlhelm.

Schauwecker, Heinz, "Erinnerungen eines Freikorps-Studenten," in *Deutscher Aufstand*, edited by Curt Hotzel (Stuttgart, 1934).

Scheidemann, Philip, *Memoiren eines Sozialdemokraten*, 2 vols. (Dresden, 1928).

————, *Der Zusammenbruck* (Berlin, 1921).

Schlageter, Albert Leo, *Deutschland muss leben: Gesammelte Briefe von Albert Leo Schlageter*, edited by Friedrich Bubendey (Berlin, 1934).

Schmidt, Oberleutnant, "Einsatz in Hannover," in *Das Buch vom deutschen Freikorpskämpfer*, edited by Ernst von Salomon (Berlin, 1938).

Sebottendorff, Rudolf von, *Bevor Hitler kam: Urkundliches aus der Frühzeit der nationalsozialistischen Bewegung* (Munich, 1934). The founder of the *Thule Gesellschaft* attempts to show that his racist society was the real precursor of National Socialism. The book was marked with the letter V (*Volkswiderlich?*) and placed in the closed archives of the NSDAP. The Nazis did not like competitors.

Seeckt, Generaloberst Hans von, *Deutschland zwischen West und Ost* (Hamburg, 1933).

————, *Gedanken eines Soldaten* (Berlin, 1929).

————, *Die Reichswehr* (Leipzig, 1933).

Seitz, Georg, "Die Eiserne Schar Berthold in Harburg," in *Das Buch vom deutschen Freikorpskämpfer*, edited by Ernst von Salomon (Berlin, 1938).

Severing, Carl, *1919–1920 im Wetter und Watterwinkel* (Biele-

feld, 1927). The memoirs of the former Reichskommissar for the Ruhr area during and after the Kapp Putsch.

Solf, Major F. E., *1934: Deutschlands Auferstehung,* 3rd ed. (Naumberg, 1922). A remarkable prophecy written by a former officer in the Ehrhardt Brigade. First published in 1920.

Stadtler, Eduard, *Als Antibolschewist 1918–1919* (Düsseldorf, 1935). The unreliable memoirs of the founder of the Anti-Bolshevist League and supporter of the Free Corps.

Stählin, Wilhelm, *Fieber und Heil in der Jugendbewegung* (Hamburg, 1924). Mystic nonsense written by one of the champions of the post World War I youth movement.

Stenbock-Fermor, Graf Alexander, *Freiwilliger Stenbock: Bericht aus dem baltischen Befreiungskampf* (Stuttgart, 1929). Reminiscences of a student volunteer in the Baltic *Landeswehr.*

Stephani, Major von, "Der Sturm auf das Vorwärts-Gebäude," in *Deutsche Soldaten,* edited by Hans Roden (Leipzig, 1935). An account written by the commander of the Potsdam Free Corps and an organizer of the Kapp Putsch.

———, "Freikorps Potsdam," in *Deutsche Soldaten,* edited by Hans Roden.

Stiewe, Willy, *Der Krieg nach dem Krieg* (Berlin, n.d.).

Strasser, Otto, *Die deutsche Bartholomäusnacht,* 7th ed. (Prague, 1938). An interpretation of the Blood Purge written by a former Nazi who bolted the party to form the Black Front in opposition to Hitler.

Tirard, Paul, *La France sur le Rhin: Douze Années d'Occupation Rhénane,* 5th ed. (Paris, 1930). An unconvincing defense written by the former High Commissioner for the Rhineland Occupation.

Toller, Ernst, *Eine Jugend in Deutschland* (Amsterdam, 1936). The memoirs of the poet who became one of the leaders of the short-lived Bavarian Republic of Soviets.

Unruh, Major von, "Einmarsch in München," in *Deutsche Soldaten,* edited by Hans Roden (Leipzig, 1935).

Vanlande, Capitaine René, *Avec le Général Niessel en Prusse et en Lithuanie, la Dernière Défaite Allemande* (Paris, 1921).

Wagener, Hauptmann Otto Wilhelm Heinrich, *Von der Heimat geächtet* (Stuttgart, 1920). The memoirs of the commander of the German Legion.

Weber, Hans Siegfried, "Das deutsche Baltentum," in *Das grössere Deutschland: Wochenschaft für deutsche Welt und Kolonialpolitik*, Nr. 50 (December 9, 1916), 1584–1592.

Wilung, Fritz "Die Jungenpflege und Jugendbewegung im Arbeitersport" in *Die deutschen Jugendverbände*, edited by Hertha Siemering (Berlin, 1931).

Winnig, August, *Am Ausgang der deutschen Ostpolitik; Persönliche Erlebnisse und Erinnerungen* (Berlin, 1921). Before becoming a pamphleteer for the NSDAP, Winnig had been a Social Democrat and the German Plenipotentiary in the Baltic from 1918 to 1919. As such, he was instrumental in calling in the Free Corps.

——, *Befreiung* (Munich, 1926).

——, *Das Reich als Republik, 1918–1928* (Berlin, 1929).

——, *Die Hand Gottes* (Berlin, 1940).

——, *Heimkehr*, 3rd ed. (Hamburg, 1935).

Witkop, Professor Doktor, ed., *Kriegsbriefe gefallener Studenten* (Munich, 1928).

Zehn Jahre deutsche Geschichte, 1918–1928, 2nd ed. (Berlin, 1928). A collection of essays written by leaders of the Republic.

Zehn Jahre deutsche Republik: Ein Handbuch für republikanische Politik (Berlin, 1928).

Zetkin, Clara, *Les Batailles Révolutionnaires de L'Allemagne en 1919*. Publication No. 47 of Editions de L'Internationale Communiste (Petrograd, 1920).

Zöberlein, Hans, *Der Glaube an Deutschland: Ein Kriegserleben von Verdun bis zum Umsturz*, 25th ed., 275th thousand (Munich, 1938).

——, *Der Befehl des Gewissens: Ein Roman von den Wirren der Nachkriegszeit und der Ersten Erhebung*, 13th ed., 280th thousand (Munich, 1931).

F. ANONYMOUS PAMPHLETS AND ARTICLES

Armee und Revolution: Entwicklung und Zusammenhänge, by "a German general staff officer" (Berlin, 1919). An example of the pamphlets issued by the OHL in an effort to prove that the Army had been "stabbed in the back" by the home front.

"Les Dessous de la Politique Réactionaire en Europe Centrale et

ses Dangers pour la France," in *L'Europe Nouvelle*, IV,
Part I, No. 15 (April 9, 1921), 475–478; Part II, No. 16
(April 16, 1921), 509–512; Part III, No. 17 (April 23, 1921),
538–543. A series of three articles written by a man close
to the leaders of the Kapp Putsch. Is the author "Doctor
Schnitzler"? Or is it Trebitsch-Lincoln?

*Deutschland als freie Volksrepublik: Den aus dem Felde heim-
kehrenden Volksgenossen* (n.p., November, 1918). A
pamphlet issued by the executive committee of the Social
Democratic Party.

Der Dritte Aufstand in Oberschlesien: Mai–Juni 1921 (n.p., n.d.).

Generalstreik und Noske-Blud-Bad in Berlin, by "Cains" (Berlin,
1919). A pamphlet issued by the *Rote Fahne*.

Geschichte des Oberschlesischen Aufstandes und seiner Resulte
(n.p., n.d.).

*Hitler Rast: die Bluttragödie des 30. Juni 1934, Ablauf, Vorge-
schichte und Hintergründe*, 3rd ed. (Saarbrücken, 1934).
On the frontispiece of this anonymous book someone has
penciled in, "Verfasser, Konrad Heiden." The book was
found in the closed archives of the NSDAP. It is rubber
stamped with the letter V.

*Das Martyrium der Deutschen in Oberschlesien: Gewaltakte und
Greuelten der Polen während des 3. Aufstandes Oberschlesien im Mai und Juni 1921* (n.p., n.d.).

Mathias Erzberger: Ein politischer Mord? by "Germanicus"
(Leipzig, 1921). A furious nationalist denial of Chancellor
Wirth's charge that "The enemy stands at the Right."

*Die Münchener Tragödie: Entstehung, Verlauf und Zusammen-
bruch der Räte-Republik München* (Berlin, 1919). Published by the USPD organ, *Freiheit*.

Naziführer sehen Dich an! 33 Biographien aus dem Dritten Reich
(Paris, 1934). Anti-Nazi but accurate sketches of leaders
of the National Socialist Party.

*Der 9. November 1923: Die Wahrheit über die Münchener Vor-
gänge* (Munich, 1923[?]). The official Nazi version of the
Beer Hall Putsch. On the frontispiece of this propaganda
pamphlet these words appear: "Preis 10 Pfg. Nachruck
erwünscht!"

Die Wahrheit über die Berliner Strassenkämpfe (Berlin, 1919).
An indictment of Noske and Ebert printed by the *Freiheit*.

Weissbuch über die Erschiessungen des 30 Juni 1934: Authentische Darstellung der deutschen Bartholomäusnacht, 3rd ed. (Paris, 1935). An anti-Nazi interpretation.

"With the Baltic Squadron 1918–1920," by "Paravane," in *The Fortnightly Review,* CIX (May 2, 1921), 705–716.

Der Zusammenbruch der Kriegspolitik und die Novemberrevolution (Berlin, 1919). A USPD interpretation.

G. MAGAZINES

Les Archives de la Grande Guerre: Revue Internationale de Documentation Contemporaire, edited by E. Chiron (Paris, 1919–1923).

Baltische Blätter, Alleiniges Mittelungsorgan der Arbeitsgemeinschaft baltischer Organisationen (Berlin, 1918–1929).

Current History: A Monthly Magazine of the New York Times (New York, 1919–1925).

Deutsche Republik, edited by Josef Wirth (Frankfurt a. M., 1926–1927).

Deutsche Revue (Stuttgart and Leipzig, 1921).

Deutsche Rundschau (Leipzig, 1919–1935).

Deutschlands Erneurung: Monatsschrift für das deutsche Volk (Munich, 1933).

L'Europe Nouvelle: Revue Hebdomadaire des Questions Extérieures, Economiques et Littéraires (Paris, 1919–1924).

The Fortnightly Review (London, 1921).

Das grössere Deutschland: Wochenschaft für deutsche Welt und Kolonialpolitik (Berlin, 1916).

The New Europe (London, 1920).

Quarterly Review (London, 1924).

Der Schulungsbrief (Berlin, 1934–1939). The official publication of the Reichsschulungsamt and the Arbeitsfront of the NSDAP.

Süddeutsche Monatshefte (Munich, 1918–1930).

Wissen und Wehr (Berlin, 1928). Semi-official Army publication.

H. NEWSPAPERS

Berliner Tageblatt, 1918–1927. (Moderate.)

Deutsche Allgemeine Zeitung, Berlin, 1918–1928. (Moderate-conservative.)

Frankfurter Zeitung, 1918–1927. (Moderate-conservative.)

Freiheit, Berlin, 1918–1923. (Organ of the USPD.)

The New York Times, 1918–1923.

Reichswehr: Soldatenzeitung für die sächsischen Grenzjäger und Sicherheitstruppen. Dresden, 1919.

Die Rote Fahne, Berlin, 1918–1920. (Organ of the Spartakusbund and the German Communist Party.)

The Times, London, 1918–1925.

Völkischer Beobachter, Munich, 1927–1935. (Organ of the NS-DAP.)

Volkswehr: Zeitung für die Soldaten der deutschen Republik, Berlin, 1919–1920.

Vorwärts, Berlin, 1918–1927. (Organ of the Majority Socialists.)

Vossische Zeitung, Berlin, 1919–1925. (Moderate, democratic.)

II. SECONDARY ACCOUNTS

A. MONOGRAPHS AND SPECIAL STUDIES

Beuter, Paul, *Wesen und Organisation des Reichsheeres und seine Bedeutung für die deutsche Wirtschaft*. Inaugural dissertation, University of Giessen (Giessen, 1926).

Böhmer, Leo, *Die rheinische Separatistenbewegung und die französische Presse*. Inaugural dissertation, University of Munich (Stuttgart and Berlin, 1928).

Braun, Richard, *Individualismus und Gemeinschaft in der deutschen Jugendbewegung*. Inaugural dissertation, University of Erlangen (Erlangen, 1929).

Gässler, Christian Walter, *Offizier und Offizierkorp der alten Armee in Deutschland als Voraussetzung einer Untersuchung über die Transformation der militärischen Hierarchie*. Inaugural dissertation, University of Heidelberg (Heidelberg, 1930).

Graham, Malbone W., *The Diplomatic Recognition of the Border States. Part III: Latvia. In Publications of the University of California at Los Angeles*. Vol. III, No. 4 (Los Angeles, 1941).

Gruss, Hellmuth, *Aufbau und Verwendung der deutschen Sturmbataillone im Weltkrieg*. Inaugural dissertation, University of Berlin (Berlin, 1939).

Huber, Theodora, *Die soziologische Seite der Jugendbewegung*. Inaugural dissertation, University of Munich (Munich, 1929).

Kandler, Johannes, *Der deutsche Heeresetat vor und nach dem*

Kriege. Inaugural dissertation, University of Leipzig (Leipzig, 1930).

Lutz, Ralph Haswell, "The German Revolution, 1918–1919," in *Stanford University Publications,* Vol. I, No. 1 (Stanford University Press, 1922).

Mattern, Johannes, "Bavaria and the Reich: The Conflict over the Law for the Protection of the Republic," in *Johns Hopkins University Studies in Historical and Political Science* (Baltimore, Md., 1923).

Meyer, Hans M., *Die politischen Hintergründe des Mitteldeutschen Aufstandes von 1921.* Inaugural dissertation, University of Berlin (Berlin, 1935).

Nothaas, Josef, *Die Kriegsbeschädigtenfürsorge unter besonderer Berücksichtigung Bayerns.* Inaugural dissertation, University of Munich (Munich, 1922[?]).

——, "Sozialer Auf- und Abstieg im Deutschen Volk," in *Beiträge zur Statistik Bayerns,* Heft 117 (Munich, 1930).

Page, Stanley, *The Formation of the Baltic States (Lithuania, Latvia, Estonia) 1917–1920.* Unpublished Ph.D. thesis, Harvard University, 1946.

Poupard, Capitaine E., *L'Occupation de la Ruhr et le Droit des Gens.* Ph.D. thesis, University of Strasbourg (Paris, 1925).

Rau, Karl, *Der Wehrgedanke in Deutschland nach dem Weltkriege von 1918–1921: Untersucht an der Weimarer Verfassung, den politischen Parteiprogrammen und der grossen Parteienpresse.* Inaugural dissertation, University of Heidelberg (Würzburg, 1936). This sorry example of the decline of German historical scholarship under the National Socialists is little more than a propaganda pamphlet.

Rittau, Josef Albert, *Dei Stellung Oberschlesiens nach dem Versailler Vertrage während der interallierten Besetzung.* Inaugural dissertation, University of Würzburg (Würzburg, 1928[?]).

Vogel, Rudolf, *Deutsche Presse und Propaganda des Abstimmungskampfes in Oberschlesien.* Inaugural dissertation, University of Leipzig (Beuthen, O.S., 1931).

B. GENERAL

Abel, Theodore, *Why Hitler Came to Power. An Answer Based on the Original Life Stories of Six Hundred of His Followers* (New York, 1938).

Das akademische Deutschland, edited by Michael Doeberl, Otto Scheel, Wilhelm Schlink, and others, 4 vols. (Berlin, 1930–1931). This massive four folio-volume study is a standard work on youth movements preceding and following World War I.

"Alter, Junius" (Franz Sontag), *Nationalisten, Deutschlands nationales Führertum der Nachkriegszeit,* new, enlarged ed. (Leipzig, 1932). Biographical sketches written by the Rightist editor of the ultrareactionary periodical, *Die Tradition.*

Becker, Howard, *German Youth: Bond or Free* (London, 1946). A scholarly and brilliantly written study. Valuable bibliography.

Benoist-Méchin, J., *Histoire de L'Armée Allemande 1919–1936,* 2 vols. (Paris, 1938). Volume one has been translated by Eileen R. Taylor under the title, *History of the German Army since the Armistice* (Zürich, 1939). While sensationalistic and at times inaccurate, this is the best general study of the German army since World War I. Valuable bibliographical suggestions.

Berendt, Erich F., *Soldaten der Freiheit: Ein Parolebuch des Nationalsozialismus, 1918–1925* (Berlin, 1935). A collection of proto-Nazi and Nazi documents joined together by sentimental nonsense. Both the documents and the editorial comment are full of factual errors. Endorsed by the NSDAP.

Bergmann, Gerhard, "Akademische Bewegungen," in *Akademisches Deutschland,* edited by Michael Doeberl, 4 vols. (Berlin, 1930–1931), Vol. II.

Beumelburg, Werner, *Deutschland in Ketten: Von Versailles bis zum Youngplan* (Berlin, 1931). An immensely popular, savage diatribe against the Weimar Republic and all its works. Before being reissued by the National Socialists, it had sold over seventy-five thousand copies.

Bevan, Edwyan, *German Social Democracy during the War* (London, 1918). Old and brief but still the best general account of the subject.

Blüher, Hans, *Führer und Volk in der Jugendbewegung* (Jena, 1924).

———, *Die Role der Erotik in der männlichen Gesellschaft* (Jena, 1919).

————, *Wandervogel: Geschichte einer Jugendbewegung*, 6th ed., two parts in one volume (Prien, 1922). Though Blüher's extremist Freudian methodology is open to criticism, his accounts are detailed and valuable.

Brauweiller, Heinz, *Generäle in der deutschen Republik: Groener, Schleicher, Seeckt* (Berlin, 1932). An enthusiastic attempt to show that his heroes were all pillars of the Republic.

————, "Der Anteil des Stahlhelm," in *Deutscher Aufstand*, edited by Curt Hotzel (Stuttgart, 1934).

Breuer, Robert, "Die Schwarze Reichswehr," in *Deutsche Republik*, Heft XXII, erster Jahrgang (1926), 11–12.

Brickner, Richard M., *Is Germany Incurable?* (New York, 1943).

Bronnen, Arnolt, *Rossbach* (Berlin, 1930). Parts of this biography are written in the first person singular without explanation.

Butler, Rohan D'O., *The Roots of National Socialism: 1783–1933* (Glasgow, 1941). Lengthy quotations from German philosophic thought to show continuity of nationalism, but not necessarily of National Socialism.

Caro, Kurt, and Oehme, Walter, *Schleichers Aufstieg: Ein Beitrag zur Geschichte der Gegenrevolution* (Berlin, 1933). The scope of this sensationalistic account written by two Independent Socialists is wider than the title suggests. Treats the Free Corps as an "ultra-reactionary" movement completely under the thumb of the OHL.

Clark, R. T., *The Fall of the German Republic: A Political Study* (London, 1935).

Coates, W. P., and Zelda K., *Armed Intervention in Russia* (London, 1935). A sensationalistic account written by Russophiles.

Cohnstaedt, Wilhelm, "Severing im Industriebezirk," in *Deutsche Republik*, Heft XXXII, erster Jahrgang (1927), 299–301. A defense written by a warm admirer.

Cron, Hermann, *Geschichte des deutschen Heeres im Weltkrieg 1914–1918*. Volume V of *Geschichte der Kgl. preussischen Armee und des deutschen Reichsheeres*, edited by Major General Jany (Berlin, 1937).

Cuno, Rudolf, *Der Kampf um die Ruhr: Frankreichs Raubzug und Deutschlands Abwehr* (Leipzig, 1923). An example of the screaming protests made by German patriots.

Daniels, H. G., *The Rise of the German Republic* (New York, 1928).

Degener, Hermann, A. L., ed., *Wer ist's?* (Berlin, 1935).

Delbrück, Hans, *Regierung und Volkswille: Eine akademische Vorlesung* (Berlin, 1914). A warm defense of the old regime made by the famous military historian.

————, *Vor und nach dem Weltkrieg: Politische und historische Aufsätze 1902–1925* (Berlin, 1926).

Demeter, Karl, *Das deutsche Heer und seine Offiziere* (Berlin, 1930[?]). A careful study written by the director of the National Archives.

Deubel, Werner, *Deutsche Kulturrevolution: Weltbild der Jugend* (Berlin, 1931).

Dreyfus, P., and Mayer, Paul, *Recht und Politik im Fall Fechenbach* (Berlin, 1925).

Ehrenthal, Günther, *Die deutsche Jungenbünde: ein Handbuch ihrer Organisation und ihrer Bestrebungen* (Berlin, 1929).

Erikson, Erik Homburger, "Hitler's Imagery and German Youth," in *Psychiatry*, V, No. 4 (November 1942), 475–493.

Espe, Walter M., editor, *Das Buch der NSDAP: Werden, Kampf, und Ziel der N.S.D.A.P.* (Berlin, 1933). An officially and very enthusiastically endorsed account written by a director of the Party Propagandaleitung.

Felgen, Friedrich von, ed., *Femgericht*, 4th ed. (Munich, 1933). Extremist nationalist interpretation. The third edition was entitled *Die Femelüge*.

Fischer, Louis, *The Soviets in World Affairs: A History of the Relations between the Soviet Union and the Rest of the World*. 2 vols. (London and New York, 1930).

Fischer, Ruth, *Stalin and German Communism: A Study in the Origins of the State Party* (Cambridge, Mass., 1948).

Frank, Walter, *Franz Ritter von Epp: Der Weg eines deutschen Soldaten* (Hamburg, 1934).

Freitag, Martin, *Albert Leo Schlageter: ein deutscher Held* (n.p., n.d.). A sentimental, trashy biography which contains a useful bibliography.

Freiwald, Ludwig, *Der Weg der braunen Kämpfer: Ein Frontbuch von 1918–1933* (Munich, 1934). A party endorsed survey of the period. Thin, inaccurate, hyperthyroid. Thesis: the National Socialists welcomed all Free Corps and activist Rightist groups into the Party.

Fried, Hans Ernst, *The Guilt of the German Army* (New York, 1942). A sensationalistic account which, though containing errors in documentation, has a very valuable bibliography.

Fromm, Erich, *Escape from Freedom* (New York, 1941). The well-known psychiatrist argues that the German middle class is sado-masochistic.

Gengler, Ludwig F., *Kampfflieger Rudolf Berthold, Sieger im 44 Luftschlägen, Erschlagen im Brüderkampfe für Deutschlands Freiheit* (Berlin, 1934). A prominent Free Corps fighter is here adopted, like Schlageter, as a National Socialist hero.

Gerth, Hans, "The Nazi Party: Its Leadership and Composition," in *The American Journal of Sociology,* XLV (January 1940), 517–541.

Gooch, G. P., *Germany* (London, 1925).

Grimm, Claus, *Jahre deutscher Entscheidung im Baltikum 1918–1919* (Essen, 1939). A packed, heavily documented National Socialist account with excellent bibliography. Weakened by the necessity of following the Nazi line. Unfortunately, narrative does not go beyond February, 1919.

Grimm, Friedrich, *Frankreich am Rhein: Rheinlandbesetzung und Separatismus im Lichte der historischen französischen Rheinpolitik* (Hamburg, 1931).

———, *Oberleutnant Schulz, Femeprozesse und Schwarze Reichswehr* (Munich, 1929[?]).

———, *Vom Ruhrkrieg zur Rheinlandräumung: Erinnerungen eines deutschen Verteidigers vor französischen und belgischen Kriegsgerichten* (Hamburg, 1930). Impassioned accounts written by the defender of Feme murderers and saboteurs.

Grote, Hans Henning, Freiherr, *Seeckt: der wunderbare Weg eines Heeres* (Stuttgart, 1938[?]). A thin encomium.

Günther, Gerhard, *Deutsches Kriegertum im Wandel der Geschichte* (Hamburg, 1934). A National Socialist glorification of "pure-souled" warrior types from the Teutonic Knights to the Free Corps and SA.

Gumbel, E. J., *"Verräter verfallen der Feme," Opfer, Mörder, Richter, 1919–1920* (Berlin, 1929).

———, *Verschwörer: Beitrage zur Geschichte und Soziologie der deutschen Nationalistischen Geheimbünde seit 1918* (Vienna, 1924).

————, *Vier Jahre politischer Mord,* 5th ed. (Berlin, 1922).

————, Jacob, Berthold, and others, *Weisbuch über die Schwarze Reichswehr* (Berlin, 1925).

————, editor, *Denkschrift des Reichsjustizministers zu "Vier Jahre politischer Mord"* (Berlin, 1924).

————, "Le Capitaine Ehrhardt et L'Organisation C," in *L'Europe Nouvelle,* VI, No. 34 (August 25, 1923), 1073–1075.

————, "La Psychologie du Meurte Politique en Allemagne," in *L'Europe Nouvelle,* V, No. 34 (August 26, 1922), 1066–1068.

Halperin, S. William, *Germany Tried Democracy. A Political History of the Reich from 1918–1933* (New York, 1946). The best political history of the Weimar Republic.

Hedemann, Wilhelm, "Die geistigen Strömungen in der heutigen deutschen Studentenschaft," in *Akademisches Deutschland,* edited by Michael Doeberl, Otto Scheel, and others, 4 vols. (Berlin, 1930–1931), Vol. III.

Heiden, Konrad, *Der Fuehrer, Hitler's Rise to Power,* translated by Ralph Manheim (Boston, 1944). A brilliant, penetrating analysis of Hitler.

————, *Geschichte des Nationalsozialismus: Die Karriere einer Idee* (Berlin, 1932). The English translation omits important sections relative to the early beginnings of the movement.

Herrle, Theo, *Die deutsche Jugendbewegung in ihren wirtschaftlichen und gesellschaftlichen Zusammenhängen,* 2nd enlarged ed. (Stuttgart, 1922).

Heyck, Hans, *Deutschlands Befreiungskampf 1918–1933* (Bielefeld and Leipzig, 1933).

Hoeppener-Flatow, W., *Stosstrupp Markmann greift an! Der Kampf eines Frontsoldaten* (Berlin, 1939). The worshipful biography of a boy who became the leader of a Storm Troop at the age of nineteen.

Hotz, Wilhelm, *Albert Leo Schlageter, Seine Sippe und seine Heimat* (Essen, 1940).

Jacob, Berthold, *Das neue deutsche Heer und seine Führer* (Editions du Carrefour, Paris, 1936). A not altogether accurate exposé of German rearmament after 1918.

Jung, Edgar J., "Die Tragik der Kriegsgeneration," in *Süddeutsche Monatshefte,* Heft 8, 27. Jahrgang (May 1930), 511–534.

Kessler, Count Harry, *Walther Rathenau: His Life and Work,* translated under author's supervision by W. D. Robson-Scott and Lawrence Hyde (New York, 1930). An able study of a complex subject by an intimate friend.

Kleinau, Wilhelm, *Franz Seldte, ein Lebensbericht* (Berlin, 1933).

Kloeber, Wilhelm von, *Vom Weltkrieg zum nationalsozialistischen Reich: Deutsche Geschichte 1914–1936,* enlarged ed. (Munich and Berlin, 1937). A typical example of Nazi historical writing.

Koch, Sturmhauptführer Karl W. L., *Das Ehrenbuch der S.A.* (Düsseldorf, 1934).

——, *Männer im Braunhemde: vom Kampf und Sieg der S.A.* (Leipzig and Berlin, 1936).

Kramer, Gerhard, "Greuelpropaganda und Wirklichkeit," in *Femgericht,* edited by Friedrich von Felgen (Munich, 1932).

Kretschmann, Hermann, editor, *Soldaten der Freiheit: Ein Parolebuch des Nationalsozialismus, 1918–1925* (Berlin, 1935). An officially authorized propaganda pamphlet.

Krumbach, Josef H., ed., *Franz Ritter von Epp: Ein Leben für Deutschland* (Munich, 1939). Songs of praise contributed by friends and admirers.

Lasswell, Harold D., "The Psychology of Hitlerism," in *The Political Quarterly,* IV (1933), 373–384.

Ledebur, Ferdinand, Freiherr von, and others, editors, *Die Geschichte des deutschen Unteroffiziers* (Berlin, 1939). A 1212-page history of the German noncommissioned officers from the Thirty Years War to Hitler.

Loessner, A., *Der Abfall Posens: 1918–1919 im polnischen Schrifttum.* Volume VI of the *Ostland Schriften* (Danzig, 1933). A valuable bibliographical essay.

Machray, Robert, *The Problem of Upper Silesia* (London, 1945). An extremely biased, pro-Polish treatment. An unreliable war book.

Medem, Walter Eberhard, Freiherr von, *Seldte-Duesterberg* in the series, *Männer und Mächte* (Leipzig, 1932).

Megede, Hans zur, "Die baltische Tragödie," in *Der Schulungsbrief,* 1. Jahrgang, 4 Folge (June, 1934), 20–29. An official NSDAP interpretation of the Baltic adventure written for the benefit of school children in the Third Reich.

Müffling, Wilhelm, Freiherr von, *Wegbereiter und Vorkämpfer für das neue Deutschland* (Munich, 1933).

Neumann, Franz, *Behemoth: The Structure and Practice of National Socialism* (New York, 1944). A brilliant analysis. By far the best thing written on the subject.

Oertzen, Friedrich Wilhelm von, *Alles oder Nichts: Polens Freiheitskampf in 125 Jahren* (Breslau, 1934).

——, *Baltenland: Eine Geschichte der deutschen Sendung im Baltikum* (Munich, 1939).

——, *Das ist Poland*, 4th ed. (Munich, 1939).

——, *Die deutschen Freikorps, 1918–1923*, 5th ed. (Munich, 1939). The best National Socialist account.

——, *Im Namen Geschichte! Politische Prozesse der Nachkriegszeit* (Hamburg, 1934).

——, *Kamerad, reich mir die Hände: Freikorps und Grenzschutz Baltikum und Heimat* (Berlin, 1933). Based in part on the author's own experience as a member of the intelligence section of the Division of Horse Guards.

Osborne, Sidney, *The Upper Silesian Question and Germany's Coal Problem*, 2nd revised ed., two parts in one volume (London, 1921). Friendly to Germany.

Posse, Ernst H., *Die politischen Kampfbünde Deutschlands*, 2nd enlarged edition, in *Fachschriften zur politik und staatsbürgerlichen Erziehung*, Ernst von Hippel, general editor (Berlin, 1931). A valuable, nationalistic study.

Rabenau, General Friedrich von, *Seeckt: Aus seinem Leben 1918–1936* (Leipzig, 1940). The chief of the army archives who edited Seeckt's posthumous memoirs (*Seeckt: Aus meinem Leben 1866–1917*, Leipzig, 1938) is the author of this definitive biography.

Rehbein, Arthur, *Für Deutschland in den Tod: Leben und Sterben Albert Leo Schlageters* (Berlin, 1933). Another thin Nazi encomium.

Reich, Albert, and Achenbach, O. R., *Vom 9. November 1918 zum 9. November 1923: Die Entstehung der deutschen Freiheitsbewegung* (Munich, 1933). A distorted and factually inaccurate account.

Reichenbrand, Johann von, *Zwanzig Jahre deutsches Ringen vom Weltkrieg über Versailles zur nationalen Erneurung* (Berlin, 1934).

Richter, Artur Georg, *So war die Jugend grosser Deutscher* (Stuttgart, 1934). Childhood sketches of Hitler, Hindenburg, Schlageter, and others.

Roegels, Fritz Carl, *Der Marsch auf Berlin: Ein Buch vom Wehrwillen deutscher Jugend* (Berlin, 1932). Whole sections copied verbatim from other books without quotations or documentation.

Rose, William John, *The Drama of Upper Silesia* (Brattleboro, Vermont, 1935). Perhaps the best account in English.

Rosenberg, Arthur, *Die Entstehung der deutschen Republik* (Berlin, 1928). A penetrating analysis of Germany before and during World War I. Rosenberg was an active member of both the Independent Socialist and Communist parties from 1919–1928; a member of the Reichstag and professor of history at the University of Berlin.

——, *Geschichte der deutschen Republik* (Karlsbad, 1935). The author was too involved personally in events to write objectively about them.

Rosinski, Herbert, *The German Army* (New York, 1940). A good general history which covers the period from Frederick William I to Hitler.

——, "Rebuilding the Reichswehr," in *Atlantic Monthly*, CLXXIII, No. 2 (February, 1944), 95–100.

Royal Institute of International Affairs, *The Baltic States: A Survey of the Political and Economic Structure and the Foreign Relations of Estonia, Latvia, and Lithuania* (London, 1938).

Rudin, Harry R., *Armistice, 1918* (New Haven, 1944).

Rzymowski, Vincent, *Pologne et Haute-Silésie*, translated from Polish by T. Warynski (Paris, 1921).

Scheele, Godfrey, *The Weimar Republic, Overture to the Third Reich* (London, 1945). In spite of the pronounced warbook tone and such phrases as "in 1914 Germany sinned against Europe" there is real value in his thesis that the Third Reich was inchoate in the Weimar Republic.

Scheer, Maximilian, ed., *Blut und Ehre*, herausgegeben vom ueberparteilichen deutschen Hilfsausschuss (Paris, 1937). An anti-Nazi exposé of Free Corps and SA atrocities. Often inaccurate in details, names of men, dates, and so forth.

Schemann, Ludwig, *Wolfgang Kapp und die Märzunternehmung*

vom Jahre 1920: Ein Wort der Sühne (Munich and Berlin, 1937). A passionate but well documented defense. Useful critical bibliography.

Schirach, Baldur von, *Die Pioniere des Dritten Reiches* (Essen, 1933[?]). Pictures and praises of the pioneers, some of whom were to die a year later in the Blood Purge.

Schmidt, Major Ernst, *Argonnen: Schlachten des Weltkrieges* (Berlin, 1927).

Schmidt-Pauli, Edgar von, *Geschichte der Freikorps 1918–1924* (Stuttgart, 1936).

——, *Die Männer um Hitler* (Berlin, 1932).

——, *General von Seeckt: Lebensbild eines deutschen Soldaten* (Berlin, 1937).

Schultze-Pfaelzer, Gerhard, *Von Spa nach Weimar, die Geschichte der deutschen Zeitwende* (Leipzig, 1929). A reliable account of the Revolution.

Schwarte, Max, ed., *Der Grosse Krieg 1914–1918*. 10 vols. (Leipzig, 1921). Vol. VIII, "Die Organisationen der Kriegführung."

Schwertfeger, Bernhard, *Das Weltkriegsende: Gedanken über die deutsche Kriegsführung 1918*, 7th ed. (Potsdam, 1938).

——, and Volkmann, Erich Otto, editors, *Die deutsche Soldatenkunde*. 2 vols. (Leipzig, 1937). A series of essays on military problems 1918–1933.

Siemering, Hertha, ed., *Die deutschen Jugendverbände: Ihre Ziele, ihre Organisation sowie ihre neuere Entwicklung und Tätigkeit* (Berlin, 1931). A valuable collection of essays on separate youth groups.

La Silésie Polonaise, Vol. II of *Problems Politiques de la Pologne Contemporaine* (Paris, 1932). Pro-Polish lectures given by members of the faculty at the Sorbonne.

Smogorzewski, Casimer, "Le Plebiscite et la Partage de la Haute-Silésie," in *La Silésie Polonaise*, Vol. II of *Problems Politiques de la Pologne Contemporaine* (Paris, 1932), 330–332. The case for Poland ably presented.

Spethmann, Hans, *Die Rote Armee an Ruhr und Rhein: Aus den Kapptagen, 1920* (Berlin, 1930).

——, *Der Ruhrkampf, 1923–1925* (Berlin, 1933). These two popular accounts are based on his larger work, *Zwölf Jahre Ruhrbergbau*.

——, *Zwölf Jahre Ruhrbergbau, 1914 bis 1925: Aus seiner*

Geschichte von Kriegsanfang bis zum Franzosenabmarsch,
4 vols. (Berlin, 1928). A fully documented nationalist
interpretation.

Spiecker, Karl, "Geheimfonds der Reichswehr?" in *Deutsche
Republik,* Heft VI, Erster Jahrgang (1926), 11–12.

Springer, Max, *Loslösungsbestrebungen am Rhein 1918–1924*
(Berlin, 1924). A careful study based on the official documents. Key documents are printed in the Appendix.

Stadler, Eduard, *Seldte, Hitler, Hugenberg: Die Front Freiheitsbewegung,* 2nd ed. (Berlin, 1930). Weak and unreliable
book written by the founder of the Anti-Bolshevist League.

Stegemann, Hermann, *Der Kampf um den Rhein: Das Stromge-
biet des Rheins im Rahmen der grossen Politik und
im Wandel der Kriegsgeschichte* (Stuttgart and Berlin,
1934 [?]). A new edition of the book written by the distinguished German historian, carries the narrative up to
Hitler.

Temperley, H. W. V., *A History of the Peace Conference of Paris,*
6 vols. (London, 1924), Vol. VI. *

Thomée, Gerhard, Major im Oberkommando der Wehrmacht,
Der Wiederaufstieg des deutschen Heeres 1918–1938 (Berlin, 1939). An official Wehrmacht interpretation.

Tötter, Heinrich, *Warum wir den Ruhrkampf verloren: Das
Versagen der deutschen Pressepropaganda im Ruhrkampf*
(Cologne, 1940). A propaganda pamphlet written with
the approval of the NSDAP.

Ullmann, Hermann, *Durchbruch zur Nation: Geschichte des
deutschen Volkes 1919–1933* (Jena 1933). Nazi propaganda.

Vegesack, Siegfried, *Die baltische Tragödie, eine Romantrilogie*
(Bremen, 1934). Typical of the romantic novels written
about the historic German mission in the Baltic.

Viereck, Peter, *Metapolitics: From the Romantics to Hitler* (New
York, 1941). A provocative study.

Volkmann, Erich Otto, *Revolution über Deutschland* (Oldenburg,
1930).

———, *Am Tor der neuen Zeit* (Oldenburg, 1933).

———, "Der internationale sozialistische Gedanke in seiner Einwirkung auf die deutsche Wehrmacht im Weltkrieg," in
Wissen und Wehr, VIII Jahrgang, 1927, Fünftes Heft, 258–
274.

———, "Das geistige Gesicht des deutschen Offizierkorps in der Zeitwende," in *Deutsche Rundschau*, CCXLIII (April, 1935), 1–7.

———, "Das Soldatentum des Weltkrieges," in *Die deutsche Soldatenkunde*. Vol. I. Volkmann was a prominent military authority and a member of the Reichsarchiv.

———, "Soziale Heeresmissstände als mitursache des deutschen Zusammenbruches von 1918," in *Die Ursachen des deutschen Zusammenbruches*, XI, Zweiter Halbband (Berlin, 1925–1929).

Vorweck, Hauptmann, *Deutschlands Zusammenbruch: Seine Ursachen und Folgen, Eine Flugschrift zur Aufklärung und Rechtfertigung* (Oldenburg, 1919).

Wambaugh, Sarah, *Plebiscites since the World War*, 2 vols. (Washington, D.C., 1933). The standard work on the subject.

Warneck, Hans, and Marschke, Willy, *Geschichte für Volkschulen* (Bielefeld and Leipzig, 1943). This history textbook shows how the Nazis urged the youth of the Third Reich to emulate the Freikorpskämpfer.

Wentzcke, Paul, *Der Freiheit entgegen! Deutscher Abwehrkampf an Rhein, Ruhr und Saar* (Berlin, 1934). A popular, nationalistic account based on his earlier and more valuable studies.

———, *Rheinkampf*, 2 vols. (Berlin, 1925).

———, *Ruhrkampf: Einbruch und Abwehr im Rheinisch-Westfälischen Industriegebiet*, 2nd ed., 2 vols. (Berlin, 1934). In spite of heavy nationalist bias, a well documented and useful study.

Wheeler-Bennett, John W., *Wooden Titan: Hindenburg in Twenty Years of German History, 1914–1934* (New York, 1936). An admirable study based upon the sources and the author's interviews with leaders of the Weimar Republic.

Wiemers-Borchelhof, Franz, "Freikorps, Arbeitsdienst, Siedlung: Das Schicksal eines Vorkämpfers der Freikorpssiedler," in *Das Buch vom deutschen Freikorpskämpfer*, edited by Ernst von Salomon (Berlin, 1938).

Wrisberg, Generalmajor Ernst von, *Heer und Heimat 1914–1918* (Leipzig, 1921).

———, *Der Weg zur Revolution 1914–1918* (Leipzig, 1921).

———, "Aufbau und Ergänzung des Heeres," in *Der Grosse Krieg*

1914–1918, edited by Max Schwarte, 10 vols. (Leipzig, 1921–1923.), Vol. VIII.

Wulfsohn, Leo, "The Enforced Demobilization of the German Army," in *The New Europe*, XII, No. 149 (August 21, 1919), 132–134.

INDEX